Visu e

Answers!

About the Author

Michael Otey is a Senior Technical Editor for *Windows NT Magazine* and *SQL Server Magazine.* He is also President of TECA, Inc., a software development and consulting company. Michael is the co-author of Osborne/McGrawHill's *SQL Server 7 Developer's Guide.* He is an avid Visual Basic supporter and has been developing projects with Visual Basic since 1992.

Visual Basic

Answers!

Michael Otey

Osborne/McGraw-Hill

Berkeley • New York • St. Louis • San Francisco
Auckland • Bogotá • Hamburg • London
Madrid • Mexico City • Milan • Montreal
New Delhi • Panama City • Paris • São Paulo
Singapore • Sydney • Tokyo • Toronto

Osborne/**McGraw-Hill**
2600 Tenth Street
Berkeley, California 94710
U.S.A.

For information on translations or book distributors outside the U.S.A., or to arrange bulk purchase discounts for sales promotions, premiums, or fund-raisers, please contact Osborne/**McGraw-Hill** at the above address.

Visual Basic Answers!

1234567890 AGM AGM 019876543210

ISBN 0-07-211895-4

Publisher Brandon A. Nordin	**Copy Editor** Bill McManus
Associate Publisher and Editor-in-Chief Scott Rogers	**Proofreaders** Linda Medoff Paul Medoff
Acquisitions Editor Wendy Rinaldi	**Indexer** David Heiret
Acquisitions Coordinator Monika Faltiss	**Computer Designer** Michelle Galicia E. A. Pauw
Project Editor Emily Rader	**Illustrators** Beth Young Robert Hansen
Technical Editor Bob Noble	**Series Design** Michelle Galicia

This book was composed with Corel VENTURA ™ Publisher.

To the glory of God

Contents @ a Glance

Contents

Acknowledgments

Books don't just appear by themselves; they begin with an idea, and if that idea is a good one, they continue to grow into reality from there. This book is no exception. The initial spark for *Visual Basic Answers!* came from Acquisitions Editor Wendy Rinaldi. I want to thank Wendy for bringing me in on this project and helping to see it through to fruition.

Next, I'd like to thank my wife, Denielle Otey, for providing coding advice and technical tips, as well as drawing several of the graphics that were used. All of this, in addition to the tons of proofreading she did, made Denielle's contribution invaluable.

Through the development of the book, Bob Noble provided the essential technical reviews for all of the chapters, as well as ongoing encouraging comments that helped keep the book on track. I wish my chapters could have been as timely as Bob's reviews always were!

I would also like to thank the staff at Osborne/McGraw-Hill for all of their help in making this book a reality. Monika Faltiss, Acquisitions Coordinator, had the thankless (until now) job of keeping up with the book's ever-changing schedule; and Emily Rader, Project Editor, once again did a fantastic job of making sure that all of the language and technical terms were consistent and correct. I am also thankful for the very thorough efforts of copy editor Bill McManus.

Michael Otey

Introduction

Like death and taxes, some things in life are certainties. For
the software developer, running into technical problems and
hurdles is a guaranteed feature of every project. In my
experience, this software axiom holds true for everything but
the simplest of applications. In the hundreds of projects that
I've worked on since I began writing software in 1983, there
were only a handful that didn't hold some hidden problem that
needed to be surmounted. It's not unusual for an entire project
to be hung up waiting for the resolution of a single technical
problem. Many times, all I needed to solve the problem was
seeing a quick example code snippet or sometimes the
not-so-obvious "magic trick" that was required to unlock the
puzzle. Scrambling to overcome these problems is where advice
from other experienced programmers, technical support calls,
and books are worth their weight in gold.

Visual Basic Answers! was written to directly address
these types of problems. It contains a collection of hundreds of
practical questions and answers that I've encountered in my
years of developing and supporting in-house applications,
shrink-wrapped products, and published applications that
have been presented in the *Windows NT Magazine* "VB
Solutions" column. This book also provides hundreds of tested
code examples that can help you solve a variety of different
problems, ranging from implementing toolbars and menus to
more advanced topics, such as dynamically creating and
resizing forms and controls.

I've found that the answer to a single question can, by
itself, make the purchase of a book worthwhile. My goal
with this book is to offer solutions to help you get past the
immediate problems you may face, as well as provide a useful
reference and code library that you can use to overcome
obstacles in future projects. While no one book can address
the infinite array of possible problems that can arise, I have
made an effort to address the majority of issues you'll likely
encounter. While there is a lot of code presented in this book,

don't worry—you won't have to manually key it all in. All the code presented in this book can be downloaded from Osborne/McGrawHill's Web site, at www.osborne.com.

This book is organized into 18 chapters and two appendixes:

- **Chapter 1** presents the ten most common questions I've encountered from beginning and intermediate VB programmers.

- **Chapters 2 through 5** address issues that the beginning Visual Basic user will need to know in order to make the most effective use of the VB development environment. These chapters deal with issues such as using VB's IntelliSense feature for productive coding, and using the debugging and source control tools that are an integrated part of the development environment.

- **Chapters 6 through 9** present questions and answers that illustrate how to solve application problems you might encounter using the core Visual Basic development objects. These chapters clarify issues such as using splash screens, dynamically resizing forms, and using the standard ActiveX controls that are supplied with Visual Basic.

- **Chapters 10 through 12** pertain to some of the thorny issues that seem to crop up in all applications. The questions and answers in these chapters show you how to read and write files, produce reports from your applications, and retrieve and format the system date and time.

- **Chapters 13 through 17** address more advanced problems you are likely to encounter in your VB development process. For example, they show you how to create objects and collections, use DAO and ADO for database access, and create Web-based applications.

- **Chapter 18** shows you how to use Visual Basic's Packaging and Deployment Wizard to distribute your VB projects.

- **Appendixes A and B** present a collection of coding conventions and commonly used constants.

Chapter 1

Top 10 Frequently Asked Questions

Top 10 FAQs @ a Glance

In this chapter, I'll cover the top 10 most frequently asked questions that I've encountered in my experience of developing and supporting a number of custom and shrink-wrapped Visual Basic applications. These questions don't fall into any specific category. Instead, they range across the board. However, they do have a common theme, they all revolve around some of the most regularly performed tasks that are required to build Visual Basic applications.

 ## 1. How do I create a menu?

Using the Menu Editor is the simplest way to add and update menus in a Visual Basic application. The Menu Editor can be used to create new menus as well as add items and commands to existing menus. You can start the Menu Editor by selecting the Menu Editor option from the Tools menu, by clicking the Menu Editor icon in the Standard toolbar, or by right-clicking the form where you want to add the menu and then selecting the Menu Editor option from the pop-up menu. The Visual Basic menu editor shown in Figure 1-1 will be displayed.

The upper half of the Menu Editor displays the menu control properties. The Caption property is used to assign the name of each menu item. The name will appear on the menu exactly as you enter it in the Caption property. The & symbol is used to add an *access key* (sometimes called an *accelerator key* or *shortcut* key) to the menu item. An access key can be used in lieu of the mouse to invoke menu items, using a combination of the CTRL key and the first letter following the & symbol. In Figure 1-1, you can see the Menu Editor displaying the value &New in the Caption property. This results in a menu item named New, which can be run using either the mouse or the CTRL+N key combination. In addition to item names, the Caption property can be used to create separator bars that divide different sections of the menu. A separator bar is created by entering a hyphen (-) in the Name property. Although no code is executed by the separator bar, a name must still be entered in the Name property. The name "separator" is a descriptive placeholder that can satisfy the Menu Editor's requirement for a name.

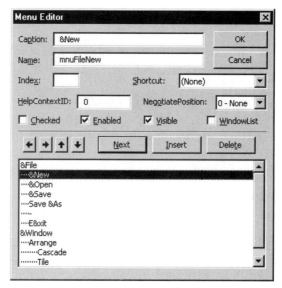

Figure 1-1   The Menu Editor

The Name property is used to specify the name of the VB function that will be executed when the menu item is selected. The name can be anything that you choose. One common convention is to prefix the function name with the object type and menu hierarchy. In the example in Figure 1-1, the object type is a menu, and the menu item is the File menu's New option. Hence the name *mnuFileNew*. Likewise, if you were entering a name for the File | Save option, you might call it mnuFileSave.

The Caption and Name properties are the only menu control properties that you need to enter. The Index property is used to identify menu control arrays, which are typically used to allow runtime control over the menu. The Shortcut property allows you to enter additional keyboard hot keys that can be used to run a menu option. The HelpContextID property links the menu item with a help file entry, and the NegotiatePosition property controls how the form will display the menu. The Checked property causes a check mark to appear next to an item that has been selected. The Enabled property allows the menu item to be selected by the user. The Visible property allows the menu item to be seen by the user. The Enabled and Visible properties are selected by default.

The WindowList property enables the menu to automatically track open MDI child forms.

The lower portion of the Menu Editor contains the *menu control list*. The menu control list allows you to specify the relationships of the different menu items. You use the menu control list to specify which menu items will be top-level items and which items will appear on submenus. Top-level menu items appear on the far left. The menu items under each top-level item are indented and prefixed with three or more dots. You can use the four arrows on the Menu Editor to alter the relationships of the different menu items. The four arrows can be used to move menu items up and down, as well as to change the indented level of each menu item. The Next button positions the cursor at the bottom of the menu control list. The Insert button is used to insert a new item at the current cursor position, and the Delete button is used to remove menu items.

In Figure 1-1, you can see that File and Window are the top-level menu items, and the menu items for the File menu are New, Open, Save, and Save As. The Window menu contains one menu entry named Arrange. The Arrange item, in turn, contains a submenu that consists of two options, Cascade and Tile. These submenu items were created by clicking the right arrow two times, specifying two indented menu levels.

 ## 2. How do I create a toolbar?

Toolbars allow you to quickly access commonly used program functions. Toolbars are used by almost all current Windows applications, and creating the toolbar is generally the next step after creating the initial menu. VB includes a toolbar wizard that runs as a part of VB's App Wizard; if you're building a new application, it's the fastest way to add a toolbar to your application. However, that wizard isn't accessible as a stand-alone after your project has been created.

The best way to add a toolbar to an existing VB project is to use a combination of the Toolbar control and the ImageList control. By itself, the Toolbar control is just a container. It can be configured in the design environment to display toolbar buttons, but it requires the ImageList control to

provide the images that will be displayed on each of these buttons. As you have probably guessed, the first steps in creating a toolbar are to add the Toolbar control and the ImageList control to the form that you want to display as a toolbar. Double-clicking the Toolbar control in VB's Toolbox automatically adds the toolbar to the top portion of the form, while double-clicking the ImageList control automatically adds it to the center of the current form.

After both of these controls have been added to your form, the next step is to insert a set of pictures into the ImageList control. To this control, you can add images that are contained in Bitmap (.bmp), Icon (.ico), GIF (.gif), or JPEG (.jpg) files.

To add these icons to your toolbar, right-click the Toolbar control that's on your VB form and then select Properties from the shortcut menu. Next, click the Images tab, and the ImageList properties window shown in Figure 1-2 will be displayed.

Initially, the list of images will be empty. To add images, click the Insert Picture button and then use the Open File dialog box to select the folder and image files that you want

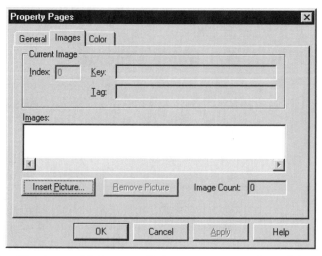

Figure 1-2 The ImageList control's Images properties with no images

to add to your toolbar. Visual Studio 6 installs a set of the common toolbar icons in the following folder:

\Microsoft Visual Studio\Common\Graphics\ Bitmaps\TlBr_W95

While you don't need to add the pictures in the same order that they appear in the toolbar, it does tend to make using the images in the Toolbar control a bit easier. Figure 1-3 shows the ImageList control after some of the common toolbar icons have been added from the Visual Studio Bitmaps folder.

You should note that as each image is added to the ImageList control, it is assigned an index. This index will be used by the Toolbar to associate the image to a toolbar button.

After the images have been added to the ImageList control, you are ready to set up the Toolbar control. The first step is to "bind" the Toolbar control to the ImageList control. To do this, right-click the Toolbar control and select the Properties option from the pop-up menu. The Toolbar

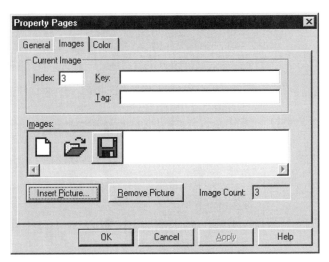

Figure 1-3 The ImageList control's Images properties window with three images

control's General properties window, shown in Figure 1-4, will be displayed.

The most important properties on this page are ImageList, DisabledImageList, and HotImageList. These properties allow you to associate one or more ImageList controls with the Toolbar control.

To create a simple toolbar, you really only need to use the ImageList property, which points to an ImageList control containing the images that will be displayed on the buttons. The DisabledImageList control allows you to set up a special set of images that are displayed when toolbar buttons are disabled. Likewise, the HotImageList control contains a set of images that will be displayed when the mouse pointer is over a clickable portion of the button. In Figure 1-4, you can see that the ImageList property contains the name ImageList1, which is the control that was populated earlier with standard toolbar images.

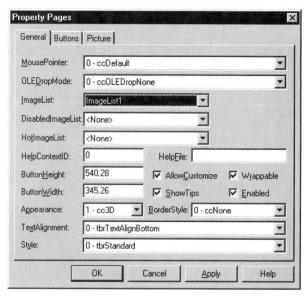

Figure 1-4 Toolbar control's General properties window

Next, to create toolbar buttons and assign images to those buttons, you need to click the Buttons tab to display the window shown in Figure 1-5.

The three most important properties on this window are the Index, Image, and Style properties. The Index property indicates which button on the toolbar you are currently working with. The Image property indicates the index of the image to use on this button, based on its index in the ImageList control. The Style property controls the button's appearance on the toolbar.

Initially, all of the properties on the Buttons tab will be disabled. Click the Insert Button button to begin adding new buttons to the toolbar. All of the property fields will be enabled, and the Index properties will be set to 1. As you insert buttons that use the tbrDefault value in the Style property, each button will appear adjacent to the one that was created immediately before. If you want to insert a separator between buttons or groups of buttons, select tbrSeparator from the drop-down Style menu on the property page for the button that you are inserting. While most

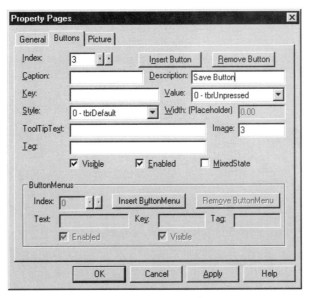

Figure 1-5 Toolbar control button properties

toolbars only display an image, you can add a text caption to any button. If you want a caption to appear on a button, enter the text for the caption in the Caption property. If you want a ToolTip to appear when the mouse pointer moves over a button, enter the text for the ToolTip in the ToolTipsText property. Finally, enter the index number from the ImageList control of the image that you want displayed on the button. In Figure 1-5, you can see the property setting for the third button in the Toolbar control. This button uses no caption or ToolTip, and it will display the third image contained in the associated ImageList control.

3. I've installed some third-party ActiveX controls, but they don't appear in VB's Toolbox. How do I add ActiveX controls to my VB development environment?

You can add ActiveX controls to VB's development environment by selecting the Components option from VB's Project menu. You might be surprised at how many controls are already loaded on your system but are not displayed in the Toolbox. Selecting the Components option displays the Components dialog box shown in Figure 1-6.

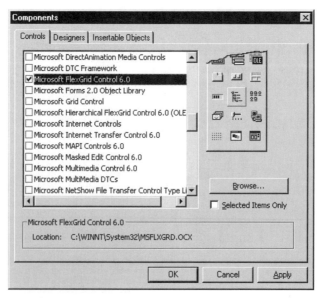

Figure 1-6 Adding ActiveX controls to Visual Basic

Scroll through Visual Basic's Components dia
you see the ActiveX control you want to use. For i
add the Microsoft Flex Grid control, scroll through
components until you see Microsoft FlexGrid Contro
click the check box immediately in front of the contro₁.
followed by the OK button. This adds the Microsoft Flexᴜ
ActiveX control to Visual Basic's Toolbox. You can now use
this ActiveX control in your Visual Basic applications.

4. I've just finished creating a VB form and laying out all of the different ActiveX controls that I want to use. However, when I run the application, the TAB key doesn't move the cursor from field to field. How can I control the tab order of the controls on a form?

You can control the tab order of the ActiveX controls on a
form by setting each control's TabIndex property, which
initially is set automatically, according to the order in which
it was placed on the form. Since ActiveX controls are rarely
created in input order, the tab order of the completed form
can be unpredictable

Figure 1-7 illustrates setting the TabIndex property of a
Text Box control.

Figure 1-7   Setting the tab order

The tab order proceeds from lowest to highest. The first control to receive input should be assigned a TabIndex value of 0, the second control should use 1, the next 2, and so on.

5. How do I make my program respond to mouse clicks?

Virtually all visible ActiveX controls provide support for mouse click events via the _Click subroutine. For a control to respond to mouse click events, you need to add your own code to its _Click event subroutine. The _Click event subroutine uses the same name as the control, with the suffix _Click appended to it. When the user clicks the control, VB automatically executes its click event subroutine. For instance, if you want your VB application to take some specific action when the user clicks a button named Command1, you would add code to the Command1_Click subroutine as is illustrated in the following example:

```
Private Sub Command1_Click()
    ' Your code that acts on the click event goes here.
    Text1.Text = "I clicked the Command1 button"
End Sub
```

When the user clicks the Command1 button, VB will run the Command1_Click subroutine and will execute the code that you have added to this subroutine as well. In the previous example, clicking the Command1 button will set the Text property of the Text1 control to the value "I clicked the Command1 button".

Visual Basic responds to all events in a similar fashion. For instance, if you want Form1 to respond to a double-click, you will need to add code to the Form1_DblClick subroutine.

You can add these subroutines manually, but it's usually easier to let VB create them for you. To create and edit subroutines using VB's IDE, you first need to add the appropriate objects to your project. Then, using VB's code editing window, you can select the desired objects from the drop-down box at the top-right portion of the window and select the appropriate supported events from the drop-down box on the left side of the window. Figure 1-8 illustrates the selection of events for a Form object.

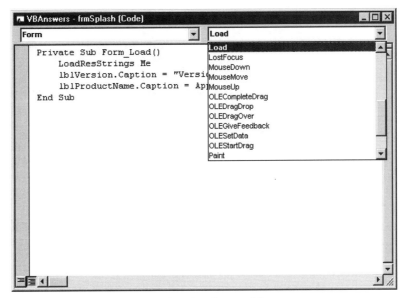

Figure 1-8 Selecting events for the form object

Because responding to click events is such a common requirement, VB has an additional shortcut for creating and editing the click event subroutine. Double-clicking the object in VB's form design window automatically starts the code editing window and creates a _Click subroutine for the object that you double-clicked.

 ## 6. How can I extract a subset of a string?

Visual Basic provides several string manipulation functions that you can use to extract a subset of a string. The following table describes the primary VB string subset functions. All of these functions return a string.

VB String Function	Description
Left(*string*, *length*)	Extracts a specified number of characters starting from the left side of the search string
Mid(*string*, start[, *length*])	Extracts a specified number of characters from the specified beginning and end points of the search string
Right(*string*, *length*)	Extracts a specified number of characters starting from the right side of the search string
LTrim(*string*)	Strips all leading blank characters from the left side of the search string

VB String Function	Description
RTrim(*string*)	Strips all trailing blank characters from the left side of the search string
Trim(*string*)	Strips all leading and trailing blank characters from the left side of the search string

The following code example demonstrates how to use these VB string functions to return a subset of a string:

```
Private Sub StringDemo()

    Dim sSource As String
    Dim sSource2 As String
    Dim sTarget As String

    sSource = "This is a sample string.    "

    sTarget = Left(sSource, 4)    'sTarget = "This"
    sTarget = Mid(sSource, 6, 2)  'sTarget = "is"
    sTarget = Right(sSource, 11)  'sTarget = " string."

    sSource2 = sTarget

    sTarget = LTrim(sSource2)     'sTarget = "string."
    sTarget = Trim(sSource2)      'sTarget = "string."
    sTarget = RTrim(sSource2)     'sTarget = " string."

End Sub
```

7. How do I display a message box?

Your application can display a simple message box by using Visual Basic's MsgBox function. The MsgBox function displays a modal dialog box that waits for the user's input. It can also return an integer value that indicates the user's response. The following example shows the prototype for the MsgBox function.

MsgBox(*prompt*[, *buttons*] [, *title*] [, *helpfile, context*])

The *prompt* parameter accepts a string that will be displayed in the message box. This first parameter is required. All of the other parameters are optional.

The *buttons* parameter accepts an integer value that controls the types of buttons that will be displayed on the message box. If this parameter is omitted, the OK button will be displayed by default. The following table lists the constants and their values that can be used in the *buttons* parameter:

Constant	Value	Description
vbOKOnly	0	Display OK button only
vbOKCancel	1	Display OK and Cancel buttons
vbAbortRetryIgnore	2	Display Abort, Retry, and Ignore buttons
vbYesNoCancel	3	Display Yes, No, and Cancel buttons
vbYesNo	4	Display Yes and No buttons
vbRetryCancel	5	Display Retry and Cancel buttons
vbCritical	16	Display Critical Message icon
vbQuestion	32	Display Warning Query icon
vbExclamation	48	Display Warning Message icon
vbInformation	64	Display Information Message icon
vbDefaultButton1	0	Make first button the default
vbDefaultButton2	256	Make second button the default
vbDefaultButton3	512	Make third button the default
vbDefaultButton4	768	Make fourth button the default
vbApplicationModal	0	Make the message box application modal
vbSystemModal	4096	Make the message box system modal
vbMsgBoxHelpButton	16384	Add Help button to the message
vbMsgBoxSetForeground	65536	Specify the message box window as the foreground window
vbMsgBoxRight	524288	Right-align the text
vbMsgBoxRtlReading	1048576	Specify that text should appear as right-to-left when read on Hebrew and Arabic systems

The *title* parameter of the MsgBox function accepts a string that will be displayed in the title of the message box. If this parameter is omitted, the application's title will be displayed by default.

The *helpfile* and *context* parameters are used to associate online help with the message box. The *helpfile* parameter accepts a string that contains the name of the specific window's help file, while the *context* parameter is an optional help context number.

The MsgBox function returns the following values, which are used to determine which button was selected on the message box:

Constant	Value	Description
vbOK	1	OK
vbCancel	2	Cancel
vbAbort	3	Abort
vbRetry	4	Retry
vbIgnore	5	Ignore
vbYes	6	Yes
vbNo	7	No

The following listing illustrates how you can use the MsgBox function in your Visual Basic applications:

```
Private Sub DemoMsgBox()
    Dim nResponse As Integer
    nResponse = MsgBox("This is an example message _
        box", vbYesNo, "VB Answers! MsgBox Example")
    If nResponse = vbYes Then    ' User chose Yes
        MsgBox "You chose Yes"
    Else                         ' User chose No
        MsgBox "You chose No"
    End If
End Sub
```

In this section of code, you can see that the first line declares an integer variable named nResponse that will be used to evaluate the value returned from the MsgBox function. Next, the MsgBox function is called using three parameters. The first parameter sets the text that will be

Figure 1-9   A example message box displayed using the Msg Box function

displayed in the message box. The value of vbYesNo in the second parameter causes two buttons, a Yes button and a No button, to be displayed on the message box. And the third parameter sets the title of the message box. Figure 1-9 presents the message box that is displayed by the preceding DemoMsgBox function.

 8. How can I trap errors that occur when my application is running?

Visual Basic's On Error statement is used to activate error handling in VB functions and subroutines: executing it enables Visual Basic to trap runtime errors. The error-handling options of the On Error statement specify where program execution will continue in the event that a trappable error is encountered. If a fatal runtime error occurs and Visual Basic's error handling is not enabled, then the program will terminate at the line where the error was encountered. Table 1-1 lists the various error-handing options provided by Visual Basic.

Error Handler	Description
On Error Goto *line*	Program execution continues with the line number or label specified. This allows you to trap and programmatically respond to runtime errors.
On Error Resume Next	Program execution continues with the next executable line. This essentially catches and ignores the trappable error condition.
On Error Goto 0	Error handling is disabled.

Table 1-1   Visual Basic's Error-Handling Options

The following ShowError subroutine illustrates how Visual Basic's On Error function can be used to trap a DAO error:

```
Private Sub ShowError()

    Dim rs As Recordset
    Dim sSQL As String
    On Error GoTo Errorhandler

    sSQL = "Select * From no_such_table"
    Set rs = db.OpenRecordset(sSQL, dbOpenDynaset)
    Rs.close
    Exit Sub

Errorhandler:
    DisplayDAOError

End Sub
```

This subroutine sets up a Select statement to query a nonexistent table appropriately named no_such_table. Before this query is executed, the On Error statement is used to specify that program execution will branch to the Errorhandler label if a runtime error is encountered. When the OpenRecordset method using the invalid SQL statement is executed, a trappable error is generated and the program execution will continue with the Errorhandler label where the DisplayDAOError subroutine will be executed.

9. What are references and how do I add them to VB's development environment?

Much like ActiveX controls, references are application objects that you can make use of in your VB applications by creating references to their libraries. Like ActiveX controls, references are COM (Component Object Model) objects. These objects are also known as OLE Automation Servers. Unlike ActiveX controls, VB references do no not have a visual representation or user interface. Instead, they extend the functions that are available to your VB application.

For instance, a common reference that you might want to add would be one to the ADO (ActiveX Data Objects) library. The ADO object library extends VB's capabilities by allowing VB applications to access data from a variety of sources including databases and spreadsheets. To add a reference to the ADO 2 object library in Visual Basic 5, you first select the References option from the Project menu, which will display the References dialog box shown in Figure 1-10.

Scroll through Visual Basic's References dialog box until you see the object library that you want to add. For ADO, this is the Microsoft ActiveX Data Objects 2.0 Library. Clicking in the check box and then clicking the OK button will add the ADO object library to Visual Basic's IDE (Interactive Development Environment). You can then use any of the ADO objects, methods, and properties in your VB application. Visual Basic's Object Browser can be used to display an object library's properties, events, and methods. Figure 1-11 displays the ADO object library using the Object Browser.

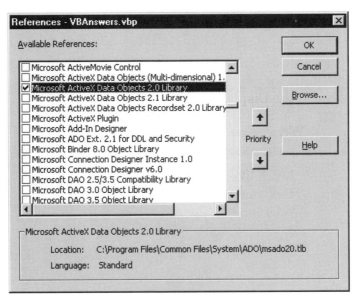

Figure 1-10   Adding a VB reference

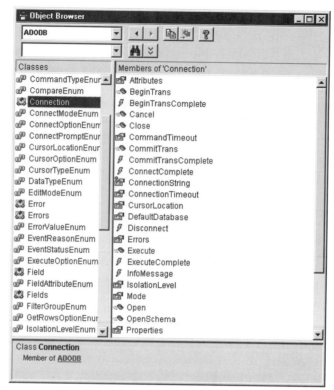

Figure 1-11   Viewing a reference using the Object Browser

 ## 10. How can I access the registry from a VB application?

Contrary to the popular myth, VB can indeed read and write to the registry. However, VB's built-in support of the registry is modeled after the old-style INI files and is quite limited. VB provides two primary functions that work with registry values: GetSetting and SaveSetting. As their names suggest, GetSetting is used to read registry values, while SaveSetting is used to write them. Both of these built-in functions can only work with a small subset of the registry. They are both limited to the following key:

HKEY_CURRENT_USER\Software\VB and VBA Program Settings

Within this key, each VB application uses the following subkey to store its information:

\appname\section\key

where *appname* is the name of the VB application, *section* is the name of the different keys under the *appname* key, and *key* is the specific registry key that is under the *section* key. The values for *appname*, *section,* and *key* are supplied as arguments to the GetSetting and SaveSetting functions. The following code listing illustrates how to use the SaveSetting function:

```
Private Sub Command_Save_Click()

        SaveSetting "VBAnswers", "Startup", _
        "Interval", Text_Time.Text
        SaveSetting "VBAnswers", "Startup", "Beep", _
        Check_Beep.Value

End Sub
```

The SaveSetting function is typically used either when the application is ended, or in a part of the application that allows the user to customize the program operations. As its name suggests, the SaveSetting function writes settings to the registry; if the specified registry keys do not exist when the function is executed, they will be created. In this example, the value of VBAnswer is used as the *appname*. The value of Startup is used for the *section,* and the values of Interval and Beep are used for the *key* parameters.

Note: *The values written to the registry in this example come from a text box and a check box that are a part of the same form that contains this function.*

The previous code listing will write values into the following registry keys:

HKEY_CURRENT_USER\Software\VB and
VBA Program Settings\VBAnswers\Startup\Interval

HKEY_CURRENT_USER\Software\VB and VBA
Program Settings\VBAnswers\Startup\Beep

After the registry keys have been created and written to using the SaveSetting function, you can use the GetSetting

function to read the keys and values later. The following code shows how to use the GetSetting function to read these values out of the registry:

```
Private Sub Form_Load()

    Text_Time.Text = GetSetting("VBAnswers", _
    "Startup", "Interval", 60)
    Check_Beep.Value = GetSetting("VBAnswers", _
    "Startup", "Beep", False)

End Sub
```

The GetSetting function is typically used in the Form_Load or other program initialization code.It returns the value of the registry key identified in the parameters of the function. In this example, you can see that the application name VBAnswers is supplied as the *appname* parameter. The value of "Startup" is supplied as the value for the *section* parameter, and the values of "Interval" and "Beep" are supplied for the *key* parameter. The value following the *key* parameter is a default, which will be returned by the GetSetting function in the event that the value is not present.

Tip: *If you attempt to use the GetSetting function and the registry key is not present, VB will issue a runtime error. This error can be trapped using the VB error handler.*

In addition to the GetSetting and SaveSetting functions, VB provides two other functions that work with registry values: GetAllSettings and DeleteSetting. As you might guess, GetAllSettings retrieves the values of multiple keys under a subkey, while DeleteSetting deletes a registry key. Both of these functions are limited to working with the same registry section as the GetSetting and SaveSetting functions.

Tip: *You can access other registry values either by incorporating third-party ActiveX controls into your application or by using the Win32 API registry functions RegOpenKeyEx, RegQueryValueEx, RegSetValueExA, RegCloseKey, and RegSaveKey within your application.*

Chapter 2

Visual Basic Fundamentals

Answer Topics!

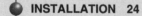

Visual Basic Fundamentals @ a Glance

This chapter covers Visual Basic fundamentals.

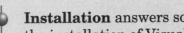 **Installation** answers some of the basic questions concerning the installation of Visual Basic.

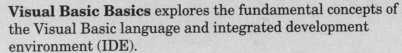 **Visual Basic Basics** explores the fundamental concepts of the Visual Basic language and integrated development environment (IDE).

INSTALLATION

The first section of this chapter covers some of the questions and answers concerning the system requirements and installation options of Visual Basic 6.

 ## What are the system requirements for Visual Basic 6?

Visual Basic 6 requires Windows 95, Windows 98, or Windows NT 4 or later. If you are installing on Windows NT 4, then Service Pack 3 is also recommended. On the hardware side, Microsoft recommends the use of a 486/66 or higher Pentium processor or any Alpha processor. A minimum of 16MB of RAM is recommended for Windows $9x$, while 32MB of RAM is recommended for Windows NT. Although these minimum levels are workable, you will definitely get better performance with additional RAM, such as 48 to 64MB. Visual Basic 6 also requires a VGA or better monitor, a CD-ROM drive, and a mouse.

 ## Can Visual Basic be installed on a network drive?

Yes, Visual Basic can be installed on a network drive that is mapped to a local drive. For instance, if you have mapped the L drive to your network share, you can install Visual Basic to the L drive. The following table lists the disk requirements for the Professional and Enterprise Editions of Visual Basic:

Visual Basic Edition	Typical Installation	Complete Installation
Professional Edition	48MB	80MB
Enterprise Edition	128MB	147MB

Although installing Visual Basic to a network drive can reduce the local disk storage requirements for Visual Basic, it doesn't entirely eliminate them. Visual Basic still installs approximately 50MB worth of dynamic-link libraries (DLLs) and OLE custom controls (OCXs) to the %system% directory. Typically, this is the \windows\system directory for a Windows $9x$ system, and the \winnt\system32 directory for a Windows NT system.

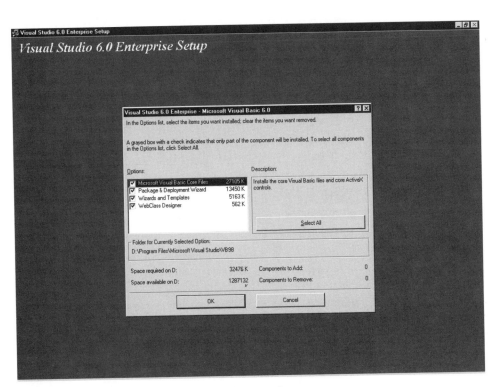

How do I change my installation options after I've already installed Visual Basic?

You can change the installation options for Visual Basic at any time after the product is installed, by rerunning the Visual Basic Setup program. You can run the Setup program either by inserting the CD-ROM and running the AutoPlay file or by executing the Setup.exe program located on the CD-ROM.

To add or remove components, select the Custom option from VB's Setup dialog box. An installation options dialog box, shown in Figure 2-1, will be displayed, and the options that have been selected previously will be checked.

To add components, select the options that you want to add by clicking the corresponding entries in the list. A check mark will appear next to each option to be added. Similarly, to

Figure 2-1 Visual Basic installation options

uninstall a component, deselect its entry in the list by clicking it, and the check mark will be removed from that entry.

After you make all the changes that you want, click Next until the final installation dialog box is displayed, and then click Finish. All the new program components that you have selected will be copied from the CD-ROM to the system. If any Visual Studio or Visual Basic service packs had been applied to the previously installed VB code, they will need to be reapplied.

I selected the Complete Installation option, but I don't seem to have the sample files. Where do I find the VB sample projects?

Unlike some of the previous versions of Visual Basic, the samples included with version 6 are not installed by running the VB Setup program. Instead, the samples are intended to be accessed via VB's Help facility, and they are installed as an optional part of the Microsoft Developers Network (MSDN) installation. This change makes finding the sample projects much more difficult than in the past. The samples, listed in the following table, are included in the \Samples\Vb98 directory of the MSDN Library CD-ROM that comes with Visual Basic and Visual Studio, and they are contained in standard, uncompressed files that can be readily copied to your system and used.

CD-ROM Folder	Description
ACTXDOC	Creating an ActiveX document
ALARM	Using the timer to create a simple alarm clock
ATM	Using a resource file
AXDATA	Using ActiveX components as data sources for other controls
BLANKER	Using general graphics techniques
BOOKSALE	Using an Automation server to encapsulate the logic of business policies and rules
CALC	Creating a simple calculator
CALLBACK	Using server-initiated callback to the client
CALLDLLS	Calling procedures in DLLs
CHRTSAMP	Using the MS Chart control for graphs

CD-ROM Folder	Description
COFFEE	Creating and using ActiveX components
CONTROLS	Using controls, such as TextBox, CommandButton, and Image
CTLPLUS	Creating an ActiveX control
CTLSADD	Adding controls to an application at run time
DATAREPT	Using the new Data Report Designer
DATATREE	Using the TreeView, ListView, and ProgressBar controls
DATAWARE	Creating classes that can act as sources or consumers of data
DHSHOWME	Using DHTML (Dynamic HTML)
DIALER	Using the MSComm control to dial the phone
ERRORS	Using error-handling techniques
FILECTS	Using a simple file find application
FIRSTAPP	Using the Data control and other data-aware controls
GEOFACTS	Using Excel objects in a VB application
HELLO	Using simple remote automation
INTRFACE	Using the Component Object Model (COM) apartment model resource allocation algorithm
IOBJSAFE	Using Internet Explorer's scripting and security interfaces
LISTCMBO	Data-binding to a list box and a combo box
MCI	Making a simple multimedia application
MDI	Making a simple multiple-document interface application
MESSAGEQ	Using Microsoft Message Queuing (MSMQ)
MSCOMM	Performing terminal emulation using the MSComm control
MSFLEXGD	Using the MS FlexGrid control
OLECONT	Using the OLE Container control
OPTIMIZE	Using optimization techniques
PALMODE	Using PaletteMode property settings
PASSTHRU	Using a simple pass-through server
PICCLIP	Creating an animation of a spinning top
POOLMGR	Using the pool manager
PROGWOB	Programming with objects

CD-ROM Folder	Description
PROPBAG	Storing state values between HTML pages
SDI	Making a simple, single-document interface application
TABORDER	Resetting the tab order of a given form
VBMAIL	Using the Messaging Application Programming Interface (MAPI)
VCR	Creating VB classes
VISDATA	Using Data Access Object (DAO) techniques
WCDEMO	Using WebClass

What products qualify for the upgrade pricing to Visual Basic?

The following products qualify for upgrade pricing to Visual Basic 6 Professional Edition:

- Microsoft Visual Basic 4 Standard Edition or higher
- Microsoft Visual Basic 5 Learning Edition or higher
- Microsoft Office 5 Professional Edition
- Microsoft Office 97 Developer Edition or higher
- Borland Delphi 2 or higher
- Sybase PowerBuilder 5 or higher

Owners of the Microsoft Visual Basic 5 Professional Edition are not eligible for the upgrade pricing but are eligible for a $50 rebate.

For the Visual Basic Enterprise Edition, the following products qualify for upgrade pricing:

- Visual Studio 97 Professional Edition or higher
- Microsoft Visual Basic 4 Professional Edition or higher
- Microsoft Visual C++ 4 Professional Edition or higher
- Microsoft Visual InterDev 1 or higher
- Microsoft Visual J++ 1.1 or higher
- Microsoft Visual FoxPro 3 or higher
- Microsoft Visual SourceSafe 3 or higher

VISUAL BASIC BASICS

The questions and answers presented in this part of the chapter deal with some of the fundamental concepts behind Visual Basic. These questions and answers start out on the ground floor by comparing Visual Basic to other BASIC dialects, and then move into some of the basic concepts that will help you understand Visual Basic better and enable you to use it more effectively.

Is Visual Basic the same thing as BASIC?

Yes and no. Visual Basic is a version of the BASIC language. However, when people refer to BASIC, they often are talking about a much older version of the language that they may have learned about in school or perhaps tinkered with on one of the old PCs that supplied a BASIC interpreter in ROM. These old versions of BASIC were intended to run on character-based operating systems, such as DOS or UNIX. They usually required that each line be numbered, and they often limited variable name lengths to two characters.

Visual Basic is derived from these BASIC roots but has extended way past these humble beginnings. Visual Basic is expressly designed as a Windows development platform and has all the primary features found in modern development languages, including long variable names, advanced program flow control operators, and the ability to use objects and generate COM components.

In addition to these essential language capabilities, Visual Basic supplies a highly productive development environment with myriad features that are aimed at helping you to rapidly develop applications. The Visual Basic Editor provides syntax checking, color-coded keywords, and IntelliSense automatic statement completion. It includes an integrated source-level debugger that enables you to step through your code, set break points, and alter the contents of variables as your application is running. As an interpreted language, Visual Basic is able to provide a highly productive development cycle that enables you to shortcut the traditional compile-test-debug cycle. Using Visual Basic, you can modify your application even while you're using the debugger, and your changes will be effective immediately.

Unlike most other compiled languages, there's no need to exit the debugger, recompile, and then retest.

Visual Basic also enables you to use ActiveX custom controls, which fulfills the promise of code reusability. The VB Professional Edition comes with over 40 ActiveX custom controls that you can snap into your application to immediately gain a wide range of additional functionality.

What is event-driven programming?

Event-driven programming means that the program flow is controlled by events generated by the user. *Events* are user actions, such as clicking with the mouse or entering a keystroke from the keyboard. Events can also be system actions, such as a timer firing. In traditional procedural programming, the application code follows a predetermined path that is coded into the program. Event-driven programs tend to be more flexible and responsive for the end user than traditional programs, because they have no rigid sequence for the application path.

The Microsoft Windows operating system supports event-driven programming by assigning a unique number (called a *handle*) to each window and then monitoring each window for mouse clicks or key presses. When an event occurs, Windows captures the event and sends a message to all open Windows applications. If the Windows application is monitoring for the event, it can take the appropriate action, such as opening a new window. Otherwise, the application can ignore the event.

Visual Basic makes it easy to capture and respond to the events that occur in your application. It insulates you from needing to deal with low-level Windows messages. An event-handling procedure is automatically created for each interface object that is added to your application. For instance, when you add a button named Command1 to your form, Visual Basic creates a subroutine shell named Command1_Click. It automatically captures the Windows messages that are generated by the system, and it it

determines that a click event was generated by the Command1 button, it will execute the Command1_Click subroutine. By adding your own code to this subroutine, you can cause your application to perform a given set of actions when the Command1 button is clicked.

 What makes Visual Basic a productive environment?

Visual Basic gets a great deal of its productivity from two main areas: its visual design environment and its interactive development cycle. Visual Basic's visual design environment allows you to create your application windows interactively by dragging and dropping interface elements from the Toolbox to the form design window. Visual Basic's Toolbox is stocked with a variety of ready-to-use interface elements, including labels, text boxes, combo boxes, lists, check boxes, and many other items that enable you to design your application quickly and easily. For each component added to the form design window, Visual Basic automatically adds subroutines that can handle the events that are generated by the application.

The other highly productive feature of Visual Basic is its interactive development cycle. In many traditional languages, you develop applications by using a code-compile-debug cycle. In this scenario, the developer edits the source code, compiles it into an executable form, and then tests and debugs it. When errors are found, the cycle begins again. The developer must make changes to the source code, compile those changes, and then retest. Visual Basic's interactive nature radically compresses this cycle.

First, the VB Editor traps syntax errors as the source code is being entered. Next, Visual Basic's IDE allows you to change the source code directly from the debugger. This enables you to make many changes while the program is being tested, and circumvents the need to interrupt testing to change and compile the program. Changes made while debugging are effective immediately. This interactive development cycle makes developing applications with Visual Basic much more productive than traditional languages.

 ## What are the differences among the Visual Basic editions?

Four different editions of Visual Basic 6 are available, all of which share the same basic IDE. The main differences among them lie in their capabilities and in the number and types of custom controls that are supplied with each version. The following describes the four editions of Visual Basic, including the intended use for each:

- **Visual Basic Control Creation Edition** Intended to create ActiveX custom controls. It is somewhat limited in that it can't produce standard VB executable programs. However, it does allow VB programs to be run from within the design environment, to facilitate testing the ActiveX controls created in it. This edition can be downloaded for free from the Microsoft Web site at http://msdn.microsoft.com/vbasic/downloads/cce/default.asp.

- **Visual Basic Learning Edition** Intended as an entry-level vehicle that will introduce a new user to Visual Basic. It is a low-cost tool designed to help you learn to program in Visual Basic, but it's not really intended to be used as a programming tool. It can be used to produce standard VB programs, and it comes with the CD-ROM–based Learn VB Now tutorial; however, it comes with only a small selection of ActiveX controls.

- **Visual Basic Professional Edition** Intended for the serious hobbyist or developer for producing stand-alone applications, or applications that run on a single system. It is the real programming entry point of the VB product line. It has all the features found in the Learning Edition, plus more than 20 additional ActiveX controls, and includes IIS Application Designer, Integrated Data Tools and Data Environment, Active Data Objects, Dynamic HTML Page Designer, and documentation on an MSDN CD-ROM.

- **Visual Basic Enterprise Edition** Intended for the corporate or professional developer who needs to produce Internet or distributed applications. It is the top of the VB product line. It includes all the features found in the Professional Edition, plus the Visual Component

Manager, Visual Database Tools, Application Performance Explorer, and developer versions of several BackOffice products, such as SQL Server, Microsoft Transaction Server, Internet Information Server, Visual SourceSafe, and SNA Server.

 ## What types of projects can Visual Basic produce?

Visual Basic 6 can produce numerous different types of projects, as listed here:

Visual Basic Project Type	Description
Standard EXE	Creates a standard executable file
ActiveX DLL	Creates an ActiveX DLL file
ActiveX EXE	Creates an ActiveX executable file
ActiveX component	Creates an ActiveX control
ActiveX document DLL	Creates an ActiveX document DLL, which essentially is a VB application that is accessible through Internet Explorer
ActiveX document EXE	Creates an ActiveX document EXE (a type of ActiveX EXE)
Visual Basic add-in	Creates a VB add-in (a type of ActiveX DLL), which adds functionality to the Visual Basic IDE
Data project	Creates a data project, which accesses information stored in a local or remote database
DHTML application	Creates a Dynamic HTML application, typically used for a Web-based application intended for use on an intranet and dependent on Internet Explorer 4
IIS application	Creates an IIS application, which uses a combination of HTML and compiled VB code in a browser-based application that is executed on a Web server

 ## What are the differences among forms, modules, and class modules?

A VB *form* is basically a window. Forms are contained in files that end with an .frm file extension. You typically have one form for each windo`w in your application. Forms contain interface objects, such as text boxes and subroutines, that

handle the events generated by the interface objects, and can also contain variable declarations, functions, and subroutines. The variables and subroutines that are contained in a form are scoped to that form. In other words, those variables and subroutines typically only work with the data and objects associated with that particular form. Although forms can be used in multiple projects, each form is more commonly used in a single project.

In contrast, a VB *module* is a file that contains variable declarations, subroutines, and functions that typically are shared between different forms as well as other modules. Modules are contained in files that end with a .bas file extension. They provide common resources for subroutines and functions that are used multiple times throughout a project. Modules are also often shared between different VB projects.

A VB *class module* is very similar to a module insofar as both contain code normally shared between forms and other modules. However, whereas a module often contains an assortment of unrelated subroutines and functions, the subroutines and functions in a class module usually all relate to the object that is instantiated by the class. In other words, all the functions and subroutines in the class module are part of the class and are related to one another. Class modules are contained in files that end with a .cls file extension.

 What's a variable?

A *variable* is a named storage space that refers to a computer memory location where you can put program information that may change while your program is running. For instance, your program might use a variable named nCount to store the number of times a loop was executed. Visual Basic insulates you from needing to know the actual memory location of the variable. Instead, you simply have to refer to the variable by name in your code to access the value stored at that location.

What are data types?

All Visual Basic variables have a *data type,* which essentially allows Visual Basic to know the internal storage structure of the variable so that it can correctly access and alter the variable's contents. For instance, numeric data types are stored differently than strings. Likewise, dates are stored differently than characters.

The default VB data type is a *Variant,* which can store many different values, including numbers, strings, dates, and characters. At first, it might seem that using the Variant data type eliminates the need to use any of the other data types that are supported by Visual Basic. However, that's not the case. Although the Variant data type can be useful when you don't know the type of value that will be used in a given variable, it also requires more internal storage space than the simpler data types. In addition, when Visual Basic accesses variables of the Variant data type, it makes assumptions about how the values contained in the storage location should be converted. This can result in some very subtle and difficult-to-find bugs. In most programming projects, you will know the types of values that are going to be stored by each variable, and using the appropriate data type will make your application more efficient and give you more control over the manner in which Visual Basic handles the data. The following table lists the data types supported by Visual Basic 6:

Data Type	Storage Size	Range
Byte	1 byte	0 to 255
Boolean	2 bytes	True or False
Integer	2 bytes	–32,768 to 32,767
Long	4 bytes	–2,147,483,648 to 2,147,483,647
Single	4 bytes	–3.402823E38 to –1.401298E-45 for negative values; 1.401298E–45 to 3.402823E38 for positive values
Double	8 bytes	–1.79769313486232E308 to –4.94065645841247E–324 for negative values; 4.94065645841247E–324 to 1.79769313486232E308 for positive values
Currency	8 bytes	–922,337,203,685,477.5808 to 922,337,203,685,477.5807

Data Type	Storage Size	Range
Decimal	14 bytes	±79,228,162,514,264,337,593,543, 950,335, with no decimal point; ±7.9228162514264337593543950335, with 28 places to the right of the decimal; smallest nonzero number is ±0.0000000000000000000000000001
Date	8 bytes	January 1, 100, to December 31, 9999
Object	4 bytes	Any object reference
String (variable length)	10 bytes + string length	0 to approximately 2 billion
String (fixed length)	Length of string	1 to approximately 65,400
Variant (with numbers)	16 bytes	Any numeric value up to the range of a Double
Variant (with characters)	22 bytes + string length	Same range as for variable-length string
User-defined (using the Type statement)	Number required by elements	Range of each element is the same as the range of its data type

What's a user-defined data type?

A user-defined data type is essentially the same thing as a C language struct. In Visual Basic, a user-defined data type allows you to combine variables of several different data types into a single named structure. This is useful when you want to combine several pieces of related information. User-defined data types are also useful when calling external API functions that require structured data in their parameters.

You create a user-defined data type by using the Type statement in the Declarations section of a form or code module. The following listing illustrates use of the Type statement to declare a new user-defined data type:

```
Type SYSTEMTIME
    wYear         As Integer
    wMonth        As Integer
    wDayOfWeek    As Integer
    wDay          As Integer
    wHour         As Integer
```

```
    wMinute         As Integer
    wSecond         As Integer
    wMilliseconds   As Integer
End Type
```

This example shows how to combine two long variables into a new data type named SYSTEMTIME. After you declare the user-defined data type, you must use the Dim statement to declare a variable of the new SYSTEMTIME type. The following listing illustrates the declaration of a new SYSTEMTIME variable and the assignment of values to two of its members:

```
Dim tSystemTime As SYSTEMTIME
tSystemTime.wYear = 1999
tSystemTime.wMonth = 3
```

Does Visual Basic have any naming restrictions?

Yes. Visual Basic enforces the following rules with regard to object and variable names:

- Must begin with an alphabetic character
- Cannot contain an embedded period
- Cannot exceed 255 characters
- Must be unique in the scope in which it is declared

What's the difference between a subroutine and a function?

Subroutines and functions are very similar. Both are blocks of code that are called from another part of the VB program. Both can accept multiple parameters that are passed into the subroutine or function as part of the call. The primary difference between a subroutine and a function is that a function can return values, and a subroutine doesn't return any values. The following code listing illustrates a simple subroutine:

```
Private Sub DemoSub(sText As String)
    MsgBox sText
End Sub
```

This simple DemoSub subroutine accepts a single String argument and displays a message box using the String parameter that was passed into the subroutine. The Sub statement indicates the beginning of the subroutine, while the End Sub statement indicates the end of the subroutine. No values are returned to the calling procedure.

In contrast, a function can return values to the calling procedure. The following listing presents a simple VB function:

```
Private Function DemoFunction _
      (sText1 As String, sText2 As String) As String
   DemoFunction = sText1 & sText2
End Function
```

The DemoFunction subroutine accepts two parameters, each containing a String data type. The Function statement indicates the beginning of the subroutine, while the End Function statement indicates the end of the subroutine. One important difference between a function and a subroutine is the function's ability to return values to the calling procedure. The data type of the returned value is declared in the final portion of the Function statement. In the preceding example, you can see the As String keywords at the end of the function statement, indicating that the DemoFunction returns a string to the calling procedure. Inside the DemoFunction block, the two String values that are supplied as parameters are concatenated and assigned to the return variable DemoFunction. Any calling procedure can use the DemoFunction function anywhere a standard string variable is used.

The following subroutine illustrates the difference between executing a subroutine and executing a function:

```
Private Sub Command1_Click()

    ' Execute a subroutine.
    Call DemoSub("This is a string parameter")
    ' or
    DemoSub "This is a string"

    ' Execute a function.
    MsgBox (DemoFunction("String1", "String2"))
End Sub
```

The first part of this subroutine illustrates the two methods of calling a subroutine, whereas the second part shows how to execute a function. A subroutine can be executed either by using the Call statement followed by the subroutine name or by executing the subroutine name inline exactly like one of the intrinsic VB functions. If the subroutine is executed by using the Call statement, then any parameters must be enclosed in parentheses. If the subroutine is executed inline, then no parentheses are allowed, and each parameter must be separated by using commas. Since a subroutine doesn't return any value, it can't be used as part of another expression.

A function is executed by using the function name inline exactly as if it were a built-in VB function or statement. Since a function returns a value, it must be used either on the right side of the equal sign, to assign a value to a variable, or as a part of an expression. Unlike the subroutine, a function call can be substituted in any expression that uses the returned data type.

In the previous example, the DemoFunction is used by Visual Basic's built-in MsgBox statement in the same parameter where the MsgBox function accepts a String argument. Visual Basic evaluates each statement from the inside out. When the line containing the MsgBox statement is executed, the DemoFunction will be the first code that is executed. Then, the results of the DemoFunction function (a concatenated string containing the value "String1String2") will be returned to the calling procedure. As far as the MsgBox statement is concerned, it doesn't know or care that the string "String1String2" was produced by a function call. It will act on the returned string exactly like a standard String data type.

 ## What's an object and how do you use one in Visual Basic?

An *object* is a combination of code and data that is used as a single unit. In Visual Basic, each object is defined by its class. The class essentially defines a generic type, whereas an object is a specific instance of that type. For instance, all buttons that are created from the standard Visual Basic

Toolbox have the class CommandButton. However, a
CommandButton object doesn't exist until you create a
specific button in your project.

Generally, objects can be readily used in your projects,
and they provide code and functions that you don't have to
write yourself. The data in a VB object is contained in an
object's properties, whereas the code provided by an object is
executed by using the object's methods. For instance, in
Figure 2-2, you can see an instance of the CommandButton
class, named Command1, displayed in the Visual Basic
Object Browser.

The Object Browser enables you to see all the properties,
methods, and events that are available in an object class. In
this figure, the object class CommandButton is highlighted in
the left pane of the Object Browser, and its properties,

events, and methods are displayed in the right pane.
Properties are marked with the small square and hand icon.

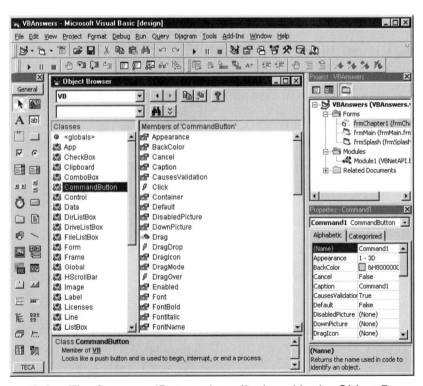

Figure 2-2   The CommandButton class displayed in the Object Browser

Methods are shown with the green rectangle icon, and events are displayed using the small lightning bolt icon.

Properties contain data that is used to influence the appearance or behavior of an object. Two properties of the CommandButton class shown in Figure 2-2 are the Appearance and the Caption properties. Setting the data in the Appearance property alters the display of the button between flat and 3-D, while the text value that's found in the Caption property is displayed on the face of the button.

Methods are functions that can be executed by other objects or by source code. Figure 2-2 shows that the CommandButton class contains the Drag method, which is executed when the user performs a drag-and-drop operation.

Events are called in response to user interface actions. For instance, Figure 2-2 shows that the CommandButton class will respond to the Click event, which occurs when the user clicks the button object by using the mouse.

Remember, the class itself is only a prototype and doesn't actually contain any data. An object of that class type must be instantiated to use its properties, events, and methods. In Figure 2-2, you can see an instance of the CommandButton class, named Command1, in the lower-right corner of the VB Properties window. You can also see examples of the actual data contained by the Command1 object.

Chapter 3

The Integrated Development Environment

Answer Topics!

The Integrated Development Environment @ a Glance

This chapter covers a range of questions and answers regarding Visual Basic's integrated development environment (IDE).

- **IDE Basics** addresses the general topics about Visual Basic's IDE.

- **Working with Projects** discusses the issues involved in using Visual Basic projects and project groups to develop and organize your application development.

- **Code Editing** explains how you can take advantage of the rapid application development features found in Visual Basic's IDE.

IDE BASICS

This first part of the chapter covers using the Visual Basic interactive development environment (IDE). The questions and answers in this part of the chapter introduce you to the different elements that comprise the Visual Basic IDE and help you understand the purpose of each element.

What are the different components of the Visual Basic IDE?

The Visual Basic IDE provides a wide range of functionality and uses numerous different components. Figure 3-1 provides an overview of the Visual Basic IDE, which consists of the following components:

- **Menu bar**   Displays a set of commands that allows you to perform all the available actions within the Visual Basic IDE.

- **Toolbars**   Provide quick access to common actions. Each toolbar contains a set of related items. Visual Basic includes Debug, Edit, Form Editor, and Standard toolbars. You can control which toolbars are displayed by selecting View | Toolbars from the Visual Basic menu bar. You can also create custom toolbars, using the View | Toolbars | Customize option. The toolbars can be either docked beneath the menu bar or free-floating windows.

- **Toolbox**   Contains a set of ActiveX controls that you can use in the Visual Basic Form Designer by dragging and dropping the controls from the Toolbox into the form design window. You can add ActiveX controls to the standard Toolbox by using the Project | Components option. You can also set up a custom Toolbox by right-clicking the toolbar and selecting the Add Tab option from the pop-up menu.

- **Project Explorer**   Lists the different forms, modules, and files that make up a Visual Basic project, a collection of files that are used to build an application. The Project Explorer window can contain one or more projects.

Menu bar

Toolbars

Toolbox

Code Editor

Object Browser

Project Explorer

Form Designer

Properties window

Immediate window

Locals window

Watch window

Form Layout window

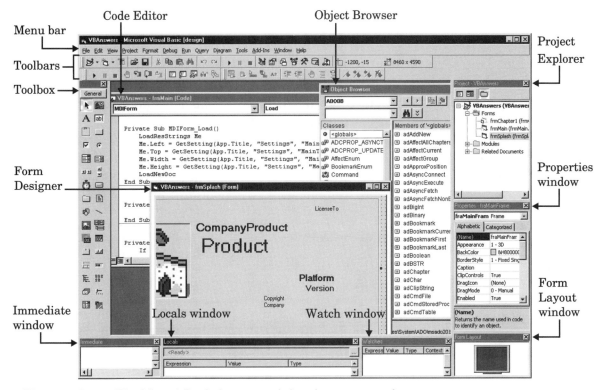

Figure 3-1 The Visual Basic integrated development environment

- **Properties window**   Lists the property settings for a selected object. These properties typically control the appearance and behavior of the object.

- **Object Browser**   Enables you to view all the objects that are used in a Visual Basic project, including the properties, events, and methods that comprise the selected object.

- **Form Designer**   One of the most commonly used windows in the Visual Basic IDE. As its name suggests, it enables you to visually design the interface used in your application. The Form Designer is used in conjunction with the Toolbox. To create a new window, you drag and drop controls from the Toolbox onto the form design window. Then, you can move and resize the objects on the form design window to create the application's interface.

- **Code Editor** The core of the Visual Basic IDE. Enables you to enter the Visual Basic source code that controls your application. The Code Editor provides color-coded keywords and syntax checking, to make entering source code easier and more productive.

- **Form Layout window** Enables you to position the forms used by your application.

- **Immediate window** Used when you debug your application; enables you to display and change the value of the variables that are used in your application. (More information about the Immediate window is presented in Chapter 4.)

- **Locals window** Used while you debug your application; automatically displays the current value of the local variables. (More information about the Locals window is presented in Chapter 4.)

- **Watch window** Another debugging tool that is available when you run your application from the IDE; displays the value of a variable or an object when the application is in break mode. (More information about the Watch window is presented in Chapter 4.)

WORKING WITH PROJECTS

The second part of this chapter presents several questions and answers that deal with Visual Basic projects. The *project* is the primary organizational unit of a Visual Basic application. Every Visual Basic application must have an associated project, and all the Visual Basic forms, code modules, and other file types are contained within a project. The questions and answers in this section will help you understand Visual Basic projects and learn how to use them to build applications.

 How do I open and save a project?

You can open an existing project in Visual Basic either by selecting File | Open Project or by clicking the Open icon on the Visual Basic toolbar. The Visual Basic Open Project dialog box, shown in Figure 3-2, is displayed.

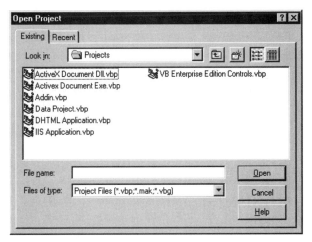

Figure 3-2 Open Project dialog box

The Open Project dialog box has two tabs at the top that help you locate quickly the project that you want to open. The Existing tab (see in Figure 3-2) enables you to navigate through the different folders on your system to find a specific project. The Recent tab presents a list of the most recently opened Visual Basic projects. The first icon that is displayed next to the folder name allows you to navigate to the next-higher level in the directory. The second icon allows you to create a new folder. The two icons on the far right toggle the file list between an icon list and a details list. You can also right-click any of the files displayed in the Open Project dialog box's file list to display the Windows Explorer pop-up menu. The pop-up menu typically allows you to delete, rename, view, and perform other file management actions to the files displayed in the list.

 Tip: *When you are actively working on a project, the Recent tab is the quickest way to reopen your project. You can also quickly reopen a project by using the most recently used project list that's displayed in Visual Basic's File menu.*

You can save a Visual Basic project either by selecting File | Save (or Save As) or by clicking the Save icon on the Visual Basic toolbar. If this is the first time that the project has been saved, a Save dialog box is displayed, which looks and acts much like the Open Project dialog box presented in

Figure 3-2. If the project has been previously saved, then selecting either of these options will immediately save the project along with the files contained in the project, and no Save dialog box will be shown.

 ## How do I add files to a project?

You can add different types of files to your Visual Basic project either by selecting one of the Add options from the Project menu or by right-clicking in the Project window and selecting the Add option from the pop-up menu. For instance, the Project menu allows you to add the following types of files: forms (FRM), modules (BAS), class modules (CLS), user controls (CTL), and property pages (PAG). Each of the different file types lists a different set of options in the Open Project dialog box. For instance, selecting Projects | Add Class Modules displays the Add Class Module dialog box, shown in Figure 3-3.

All the different Add dialog boxes use the New and Existing tabs, enabling you to either add a new file to your

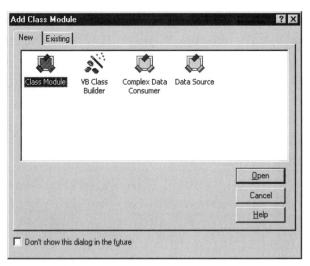

Figure 3-3 Adding files

project or locate and add an existing file to your project. In Figure 3-3, you can see that the New tab for adding a class module enables you to add either a class module, a VB class builder, a complex data consumer, or a data source. All the options add a CLS file to your project. The main difference among them is in the code stubs that are included in the file that is added. For instance, whereas adding a regular class module adds an empty file, adding a data source adds a file that contains many prebuilt property and method declarations. The Existing tab presents a standard Open dialog box that allows you to traverse the directory and select the desired file to add to your project.

In addition to these options that add specific types of files to a Visual Basic project, the Projects menu and the pop-up menu both offer a generic Add Files option that displays an Add File dialog box that allows you to add any type of file to your project. The generic Add File option mainly is used when adding text files or resource files to your Visual Basic projects.

Tip: *Because adding new forms is one of the most common development activities, the Visual Basic toolbar includes an icon that provides a shortcut for adding new forms to a project.*

How do I add ActiveX controls to a project?

You can add ActiveX controls to the Visual Basic IDE by selecting Project | Components, which displays the Components dialog box, shown in Figure 3-4.

Scroll through Visual Basic's Components dialog box until you see the ActiveX control that you want to add. For instance, to add the Microsoft Flex Grid control, scroll through the list of components until you see Microsoft FlexGrid Control 6.0. Click the check box immediately in front of the control's name on the list, and then click the OK button. This adds the Microsoft Flex Grid ActiveX control to Visual Basic's Toolbox. After you add a control to the Toolbox, you can use it in your Visual Basic project by dragging and dropping it onto a Visual Basic form.

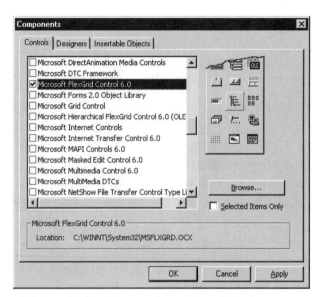

Figure 3-4   Adding ActiveX controls to Visual Basic

Tip: *You can also add ActiveX controls to your project by dragging and dropping the controls from Windows Explorer onto Visual Basic's Toolbox.*

How do I add references to a project?

Much like ActiveX controls, *references* are COM objects that add functionality to your Visual Basic application. References are also known as *OLE type libraries* (or sometimes *OLE libraries*). Unlike ActiveX controls, VB references do not have a visual representation or user interface. Instead, they are used (or "referenced") in code. For instance, one common reference that you might want to add is a reference to the ADO (ActiveX Data Objects) library. The ADO reference library extends VB's capabilities by allowing VB applications

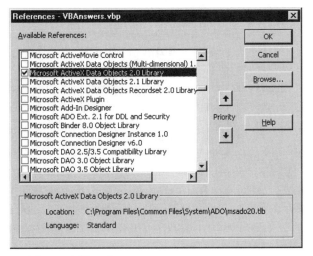

Figure 3-5 Adding a VB reference

to access data from a variety of sources, including databases and spreadsheets.

To add a reference in Visual Basic, select Project | References, which displays the References dialog box, shown in Figure 3-5.

Scroll through Visual Basic's References dialog box until you see the reference library that you want to add. For instance, to add the ADO library, you select Microsoft ActiveX Data Objects 2.0 Library. Clicking the corresponding check box and then clicking the OK button adds the ADO library to Visual Basic's IDE. You can then use any of the ADO objects, methods, and properties in your VB application.

 How do I add resources to a project?

Resource files contain bitmaps and other binary resources that you may need to use in your Visual Basic project. To add

a resource file to your VB project, you need to right-click Visual Basic's Project window and select the Add option, which displays the pop-up menu shown in Figure 3-6.

The pop-up Add menu enables you to add several different types of files to your VB project. To add a resource file, select the Add File option, which then displays the Add File dialog box, shown in Figure 3-7.

The Add File dialog box uses an *extension filter* that restricts the list to just the file types that VB expects to use. Resource filenames end with an extension of .res. Selecting a RES file from the list and then clicking OK adds the resource file to your VB project. After the resource file has been added, you see a Related Documents section appear in your VB Project window, as shown in Figure 3-8.

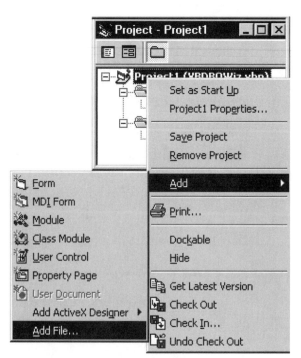

Figure 3-6 Pop-up Add menu

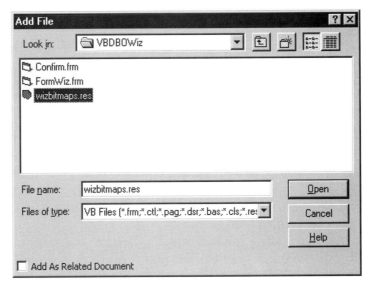

Figure 3-7   Add File dialog box

After you add the resource file to your project, you can use VB's LoadResData, LoadResPicture, or LoadResString functions to use the contents of the resource file in your application.

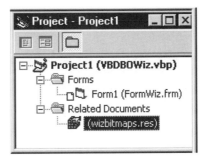

Figure 3-8   Project window with a resource file

 ## How do I make an executable file?

After you design the forms and add the code you want to your project, you can make your project into an executable file by selecting File | Make, which displays the Make Project dialog box, shown in Figure 3-9.

The Make Project dialog box enables you to select the folder that will contain your project's executable file. By default, the executable filename is the same as the Visual Basic project name, with the extension .exe appended to the end. However, you can easily assign the project a new name simply by typing over the name shown in the Make Project dialog box.

The Make Project dialog box works exactly like the Visual Basic Open Project and Save dialog boxes. The drop-down combo box at the top of the screen allows you to navigate to different directories. The first icon that is displayed next to the folder name allows you to return to the next-higher level in the directory. The second icon allows you to create a new folder. The two icons on the far right toggle the file list between an icon list and a details list. You can also right-click any of the files displayed in the Make Project dialog box's file list to display the Windows Explorer pop-up menu.

In addition to these options, the Make Project dialog box provides an Options button that enables you to assign the

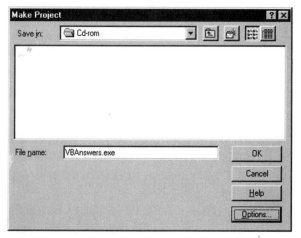

Figure 3-9 Make Project dialog box

properties that will be applied to the executable file. The Make options are shown in Figure 3-10.

The Make options allow you to assign to your project a version number, version information, application title, and application icon. By checking the Auto Increment check box, you can cause the revision number of your project to increment automatically each time you run the Make command. The Version Information field is used to enter company name, description, legal copyright, legal trademarks, product name, and any other comments that you may want to attach to this executable file. The Command Line Arguments field enables you to supply a set of command-line arguments that will be used by default if the executable file is started from the Run menu. The Conditional Compilation Arguments field allows you to specify constant declarations that control conditional compilation of the Visual Basic source code.

The Compile tab (the top of which you can see in Figure 3-10) presents options that allow you to specify whether your project should be compiled to p-code or to native code. The Compile to Native Code option indicates that the resulting executable file will be built in the machine code for the current system type. In most cases, this is in Intel format, but

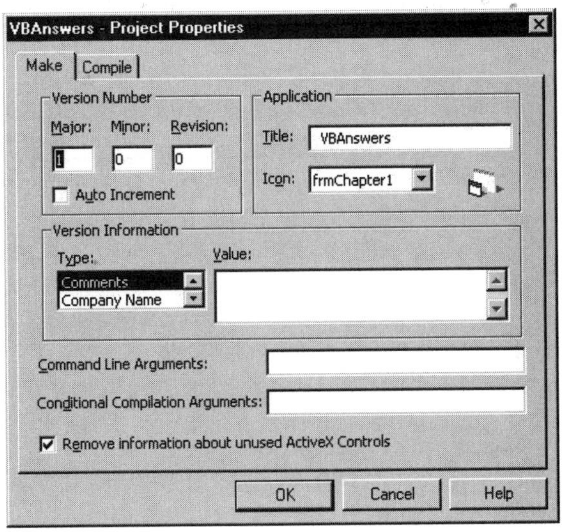

Figure 3-10 Make options

Visual Basic also supports the Alpha processor. The Compile to P-Code option specifies that the resulting executable file will be in an intermediate format that must be transformed into machine instructions before it is executed. The Compile to P-Code option produces smaller Visual Basic executable files, whereas the Compile to Native Code option produces faster executable files.

Note: *Unlike most other development languages, executable programs developed with Visual Basic are not completely stand-alone programs. To be executed, the Visual Basic runtime files must be present on the target system. The most important of these files is msvbvm60.dll. This is true even if you use the Compile to Native Code option on the Project Properties dialog box's Compile tab. The Visual Basic license allows you to distribute these runtime files freely with your application. The Visual Basic Setup Wizard and other third-party installation utilities help you bundle these files together with your application.*

 How do I use add-ins?

An *add-in* is a customized tool that adds functionality to the Visual Basic IDE. Visual Basic is shipped with many add-ins, and you can obtain other specialized add-ins from various third parties. To use an add-in, you must first register it by using the Visual Basic Add-In Manager. You start the Add-In Manager by selecting Add-Ins | Add-In Manager. You can see the Add-In Manager in Figure 3-11.

To install an add-in, scroll through the list of add-ins on the Add-In Manager, select the add-in that you want to use, and then click one of the following Load Behavior check boxes:

- **Loaded/Unloaded**   Causes the add-in to be loaded immediately.

- **Load on Startup**   Causes the add-in to be loaded the next time that the Visual Basic IDE is started.

- **Command Line**   Causes the add-in to be loaded when the IDE is started from a command line.

Installing a new add-in will add a new option to the Visual Basic Add-In menu.

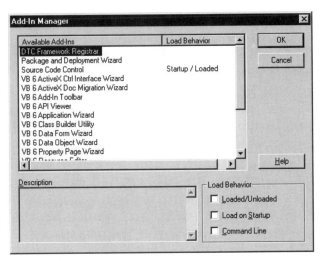

Figure 3-11 Add-In Manager

 Tip: *To unload an add-in, uncheck all the Load Behavior check boxes.*

What is a project group?

A Visual Basic *project group* contains one or more related projects. The main purpose of the project group is to enable you to create and test ActiveX controls and other COM components, which generally provide methods and properties that are intended to be used and reused by other applications. To test this type of COM component, you need to have a *container* (a standard application) in which you can place the component. You can then build functions into the container (in other words, the functions that enable you to test the application) that can call and query the various methods and properties that are provided by the component.

Visual Basic's project group enables you to create both COM components and standard applications in the same project group. Figure 3-12 shows an example Visual Basic project group.

This project group consists of an ActiveX control project group named NetworkSystems, and a standard Visual Basic EXE project named Test NetworkSystems. Here, all the code for the NetworkSystems ActiveX control is contained in the NetworkSystems project, whereas the TestNetworkSystems

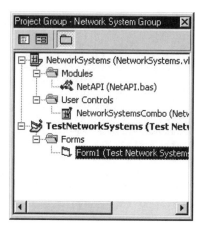

Figure 3-12   The Visual Basic project group

project is simply used as a convenient container to test the NetworkSystems ActiveX control.

Although Visual Basic's project group is primarily intended for creating and testing COM components, it certainly isn't limited to just these types of projects. You can make a project group that contains any combination of Visual Basic project types.

The New Project and Open Project options both just replace my current project group. How can I add a project to a project group?

You can add a project to an existing project group by selecting File | Add Project, which displays the Add Project dialog box, shown in Figure 3-13.

The Add Project dialog box has the following three tabs that you can use to add either a new project or an existing project to your current Visual Basic project group:

● **New**   Enables you to add a new project consisting of one of the various Visual Basic project types. For instance, if your current Visual Basic project is an ActiveX control and you want to add a standard EXE project to your project group to test the control, select the Standard EXE project type from the list of new projects displayed. Then, click the Open button to add the project and its associated files to your current project group.

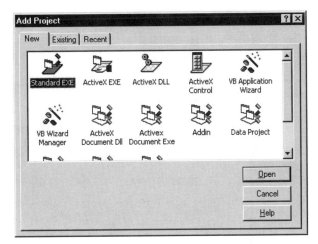

Figure 3-13   Add Project dialog box

● **Existing**   Enables you to navigate through the different folders on your system, to find a specific project.

● **Recent**   Presents a list of the most recently opened Visual Basic projects. In each case, after the project is located, you click the Open button to add the project to the project group in Visual Basic's IDE.

Tip: *A Visual Basic project can belong to more than one project group.*

CODE EDITING

The first section of this chapter answers questions about the general use of the Visual Basic IDE. The questions and answers in this section deal with some of the issues that turn up while writing code in the Visual Basic IDE.

How do I open a window to write code?

The best method for opening a window to write code depends on the type of module that you are working with. If you are working with a Form module or one of the visual designers, such as the Data Environment or Data Report, the easiest way to open a window that allows you to edit code is to right-click the desired object name in the Project window and select the Edit Code option from the pop-up menu. Alternatively, if you are working with one of the code-based objects, such as a BAS

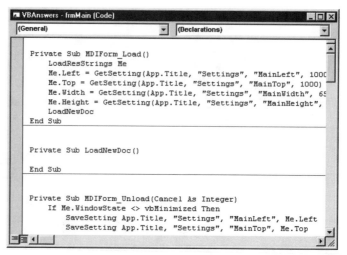

Figure 3-14 The Visual Basic Code window

or CLS module, you can simply double-click the object name in the Project window. In each case, the Visual Basic Code window shown in Figure 3-14 is displayed.

The Code window allows you to type the Visual Basic source code for your application. By default, the Code window color-codes the Visual Basic keywords, and automatically checks the syntax of each line when you move your cursor off the line. As Figure 3-14 shows, all the Visual Basic subroutines contained in the module are displayed in the Code window, and each subroutine is bordered by a set of horizontal lines.

 How do I create an event procedure?

An *event procedure* is a specially named subroutine that Visual Basic executes in response to a user event. When you add a user interface object (such as a button) to a Visual Basic form, Visual Basic automatically generates event procedure stubs for that user interface object. For instance, when a button is added to a Visual Basic form, several event procedure stubs are added to handle events such as mouse clicks and double-clicks. When a user clicks a button, a click event is generated. Visual Basic captures that click event and executes the corresponding click event procedure.

By adding your own custom code to Visual Basic's event procedure stubs, you can make your application respond to different user actions. An event procedure is named by combining the control's name, an underscore, and the name of the event. For instance, the event procedure that handles mouse clicks for a button named Command1 would be named Command1_Click.

You can create an event procedure for a button from either the Form Designer or directly from the Code Editor. To create an event procedure from the form design window, simply double-click the interface object. The Visual Basic Code window appears, with the default event procedure automatically displayed. To create an event procedure from the Code window, select the desired object in the object list box and then use the procedure list box to select the event procedure for that object. Figure 3-15 illustrates the procedure drop-down list box for a command button.

In Figure 3-15, you can see that the Command1 object has been selected in the object list box, located in the upper-left portion of the Code window. The procedure list box, located in the upper-right portion of the Code window, lists the available

Object list box   Procedure list box

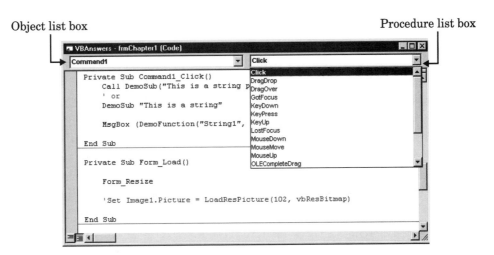

Figure 3-15 Creating an event procedure

event procedures for the Command1 button. Selecting one of
the entries in the procedure list box automatically creates an
event procedure for that event in the main portion of the Code
window. You can then enter your own VB code into the event
procedure to enable your application to take some action based
on the event.

How do I use the splitter window in Visual Basic's Code Editor?

The splitter window in Visual Basic's Code Editor allows you
to edit simultaneously two different sections of a Visual Basic
source file. The splitter window allows you to get around the
limitation of the Visual Basic IDE that restricts multiple
editing windows from being open for a single module. By
default, the splitter window is closed. You can open the
splitter window by positioning the mouse pointer over the
small horizontal bar at the top of the Code window's scroll
bar. When the mouse pointer turns into a pair of horizontal
bars, hold down the left mouse button and drag the splitter
bar to a new position on the scroll bar. This creates two
separate scrollable sections in the Code window. Figure 3-16
shows the Code Editor's splitter window.

Figure 3-16   Code Editor splitter window

When the splitter window is displayed, you can edit code in both the upper and lower sections of the Code window. If you position both windows to the same section of code, all the changes you make in one window are displayed in the other window. You can close the splitter window by dragging the splitter bar back to the top of the scroll bar.

What's automatic code completion and how do I use it?

The automatic code completion feature is also known as *IntelliSense*. IntelliSense allows Visual Basic to display interactive prompts that can help you complete the current statement that you are editing. Visual Basic automatically displays the interactive prompt as soon as you complete typing either a valid Visual Basic function name or the name of a function or object that's used in your Visual Basic application. Figure 3-17 demonstrates Visual Basic's IntelliSense feature in action.

In Figure 3-17, you can see that typing the dot following the name of a valid form causes Visual Basic to display a drop-down list that contains all the valid properties and

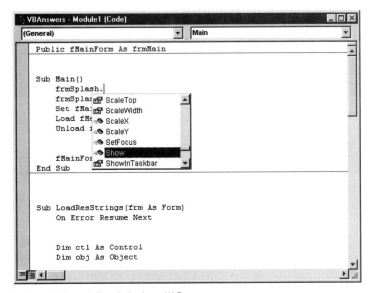

Figure 3-17　Visual Basic's IntelliSense

methods for that form. In this case, the list contains all
the properties and methods for the form named frmSplash.
Selecting the desired object in the list and then pressing the
TAB key allows Visual Basic to write the selected source code
automatically in the Code Editor. IntelliSense can help you
avoid syntax errors, and it often eliminates the need to use
online help to learn the correct parameters and constants
required by a particular function or object.

How can I turn off Visual Basic's syntax checking?

Visual Basic's auto syntax checking feature can be an
important productivity feature, especially for beginning and
intermediate programmers. However, it can also be an
annoyance for experienced developers who are very familiar
with Visual Basic's syntax. Fortunately, turning off auto
syntax checking is quite simple. Select Tools | Options to
open Visual Basic's Options dialog box, shown in Figure 3-18.

The Auto Syntax Check option is turned on by default.
To turn off auto syntax checking, select the Editor tab on
the Options dialog box and uncheck the Auto Syntax Check
check box. To save and activate the new configuration, click
the OK button.

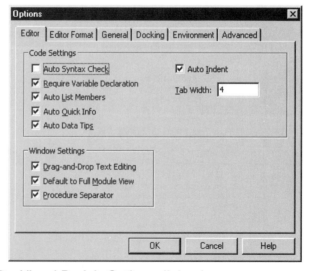

Figure 3-18   Visual Basic's Options dialog box

How can I change the Code window to display a single procedure, just like Visual Basic 4 used to do?

The ability of Visual Basic's Code window to display multiple subroutines makes it much easier to see and move between the different procedures that are contained in a given module. However, if you're more comfortable restricting the Code window to a single procedure, as in Visual Basic 4, you can do this in the Visual Basic project options: select Tools | Options. When the Visual Basic Options dialog box is shown, deselect the Default to Full Module View option on the Editor tab and then click OK. The Code window now displays only a single procedure. In this mode, you must use the object and procedure drop-down list boxes to display different procedures in the Code window.

Are there any keyboard shortcuts for editing?

The most useful keyboard shortcuts for editing are CTRL+Z, CTRL+X, CTRL+C, and CTRL+V. These shortcuts basically have the same use in the Visual Basic Code Editor as they have in the Microsoft Office applications. The CTRL+Z shortcut performs a multilevel undo. The CTRL+X shortcut cuts the selected section of text to the Clipboard. The CTRL+C shortcut copies the selected section of text to the Clipboard. The CTRL+V shortcut pastes the contents of the Clipboard to the current cursor location.

Do you have any tips about how to set up the Visual Basic development environment?

Yes. The following list presents the Visual Basic IDE options that I usually use:

- *Leave on the option for syntax checking.* Turning off the syntax checking option does give you a bit more freedom in the Code window, because you can freely jump between lines without needing to complete the syntax of the current line. However, I find that allowing Visual Basic to check the syntax automatically as I enter each line results in substantially more time saved than easier editing.

● *Turn on the Prompt to Save Changes option.* Enabling the Prompt to Save Changes option can save you from loosing hours of programming time. When you're deep in the editing and testing cycle, it's a certainty that at some time or another, you'll lock up your test program. If this happens, all the code changes that you made will be lost. The *Prompt to Save Changes* option gives you the option to save the project before the program starts. Responding to the Save dialog box takes only a second. If you make numerous changes that you don't want to lose, you can save the project; otherwise, you can skip the save and just run the program.

● *Close the Form Layout window.* With every new release of Visual Basic, screen real estate seems to become an ever-more-precious commodity. The Form Layout window presents a miniature view of the current form, but it's too small really to be helpful, and most of the time it just wastes a section of your development space.

● *Close the Toolbox when coding.* Although the Toolbox is really handy while you're working in the form design window, when you're coding, you'll probably find that the Toolbox just takes up precious space that could be used by the Code window. Closing the Toolbox significantly expands the size of the Code window. To bring back the Toolbox, just click the View | Toolbox menu option.

● *Add the Edit toolbar when coding.* When you're performing a lot of coding, the Formatting toolbar can really come in handy. It's especially useful for indenting as well as commenting and "uncommenting" blocks of code. You can add the Editing toolbar by selecting View | Toolbars | Edit.

● *Use the CTRL+C, CTRL+V, and CTRL+X keyboard shortcuts.* When you're entering code, using the keyboard shortcuts to perform cut-and-paste actions often is easier than using the mouse. These keyboard shortcuts enable you to perform the most common editing actions without having to remove your hands from the keyboard. The CTRL+V (paste) operation can be particularly useful when you need to insert the same text multiple times.

- *Make liberal use of IntelliSense.* Visual Basic's IntelliSense code-completion feature can provide a big productivity boost when you are entering code. You can use the IntelliSense feature to have Visual Basic enter method, property, and constant names that you might otherwise need to look up in the online help or via the Object Browser.

- *Add the Debug toolbar when testing.* When you're ready to test and debug your application, be sure to add the Debug toolbar to the Visual Basic IDE. The Debug toolbar has icons that allow you to easily set breakpoints, single-step through the application source code, and view and change variables. More information about the Debug toolbar is presented in Chapter 4. You can add the Debug toolbar by choosing View | Toolbars | Debug.

Chapter 4

The Visual Basic Debugger

Answer Topics!

The Visual Basic Debugger @ a Glance

This chapter presents a set of questions and answers that deal with using the debugging features that are provided by Visual Basic.

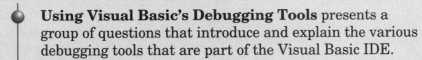

Using Visual Basic's Debugging Tools presents a group of questions that introduce and explain the various debugging tools that are part of the Visual Basic IDE.

Debugging a Program illustrates how you use those tools to perform some of the most common Visual Basic debugging tasks.

USING VISUAL BASIC'S DEBUGGING TOOLS

The questions in this section of the chapter explore the different debugging tools that are provided as part of the Visual Basic integrated development environment (IDE). The debugging tools discussed are the Debug toolbar, the Quick Watch dialog box, the Immediate window, the Watch window, and the Locals window.

 How do I use the Debug toolbar?

The Debug toolbar gives you easy access to Visual Basic's most frequently used debugging options. The Debug toolbar is not displayed, by default. To display the Debug toolbar, select View | Toolbars | Debug from Visual Basic's menu. The Debug toolbar can be either free-floating or docked to any side of the IDE. To undock the docked toolbar, simply click its handle and drag it to its new location. To dock the free-floating toolbar, click its title bar and drag it to its new location. In either situation, the toolbar's new status as either docked or undocked depends on the location to which you drag it. If that location is adjacent to one of the sides of the IDE, the toolbar automatically docks to that side. Otherwise, it is free-floating. Thus, if you click and drag the free-floating toolbar, with the intention of docking it, but then release it before it's adjacent to the side of the IDE, it remains free-floating. The Debug toolbar buttons are shown in Figure 4-1.

The following is a list of the various buttons shown in the Debug toolbar, including a description of the result of clicking each icon:

- **Run**   Runs the current project from the Visual Basic IDE, which automatically enables the debugging environment.

- **Break**   Pauses the execution of the program currently running in the Visual Basic IDE. Puts the program in break mode, during which you can set breakpoints and examine and modify the contents of program objects and variables.

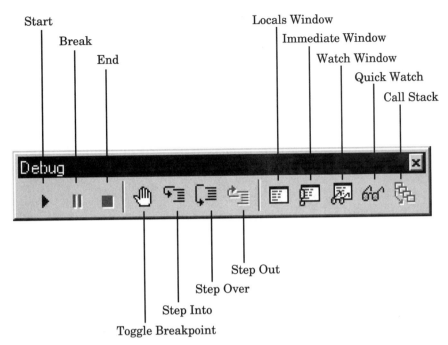

Figure 4-1 The Visual Basic Debug toolbar buttons

- **End** Terminates the execution of the program and returns the IDE to development mode.

- **Toggle Breakpoint** Adds or removes breakpoints from the Visual Basic source code. Adding a breakpoint causes the execution of the program to stop when the breakpoint is encountered. Clicking the Toggle Breakpoint icon when the cursor is positioned on an executable line causes a breakpoint to be placed on the line. Breakpoints are indicated in the IDE by a red dot in the left margin of the Code window. To remove a breakpoint, you simply click the Toggle Breakpoint icon when the cursor is positioned on a line that has a breakpoint.

- **Step Into** Causes the program to *single-step,* executing one line at a time in the current project. If the current

line is a subroutine or function, the debugger breaks program execution at the first executable line in the procedure or function. Otherwise, the program execution breaks at the next executable line of source code.

- **Step Over** Also causes the program to single-step. If the current line is a subroutine or function, the debugger breaks program execution at the first executable line following the call to the subroutine or function. The program will not go into break mode at any of the lines contained in the subroutine or function unless a breakpoint was previously placed in the subroutine or function.

- **Step Out** Also causes the debugger to single-step. If the current line is within a subroutine or function, clicking the Step Out icon causes the program execution to break at the first executable line following the subroutine or function.

- **Locals Window** Causes the Locals window to be displayed, which displays the contents of all the variables that were declared in the current procedure, but does not include global variables or variables that were declared in other procedures.

- **Immediate Window** Causes the Immediate window to be displayed, which is used to enter lines of code that will be executed while the program is in break mode.

- **Watch Window** Causes the Watch window to be displayed, which lists all the watch expressions that have been added to the watch list. A watch expression can be a variable name, an object name, a procedure name, or a Visual Basic expression.

- **Quick Watch** Displays Visual Basic's Quick Watch dialog box, which enables you to view the contents of a variable and optionally add it to the current list of watch expressions.

- **Call Stack** Displays the Call Stack window, which lists the stack of active procedures.

 What's the purpose of the Quick Watch dialog box?

The Quick Watch dialog box displays the contents of a variable or an expression and, optionally, can add the variable or expression to the list of watched expressions. To use the Quick Watch dialog box, position your cursor on the variable that you want to view and then click the Quick Watch icon on the Debug toolbar. To view the results of an expression, highlight the expression and then click the Quick Watch icon, which displays the Quick Watch dialog box, shown here:

```
Quick Watch                                                  ☒
┌Context────────────────────────────────────────────────────┐
│ VBAnswers.frmChapter1.Command1_Click                       │
└───────────────────────────────────────────────────────────┘
┌Expression───────────────────────────────┐   ┌───────────┐
│ sTextString                              │   │    Add    │
└──────────────────────────────────────────┘   └───────────┘
                                                ┌───────────┐
┌Value─────────────────────────────────────┐   │  Cancel   │
│ "This is a string parameter"             │   └───────────┘
└──────────────────────────────────────────┘   ┌───────────┐
                                                │   Help    │
                                                └───────────┘
```

The Context box identifies the project, module, and procedure that are currently active. The Expression box displays the name of the program variable. The Value box displays the contents of the variable. Clicking the Add button enables you to add the variable or expression to the list of watched expressions.

 What's the purpose of the Immediate window?

Visual Basic's Immediate window enables you to enter and execute code while your Visual Basic application is in debug mode. By using the Immediate window, you can display or change the contents of a variable, as well as perform any other action allowed in Visual Basic code. In addition, you can cut and paste between the Immediate window and the Code window.

The Immediate window is displayed by default when a program is executed using the IDE. If the Immediate window is closed, you can open it either by selecting View | Immediate or by pressing CTRL+G. Like most of the other Visual Basic windows, the Immediate window can be either docked to the side of the IDE or free-floating. Figure 4-2 illustrates using the Immediate window.

The first line in the Immediate window illustrates displaying the contents of a variable by using the question mark command. To display the contents of a variable by using the Immediate window, enter a question mark, followed by the variable name, and then press the ENTER key. The value of the variable will be displayed on the following line. To change a variable or to execute a line of code, type the code into the Immediate window and then press the ENTER key. If the code entered is correct and free of syntax errors, it will be executed. In Figure 4-2, you can see that the content of the variable named sTextString has been changed by using a simple assignment statement.

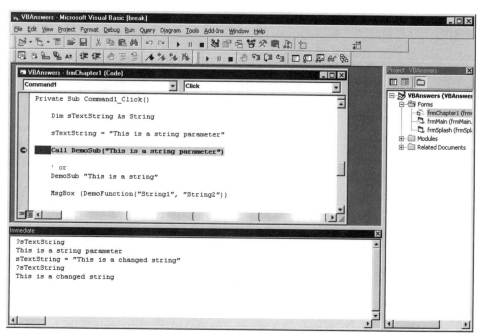

Figure 4-2   Using the Immediate window

The Immediate window lists all the actions performed using the Immediate window during the debugging session, and is cleared either when the session ends or manually. To clear the Immediate window manually, select the text in the Immediate window and press the DELETE key.

What's the purpose of the Watch window?

Visual Basic's Watch window enables you to view and change the contents of variables dynamically while a program is running from the IDE. The values of the variables shown in the Watch window are automatically updated as the program is executed.

The Watch window is displayed automatically when a watch expression is added to the project being debugged. A watch expression must be added to the Watch window, before any values will be shown in the Watch window. You can add a watch expression by selecting the Add Watch option from the Debug menu, by clicking the Watch icon on the Debug toolbar, or by clicking the Add Watch button in the Quick View dialog box. The Add Watch dialog box is shown in Figure 4-3.

To add a watch expression, enter the variable name, the object name, the function name, or any other valid Visual Basic expression into the Expression field of the Add Watch dialog box. Then, click the OK button. The Watch window, shown in Figure 4-4, will be displayed.

The example Watch window in Figure 4-4 contains both a standard program variable and an object. The variable or object name is shown in the Expression column, and the current value is shown in the Value column. The Type column shows the variable's data type. The Context column lists the current form or module and procedure of the watch expression.

As the program is single-stepped or run, the variable values shown in the Watch window's Value list will be updated as the contents of the variables are modified. To manually change the contents of a variable shown in the Watch window, simply type over the value of the variable and press the ENTER key. If the value entered is valid, then the variable will be changed.

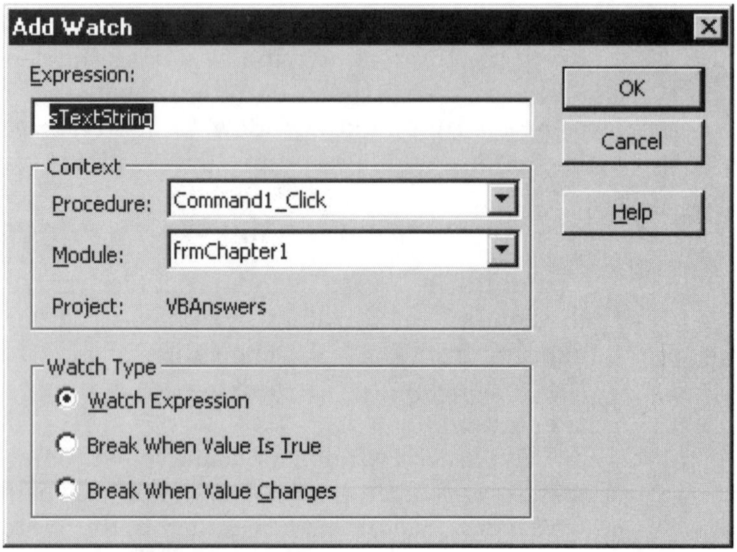

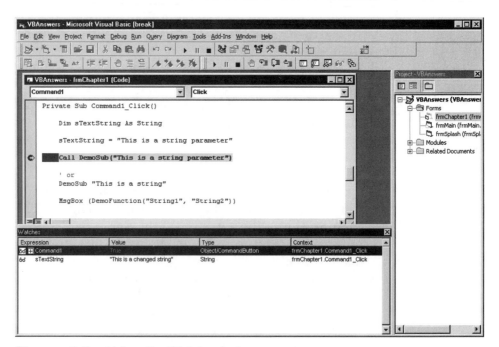

Figure 4-3 Add Watch dialog box

Figure 4-4 Using the Watch window

In addition to working with regular variables, the Watch window can work with objects. When an object is displayed in the Watch window, a plus sign is shown. Clicking the plus sign expands the list in the Watch window to show all of the object's properties and their values.

Tip: *The value of an object can't be displayed using Visual Basic's Quick View option. To display the contents of an object, you must use the Watch window.*

What's the purpose of the Locals window?

Visual Basic's Locals window automatically displays all the variables that are declared in the current procedure. By using the Locals window, you can both display and modify the values of the variables and objects found in the current procedure.

You can view the Locals window by selecting View | Locals Window or by clicking the Locals Window icon on the Debug toolbar. Like the other Visual Basic debugging windows, the Locals window can be either docked or free-floating. Figure 4-5 presents the Locals window.

The button with an ellipsis, in the upper-right corner of the Locals window, is the Call Stack button. Clicking this button displays the Call Stack dialog box, which displays the current list of active procedures. The Expression column lists the names of all the local variables and objects. The Value column displays the current contents of each of the local variables and objects. The Type column displays their data types.

In addition to displaying local variables, the Locals window enables you to change the contents of those variables. You can edit the value of a variable by clicking the variable's value in the Value column. When the cursor changes to an I-beam, you can edit the variable's value.

The variables and their values shown in the Locals window are updated whenever the program is changed from run to break mode.

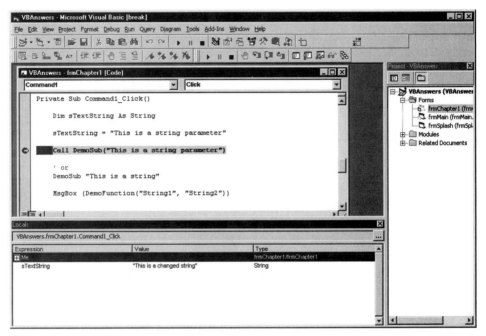

Figure 4-5 Using the Locals window

Tip: *You can also add program variables and objects to the Watch window or the Immediate window by dragging and dropping variable and object names from the Code window to the Watch window or the Immediate window when the program is in break mode.*

DEBUGGING A PROGRAM

This section addresses using the Visual Basic debugger to perform some of the common debugging tasks. The questions and answers in this section deal with topics such as starting the debugger, working with breakpoints, viewing the value of variables and objects, and stepping through the code of the program being debugged. This section ends with a set of tips to help you make the best use of the Visual Basic debugging environment.

What is break mode?

The Visual Basic IDE has three basic modes:

- **Design mode**   Use to develop your application, by visually designing windows and entering source.

- **Run mode**   Use when you run your application from Visual Basic's IDE.

- **Break mode**   Use to debug your application.

Visual Basic's current mode is displayed in the title bar. Figure 4-6 shows the Visual Basic IDE in break mode.

Break mode is entered when you run your application from the Visual Basic IDE and the program encounters a breakpoint. Program execution is suspended before the line containing the breakpoint is executed, and the debugger provides a snapshot of the current program state. When a program is in break mode, you can view and edit code, inspect and change the value of variables, and perform other debugging actions such as setting breakpoints. You can reenter run mode by clicking the Run button or by clicking one of the Step icons on the Debug toolbar.

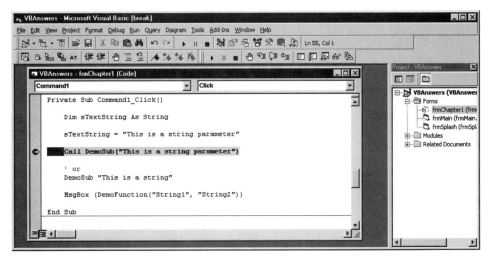

Figure 4-6   Break mode

 ## How do I start the Visual Basic debugger to debug my program?

Visual Basic makes debugging your programs very easy. Any time you run your Visual Basic program from the IDE, you start the Visual Basic debugger. You can run Visual Basic programs from the IDE by selecting Run | Start, by clicking the Start icon on Visual Basic's Standard or Debug toolbars, by pressing the F5 key from the IDE, or by clicking one of the step icons on the Debug toolbar. After you start the program from the IDE, it will run until it encounters a breakpoint, you end the program, you select the Break option from the Run menu, or you click the Break icon from the Debug toolbar. When the program is in break mode, you can perform all the available debugging options. For instance, you can inspect and change any value of the program variables, as well as edit the application source code. After you perform the necessary debugging activities, you can resume the program's execution by using any one of the start options.

 Tip: *Running your Visual Basic program from the IDE causes the current directory to become the directory that contains your VB6.EXE executable file—it is not the directory in which your VB project is stored. If your Visual Basic project uses file system objects that are found in your project's directory, they will not be found when you run your application through the IDE. To work around this situation, you can either include the entire path for the file while you are debugging your project or copy the files to the directory that contains the VB6.EXE file.*

 ## How do I set a breakpoint?

The easiest way to set a breakpoint is to open the Code window and single-click the gray margin to the left of the executable line on which you want the program execution to stop. After you set a breakpoint, a red dot appears in the gray margin, and the line is highlighted in red. Figure 4-7 shows a break set in the Code window.

```
VBAnswers - frmChapter1 (Code)                                    _ □ ×
Command1                          ▼   Click                          ▼
    Private Sub Command1_Click()                                      ▲

        Dim sTextString As String

  ●     sTextString = "This is a string parameter"

        Call DemoSub("This is a string parameter")
        ' or
        DemoSub "This is a string"

        MsgBox (DemoFunction("String1", "String2"))

    End Sub                                                           ▼
```

Figure 4-7 Setting a breakpoint

Running the program from the Visual Basic IDE then causes the program to go into break mode immediately before the line containing the breakpoint is executed. When the program is in break mode, you can examine and change the contents of program variables and objects. Clicking the Run icon in the Visual basic toolbar causes resumption of the program's execution.

To remove the breakpoint, simply click the red dot in the margin. The breakpoint will be removed, and the red dot and highlighting will disappear.

Can I clear all the breakpoints in a program simultaneously?

Yes. You can clear all the breakpoints in a program at one time by selecting the Clear All Breakpoints option from the Debug menu or by pressing CTRL+SHIFT+F9. This option is available in both edit mode and break mode.

Breakpoints are not maintained between development sessions. Closing and then reopening your Visual Basic project also clears all existing breakpoints.

How can I see the value of a variable while I'm debugging a program?

The easiest way to see the value of a variable is simply to position the mouse pointer over the variable. A pop-up window

will appear that displays the variable's value. Figure 4-8 shows an example of Visual Basic's instant-information feature.

You can also use the Quick Watch feature to display the value of a variable. To use Visual Basic's Quick Watch feature, click the variable that you want to display and then click the Quick Watch icon on the Debug toolbar. The Quick Watch dialog box, shown earlier in this chapter, will be displayed.

Unfortunately, these same techniques can't be used to display the value of an object. Objects are more complex than simple variables and generally contain multiple values that can't be displayed in a single text box such as the one used by the Quick Watch dialog box. To display the contents of an object, you first must add the object to Visual Basic's list of watched expressions. An object is added to the watch expressions list either by clicking the Add Watch button in the Quick Watch dialog box or by dragging and dropping the object name from the Code window to the Watch window. When the program is in break mode, you can expand the object's properties by clicking the plus sign in the Watch window. The values of all the object's properties will be displayed in the Watch window.

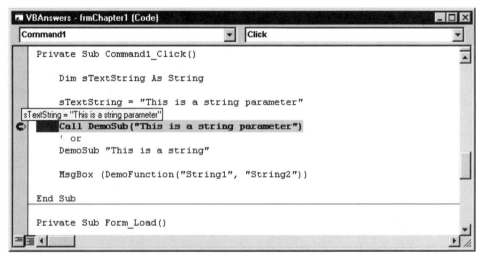

Figure 4-8   Showing the value of a variable

How can I change the value of a variable while I'm in debug mode?

You can change the value of a variable in several different ways. Probably the easiest way to change the value of a variable while you're in break mode is to open the Locals window and then click the value of the variable that you want to change. Figure 4-9 illustrates using the Locals window to alter the contents of a variable.

Clicking the Value column of the variable that you want to change causes the cursor to change into the I-beam. Then, you can type a new value for the variable.

Alternatively, you can add the variable to the list of Watched Expressions and then open the Watch window and type a new value in the Value column. In addition to these direct methods, you can change the value of a variable by executing an assignment statement in the Immediate window.

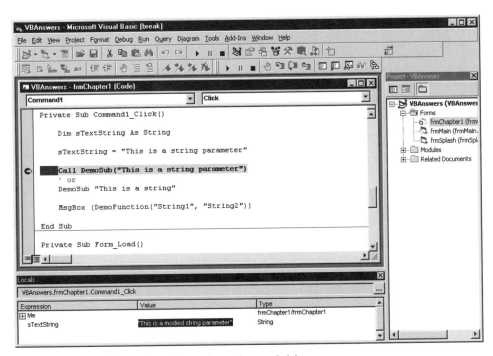

Figure 4-9   Changing the value of a variable

 ### How do I make the program single-step through one line of code at a time?

The Visual Basic debugger makes single-stepping through your code very simple. When your program is in break mode, to single-step, simply click the Step Into, Step Over, or Step Out icon on the Debug toolbar. The next line of code will be executed and the source line will be highlighted yellow. The Step Into icon enables you to continue single-stepping inside of functions and subroutines. The Step Over icon runs through the contents of subroutines and functions and continues single-stepping with the next line of the current procedure. The Step Out icon runs through the remaining contents of the current procedure and then breaks execution at the line following the call to the current procedure.

 ### Can I make the program execution stop when a variable contains a specific value?

Yes. Using Visual Basic's Watch window, you can add a watched expression that will break the program's execution when that expression becomes true or when it becomes false. For instance, Figure 4-10 shows how an expression can be used in the Watch window.

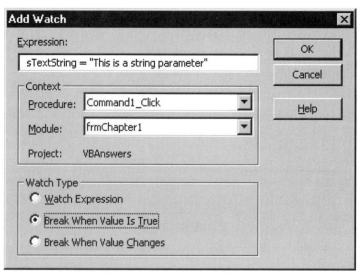

Figure 4-10 Breaking program execution based on a variable's value

The expression in Figure 4-10 tests the string variable named sTextString for the value "This is a string parameter". The Context box is used to identify the section of the program where the watch expression will be evaluated. The expression could be evaluated for either the entire scope of the project or just a single procedure. In the Add Watch dialog box shown in Figure 4-10, the expression will be evaluated or watched only in the Command1_Click subroutine of the form named frmChapter1.

The Watch Type box at the bottom of the dialog box specifies the watch condition. The following lists the radio buttons in the Watch Type box and describes the result of selecting each of them:

- **Watch Expression** Adds the expression to the list of watched expressions, which causes the value of the expression to be shown in the Watch window.

- **Break When Value Is True** Cause the program execution to halt when the watch expression becomes true. In other words, in the example in Figure 4-10, the program will break when the string variable named sTextString contains the value "This is a string parameter".

- **Break When Value Changes** Cause the program execution to break when the value of the watch expression becomes a different value than the value specified in the Watch Expression box.

Can I change the code while I'm in debug mode?

Yes. One of the features that makes Visual Basic such a productive development environment is that it enables you to bypass the traditional edit-compile-debug cycle and make changes to your source code while the program is in break mode. Those code changes are then executed immediately without leaving debug mode. After running a program from the IDE, the program enters break mode either when it encounters a breakpoint or when a watched expression is activated. At that point, the Code window is displayed at the current procedure containing the breakpoint or watch

expression. The next line to be executed will be highlighted in yellow, and a red breakpoint dot will be displayed in the left margin.

You can make code changes anywhere in the current project or procedure. However, only changes to those lines following the breakpoint will be executed immediately. Changes to the lines preceding the breakpoint will be executed the next time that the program executes that portion of the procedure.

I positioned the mouse pointer on an object, but no pop-up value window was displayed. How do I see the value of an object?

Unlike standard variables, the value of an object is not displayed in either the Visual Basic instant pop-up window or the Quick Watch dialog box. Simple variables contain only a single value that can easily be displayed in a single text box. More complex objects usually contain multiple properties—each having different values. Multiple values don't fit within the constraints of a single text field, such as those used by the instant pop-up window or the Quick Watch dialog box. To display the value of an object, you must add the object to Visual Basic's Watch window.

You can add an object to the Watch window in any of several ways. Probably the easiest method is to open the Watch window and then drag and drop the object name from the Code window into the Watch window. The object name will appear in the list of Watch Expressions along with a plus sign. Clicking the plus sign expands the object's properties, and their respective values are shown in the Value column of the Watch window.

One of the applications I'm maintaining has a Stop statement in it. What does that do?

The Stop statement causes the execution of the program to break very much like using a standard breakpoint causes it to break. However, because it is source code, the Stop statement can also be compiled into a Visual Basic executable program. When a program running from the IDE encounters a Stop statement, the program execution breaks and the Code window displays the procedure containing the Stop statement. Clicking the run icon or one of the step icons will cause the program execution to resume. When a Stop statement is encountered in a Visual Basic executable program, a message box is displayed and the program ends. Here is the message box that's displayed when a Visual Basic executable program encounters a Stop statement:

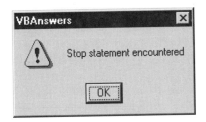

Can I make the program execution jump back to a section of code so that I can execute it again?

Yes. Visual Basic's Set Next Statement command enables you to set the execution point to a new location within the current procedure. To use the Set Next Statement command, do either of the following:

● Click the line where you want to set the new execution point and then select the Set Next Statement option from the Debug menu.

● Drag the current line of execution indicator (yellow arrow) that's shown in the left margin to the next statement that you want to execute. For instance, if the current execution point is within a loop, you can click the current line of execution indicator and drag it back to a line before the loop. When the program resumes running, it will then execute the loop again. Similarly, if you want to skip the execution of a section of code, you can click the current line of execution indicator and drag it past the section of code that you want to skip. When the program's execution resumes, it will begin at the line where you positioned the current line of execution indicator.

 Do you have any tips for debugging?

The following are some general tips for more productive application debugging:

- *Add the Debug toolbar to Visual Basic's IDE.* Adding the Debug toolbar to the IDE is the first step to productive debugging of Visual Basic applications. The Debug toolbar provides quick access to the most common debugging features. Use the View | Toolbars | Debug menu option to add the Debug toolbar to Visual Basic's IDE.

- *Use the F5 key to quickly run an application.* Using the F5 key is handy after you've just entered several lines of code, because it enables you to run the program quickly without having to move your hands away from the keyboard.

- *Comment out the current line to get past runtime errors.* Occasionally, when testing your applications, you will encounter runtime errors that break the program's execution and display the Code window in break mode. The line that caused the runtime error will be highlighted in yellow. These kinds of errors often are not serious, but they may stop you from debugging other parts of the application. One simple way to get past these errors is simply to type a comment symbol in the beginning of the line that caused the error, and then click the Run icon to continue running your application.

- *Set breakpoints before and after loops.* When debugging logic errors, common practice is to use the single-step feature to watch lines of code executing. Although this often can be very enlightening regarding the cause of various problems, it also can be very tedious when you encounter loops and other repeating code structures. Setting breakpoints at the beginning and end of these loops enables you to use the Run feature to execute the loop quickly. Then, you can resume single-stepping in the code that follows the loop.

- *Use the Set Next Statement command to reposition the current execution point.* Sometimes, when you're debugging code, you may want to skip over a section of code or re-execute a section of code. The Set Next Statement command enables you to do either one of these things. You can set the execution point of the next statement to any point within the current procedure by dragging the yellow current line of execution indicator to the statement that you want to execute next.

- *Use full path names to locate files and other external objects.* When you are running applications from Visual Basic's IDE, you need to be aware that the current directory is the directory from which Visual Basic's own IDE is run, not the directory containing your application. This can cause your application to have problems locating various external objects, such as files.

  To avoid such problems, you should consider using the full path to locate objects during development. When the debugging process is finished, you can remove the absolute references and allow your program to find objects by using the relative path.

- *Use the Option Explicit keyword to help you avoid using the debugger.* Using the Option Explicit keyword can help you avoid needing to use the debugger. The Option Explicit statement should be used for all Visual Basic projects.

  Visual Basic doesn't require that variables be declared before they are used. Although this may seem like a convenient feature, it isn't, and can actually introduce very subtle, difficult-to-find bugs into your programs. For instance, suppose that you declare in your script a variable named nCount, which you intend to use as a loop counter. However, in your code, you inadvertently use nCoun*ter*. Visual Basic allows this, but treats each instance as a totally separate variable, which probably isn't what you intended and can cause unpredictable results. This type of error can also be very difficult to find. The Option Explicit statement requires that all variables must be declared before they can be used, which prevents this type of problem from occurring.

Chapter 5

Visual Basic's Version Control

Answer Topics!

Visual Basic's Version Control @ a Glance

This chapter covers some of the common questions about using Microsoft's Visual SourceSafe (VSS) version control software with Visual Basic.

- **Using Visual Basic's Source Control Tools** explores the version control tools that are provided with Visual SourceSafe.

- **Using Visual SourceSafe with Visual Basic** dives into the questions that arise when using Visual SourceSafe to perform some of the common version control tasks from Visual Basic.

USING VISUAL BASIC'S SOURCE CONTROL TOOLS

The questions and answers in the first part of this chapter help to introduce the different version control tools that are provided with Visual SourceSafe 6, the VSS version integrated with Visual Basic.

 ## What is Visual SourceSafe?

Visual SourceSafe is Microsoft's version control software that is included both in the Enterprise Edition and Visual Studio Enterprise Edition of Visual Basic. The main purpose of Microsoft's Visual SourceSafe version control system is to facilitate team development for Visual Basic projects as well as for software projects developed using the other members of the Visual Studio family of development products. *Version control* essentially provides a mechanism that safeguards developers from overwriting each other's changes. Some of the other Microsoft products that are integrated with VSS include Visual C++, Visual InterDev, and Visual J++.

Visual SourceSafe provides software version control by implementing a project archival system that stores both the source and binary files used in a Visual Basic project. VSS then manages those files by controlling access to them. VSS keeps track of each project's status, whether the project is checked in or out, as well as who has checked out each project.

To makes changes to a project, a developer must first "check out" the project from VSS. When a project is checked out, VSS restricts access to that project until it is checked back in. Basically, a developer checks out a project to make a set of changes, and then checks the project back in after completing those changes. The check in/out system prevents two different developers from simultaneously working on the same project files. Because the current version of the project is available only to one developer at a time, multiple developers can't overwrite the changes made by other developers.

From the preceding description, Visual SourceSafe may seem to restrict the use of the project to one developer at a time, thereby limiting team development. However, that's not really the case. VSS's check in/out facility works at the file

level, not the project level. Although no two developers can check out the same file at the same time, they can each check out different files from the same project. For instance, one developer might check out the Module.bas file from Project1 at the same time that another developer has Form1.frm checked out from Project1.

What are Visual SourceSafe's client and server installations?

Installing the server portion of Visual SourceSafe installs the database that will contain your Visual Basic project source code and binary files. The VSS server component is typically installed on a network share that can be accessed by multiple developers. This provides a central code repository that can be readily shared. However, the VSS server can also be installed on a stand-alone system, for single-user version control. Table 5-1 describes the folders that are created on the server.

When the VSS server is installed, the Visual SourceSafe Explorer and Administrator are also installed.

The VSS client installation installs the portion of VSS that integrates it with the target development environment and enables each client system to access the shared VSS server database. The client portion can be installed either from CD-ROM or by running the Netsetup.exe program located in the server's Netsetup folder.

Folder	Description
\Data	Contains the project database
\Users	Contains the user initialization files
\Temp	Contains the temporary work files used by VSS
\Win32	Contains the setup files used by Windows 95 and NT installations on Intel platforms
\Setup	Contains the files used by the VSS server installation to add or remove components
\Netsetup	Contains the files required to perform the VSS client installation
\Ntaxp	Contains the setup files used by Windows NT installations on Alpha platforms

Table 5-1   Folders Installed with the Visual SourceSafe Server

 How do I get started using Visual SourceSafe?

The following are the general steps for getting started using Visual SourceSafe:

1. Create a new VSS database. A default VSS database is created when you install the VSS server. The database contains an archived copy of the projects that you want to maintain under version control. For a single developer, the VSS database can be located on your own local system. However, it's more common to install VSS to a network share where it can be used by multiple developers.

2. Add user IDs and passwords for the users that are permitted to access the VSS database.

3. Create projects within VSS. A new VSS project contains all the files that are used within a given development project. You typically create the VSS project after you create a project by using one of the supported development platforms, such as Visual Basic.

4. Set the working directory for the project. The *working directory* typically refers to the location on your local hard drive where your copy of the Visual Basic development project is located.

5. Copy the files that comprise the local development project into Visual SourceSafe. The VSS project can include both the source and the different binary files that are used in your project. After you add the local development files to the VSS project, you can then use VSS for version control.

 What is Visual SourceSafe Explorer?

Visual SourceSafe Explorer is the primary management tool for Visual SourceSafe. You can use it to create new VSS projects, add and remove files for VSS projects, and check files in and out of VSS. After you install the VSS client on your development system, you can run Visual SourceSafe

Explorer from Visual Basic by selecting Tools | SourceSafe | Run SourceSafe. If you installed VSS as part of Visual Studio, you can also run Visual SourceSafe Explorer from Windows, by selecting Start | Microsoft Visual Studio 6.0 | Microsoft Visual SourceSafe | Microsoft Visual SourceSafe 6.0. Figure 5-1 presents the Visual SourceSafe Explorer.

The Visual SourceSafe Explorer uses three main window panes. The upper-left pane, known as the *project pane,* lists the different projects that have been added to VSS. The upper-right pane, called the *files pane,* lists the files that are contained within a VSS project. The pane in the lower portion of the window is the *results pane,* which lists status messages that report on the results of check-in and check-out operations. Figure 5-1 shows that the project called VBAnswers is highlighted in the project pane. The files pane lists all the files that make up the VBAnswers project. The results pane currently is empty.

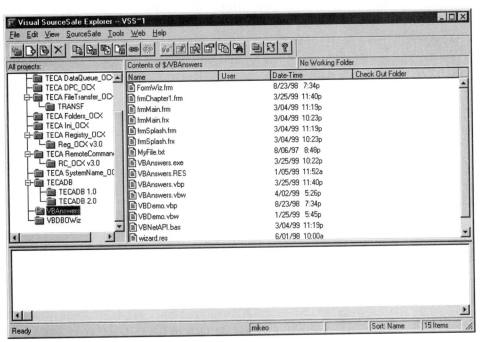

Figure 5-1 Visual SourceSafe Explorer

The Visual SourceSafe toolbar enables you to perform the common VSS operations. The following illustration identifies the name of each icon on the Visual SourceSafe toolbar.

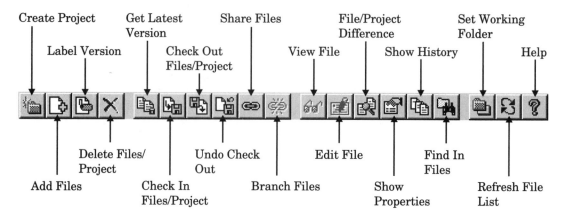

The result of clicking each of these icons is described next:

- **Create Project**　Creates a new VSS project. The project is empty until a working directory is set and files are added to the project.

- **Add Files**　Displays a dialog box that enables you to select the files to add to a VSS project. You can also add files to a VSS project by dragging and dropping them from Windows Explorer.

- **Label Version**　Displays a dialog box that enables you to assign an optional descriptive text string to a version of the file or project.

- **Delete Files/Project**　Deletes files and projects from the VSS database. This command does not delete projects and files that are in your working folder.

- **Get Latest Version**　Enables you to refresh the files contained in the VSS database from the contents of the working folder.

- **Check In Files/Project**　Displays a dialog box that enables you to check in an entire project or individual files from the project to your working folder. To check in an entire project, select the project from the project pane and then click the Check In icon. To select individual files, highlight on the files pane the files to be checked in and then click the Check In icon. You can check in only the files that you have previously checked out.

- **Check Out Files/Project**   Displays a dialog box that enables you to check out an entire project or individual files from the project to your working folder. To check out an entire project, select the project from the project pane and then click the Check Out icon. To select individual files, highlight in the files pane the files to be checked out and then click the Check Out icon. A red check-mark icon is displayed in front of all files that have been checked out. You can't check out a file that is already checked out by someone else.

- **Undo Check Out**   Enables you to undo the previous check-out operation. Undoing a check out enables the files in a VSS project to be checked out by another user.

- **Share Files**   Displays a dialog box that enables you to share one or more files between multiple VSS projects. Sharing a file between two projects creates a link between the two projects, and any subsequent updates to the shared files automatically update both projects. The Share Files dialog box also gives you the option to create a *branch after share*—a separate copy of the current project—which will essentially unlink the projects creating two separate archives of the shared code.

- **Branch Files**   Enables you to create separate, unlinked copies of a shared file. This icon is enabled only if you select a shared file in the VSS files pane.

- **View File**   Displays a dialog box that enables you to either view the source of a file contained in a VSS project or check out the file to edit it.

- **Edit File**   Displays the same dialog box that is displayed when you click the View File icon, and gives you the same options to view or check out the file.

- **File/Project Difference**   Runs a utility that visually displays the differences between two files. This utility is good for seeing the changes that have been made to a file.

- **Show Properties** Displays a dialog box that shows the various properties associated with a project or a file contained within VSS. For files, this dialog box shows the file's version, its check in/out status, who checked out the file, and the path to the working folder.

- **Show History** Displays a dialog box that lists the different VSS operations that have been applied to a given file or project.

- **Find In Files** Displays the Find in Files dialog box, which enables you to search for a text string in one or more files contained in a VSS project.

- **Set Working Folder** Displays a dialog box that enables you to set the working folder for a VSS project or file. The working folder essentially is a local directory on your system's hard drive that contains a version of the project that will be modified. The check-out operation copies a project or selected files in the project to the working folder. Similarly, the check-in operation copies the updated files from the working directory back to the Visual SourceSafe archive.

- **Refresh File List** Updates the list of files displayed in Visual SourceSafe Explorer from VSS's database. This enables you to see any changes that have been made to the file by other developers.

- **Help** Displays the online help for Visual SourceSafe.

Tip: *As the second part of this chapter explains, many of these functions are also available from the Visual SourceSafe menu that is integrated into the Visual Basic development environment.*

 ## How do I use Visual SourceSafe Administrator?

The Visual SourceSafe Admin application enables Visual SourceSafe Administrator to set up the users that are authorized to use the VSS database. A user ID must be added, using Visual SourceSafe Administrator, before the user can access a project that is archived in the Visual Studio database.

Tip: *Visual SourceSafe initially provides the Admin user ID with a blank password. You can use this ID to log in initially and run Visual SourceSafe Administrator.*

Visual SourceSafe Administrator is not started through the Visual Basic IDE. Instead, you select Start | Visual Studio | Visual SourceSafe | Visual SourceSafe Admin. Figure 5-2 shows VSS Administrator.

Visual SourceSafe Administrator lists all the users that have been added to VSS and shows the current status of each user. Figure 5-2 shows that two users are currently logged in to Visual Source Safe.

VSS Administrator has the following four menus:

- **Users** Provides the main administrative functions of VSS Administrator. Enables you to add, edit, and delete users, and open a new VSS database.

- **Tools** Provides options that enable you to perform various maintenance functions on the VSS database, such as lock the database for exclusive use, clean up the temporary work directory, and create a new database.

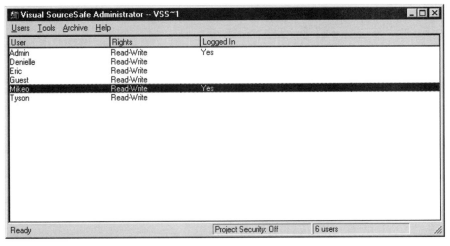

Figure 5-2   Visual SourceSafe Administrator

● **Archive** Enables you to free up disk space by saving projects offline. It also provides an option for restoring archived projects.

● **Help** Enables you to access Visual SourceSafe's online help.

 Tip: *In addition to these graphical management utilities, VSS provides a command-line interface that enables you to perform most of the same actions that you can perform using VSS Explorer and VSS Administrator. Using Visual SourceSafe's command-level interface enables you to create batch files for automating various common administrative functions.*

USING VISUAL SOURCESAFE WITH VISUAL BASIC

The questions and answers in the second part of this chapter explain the various common topics that arise while using the Visual SourceSafe version control system with Visual Basic. The questions in this section relate to getting started using VSS, adding a Visual Basic project to VSS, and checking in/out files and projects with VSS.

 How do I get started using source control with Visual SourceSafe?

The first step to getting started with Visual SourceSafe is to install the VSS server and then install the VSS client. The VSS server typically is installed on a shared network server that can be accessed by the client systems that are running Visual Basic. After the VSS server is installed, the person responsible for version control administration must run Visual SourceSafe Administrator and add the user IDs and passwords for the developers who will be accessing the VSS version control system. These IDs and passwords can be the same as the developers' existing network logons and passwords, but they do not have to be the same.

The next step is to install the VSS client on the client systems. The VSS client can be installed either from

CD-ROM or by running the Netsetup.exe program located in the \Netsetup folder of the shared Visual SourceSafe directory. Running the client installation adds the SourceSafe submenu, shown here, to the Visual Basic Tools menu:

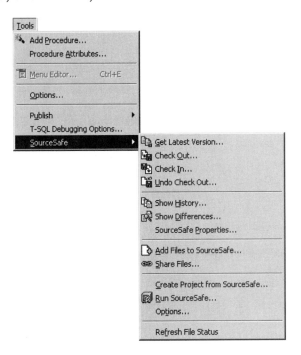

The SourceSafe menu enables you to perform all the common operations that are available from VSS Explorer directly from within the Visual Basic IDE. In many cases, the integrated options are even more convenient, because they automatically use the current files in the Visual Basic IDE. You don't need to select the appropriate files or project for the lists displayed by VSS Explorer.

After both the server and the client portions of Visual SourceSafe are installed, you can create a new VSS project and add the files from your current Visual Basic development project to the new VSS project.

How do I add source control to a project?

Visual Basic's tight integration with Visual SourceSafe makes placing a project under source control very easy. In fact, after you install the VSS client utilities, when you save each new

project, Visual Basic automatically prompts you to add the project to VSS. Here is the automatic Source Code Control dialog box that Visual Basic displays for each new project:

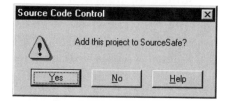

Adding new Visual Basic projects to VSS is so easy that you almost need a reason *not* to add them:

1. Click the Yes button of the Source Code Control dialog box. This will display the Visual SourceSafe Login dialog box, which prompts you to enter your Visual SourceSafe user ID and password, along with the name of the project archive database.

2. Fill in this dialog box and then clicking OK to display the Add to SourceSafe Project window, shown in Figure 5-3.

   This dialog box enables you to assign a name to the new VSS project.

3. Enter a project name and then click OK to automatically create a new VSS project and display the Add Files To SourceSafe dialog box, shown in Figure 5-4.

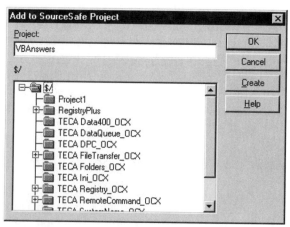

Figure 5-3 Add To SourceSafe Project dialog box

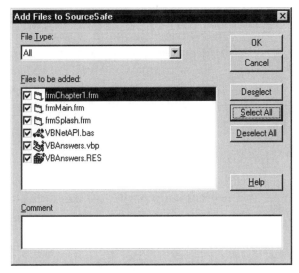

Figure 5-4 Add Files To SourceSafe dialog box

All the files from the current Visual Basic project are displayed in the Add Files To SourceSafe dialog box. You can individually select files by clicking each check box, or you can click the Select All button to place a check mark in front of all the files in the list.

4. Select the files you want to add, and click OK to add the files to the VSS database.

Adding an existing Visual Basic project to VSS is almost as easy as adding a new VB project:

1. Select the Add Project To SourceSafe option from the SourceSafe menu, shown here:

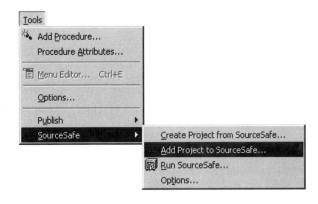

When a Visual Basic project has not been added to VSS, the SourceSafe menu shown in the Visual Basic IDE is different from the menu that is available after a project is under version control. Instead of the primary source control options, an option to add the project to SourceSafe is displayed.

2. Select Add Project To SourceSafe to display a login dialog box for VSS. After logging into VSS, the Add Projects dialog box, shown earlier in Figure 5-3, is displayed, and the name of the current Visual Basic project is displayed as the default VSS project name.

3. Click OK to display a prompt to create a new VSS project, shown here:

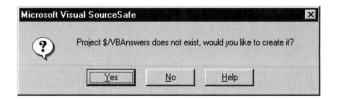

4. Click the Yes button to create a new VSS project. The Add Files to SourceSafe dialog box, shown earlier in Figure 5-4, is displayed.

5. Just as when you work with a new project, select the files to include in the version-control database, and then click OK. All the files initially have a status of "checked in."

Visual SourceSafe's tight integration with Visual Basic enables you to perform all the required functions to create a new project and add the files to the project directly from Visual Basic's IDE.

 When I put my project into Visual SourceSafe, where does it go?

When a Visual Basic project is added to Visual SourceSafe, the project files are compressed and copied into the VSS database, which is contained in the /Data folder of the VSS server. The format of this database is proprietary to Visual SourceSafe and can be readily accessed only by using the Visual SourceSafe interface or commands.

 ## How do I check out a project?

You can check out an existing Visual SourceSafe project from Visual Basic as follows:

1. Select Tools | SourceSafe | Check Out, which displays the Check Out Files From SourceSafe dialog box shown in Figure 5-5.

   When this dialog box is first opened, just the file that is selected in the Visual Basic Project window is checked.

2. To check out all the project's files, click the Select All button to select all the project's files, and then click OK to check them out of VS.

After the files have been checked out, the files in the development environment are refreshed from the files that were checked from the VSS archive. After the files have been checked out of VSS, they can't be checked out by other developers until after they are checked back in.

The Visual Basic Project window displays a red check mark immediately before each file that has been checked out from VSS. Figure 5-6 shows the Visual Basic Project window for a Visual SourceSafe project.

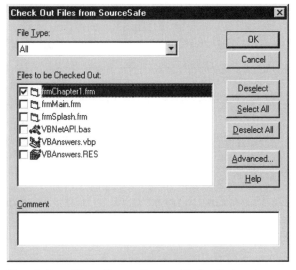

Figure 5-5   Check Out Files From SourceSafe dialog box

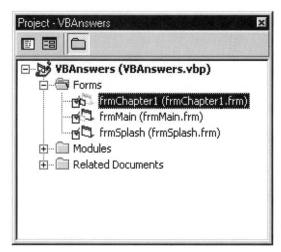

Figure 5-6 The Visual Basic Project window for a SourceSafe project

How do I check in a project?

You can check in a project as follows:

1. Select Tools | SourceSafe | Check In from the Visual Basic menu.

2. Select the Check In option to display the VSS Check In Files To SourceSafe dialog box, shown in Figure 5-7.

   By default, the current file in the development environment is selected. You can select all files in the list by clicking the Select All button.

3. After you select the files that you want to check in, click OK to copy the files from the working folder of the Visual Basic IDE into the VSS database. (Optionally, you can leave the files checked out by checking the Keep Checked Out box near the bottom of the dialog box.)

After the files have been checked into Visual SourceSafe, they are then available to be checked out by another developer.

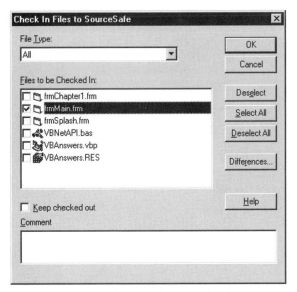

Figure 5-7   Check In Files To SourceSafe dialog box

Can I check out a project that someone else has already checked out?

In its default setting, Visual SourceSafe doesn't allow two different developers to check out the same file or project simultaneously. This behavior is by design, to provide a safeguard that prevents one developer from saving over changes that may have been made by another developer. However, Visual SourceSafe 6 does have an option that allows multiple users to check out the same files. To enable VSS 6 to check out multiple files:

1. Select the Tools | Options menu from Visual SourceSafe Administrator. The SourceSafe Options dialog box, shown in Figure 5-8, is displayed.

2. Check the box labeled Allow Multiple Checkouts to change Visual SourceSafe's configuration to permit multiple developers to check out the same files.

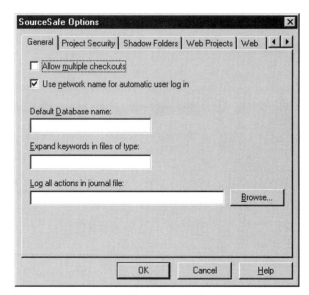

Figure 5-8   Visual SourceSafe Options dialog box

When the Allow Multiple Checkouts option is enabled, VSS keeps track of all users who have checked out each file. Then, when the files are checked back in, VSS performs a file comparison to see which lines of code in the file were changed. If the changes were to different sections of code, VSS automatically merges all the changes into a master copy of the file. If VSS determines that the changes were to the same lines in the files, it displays a warning error during the check-in process and prevents any check in from occurring.

> **Tip:**   *Generally, you are better off not enabling Visual SourceSafe's Multiple Checkouts option. Separating each developer's work according to source files is best. However, some projects with large Visual Basic modules can make this difficult.*

 Someone else has checked out a project that I need to see. I don't need to change anything, but I do want to copy some of the code. Can I access the project?

Yes. You can use the Get Latest Version option from Visual Basic's Tools | SourceSafe menu to make a read-only copy of

a file or an entire project contained in VSS. This copy can be used to view the source code, make a new project, or compile an executable program.

Does any way exist to determine what's been changed in a file that's been checked out?

You can see the changes in a file by using the Show Differences menu option from Visual Basic's Tools | SourceSafe menu. Selecting the Show Differences option first displays the Difference Options dialog box, show in Figure 5-9.

VSS's Difference Options dialog box enables you to select the files to compare as well as the comparison format to use. By default, the files that are compared are the file that is selected in Visual Basic's Project window and the archived version of that file. You can also use the Difference Options window to point to other files. The default comparison format is Visual, which displays the two versions side by side with their differences highlighted. You can also select either the SourceSafe option, which displays a summary window listing the changed lines, or the Unix option, which shows a summary window in which changed lines are indicated with arrows. Figure 5-10 shows the VSS Differences window displayed using the Visual format.

The Differences window in Figure 5-10 shows the archive version of the file in the left pane, and the updated version from the Visual Basic IDE in the right pane. The changed lines are highlighted in the center of the screen. The arrows

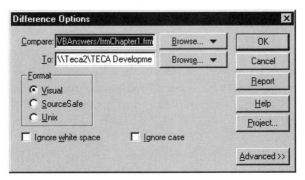

Figure 5-9 Visual SourceSafe's Difference Options dialog box

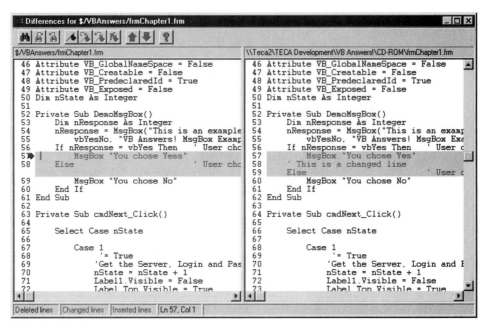

Figure 5-10 Visual SourceSafe Differences window

on the Differences window toolbar enable you to navigate quickly between the changed sections of the file.

 I'm the only developer in my shop, so I don't have to worry about anyone else working on my projects. Do I have any reason to use source control?

Yes. Although the main reason to use Visual SourceSafe is to provide central project management for multiple developers, single developers can also benefit from the features provided by VSS. One of the main benefits of VSS for the single developer is that it provides a code repository that's separate from your working development directory. If the development directory is accidentally deleted or otherwise corrupted, you can easily restore your projects from the VSS archive.

Another reason that a single developer would benefit from VSS is its project-versioning feature. VSS's tools facilitate the ability to "freeze" a production version of the project. You can then use VSS's Branch option to create a new version of the project without fear of altering your previous versions of the project. Finally, VSS provides several tools that can assist your development effort. For instance, the Project History shows the dates various changes were implemented, and the File Differences option can help you to easily locate changed sections of code.

Chapter 6

Basic Forms and Dialog Boxes

Answer Topics!

Basic Forms and Dialog Boxes @ a Glance

This chapter presents a set of questions and answers that provide a basic understanding of Visual Basic forms.

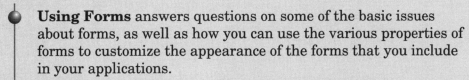

- **Using Forms** answers questions on some of the basic issues about forms, as well as how you can use the various properties of forms to customize the appearance of the forms that you include in your applications.

- **Using Basic Dialog Boxes** answers questions about using dialog boxes. In this part of the chapter, you'll see how you can display message boxes and prompt the user for input.

Apart from the syntax of the language itself, the form is probably the most essential part of Visual Basic's integrated development environment (IDE). Although you can write a VB program that doesn't use a form, that certainly isn't the norm. In fact, a "formless" VB program is so uncommon that many new VB developers don't even know that you can write a VB program without using forms. While writing formless VB programs is addressed in one of the questions near the end of this chapter, the fact that they are so little used points out how prevalent forms are to the Visual Basic IDE. A solid understanding of VB forms is essential to writing good applications using Visual Basic.

USING FORMS

The first part of this chapter presents some basic questions and answers that explore the fundamental characteristics of VB forms. The questions and answers in the later part of this chapter illustrate some of the common programming functions that you can perform by setting the various form properties.

What's a form?

From a user's standpoint, a VB form essentially equates to a window. In other words, each window that's used in your application is implemented by using a VB form. So, to the user, a form is basically the same thing as a window. The appearance of that window is controlled by the form's different properties.

From a programming standpoint, a form is a class that contains properties and methods. Like any other class, a specific instance of a form is an object.

What's the difference between an SDI form and an MDI form?

A Single Document Interface (SDI) form basically presents one window per screen, whereas a Multiple Document Interface (MDI) form presents a parent window that contains all the child windows that are used by the application—for example, with an SDI form, the menu, toolbar, and any input or output fields are all part of the same window. If an SDI application opens other windows, they also are displayed as free-floating windows that can be used and moved independently from the original window. Figure 6-1 presents an example of a simple SDI form.

In contrast, with an MDI form, all the windows that are used in an application must be presented within the confines of the parent window. These child windows are dependent on the parent window and can't be moved outside the bounds of the parent window. Likewise, moving the parent window also moves all the child windows that are contained within that parent window. Each child window can present its own input and output fields, but the application's menu and toolbar

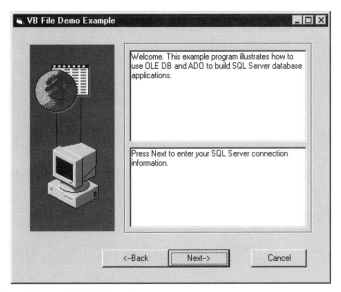

Figure 6-1   Sample SDI interface

typically are displayed only on the parent window. Figure 6-2 illustrates a simple MDI interface that contains multiple child windows.

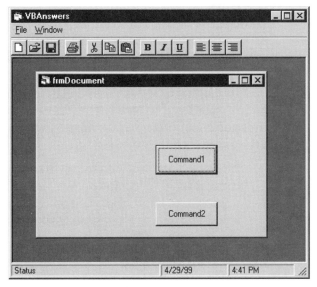

Figure 6-2   Sample MDI interface

 ## How do I put interface elements from the Toolbox onto a form?

The first step in creating your VB application is to add interface objects to your forms. Visual Basic provides a powerful and productive graphical development environment that enables you to quickly and easily build applications by dragging and dropping ActiveX controls from the Toolbox onto your forms. After you add the controls to your forms, you can visually move and resize them in Visual Basic's design environment.

Adding Controls to a Form

The following example explains how to put one of the most common sets of ActiveX controls on a VB form: the Label control and the TextBox control. These controls are often used together. The Label control is used to display text on a form, and it's usually used to help the user know what type of data to enter in the associated text box. As you would expect, the TextBox control allows the user to enter either text or numeric data. Using the Label and the TextBox controls on a VB form is very much like using any other visible control:

1. Click the Label control in the VB Toolbox to select it and drag it to the VB form. It's best to click the upper-left point on the form where you want the Label control to be displayed, and then drag the mouse pointer to the lower-right point before releasing the mouse button. In Figure 6-3, you can see that an outline of the control is displayed where the borders of the control will be, and a pop-up window displays the width and height of the control.

2. Add the TextBox control to the form. Click the TextBox control in VB's Toolbox (conveniently located immediately adjacent to the Label control) and then click the upper-left point on the form where you want the TextBox control to be positioned.

3. Without releasing the left mouse button, drag the mouse pointer to the lower-right point for the control. When the

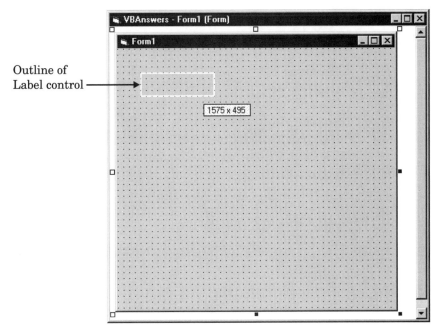

Outline of
Label control

Figure 6-3 Drawing a Label control

mouse pointer is in the appropriate position, release the
left mouse pointer.

Figure 6-4 shows the TextBox control positioned
immediately to the right of the Label control that was
created previously.

Moving and Resizing Controls on a Form

After you place the desired controls on the target form, you
can easily move and resize them. To move a control, simply
click the control and, with the mouse button held down, drag
the control to its new location. The control's current width
and height will be unchanged.

To resize the control, first click the control to display the
resizing handles—a set of blocks that are displayed on the
borders of the control. Then, position your mouse pointer over
the resizing handle on the side of the control that you want to

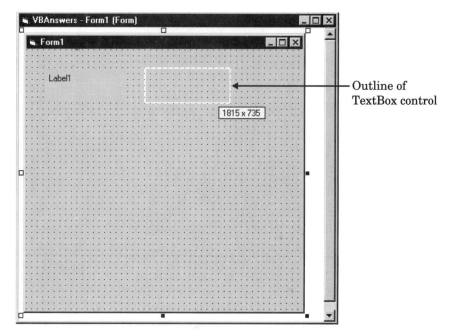

Figure 6-4 Drawing a TextBox control

change. When your mouse pointer changes into a double arrow, you can click and drag the border of the control to its new location.

As you can see, adding and positioning ActiveX controls on a VB form is very fast and easy. With a little practice, you'll see that this is a very productive environment that enables you to create graphical interfaces very quickly.

Customizing a Control's Appearance Attributes

After the control is positioned and sized, you can customize its other appearance attributes. For instance, the first action that is typically performed with a Label control is to change the text that's displayed on the screen. Figure 6-5 shows how to assign a new text string to the Label control.

After you add the Label control to the form, pressing the F4 key displays the Label control's Properties window. To display a more descriptive text string in the Label control, move to the Text property, as shown in Figure 6-5, and simply enter the desired text string. As soon as you enter the

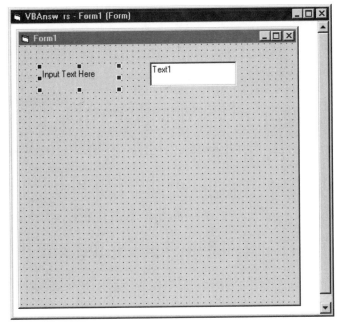

Figure 6-5 Changing the display properties

new text into the Text property of the Label control, it is displayed in the Visual Basic IDE.

How do I make a form my project's startup form? My project has multiple forms, and now I don't want the original form to be the first form displayed.

Follow these steps to change your project's startup form:

1. Select Project | Properties, which displays the VB Project Properties dialog box, shown in Figure 6-6.

    The General tab of the Project Properties dialog box contains the setting that controls the startup form that will be used by your project.

2. Click the drop-down arrow for the Startup Object list box. All the forms contained in your project are displayed in the drop-down list.

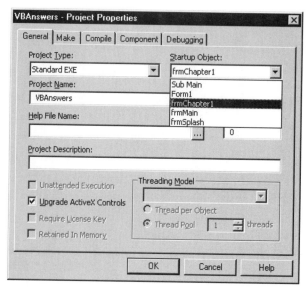

Figure 6-6 Changing the startup form on VB's Project Properties dialog box

3. Choose the new startup form by clicking its entry in the list. The new startup form name is displayed in the Startup Object field.

4. Click the OK button to save your changes.

The next time you run your project, it will begin with the new startup form.

 How do I assign an icon to my Visual Basic program?

By default, all VB forms will display the standard VB form icon, which appears as a small white screen with a blue bar across the top. This icon is displayed in the upper-left corner of the page when the form is viewed in its normal screen mode, and it is also displayed in the left side of the programs taskbar entry when the form is minimized.

You can assign a custom icon to a VB form by assigning the name of a bitmap file to the form's Icon property. You can change a form's Icon property by selecting the form in the IDE and then pressing the F4 key to display its properties. Figure 6-7 presents an example of a form's Icon property.

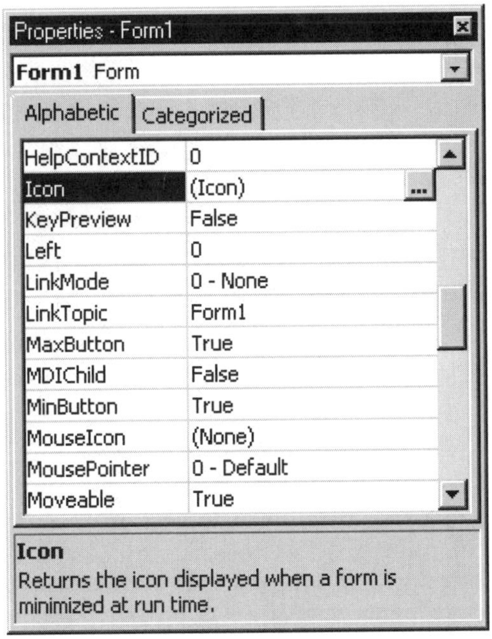

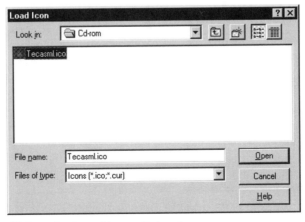

Figure 6-7 Setting a form's Icon property

To select a custom icon, click the ellipses button to display the Load Icon dialog box, shown in Figure 6-8.

Use the Load Icon dialog box to locate the file containing the icon that you want to add to your form. Select the desired icon from the list and then click the OK button to add the icon to your form. If the selected file contains a valid icon, it will be added to your VB form, and the icon shown on the selected form in the IDE will be immediately updated.

Figure 6-8 Using the Load Icon dialog box

 Note: *Icon bitmaps are created using a graphical editing program, such as Microsoft Paint. A valid icon bitmap is either 32 × 32 pixels or 16 × 16 pixels. They typically end in an extension of .ico.*

Can I remove the Min and Max buttons that are on a form? I want my form to appear like a dialog box, and a dialog box doesn't display these buttons.

Yes. You can remove both the Min and Max buttons from a form by changing the MinButton and MaxButton properties of the form. Figure 6-9 illustrates how you can remove the Min and Max buttons by changing the form's properties.

Changing the MinButton and the MaxButton properties to False removes the Min and Max buttons from the form, leaving only a Close button. As soon as each setting is changed, the form displayed in Visual Basic's IDE immediately shows the results of the form's property changes.

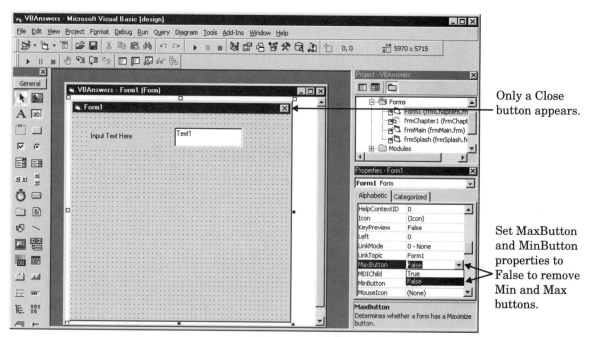

Figure 6-9 Changing the form's MinButton and MaxButton properties

How do I change the font that's used on a form?

It's very easy to change the font that's used on a form. By default, the font that's used on all VB objects is MS San Serif 8 point. To change the font for a specific form, follow these steps:

1. Open the form in the IDE and press the F4 key to display the form's properties.

2. Scroll down until you see the form's Font property and then click the ellipsis button. The Font selection dialog box shown in Figure 6-10 will be displayed.

   The form's current font, font style, and size settings are displayed in the text boxes at the top of the dialog box.

3. To change these settings, scroll down in each of the respective lists until you find the desired font selection; then click the desired entry in the list, which causes it to be displayed in the list box.

4. After you make all of your font selections, click OK to apply your changes to the current font.

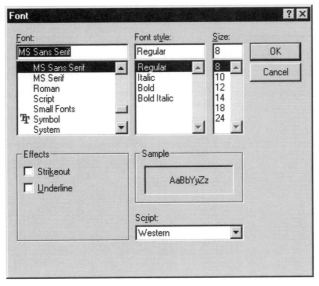

Figure 6-10 Changing a form's font

The form's display properties are immediately updated in the IDE.

How do I change the background and foreground colors used on a form?

To change the foreground and background colors used on a specific form is easy. For example, to change the background color, follow these steps:

1. Open the form in the IDE and display the form's properties by pressing the F4 key.

2. Scroll down until you see the form's BackColor property and click the drop-down button. The Palette selection drop-down box shown in Figure 6-11 is displayed.

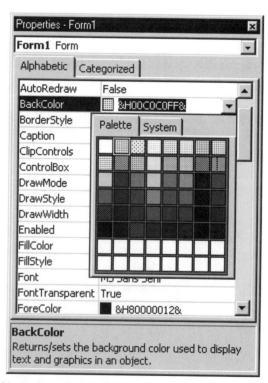

Figure 6-11 Choosing new form colors with the Palette selection drop-down box

3. Select a new background color by clicking the desired color in the Palette.

The BackColor property will be updated and the form will be redrawn with the new background color. The process for selecting a new foreground color is almost identical, except that you use the form's ForeColor property to set the foreground color.

You can also change a form's foreground and background color by using code. Sometimes this is useful to indicate a change of program status or notify of an error condition. The following code illustrates how you can change the form's ForeColor and BackColor properties by using code:

```
Form1.ForeColor = &HFF0000
Form1.BackColor = &H80FFFF
```

 Note: *Changing the form's ForeColor and BackColor properties affects only that specific Form object. It does not automatically change the colors that are used by any ActiveX controls that are on the form. You need to change the foreground and background colors of each control independently from the form that the controls are placed on.*

Can I change the string that's displayed in the title bar?

You can change the text that's displayed in a form's title bar by assigning a new value to the form's Caption property. In Figure 6-12 you can see where the Caption property of Form1 has been changed to the new value "This is a new title."

Likewise, you can change the text that's displayed in the title bar by using code. This is typically done to display your application's name in the title bar of each form or to assign a dynamic title to the form. The following code illustrates how to change the text that's displayed in the form's title bar using code:

```
Dim sTitleText As String
sTitleText = "New Form Title"

Form1.Caption = sTitleText
```

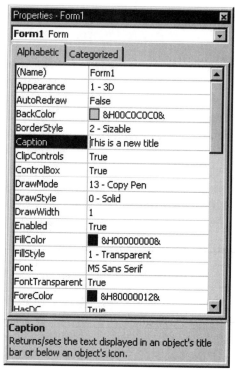

Figure 6-12   Changing a form's title text

 How do I center a form on the screen?

Before the introduction of Visual Basic 5, you needed to use
code to position your form in the center of the screen.
Fortunately, the StartUpPosition property was introduced in
Visual Basic 5 and continues to be supported in Visual Basic 6.
Setting a form's StartUpPosition property enables you to
control where a form will be displayed when it is initially
opened. In Figure 6-13, you can see how the StartUpPosition
property can be used to center a form when it is first displayed.

The StartUpPosition property specifies the position where
a form will first appear. Setting the StartUpPosition property
to 2 - CenterScreen automatically centers your form on the
screen when it is first displayed.

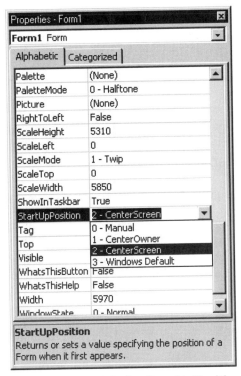

Figure 6-13   Centering forms with the StartUpPosition property

The other allowable values in the StartUpPosition property are as follows:

- **0 - Manual**   Specifies that no initial positioning will be performed.

- **1 - CenterOwner**   Specifies that the form will be centered over the owner form. This setting is mainly for forms that are MDI child forms.

- **3 - Windows Default**   Specifies that the form will be positioned in the upper-left portion of the screen.

If you're using a setting of Manual in the StartUpPosition property or want to center a form at some time other than when the form is initially opened, you can still perform this

action in code by assigning values to the form's Left and Top properties, as follows:

```
Form1.Left = (Screen.Width - Width) / 2
Form1.Top = (Screen.Height - Height) / 2
```

In this example, the center of the window is determined by dividing the width and height of the window in half. The resulting value is assigned to the Left and Top properties of a form named Form1.

 ## How can I programmatically minimize a form?

You can minimize a form by changing its WindowState property. Setting the WindowState property to 1 causes the form to be minimized. Setting the WindowState property to 2 causes the form to be maximized. Setting the WindowState property to 0 causes the form to be displayed as a normal window. The following code shows how to minimize a window in code:

```
' vbMinimized = 1
Form1.WindowState = vbMinimized
```

 Note: *If the form being minimized is an MDI child form, it will be minimized within the borders of the MDO parent. If the form is an SDI form, then it will be minimized to the Windows taskbar.*

Likewise, you can also maximize and restore a form to a windowed appearance by using VB code. You might want to do this when your application is in the minimized state and it's waiting for some event to occur. In response to the event, your application can be restored to its normal appearance. The following code shows how to restore a form to its normal appearance.

```
' vbNormal = 0
Form1.WindowState = vbNormal
```

 ## How can I move a form to a different screen location by using code?

You can move a form to a different location on the screen by changing the form's Top and Left properties. The values used in these properties are expressed in *twips*, a screen-resolution–independent measure that is approximately one twentieth of an inch per twip. The screen coordinates are measured beginning with the upper-left corner of the screen, which has a Top value of 0 and a Left value of 0. The following code illustrates how you can move a form to the upper-left corner of the screen.

```
' Screen coordinates begin at 0,0.
' Move to upper-left screen corner.
Form1.Top = 0
Form1.Left = 0
```

Tip: *The read-only Screen.Height and Screen.Width properties return the maximum number of twips available for the system.*

How do I display a new form?

You can display a new form by using the form's Show method. The following code illustrates how to use the Show method to display a form named frmMain:

```
' Display the form named frmMain.
frmMain.Show
```

Executing the form's Show method displays the form, and the focus is given to the new window. If the form isn't already loaded into memory, it will be loaded automatically when the Show method is executed. The Show method accepts two optional parameters. The first parameter determines whether the form is modal or modeless. The second, optional parameter specifies the owner form, which normally defaults to Me (the current form).

How do I close a form by using program code?

You can close a given form by using the Unload function, which both closes the form and removes it from memory. The following example illustrates the use of the Unload function:

```
' Close the form and remove it from memory.
Unload frmMain
```

+ ***Tip:***   *The Unload function only removes the code that displays the form on the screen. Any code associated with the form's module will remain loaded.*

Should I unload my form or just make it invisible?

If the form will be reused often, then it's better to make the form invisible rather than unload the form. The process of loading and unloading a form incurs more overhead than simply making the form invisible. However, if the form generally won't be reused very often, then it's probably better to free up the memory used by unloading the form. The following code illustrates how to make a form invisible and then visible again:

```
' Make the form invisible.
frmMain.Visible = False

' Now make the form visible again.
frmMain.Visible = True
```

What is a modal form?

Modal forms retain the input focus until the form is explicitly closed. In other words, a modal form requires that the user's input be directed solely to the modal form while it is displayed. No other form or window can be interacted with until the modal form has been responded to. In contrast, a modeless form (that is, a standard VB form) allows the user to move freely between the modeless form and other parts of the application. Modal forms and dialog boxes are typically used in parts of the application where obtaining user input is critical to the application's function. The following are the two basic types of modal forms:

- **Application modal form**   Does not allow the user to work with other windows in the specific application.

- **System modal form**   Even more restrictive than the application modal form, it doesn't allow the user to work with any other window in the system until the system modal window is closed.

The following code listing shows how to display an application modal form:

```
' Show the frmMain form as modal.
frmMain.Show (vbModal)
```

Tip: *Only an SDI form can be displayed modally. Attempting to display an MDI form modally results in an error.*

I understand how to output text to a Label or a ListBox control, but I simply want to display some text on the form itself. How can I print lines directly on a form?

You can print directly to a form by using the Print method. The Print method displays text on the Immediate window and it can be used with the Form object, the Debug object, or a UserControl object. The Print method accepts one optional parameter that controls how the output is displayed. The following code listing shows how you can use the Print method to display text on the background of a VB form:

```
Form1.Print "Screen.Height=" & Screen.Height
Form1.Print "Screen.Width=" & Screen.Width
```

In this example, the Print method is used to display a simple string that contains some text and the value of the current screen's Height and Width properties.

However, the Print method also accepts some special control characters that can be used to format the output string. The following line presents the output control options that are allowed by the Print method:

```
{Spc(n) | Tab(n)} expression charpos
```

The optional Spc() function inserts a specified number of spaces before the string expression that will be printed.

Likewise, the Tab() function can be used to insert a specified number of tab characters. The expression that is printed can be any valid string expression. The optional charpos portion controls the character position where the next Print method will begin inserting characters. Leaving the charpos blank causes the next Print method to begin printing on the next line. A value of ; (a semicolon) causes the printing to begin immediately after the last character printed on the current line. The value of Tab(*n*) will insert a specified number of tab characters before the next insertion point.

How can I access objects and controls, such as list boxes and text boxes, that are on a different form?

To access controls and other objects that are on a different form, you must qualify the name of the object with the form's name. For instance, if you have two forms called Form1 and Form2, and Form2 has a text box named Text1, then you can access the Text1 text box from Form1 by using the following code:

```
' This code is in Form1.
Form2.Text1.Text = "Text data on Form2"
```

Executing this code from Form1 sets the Text property of the Text1 TextBox control with the value of Text data on Form2. However, for this to work, Form2 must have already been created and loaded by using the Show method.

When I display a new form, I want to take some of the data that's contained in my first form and pass it to the second form. How can I pass a value from one form to another?

Although no direct way exists to pass data from one form to another, you can work around this by using the form's Tag property, which is the only property contained in the form that's not explicitly used by Visual Basic. The Tag property is implemented to enable you to associate any additional information you may need with a given form. The following listing shows how you can pass information between two forms by taking advantage of the Tag property:

```
' Display a new form.
frmMain.Show

' Pass data using the Tag property.
frmMain.Tag = "DATA passed from form1"
```

After assigning the new value to Form2's Tag property, you can freely use the value of the Tag property in Form2 and in any of the controls contained in Form2.

Tip: *The Tag property is also provided by most of the ActiveX controls that are supplied with Visual Basic.*

How can I write a VB program that doesn't use any forms?

Visual Basic's real strength lies in its ability to quickly and easily produce graphical programs. Even so, you can also write programs in Visual Basic that do not use any forms at all.

One of the properties of a VB project is the project's Startup Object. By default, the Startup Object is set to the first form in the program. However, the Startup Object can also be set to a special subroutine, called Sub Main. Setting the VB project's Startup Object to Sub Main causes the VB application to begin execution with the Sub Main subroutine. This can be useful when you want to write VB programs that are not graphical or when you need to explicitly code the processing that happens before the first form is displayed.

To set the project's Startup Object, follow these steps:

1. Select Project | Properties. The Project Properties dialog box, shown in Figure 6-14, is displayed.

   The project's Startup Object drop-down box is located under the General tab.

2. Click the drop-down arrow to display a list that contains the names of all the forms in the project, including the entry for Sub Main.

3. Select Sub Main from the list and click OK to cause your program to begin its execution with the subroutine named Main.

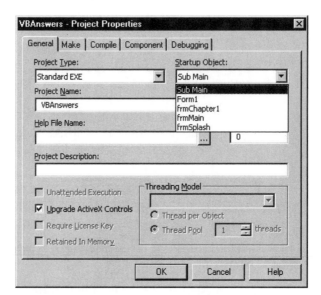

Figure 6-14 Setting the Startup Object to Sub Main

Apart from its name, the Main subroutine is no different from any other VB subroutine. The following listing shows a simple Sub Main example:

```
Sub Main()

    Dim sSource As String
    Dim sDestination As String

    sSource = "fileold.txt"
    sDestination = "filenew.txt"

    FileCopy sSource, sDestination

End Sub
```

In this example, you can see that the entire VB program consists of just a few lines and does not display any windows. This simple program declares two string variables and then assigns a filename to each of the strings. Then, the FileCopy statement is used to copy the fileold.txt file to the filenew.txt file. The program ends following the FileCopy statement.

How do I end my application?

The correct way to end your application is to unload all the forms in your application. When the last form is unloaded, the program will close. The following listing shows an example of using the Unload function within a button's Click subroutine to end an application:

```
Private Sub cmdExit_Click()
    Unload Me
End Sub
```

You can also end your VB program by using the End function. However, unlike the Unload method, which ends your program cleanly, the End method terminates your application immediately. The following listing shows how you can place the End function within a button's Click subroutine:

```
Private Sub cmdExit_Click()
    End
End Sub
```

Note: *The End function terminates the program immediately and does not execute any code that may be contained in your Form_Unload subroutines.*

Can I design my program so that its cleanup code always executes, even if the user doesn't click the Exit buttons that I've placed on my form?

Yes, the Form_Unload subroutine is always called when a form is unloaded. The Form_Unload subroutine is called either when the form is unloaded using the Unload function or when the user exits the form by clicking the Exit button. The following listing illustrates using the Form_Unload subroutine to make sure the current window settings are saved in the Registry:

```
Private Sub frmMain_Unload(Cancel As Integer)
    If Me.WindowState <> vbMinimized Then
        SaveSetting App.Title, "Settings", _
```

```
            "MainLeft", Me.Left
        SaveSetting App.Title, "Settings", _
            "MainTop", Me.Top
        SaveSetting App.Title, "Settings", _
            "MainWidth", Me.Width
        SaveSetting App.Title, "Settings", _
            "MainHeight", Me.Height
    End If
End Sub
```

In this example, the WindowState property of the current window is checked to make sure the application is not minimized. If the window isn't minimized, then the current window coordinates are saved, which enables the application to resume using its previous position. Placing this code in the Form_Unload subroutine even ensures that it will be executed when the program is terminated normally.

Tip: *The Form_Unload event is not called when the program is terminated externally by using either the Visual Basic debugger or the Task Manager. It also isn't called when the program is terminated by the End function.*

How can I load initial startup values into my form?

You can use the Form_Load subroutine to perform any initial processing that your form requires. The Form_Load subroutine is executed immediately before the form is displayed. The following example shows how you can initially set the form's startup size and position based on a set of values that were saved to the Registry when the form was unloaded:

```
Private Sub frmMain_Load()
    Me.Left = GetSetting(App.Title, "Settings", _
        "MainLeft", 1000)
    Me.Top = GetSetting(App.Title, "Settings", _
        "MainTop", 1000)
    Me.Width = GetSetting(App.Title, "Settings", _
        "MainWidth", 6500)
    Me.Height = GetSetting(App.Title, "Settings", _
        "MainHeight", 6500)
End Sub
```

After the Form_Load subroutine is executed, the form will be displayed on the screen.

USING BASIC DIALOG BOXES

The last part of this chapter deals with using basic message boxes and dialog boxes. Like forms, message boxes and dialog boxes are very important to the usability of your application. Message boxes and dialog boxes display windows in much the same way as a form. However, unlike a form, message boxes and dialog boxes tend to be used for specific functions and don't have the same types of properties and methods that are supported by forms. This tends to make them less flexible but much simpler to use than a form.

 How do I display a message box?

Your application can display a simple message box by using Visual Basic's MsgBox function. The MsgBox function displays a modal dialog box that waits for the user to click one of the buttons displayed on the message box window. The MsgBox function can optionally return an integer value that indicates the user's response. The following listing shows the prototype for the MsgBox function:

```
MsgBox(prompt[, buttons] [, title] _
    [, helpfile, context])
```

The prompt parameter accepts a string that will be displayed in the message box. This first parameter is required. All the other parameters are optional.

The buttons parameter accepts an integer value that controls the type of buttons that will be displayed on the message box. If this parameter is omitted, then the OK button is displayed by default. The following table lists the constants and their values that can be used in the buttons parameter.

Constant	Value	Description
vbOKOnly	0	Display OK button only.
vbOKCancel	1	Display OK and Cancel buttons.
vbAbortRetryIgnore	2	Display Abort, Retry, and Ignore buttons.
vbYesNoCancel	3	Display Yes, No, and Cancel buttons.
vbYesNo	4	Display Yes and No buttons.
vbRetryCancel	5	Display Retry and Cancel buttons.

Constant	Value	Description
vbCritical	16	Display Critical Message icon.
vbQuestion	32	Display Warning Query icon.
vbExclamation	48	Display Warning Message icon.
vbInformation	64	Display Information Message icon.
vbDefaultButton1	0	First button is default.
vbDefaultButton2	256	Second button is default.
vbDefaultButton3	512	Third button is default.
vbDefaultButton4	768	Fourth button is default.
vbApplicationModal	0	Application modal.
vbSystemModal	4096	System modal.
vbMsgBoxHelpButton	16384	Adds Help button to the message.
vbMsgBoxSetForeground	65536	Specifies the message box window as the foreground window.
vbMsgBoxRight	524288	Text is right-aligned.
vbMsgBoxRtlReading	1048576	Specifies that text should appear as right-to-left reading on Hebrew and Arabic systems.

The title parameter of the MsgBox function accepts a string that is displayed in the title of the message box. If this parameter is omitted, the application's title is displayed, by default.

The helpfile and context parameters are used to associate online help with the message box. The helpfile parameter accepts a string that contains the name of the specific Windows help file, whereas the context parameter is an optional help context number.

The MsgBox function returns the following values that are used to determine which button was selected on the message box:

Constant	Value	Description
vbOK	1	OK
vbCancel	2	Cancel
vbAbort	3	Abort

Constant	Value	Description
vbRetry	4	Retry
vbIgnore	5	Ignore
vbYes	6	Yes
vbNo	7	No

The following listing illustrates how you can use the MsgBox function in your Visual Basic applications:

```
Private Sub DemoMsgBox()
    Dim nResponse As Integer
    nResponse = MsgBox("This is an example message _
        box", vbYesNo, "VB Answers! MsgBox Example")
    If nResponse = vbYes Then    ' User chose Yes
        MsgBox "You chose Yes"
    Else                         ' User chose No
        MsgBox "You chose No"
    End If
End Sub
```

In this section of code, the first line declares an integer variable named nResponse that is used to evaluate the value returned from the MsgBox function. Next, the MsgBox function is called using three parameters. The first parameter sets the text that will be displayed in the message box. The value of vbYesNo in the second parameter causes two buttons, a Yes button and a No button, to be displayed on the message box. The third parameter sets the title of the message box. Here is the message box that's displayed by the preceding DemoMsgBox function:

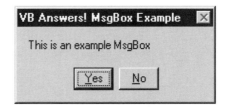

 How do I prompt a user for a simple input value?

You can use the InputBox function to capture one input value from the user. The InputBox function displays a modal dialog

box that waits for the user's input. It can also return an integer value that indicates the user's response. The following listing shows the prototype for the InputBox function:

```
InputBox(prompt[, title] [, default] [, xpos] _
    [, ypos] [, helpfile, context])
```

The prompt parameter accepts a string that is displayed in the message box. This first parameter is required. All the other parameters are optional.

The optional title parameter accepts a string that will be displayed in the title of the message box. If this parameter is omitted, the title of the application is displayed, by default.

The default parameter is also optional. Supplying a value in the default causes that value to be displayed in the input field of the InputBox. Otherwise, the input field initially is blank.

The optional xpos and ypos parameters control where the InputBox initially is displayed. As you might guess, the xpos parameter controls the position from the left edge of the screen, and the ypos parameter controls the vertical position from the top of the screen. Both parameters accept a value in twips. If these parameters are omitted, the InputBox is displayed in the center of the screen, about one third down from the top.

Like the MsgBox function, the helpfile and context parameters are used to associate online help with the message box. The helpfile parameter accepts a string that contains the name of the specific Windows help file, whereas the context parameter is an optional help context number.

The following listing illustrates how you can use the InputBox function in your VB applications:

```
Private Sub DemoInputBox()

    Dim sMessage As String
    Dim sTitle As String
    Dim sInputValue As String

    ' Set up the message and the title.
    sMessage = "Enter your name"
    sTitle = "DemoInputBox"
```

```
' Put the user input value into sInputValue.
sInputValue = InputBox(sMessage, sTitle)

End Sub
```

In the beginning of this example, two string variables are declared that will contain the title and the prompt message to be displayed by the InputBox function. Next, values are assigned to each of these string variables and then the InputBox function is executed using these variables as parameters. The value returned by the InputBox function is assigned to the string variable named sInputValue.

Here is the message box that's displayed by the preceding DemoInputBox function:

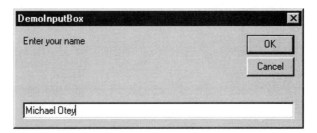

How do I use the CommonDialog control to open a file?

The CommonDialog control enables you to display the same Open, Save, Save As, and Print dialog boxes that are used by most Windows applications. Visual Basic's CommonDialog control is implemented as an ActiveX control and is used quite a bit differently than the MsgBox and InputBox functions. The CommonDialog control essentially allows VB applications to easily use Window's COMMDLG.DLL, which provides the underlying support for the different types of common dialog boxes used in Windows applications.

To use the CommonDialog control, you must first add it to the VB form that will call the control. To do this, simply double-click this control's name in the Visual Basic Toolbox. This adds an instance of the CommonDialog control to the current form. The CommonDialog control is an invisible control. It is displayed at design time, but it is not displayed at runtime until one of its open methods are executed. Figure 6-15 shows the CommonDialog control added to a VB form in design mode.

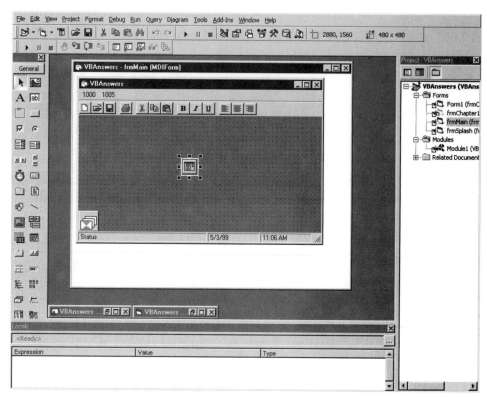

Figure 6-15   Adding the CommonDialog control to a form

After you add the CommonDialog control to your form, you can use it in your code to display different types of common Windows dialog boxes. The type of dialog box that is displayed depends upon which of the following CommonDialog control open methods is used:

Method	Description
ShowOpen	Displays the Open dialog box
ShowSave	Displays the Save As dialog box
ShowColor	Displays the Color dialog box
ShowFont	Displays the Font dialog box
ShowPrinter	Displays the Print Options dialog box
ShowHelp	Displays the Windows Help engine

In addition to these methods, the CommonDialog control has a few important properties that control its appearance

and function. The first such property is the CancelError property. Setting the CancelError property to True can help to improve the structure of your code that handles the CommonDialog control. When this property is set to True, Visual Basic's error handler is automatically invoked when the user clicks Cancel on the CommonDialog control.

The next important property of the CommonDialog control is the Filter property, which controls the types of files that are displayed by the CommonDialog control. The format for the CommonDialog control's Filter property follows:

description1 | *filter1* | *description2* | *filter2*...

The Filter property can accept multiple pairs of filter values. Each filter pair consists of a description and its corresponding filter, separated by a vertical bar. The description is the text that will be displayed in the CommonDialog window, and the filter is the actual mechanism that the CommonDialog uses to limit the files that are displayed at runtime.

Finally, the FilterIndex property is used to set the default filter that's used by the CommonDialog control. The default filter is the filter that is displayed when the CommonDialog is initially opened.

The following listing illustrates how to use the CommonDialog control to display a File Open dialog box:

```
Private Sub DemoCommonDialog()

    ' Error handler to capture Cancel button
    On Error GoTo DialogError

    ' Set up an Open dialog box with filters.
    CommonDialog1.Filter = "All Files (*.*)|*.*|Text" _
    & "Files (*.txt)|*.txt|Batch Files (*.bat)|*.bat"

    ' Specify default filter.
    CommonDialog1.FilterIndex = 2

    ' Display the Open dialog box.
    CommonDialog1.ShowOpen

    ' Display the selected file.
    MsgBox "The user selected: " & _
```

```
                    CommonDialog1.FileName, vbInformation, _
                    "Demo CommonDialog"

        Exit Sub

    DialogError:
        MsgBox "The user pressed Cancel", vbInformation, _
            "Demo CommonDialog"

    End Sub
```

Figure 6-16 illustrates the CommonDialog control that's displayed by this code listing.

Near the top of the Demo CommonDialog subroutine, you can see where the VB error handler is activated. Using the error handler enables Visual Basic to transfer control to the DialogError tag in the event that the user clicks the Cancel button on the CommonDialog control. For this to work, the CancelError property of the CommonDialog control must be set to True.

Next, the CommonDialog control's Filter property is assigned three filters. The first filter displays the text "All Files" and uses *.* as the file filter. The second filter displays the text "Text Files" and uses the filter *.txt to control the files that will be displayed. Finally, the third filter displays the text "Batch Files" and uses the filter *.bat to limit the files that will be displayed by the CommonDialog control.

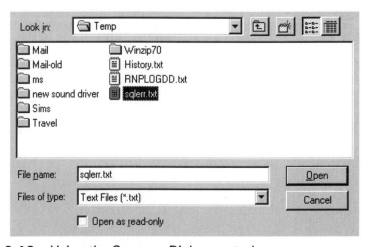

Figure 6-16   Using the CommonDialog control

After the filters are set, the FilterIndex property is set to 2, which causes the filter "Text Files ! *.txt" to be used as the default filter.

Next, the ShowOpen method is used to display a File Open type of dialog box. After the ShowOpen method is executed, the DemoCommonDialog subroutine waits for the user to respond to the Open dialog box that's displayed. If the user clicks the Cancel button, the control will branch to the DialogError tag. If the user selects a file in the dialog box and clicks the OK button, then the execution of the subroutine resumes with the next line following the CommonDialog1.ShowOpen method. In this case, a message box is displayed that shows the filename selected by the user. You should note that the filename selected on the CommonDialog control is available in the CommonDialog1.FileName property.

Chapter 7

Advanced Forms

Answer Topics!

Advanced Forms @ a Glance

The questions and answers in this chapter involve some of the more advanced issues that arise regarding forms during application development. The topics covered by these questions and answers are not required for the majority of the Visual Basic applications that you will develop. However, the information provided here does pertain to some of the more specialized application requirements that come up with some regularity.

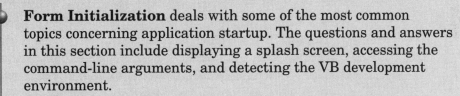

- **Form Initialization** deals with some of the most common topics concerning application startup. The questions and answers in this section include displaying a splash screen, accessing the command-line arguments, and detecting the VB development environment.

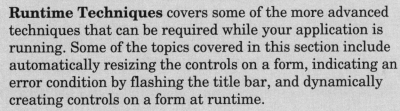

- **Runtime Techniques** covers some of the more advanced techniques that can be required while your application is running. Some of the topics covered in this section include automatically resizing the controls on a form, indicating an error condition by flashing the title bar, and dynamically creating controls on a form at runtime.

FORM INITIALIZATION

The first part of this chapter covers some common questions and answers regarding the startup processing that may be required by your application.

 What's the order and purpose of the Form_Load, Form_Initialize, Form_Unload, and Form_Terminate events?

All of these different event subroutines are called during the form's startup and shutdown process. Table 7-1 describes the different form event subroutines.

 Tip: *Executing the End function bypasses the Form_Unload and Form_Terminate subroutines.*

Order	Event	Purpose
1	Form_Initialize	Called before the form is loaded, providing an opportunity to instantiate objects and perform any other processing that is required before the form is loaded.
2	Form_Load	Called just after the Form_Initialize subroutine and just before the form is displayed. For simple programs, it typically is used to perform startup processing. It also is typically used to control the display of the form.
3	Form_Unload	Called immediately after the form is closed, which typically occurs when the user clicks the Close button or when the Unload function is executed. Any cleanup code for the form usually is placed in this subroutine.
4	Form_Terminate	The last form event procedure that's called. This subroutine is called after the form is unloaded and immediately before the program is ended.

Table 7-1   Call Order of the Form Event Subroutines

 ## How do I make my application display a splash screen?

Splash screens are often used to provide immediate feedback to the user while an application performs its initialization functions. Immediately displaying the splash screen allows the user to see that the application is loading and that it is proceeding normally. Without a splash screen, the user may be required to wait several seconds with no feedback while the application performs its startup function. Delays without feedback can easily make the user think that something is wrong. In addition, the splash screen can help brand your applications, by making them easy for the end user to identify. The best way to make your application display a splash screen is to build a form that will be used as the splash screen and then show that form for a limited period of time by using Sub Main as your startup function.

The first step to implementing a splash screen in your application is to create a form that will be used as the splash screen. The forms used as splash screens typically display a graphic element, by using the PictureBox control, as well as the application's name and version information. A form that's used as a splash screen is no different from any other form, except that its property settings are configured to allow the form to appear as a splash screen rather than a standard window. Table 7-2 shows the typical property settings that are used on a form that is displayed as a splash screen.

Property	Value
BorderStyle	3 - Fixed Dialog
MaxButton	False
MDIChild	False
MinButton	False
ShowInTaskbar	False
StartUpPosition	2 - CenterScreen
WindowState	0 - Normal

Table 7-2   Form Properties for Splash Screen

After you create the form that will be the splash screen, the next step is to set up your application to display the splash screen form upon startup. One option to accomplish this is simply to set up the splash screen form as your project's startup form. However, this isn't the best option, and it typically defeats the purpose of having a splash screen. The splash screen is intended both to provide user feedback while your application loads and to make your application seem more responsive. Using a splash screen accomplishes this by allowing all the initialization functions to be executed in the background while the splash screen is being displayed. When the main form appears, it is ready to run. Setting up the splash screen as the startup form means that all the initialization still needs to be run when the application moves from the splash screen to the main form. In addition, using the splash screen form as the startup form requires you to place the show and unload code within the splash screen form itself, making it difficult to find and maintain.

A better option is to control the display of the splash screen and the main form from the application's Main subroutine. The Sub Main can provide a central control point that is easily maintained and it moves all the required Form Load, Show, and Unload code out of the form itself and into a common code module. The following code illustrates using Sub Main to display a splash screen:

```
Sub Main()
    Dim fMainForm As New frmMain
    Dim nStartTime As Single
    Dim nEndTime As Single

    ' First show the splash form.
    frmSplash.Show
    frmSplash.Refresh

    ' Next load the main form.
    Load fMainForm

    ' Optional - delay 1 second.
    nStartTime = Timer
```

```
nEndTime = Timer + 1
Do Until nStartTime >= nEndTime
    nStartTime = Timer
Loop

' Unload the splash form.
Unload frmSplash

' Now show the main form.
fMainForm.Show

End Sub
```

In the beginning of this listing, three working variables are declared. The fMainForm variable is used to enable the main form to be loaded by using the Load function. This causes any code located in the Form_Load subroutine to be executed without displaying the form. To use the fMainForm as a variable, a declaration of a form object, such as the following, must be supplied:

```
Public fMainForm As frmMain
```

Next, the nStartTime and nEndTime variables are declared. These variables allow the splash form to be displayed for a specific amount of time.

After these working variables are declared, the next action that takes place in Sub Main is to display the splash form. In this example, the splash form is named frmSplash. The Show method is used to display the form initially, and the Refresh method is used to ensure that the frmSplash form is completely displayed while any other program actions (such as loading the main form) take place.

Next, the main form is loaded by using the Load method. Using the Load method causes any of the initialization code that is located in the form's Form_Load subroutine to be executed without displaying the form.

The next section of code merely delays the program for a period of one second. This delay code allows the splash screen to be displayed for at least one second, which is useful when the initialization code in the main form runs very quickly.

Otherwise, if the initialization code takes a few seconds to run, this code should be removed.

 Tip: *The Sleep function from the Win32 API provides an alternative method of pausing your application. Using the Sleep function is described in Chapter 12.*

After the delay, the splash screen is unloaded by using the Unload function, and the main form is displayed by using the Show method. At this point, using the Show method displays the main form almost immediately, because all the initialization code has already been executed.

 Tip: *Visual Basic's Add Form Wizard can help to create a new splash screen for your application. Select Project | Add Form and then select the Splash Screen option from the list of form types.*

 ## How can I make my program accept command-line arguments?

Command-line arguments are useful for passing in control values or other custom data to your program. Visual Basic can access command-line arguments by using the Command function. However, Visual Basic's Command function simply returns the entire command line as a string—it doesn't parse out each of the different arguments that may be supplied to the program. The following GetCommandArgs subroutine shows how you can parse the command line and extract the values from all the arguments that are passed to the program:

```
Function GetCommandArgs() As Variant()

    Dim vArgArray() As Variant
    Dim cChar As String
    Dim sCmdLine As String
    Dim nCmdLineLen As Integer
    Dim nArguments As Integer
```

```
    Dim nCount As Integer
    Dim bBuildingArg As Boolean

' Get command-line arguments.
sCmdLine = Command()

' Initialize working variables.
nCmdLineLen = Len(sCmdLine)
bBuldingArg = True

' Parse each character of the command line.
For nCount = 1 To nCmdLineLen

    sChar = Mid(sCmdLine, nCount, 1)
    ' Test for space or tab.
    If (sChar <> " " And sChar <> vbTab) Then

        ' Check if we are building the argument.
        If Not bBuildingArg Then
            'Build a new argument
            ReDim Preserve vArgArray(nArguments)
            bBuildingArg = True
        End If

        ' Concatenate character to current argument.
        vArgArray(nArguments) = _
            vArgArray(nArguments) & sChar

    ' A space or tab was found.
    Else
        ' Set building argument to False.
        bBuildingArg = False
        nArguments = nArguments + 1
    End If

Next nCount

' Return array.
GetCommandArgs = vArgArray()

End Function
```

The first bit of code in this listing declares that the GetCommandArgs function will return an array of Variants. Using an array allows the value of each argument to be placed in a different array element. The Variant data type provides maximum flexibility, which is needed, because no way exists to know the data type of each argument.

Next, a work array of Variants is declared along with several variables that will be used to parse the command-line string. After all the working variables have been declared, the Command function is used to extract the command-line data and assign it to the string variable named sCmdLine.

After the command line has been extracted, the next section of code illustrates how you can parse the command-line string and assign each argument to a separate array element. First, the total length of the command line is assigned to the nCmdLineLen variable, and then the bBuildingArg flag, which indicates that the routine is currently in the process of building an argument, is set to True.

The actual string parsing is performed within the following For Next loop, which checks each character of the command string. The character is first tested to determine whether it is a space or a tab. If it's neither and no current argument is being constructed, then a new argument is about to be processed. To prepare for the new argument, the vArgArray is resized to accommodate the new argument, and the flag is set to True. Otherwise, if the character is not a space or a tab and the bBuildingArg flag indicates that an argument is currently being constructed, then the character is appended to the current array item.

The section following the Else keyword is performed if the current character is a space or a tab. If the character is a space or a tab, then the current argument is ended. The bBuildingArg flag is set to False, showing that no current argument is being processed, and the nArgument counter that tracks the number of arguments is incremented.

The For Next loop is ended when all the characters in the command-line string have been parsed into the vArgArray Variant array. After the For Next loop has ended, the GetCommandArgs variable is assigned the value of the vArgArray. This value is returned to the calling function.

The GetCommandArgs function typically is called as part of an application's initialization routine. Usually, this means that it is executed either in a form's Form_Load subroutine or in Sub Main. The following listing illustrates how to call the GetCommandArgs function to retrieve the command-line arguments into an array:

```
Private Sub Form_Load()

    Dim vArguments() As Variant

    vArguments = GetCommandArgs

End Sub
```

The Form_Load subroutine shows how you can call the GetCommandArgs function when your application first starts. Before the GetCommandArgs function is called, an array of Variants is declared to contain the values returned by the GetCommandArgs function. The GetCommandArgs function is then called to fill the array.

Passing command-line arguments in from the command line is easy, but testing them from Visual Basic's IDE is another matter. Fortunately, Visual Basic provides a handy method for passing command-line variables to a project that executed from the IDE. To assign a set of command-line variables to the IDE, select Project | Properties and then select the Make tab in the Project Properties dialog box, shown in Figure 7-1.

In Figure 7-1, you can see that a set of test arguments has been entered into the Command Line Arguments text box. These values will be passed as command-line arguments to the program that's run from the Visual Basic IDE.

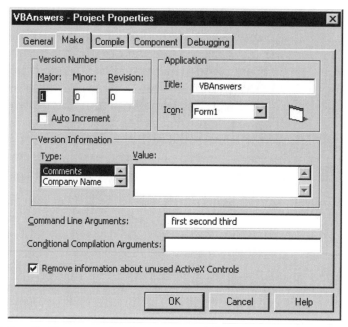

Figure 7-1 Setting a project's command-line arguments

How can I make sure that only one instance of my program runs?

You can use Visual Basic's App object to determine easily whether an instance of your application is already running. The App object provides information about the current VB program and its properties, including information about the executable filename, the version number, the company name, the path, and the application's title. The following code illustrates how to use the App object to check whether an instance of your application is already running:

```
Private Sub Form_Load()
    If App.PrevInstance Then
        MsgBox "An instance of this program " _
            & "is already running."
        Unload Me
    End If
End Sub
```

In this example, the PrevInstance property of the App object is tested as part of the Form_Load subroutine to determine whether the program is already running. The

PrevInstance property contains a Boolean data type, where a value of True means that the application is already active, and a value of False means the application is not active. In the prior listing, if an instance of the application is already active, then a message box is displayed to inform the user about the condition, and then the current form is unloaded, ending the application.

Can I determine whether my program is running within the VB IDE?

Yes. You can find out whether your application is being run from the Visual Basic IDE by checking the name of the base window that's being executed. You can get this name by using two Win32 APIs: the GetWindowWord API and the GetModuleName API. Like the other Win32 APIs, you must create function declarations in your program before you can call the API functions from your VB code. The easiest way to create the Win32 function declarations is by using API Viewer, which automatically generates the Win32 API declarations for you to use in your program. The declarations for the GetWindowWord and GetModuleFileName functions are shown in the following listing:

```
Global Const GWW_HINSTANCE = (-6)

Public Declare Function GetWindowWord Lib "user32" _
    (ByVal hwnd As Long, ByVal nIndex As Long) _
    As Integer

Public Declare Function GetModuleFileName _
    Lib "kernel32" Alias "GetModuleFileNameA" _
    (ByVal hModule As Long, ByVal lpFileName _
        As String, ByVal nSize As Long) As Long
```

The GetWindowWord function returns information about the window specified in the first parameter. The GWW_HINSTANCE constant is used with the second parameter of the GetWindowWord function to cause it to return the instance handle of the specified window. The GetModuleFileName function retrieves the filename of a module where a module refers to either a Dynamic Link Library (DLL) or a standard Windows executable program.

After these function declarations have been created, you can call them in your application, to determine the name of the currently executing module. If the program is running in the Visual Basic IDE, then they return the name VB6.EXE. Otherwise, they return the name of your VB application. The following Form_Load subroutine illustrates how to get the current module name by using the GetWindowWord and GetModuleFileName functions:

```
Sub Form_Load()

    Dim sModuleName As String
    Dim sFileName As String
    Dim hInstance As Long
    Dim lReturnCode As Long

    ' Size the return string.
    sModuleName = String$(260, Chr$(0))

    ' Get the hInstance application.
    hInstance = GetWindowWord(Me.hwnd, GWW_HINSTANCE)

    ' Get the module name.
    sModuleName = Left$(sModuleName, _
       GetModuleFileName(hInstance, sModuleName, _
          Len(sModuleName)))

    ' Check for the module named VB6.EXE.
    If InStr(sModuleName, "VB6.EXE") Then
       MsgBox App.EXEName & " In VB development Shell"
    Else
       MsgBox App.EXEName & _
          " Not in VB development Shell"
    End If

End Sub
```

At the top of the Form_Load function, you can see where the working variables for the subroutine are declared. Next, the sModuleName variable, which will be used to hold the string name, is sized to the maximum Windows 9x path size of 260.

Tip: *When calling Win32 API functions that return string values, it's very important to size the variable large enough to contain the largest possible return value. Failure to do so could result in an abnormal program termination.*

Next, the GetWindowWord function is called to get the Instance handle of the current window. The Me.hwnd property provides the Window's handle of the current application, and the GWW_HINSTANCE constant tells the GetWindowWord function to return the current window's instance handle.

After the instance handle has been retrieved, it's used in the GetModuleFileName function to get the name of the currently executing module. The GetModuleFileName function returns a string containing the path of the currently executing module in its second parameter. This string will be contained in the sModuleName variable.

Next, the contents of the sModuleName variable are checked, using the InStr function, to see whether it contains the module name VB6.EXE. If the string "VB6.EXE" is found, then the program is running in the VB IDE. Otherwise, the program is being run directly from Windows and isn't being run from the IDE.

RUNTIME TECHNIQUES

The questions and answers presented in the second section of this chapter address some of the more common advanced issues that your applications may need to address during runtime.

How can I dynamically resize all the controls on my form when I resize the form?

Enabling your form to be resized is really easy. You simply need to set the form's BorderStyle to 2 - Resizable, and you're finished. However, as soon as you attempt to resize your application, you'll find that this method falls short of what you really need. Although setting the form's BorderStyle allows the form to be resized, this property has no effect on all the controls that are placed on the form. When the form is resized, all the controls maintain their original location and size—they do not dynamically grow and shrink as the form is resized. This causes the application's appearance to be less than optimal after the form has been resized.

Fortunately, by taking advantage of the Tag property and using a little bit of custom code, you can enable all the controls on a form to be dynamically resized as the form itself is resized. To make this work, your code needs to be executed when the form is first loaded, and then again when the form is resized.

First, the Form_Load subroutine is fired when the form is initially loaded. At that point, the original position of each control is recorded in the control's Tag property. Then, the Form_Resize subroutine is executed when the form is resized. The code that's executed after the Resize event modifies the position of each control relative to the changes that occurred in the parent form. The following listing shows how you can initially assign the position values to each object's Tag property:

```
Public Sub InitObjectsToResize(frm As Form)

    Dim obj As Object

    On Error Resume Next

    ' Initialize the Tag property with the object's
    ' relative position.
    For Each obj In frm.Controls
      obj.Tag = _
      Format$ (obj.Left / frm.ScaleWidth, ".0000") _
      & Format$(obj.Top / frm.ScaleHeight, ".0000") _
      & Format$(obj.Width / frm.ScaleWidth, ".0000") _
      & Format$(obj.Height / frm.ScaleHeight, ".0000")
    Next obj

End Sub
```

The InitObjectsToResize subroutine accepts a single parameter that contains a reference to the form whose objects will be resized. Next, a working variable named obj is declared as an Object data type and error handling is enabled. Error handling is used to allow the subroutine to continue to function even if one of the objects on the form does not support the Tag property.

Next, a For Each loop is used to iterate through all the objects that are contained on the form. Each object that's on a given form is a member of the form's Controls collection, and iterating through the Controls collection enables you to programmatically access all the objects on the form. Within the For Each loop, the Tag property of each object is assigned a coordinate value that defines the object's starting position on the form and its size.

The InitObjectsToResize subroutine is typically called from the Form_Load event, as the following listing demonstrates:

```
Private Sub Form_Load()
    ' Set up the objects that will be resized.
    InitObjectsToResize Me
End Sub
```

The Me value that's passed to the InitObjectsToResize subroutine contains a reference to the current form.

After the Tag properties of all the objects on the form have been assigned with its starting coordinates, the next step to enable dynamic control resizing is to execute code from the Form_Resize event that will move and size each object relative to the parent form. The following ResizeObjects subroutine shows how you can modify the position of each object on the form:

```
Public Sub ResizeObjects(frm As Form)

    Dim obj As Object

    On Error Resume Next
```

```
' Resize each object based on the tag coordinates.
For Each obj In frm.Controls
    obj.Move _
      Val(Mid$(obj.Tag, 1, 5)) * frm.ScaleWidth, _
      Val(Mid$(obj.Tag, 6, 5)) * frm.ScaleHeight, _
      Val(Mid$(obj.Tag, 11, 5)) * frm.ScaleWidth, _
      Val(Mid$(obj.Tag, 16, 5)) * frm.ScaleHeight
Next obj

End Sub
```

Like the InitObjectsToResize subroutine that was
shown earlier, the ResizeObjects subroutine accepts a single
parameter that contains a reference to the form whose objects
will be dynamically resized. As you should expect, the form
reference passed to the ResizeObjects subroutine must
have been processed earlier, using the InitObjectsToResize
subroutine. Next, the working obj Object variable is declared
and then Visual Basic's error handling is enabled.

The real action in the ResizeObjects subroutine is
performed within the For Each loop that processes each of
the objects that are on the form. Like you saw earlier, the
Controls collection contains all the objects that are on a VB
form, and the For Each loop is the mechanism used to read
through the collection.

Within the loop, the Move method is called for each
object. The Move method accepts four parameters that
correspond to the four coordinate values that were assigned
to each object's Tag property by using the InitObjectsToResize
subroutine. The following are the Move method's four
parameters:

● **left**   The distance from the left side of the object to the
left edge of the form

● **top**   The distance between the top of the object and
the top edge of the parent form

● **width**   The width of the object

● **height**   The height of the object

All of the parameter values are expressed in twips (described in Chapter 6). The value for each parameter is extracted from the data that's contained in the Tag property and then multiplied by the value from the form's ScaleWidth or ScaleHeight property. The ScaleWidth and ScaleHeight properties indicate the interior measurement of each respective edge of the parent form. The result of this calculation yields the new location and size for each object on the form.

The ResizeObjects subroutine must be called from the Form_Resize event, as shown in the following listing:

```
Private Sub Form_Resize()

    ' Resize the form's objects.
    ResizeObjects Me

End Sub
```

The Form_Resize subroutine is executed whenever the user resizes the form. The Me value that's passed to the ResizeObjects subroutine provides a reference to the current form that's being resized.

I've seen some of the Microsoft Office applications flash the title bar to indicate an error. How do I make the title bar of my application flash?

This technique is often used to draw the user's attention to a problem or error condition. It can be especially effective in alerting the user about an error condition in a minimized window, because it also causes the icon in the taskbar to flash. You can make the title bar of an application flash by calling the GetCaretBlinkTime and FlashWindow Win32 API functions from your VB application. The GetCaretBlinkTime function returns a value that reflects the speed that the system blinks the cursor. The FlashWindow function causes the specified window to flash in a similar manner to when the window changes from active to inactive. Before either of these functions can be used in your VB application, you need to create declarations for them in a VB BAS module.

The following code illustrates the declarations for the GetCaretBlinkTime and the FlashWindow functions:

```
Declare Function GetCaretBlinkTime _
    Lib "user32" () As Long
Declare Function FlashWindow _
    Lib "user32" (ByVal hwnd As Long, _
    ByVal bInvert As Long) As Long
```

 Tip: *Using Visual Basic's API Viewer is the easiest way to create function declarations for the Win32 APIs that you want to use in your Visual B applications. To create function declarations by using API Viewer, select File | Load Text File and then select the win32API.txt file. You can then select the Declarations option and the desired Win32 functions from the list of functions that is displayed. The API Viewer, shown in Figure 7-2, will generate function declarations that you can copy into your VB application.*

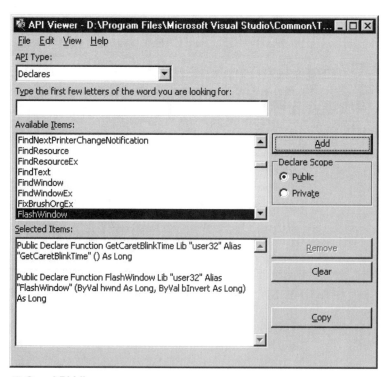

Figure 7-2 API Viewer

After the function declarations have been created, these two Win32 API functions can be called in your application. The first bit of code that's required to make the title bar of an application flash is code to set up a timer. First, add an instance of the Timer control to your VB form by dragging and dropping the Timer control from the Toolbox onto your VB form. Then, before you want the title bar to begin flashing, you need to execute the following code to enable the timer:

```
Timer1.Interval = GetCaretBlinkTime()
Timer1.Enabled = True
```

In the preceding listing, the Interval property of the timer named Timer1 is set using the GetCaretBlinkTime function. This sets the timer to fire at the same rate as the system cursor blinks—approximately once per second. Next, the Timer1.Enabled property is set to True, which starts the timer.

After the timer is enabled, its Timer event is fired each time the time interval expires. In this example, executing the FlashWindow function from the timer's Timer event causes the window to flash:

```
Private Sub Timer1_Timer()
    Dim lReturnCode As Long
    lReturnCode = FlashWindow(Form2.hwnd, 1)
End Sub
```

The FlashWindow function accepts two parameters. The first parameter is a handle to the window that will be flashed. The second parameter specifies whether the window's title bar will be inverted. A value of 1 indicates that the window will be inverted. The act of inverting the title bar and then returning it to its normal state causes the window to flash. Like the majority of the Win32 APIs, the FlashWindow function returns a Long value. For the FlashWindow function, the return value indicates whether the window was active before the call. In this example, the return value is not used.

Setting the timer's Enabled property to False turns off the timer and stops the window from flashing. The following code illustrates turning off the timer, thus causing the flashing to cease:

```
Timer1.Enabled = False
```

 ## How can I animate the icon and text that's displayed on a minimized window?

Animating the icon and text of a minimized window is a technique that is used to show the progress of long-running background jobs. This technique enables you to display a series of small icon graphics to show that the task is progressing, as well as updating text, to indicate the running percentage of the job that is complete. You can dynamically update the text and icon that are displayed on a minimized window by updating the form's Caption and Icon properties. You can create an animation effect by using the timer to display a sequence of different icons in succession.

The first step to setting up this technique is to configure the timer to fire at a predetermined interval. The following code illustrates how to minimize the window and set up the timer to fire once per second:

```
Form2.WindowState = vbMinimized
Timer2.Interval = 1000
Timer2.Enabled = True
```

Setting the WindowState property to vbMinimized causes the window to be minimized. Next, the Interval property of the timer named Timer2 is set to 1000. The timer's Interval property accepts a Long value that represents a time interval in milliseconds. The value of 1000 sets the interval to one second. Next, the timer's Enabled property is set to True, which starts the timer.

After the window is minimized and the timer is started, the next step is to update the form's Icon and Caption properties when the timer fires. Changing these properties on the form also updates the display that's presented on the taskbar. The following code listing shows how you can dynamically assign values to the form's Caption and Icon properties:

```
Private Sub Timer2_Timer()

    ' Display the red icon.
    If bYellowFlag = True Then
        Form2.Icon = LoadPicture("red.ico")
```

```
        bYellowFlag = False
        Form2.Caption = "Red"

    ' Display the yellow icon.
    Else
        Form2.Icon = LoadPicture("yellow.ico")
        Form2.Caption = "Yellow"
        bYellowFlag = True
    End If

End Sub
```

The code within the timer's Timer event is executed
whenever the timer Interval property has elapsed. In this
simple example, the form's Icon and Caption properties
are merely alternated between red and yellow. However,
using a very similar technique, you can also easily display
a sequence of different icons to provide a more sophisticated
animation effect. The more icons that you use in the series,
the smoother your animation will appear to be. Here, the
bYellowFlag variable contains the form's current state. If the
yellow icon is currently displayed, then it will be replaced
with the red icon and caption setting.

Whereas setting the Caption property is very straightforward, setting the Icon property is a little more involved. To
dynamically set a form's Icon property, you must use the
LoadPicture function. The first required parameter
of the LoadPicture function accepts a string that contains the
name of the image file that will be loaded. The LoadPicture
function can be used to load the following types of files (with
extensions shown in parentheses): bitmap (.bmp), icon (.ico),
cursor (.cur), run-length encoded (.rle), metafile (.wmf),
enhanced metafile (.emf), GIF (.gif), and JPEG (.jpg). In this
previous listing, the LoadPicture function is used to load
either an icon named red.ioc or an icon named yellow.ico.
Setting these properties causes the minimized window's
display characteristics to be immediately altered.

Setting the timer's Enabled property to False turns off
the timer and stops the minimized icon's animation. The
following code illustrates turning off the timer:

```
Timer2.Enabled = False
```

 Can I dynamically add controls to a form at runtime using program code?

Yes. Although controls normally are created using Visual Basic's Form Designer, they can also be created using code. While this is obviously a bit more complicated than using the standard VB Form Designer, it also gives your program a great deal more flexibility. Dynamically creating forms enables you to create custom windows on-the-fly in response to either the user's custom program settings or other application choices. The following are the two basic steps required to dynamically create controls on a form:

1. Create an instance of the object and display it on the desired form.

2. Handle the events that are generated by these dynamically created controls.

Before an ActiveX control can be created and used, an object of that control type must be declared. The following listing illustrates how you can declare three control objects: a Label, a TextBox, and a CommandButton:

```
Dim WithEvents ctlLabel As VB.Label
Dim WithEvents ctlText As VB.TextBox
Dim WithEvents ctlCommand As VB.CommandButton
```

Declaring dynamic control objects is very much like declaring a standard object. However, in the case of dynamically created runtime controls, the WithEvents keyword is used to indicate that the object being declared can respond to events generated by ActiveX controls. Using the WithEvents keyword enables dynamically created objects to utilize standard event procedures, in the same way that ActiveX controls created at design time can.

The Dim statements that are used to create control objects typically are placed in a form's Declarations section. This permits them to have module-level scope so that they can interact with the event subroutines that are present in the form module. All the standard VB controls, such as the Label, TextBox, and CommandButton that are used in this example, are found in the VB OLE library.

Tip: All the standard VB controls are referenced within the VB object library. This allows them to be declared directly by using the appropriate data type. For instance, the Label control can be directly declared as VB.Label object type. Controls that are not already referenced in the VB library, such as Microsoft FlexGrid, Microsoft Internet Controls, Microsoft TreeView, or any user-created ActiveX controls, can be declared by using the generic VBControlExtender object type. You can see all the controls that are part of the VB object library by using the Object Browser.

After the control objects are declared, they can be created in code. The following Form_Load subroutine illustrates how you can dynamically create three new controls and add them to an existing form:

```
Private Sub Form_Load()

  ' Dynamically add a label.
  Set ctlLabel = _
    Controls.Add("VB.Label", "ctlLabel", Me)
  ' Position the label on the form.
  ctlLabel.Move 1, 100, 1300, 400
  ' Set the display properties.
  ctlLabel.Caption = "Dynamic Label"
  ctlLabel.Visible = True

  ' Dynamically add a text box.
  Set ctlText = _
    Controls.Add("VB.TextBox", "ctlText", Me)
  ' Position the text box relative to the label.
  ctlText.Move _
    (ctlLabel.Left + ctlLabel.Width + 50), _
    ctlLabel.Top, 3200, 400
  ' Set the display properties.
  ctlText.Visible = True

  ' Dynamically add a command button.
  Set ctlCommand = Controls.Add _
    ("VB.CommandButton", "ctlCommand", Me)
  ' Position the command button relative to the label.
  ctlCommand.Move _
```

```
       (ctlLabel.Left + ctlLabel.Width + 50), _
        ctlLabel.Top + ctlLabel.Height + 150, 1500, 400
   ' Set the display properties.
   ctlCommand.Caption = "Display text"
   ctlCommand.Visible = True

End Sub
```

Inside the Form_Load subroutine, you can see where the three controls are dynamically created. The first control that's created is a Label control. A new instance of the Label control is created by using the Controls.Add method, which adds a new control object to the collection of control objects that are on the current form.

The first parameter of the Controls.Add method is a string that identifies the control that will be added to the Controls collection. For the standard VB controls, the name that's used here can be found by using the Visual Basic Object Browser to view the contents of the VB object library. In this case, the value of VB.Label specifies that a Label control object will be added to the Controls collection.

The second parameter is a string that provides the name of the object as it will be used in your application. The value of ctlLabel in the second parameter means that this control is named ctlLabel.

The third, optional parameter identifies the object container that holds the Controls collection. If this parameter is not specified, then the current object is used. In this case, the value of Me causes the control to be explicitly added to the current form.

After the Label object is created, the object's Move method is used to set the control's initial size and position on the form. The first two parameters set the object's Left and Top properties, whereas the second two parameters set the object's Width and Height properties. The values of 1 and 100 place the object near the upper-left corner of the form, while the values of 1300 and 400 size the object to a little smaller than the default label size.

Next, the text that's displayed by the ctlLabel object is assigned to the object's Caption property. Then, the control's Visible property is set to True, which causes the control to appear on the form.

The following code that adds the TextBox and CommandButton objects is very similar. As you can see in the previous listing, the TextBox control uses the object name VB.TextBox, and the CommandButton is created by using the VB.CommandButton object identifier. The TextBox control is named ctlText, and the CommandButton is named ctlCommand.

The primary difference between these controls and the Label control is the manner in which the controls are placed on the form. The ctlTextBox and ctlCommand Move method uses screen coordinates that are relative to the ctlLabel control that was previously created. This makes adjusting these controls' positions on the form much easier. If absolute screen coordinates were used, then every time you needed to adjust the appearance of the screen, you potentially would be required to adjust the values in each object's Move method. Using coordinates that are relative to the upper-left control on the form enables you to limit your adjustment to a single Move method. All the objects that are subsequently created will automatically adjust to any changes that occur to that object's position on the form.

Dynamically creating and displaying the controls allows the controls to appear on the target form. However, to allow the user to interact with these controls, you still need to provide event-handling subroutines. The following listing shows an example subroutine that handles the Click event of a CommandButton control named ctlCommand:

```
Private Sub ctlCommand_Click()
    ctlText.Text = "You clicked the dynamic _
        CommandButton"
End Sub
```

This ctlCommand_Click subroutine will be executed whenever the user clicks the CommandButton control named ctlCommand. In this example, the ctlCommand_Click subroutine simply assigns a text string to the Text property of the TextBox control named ctlText.

It's important to note that the first part of the name used here must match the name of the object that was assigned earlier using the Controls.Add method. For example, for this ctlCommand_Click subroutine to be executed when the user clicks the Command button, the earlier Controls.Add method must have assigned the control name of ctlCommand in the second parameter of the Add method. You can see an example of this in the earlier Form_Load subroutine.

Chapter 8

ActiveX Controls

Answer Topics!

ActiveX Controls @ a Glance

This chapter presents a set of questions and answers that provide a basic understanding of using ActiveX controls in Visual Basic. Effectively using ActiveX controls is the primary key to rapid application development using Visual Basic. The VB component model enables you to achieve high productivity, by providing a set of easily reusable components that can be immediately snapped into a variety of applications.

General Questions About ActiveX Controls explains some of the basic issues about the ActiveX controls that are supplied with Visual Basic. The questions and answers in this section address topics that are common to most controls.

Using the Basic ActiveX Controls answers specific questions concerning using Visual Basic's ActiveX controls to perform application development. This section shows how you can effectively use these controls in your own applications.

GENERAL QUESTIONS
ABOUT ACTIVEX CONTROLS

The first part of this chapter presents some basic questions and answers that explore the fundamental characteristics of Visual Basic forms. The questions and answers in the later part of this section illustrate some of the common programming functions that you can perform by setting the various form properties.

 ## How do I add an ActiveX control?

You can add ActiveX controls to Visual Basic's integrated development environment (IDE) by selecting Project | Components. You might be surprised at how many controls are already loaded on your system that are not displayed in the Toolbox. Selecting the Components option displays the Components dialog box, shown in Figure 8-1.

The Components dialog box is initially displayed at the Controls tab, which lists all the ActiveX controls available on the system. Scroll through Visual Basic's Components dialog

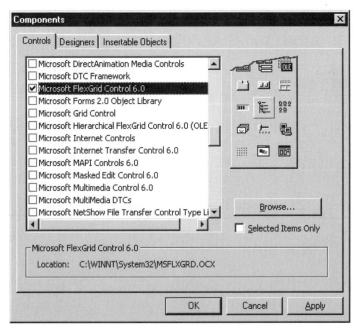

Figure 8-1 Adding ActiveX controls to Visual Basic

box until you see the ActiveX control that you want to use. For instance, to add the Microsoft FlexGrid control, scroll through the list of components on the Controls tab until you see Microsoft FlexGrid Control 6.0. Click the check box next to the control's name, and then click the OK button. This adds the Microsoft FlexGrid ActiveX control to Visual Basic's Toolbox. You can then use the MSFlexGrid control in your VB applications.

 Tip: *The ActiveX controls displayed in the Toolbox are project-specific. If you want a particular ActiveX control to be automatically added to the Visual Basic IDE each time you open a specific project, you must add the control to one of that project's forms.*

 I worked for quite a while sizing my control just how I want it. Now I need a few more controls like it. Can I copy my control?

Yes. Visual Basic's Form Designer supports cut-and-paste operations that enable you to copy existing controls quickly and easily. To use the Form Designer's cut-and-paste capability, perform the following steps:

1. Click the control that you want to copy. Resizing handles will appear around the border of the control.
2. Press CTRL+C to copy the control.
3. Click the form that will contain the copied control.
4. Press CTRL+V to paste the control onto the target form. If the paste operation is performed on the same form, you are prompted to create a control array, because the pasted control has the same name as the original control. Typically, you don't want to create a control array and thus should select No. After you complete the paste operation, the control will be initially displayed in the upper-left portion of the form.
5. Left-click the control and drag it to the desired location on the form. When the control is positioned correctly, release the left mouse button to drop the control onto the form.

You can also use Visual Basic's Format menu to adjust the size and alignment of the controls that are on a form. To adjust the size and alignment of two controls by using the Format menu, perform the following steps:

1. Left-click the target control that you want to resize. Resizing handles will appear around the border of the control.

2. Hold down the CTRL key and then left-click the second control that will be used as the resizing template. Resizing handles will appear around the border of the second control.

3. Select Format | Make Same Size | Both. The first control will be sized according to the dimensions of the second control that was selected.

4. Select Format | Align | Lefts. The first control will be aligned with the left edge of the second control.

Can I move multiple controls simultaneously by using the Form Designer?

Yes. This technique can save you a lot of time when you need to move multiple controls and you want to maintain their relative position to one another. Instead of individually selecting and positioning each control, you can select multiple controls by drawing a selection box over them and then moving the entire contents of the selection box simultaneously. To select and move multiple controls, perform the following steps:

1. Left-click the upper-left corner of the group of controls that you want to move. Do not release the left mouse button.

2. Drag the mouse pointer to the lower-right corner of the group of controls that you want to move. As you do so, a selection box is drawn on the form around all the controls that you select.

3. After you select all the controls that you want to move together, release the left mouse button. The resizing handles will appear around the border of all the selected controls.

4. Left-click any of the controls that are displaying the resizing handles and, without releasing the left mouse button, drag the group of controls to the desired position. All the controls in the selected group will move as a single unit. The relative position of each of the selected controls will be maintained.

5. After you drag the group of controls to the desired location, release the left mouse button. This drops the entire group of controls onto the new location on the form.

I've spent a long time positioning and sizing all the controls on my form. Can I prevent them from being accidentally moved?

Yes. You can use the Form Designer's Lock Controls option to lock the position of all the controls that are displayed on a specific form. To lock in place all the controls on a form, right-click the form, which displays the pop-up menu shown in Figure 8-2.

After you select the Lock Controls option from the pop-up menu, all the controls on the current form will be locked into place. After the controls are locked, you can't change their position on the form. When you click a locked control, the resizing handles are displayed as white boxes rather than in their standard, blue color.

To unlock the controls on a form, simply follow the same procedure. You can unlock the controls on a form by right-clicking the form to display the pop-up menu. The Lock

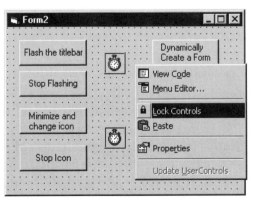

Figure 8-2 Locking controls on a form

Controls option will appear indented (or selected). Selecting the Lock Controls option toggles off the lock, and all the controls on the form will be moveable.

 ## How do I position the cursor to a specific control?

You can position the cursor to a specific control on a form by using the control's SetFocus method. The SetFocus method can be used with a form or a control that's visible and that can accept user input. As its name suggests, the SetFocus method shifts the focus to the object that executed the SetFocus method. After executing the SetFocus method, the user's next keystrokes are directed to the control. The following code illustrates how to use the SetFocus method to set the focus to a command button:

```
' The form must be visible to get focus.
Me.Show
' Set the focus to the cmdNextForm button.
cmdNextForm.SetFocus
```

You can move the focus only to a form or a control that's visible and enabled. If the SetFocus method is used within the Form_Load subroutine, then the form's Show method must be executed before the SetFocus method. Only one control can have the focus at any given time.

 Tip: *You can use the SetFocus method only on a control whose Visible and Enabled properties are set to True.*

 ## How do I control the tab order of the controls on a form?

You can control the tab order of the ActiveX controls on a form by setting each control's TabIndex property. Initially, each control's TabIndex property is set automatically according to the order in which it was placed on the form. Since the ActiveX controls on a VB form are rarely created in input order, this causes the tab order to be unpredictable after the form has been created and all the desired ActiveX controls have been placed on the form.

Figure 8-3 illustrates setting the TabIndex property of a TextBox control.

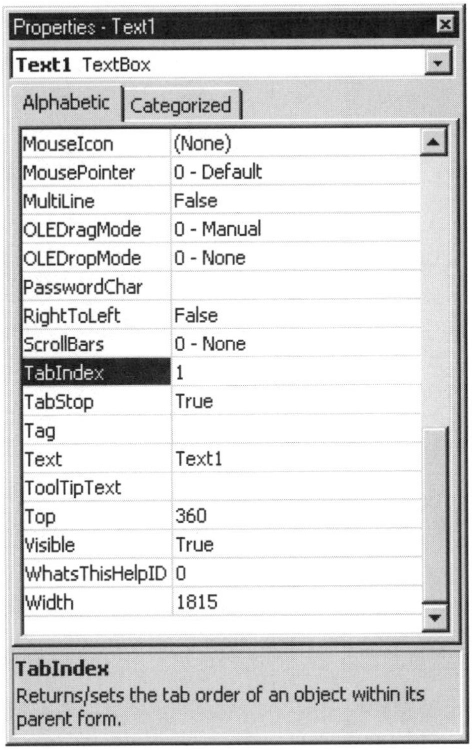

Figure 8-3   Setting the tab order

The tab order proceeds from lowest to highest. The first control that should receive input should use a TabIndex value of 0. The second control should use 1, the next 2, and so on.

How do I change the foreground and background colors of a control?

Changing the foreground and background colors of a control is very easy. Most visible controls have a ForeColor and a BackColor property that you can use to adjust the control's appearance. To change the foreground and background colors used on a specific control, follow these steps:

1. Select the control in the form design window and then display its properties by pressing the F4 key.

2. Scroll down until you see the BackColor property and then click the drop-down button. The Palette selection dialog box, shown here, is displayed:

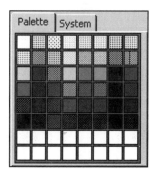

3. Select a new background color for the control by clicking the desired color in the Palette. The BackColor property is then updated and the control is redrawn in the IDE with the new background color. Altering the control's ForeColor property sets the foreground color.

You can also use code to change a control's foreground and background color. The following code illustrates how you can change the ForeColor and BackColor properties of a TextBox control:

```
Text1.ForeColor = &HFF0000
Text1.BackColor = &H80FFFF
```

 Note: *Changing a control's foreground or background color only affects that specific control. It does not change the colors that are used by any other ActiveX controls. You must change the attributes of each control independently*

How can I make a control invisible?

Making a control invisible is very easy. You can change a control's visibility by setting its Visible property to True or False. Controlling the Visible property of your control also provides an easy way to make your applications more dynamic and responsive to user input. For instance, you can selectively alter your application's appearance by programmatically controlling the visibility of different user interface components based on the user's actions. The

following code shows how you can set a TextBox control to become invisible:

```
' Hide the text box.
Text1.Visible = FALSE
```

Likewise, to make the control visible again, simply set its Visible property to True:

```
' Show the text box.
Text1.Visible = True
```

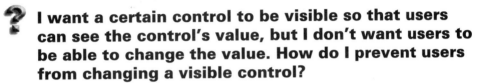

I want a certain control to be visible so that users can see the control's value, but I don't want users to be able to change the value. How do I prevent users from changing a visible control?

You can prevent users from being able to use a visible control by disabling the control. When a control is disabled, it remains visible but appears to be dimmed or "grayed out" to users. Although the control remains visible on the form, it can receive focus neither from the keyboard nor the mouse, nor can you use the SetFocus method from your VB code to give it focus. A runtime error is generated if you attempt to use the SetFocus method to set the focus to a disabled control.

You can disable most visible controls by setting the Enabled property to False. You can set the control's Enabled property in the IDE by clicking the control in the Form Designer and then pressing the F4 key to display the control's properties. Figure 8-4 illustrates setting the Enabled property of a TextBox control named Text1.

You can also disable a control by using code. The following code illustrates how to disable a TextBox control named Text1:

```
' Disable the text box.
Text1.Enabled = False
```

Likewise, to reenable the TextBox control, simply set its Enabled property to True:

```
' Enable the text box.
Text1.Enabled = True
```

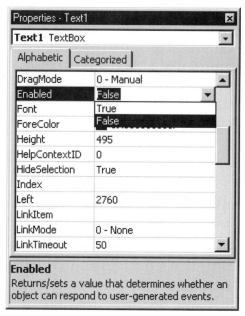

Figure 8-4 Disabling a control

 ## What's a control array and why would I want to use one?

A control array is a set of similar controls that share the same name and event procedures. Just like a standard variable array, each different control in the control array is identified by using a unique index. Control arrays are typically used to conserve system resources, by sharing the same name and event procedures for multiple controls. Control arrays are often used for menus and option buttons. Although all the elements of a control array share a common name and event procedure, each control in the array has its own properties. The maximum number of controls that can be in a control array depends on the available system resources, but the theoretical maximum is 32,767.

 ## Can I add items to a control array at runtime?

Yes. The ability to change control arrays dynamically at runtime enables you to customize the display of your forms and dialog boxes based on individual user choices and configuration values. You can add and remove controls from a control array at runtime by using the Load and Delete functions. The Load function adds a control to a control array, whereas the Delete function removes a control from a control array. The following listing illustrates dynamically adding option buttons to a control array:

```
' One option button named optButton must be
' present. nButtonIndex is declared at the form
' level. Increment the array index and add the
' new control.
nButtonIndex = nButtonIndex + 1
Load optButton(nButtonIndex)

' Set the new control's display attributes.
optButton(nButtonIndex).Top = _
    optButton(nButtonIndex - 1).Top + 400
optButton(nButtonIndex).Visible = True
optButton(nButtonIndex).Caption = _
    "Option" & nButtonIndex + 1

' Set the focus to the new option button.
optButton(nButtonIndex).SetFocus
```

In this code, the integer variable named nButtonIndex is used to keep track of how many controls are present in the optButton control array. After the nButtonIndex variable is incremented, the Load function is used to add a new item to the optButton control array. After you add the new control, you can assign values to the Top, Visible, and Caption properties to set its display attributes. The Top property controls where the new control appears in relation to the existing optButton controls. Setting the Visible property to True makes the control visible to users. The Caption property controls the text that's displayed by the control.

Setting the focus to the new control, as follows, causes it to be selected:

```
' Keep the first button.
    If nButtonIndex = 0 Then Exit Sub

    ' Delete the button and decrement the index.
    Unload optButton(nButtonIndex)
```

```
nButtonIndex = nButtonIndex - 1

' Set the focus to the last button.
optButton(nButtonIndex).SetFocus
```

Option buttons are removed by the Unload function. In the preceding section of code, the nButtonIndex variable is checked for the value 0, to prevent the first control in the array from being deleted. If the nButtonIndex value is 0, then the subroutine is exited. Otherwise, the Unload function is used to remove the control from the array, and the nButtonIndex variable is decremented by one.

Does any limit exist to the number of controls that can be placed on a form?

Yes. Any given form can have a maximum of 254 controls. A control array only counts as one control toward this limitation, because all the controls in the array share a single name.

USING THE BASIC ACTIVEX CONTROLS

The questions and answers in this part address some of the most common questions regarding the use of the controls that are supplied with Visual Basic. Learning how to effectively use Visual Basic's component model is the most important key to effective application development. Taking advantage of the prebuilt components that are supplied with Visual Basic enables you to utilize these components immediately in your applications without requiring you to "reinvent the wheel." In this part of the chapter, you'll see how you can perform some common programming tasks using Visual Basic's ActiveX controls.

How can I restrict a TextBox control to allow only numeric input?

You can edit for numeric input in a few ways. Often, the easiest way is simply to use the Masked Input TextBox control, but you can also add code to the normal TextBox control's KeyPress event to trap and evaluate each keystroke. Although the Masked Input TextBox control enables this type of editing with no coding, using it is more difficult than using the standard VB TextBox control. Furthermore, the Masked Input TextBox control's runtime behavior may not be exactly what you expect. The following subroutine shows how you can add code to a TextBox control's KeyPress event to edit for numeric input.

```
Private Sub Text1_KeyPress(KeyAscii As Integer)

    Select Case KeyAscii

        ' Allow numbers.
        Case vbKey0 To vbKey9

        ' Allow the decimal.
        Case vbDecimal

        ' Allow tab and directional keys.
        Case vbKeyBack, vbKeyClear, vbKeyDelete, _
            vbKeyLeft, vbKeyRight, vbKeyTab, vbKeyUp, _
            vbKeyDown

        ' Cancel all other keystrokes.
        Case Else
            KeyAscii = 0
            Beep

    End Select

End Sub
```

The heart of this subroutine is the Select Case statement. The selection evaluates the ASCII value of the key that was pressed and either accepts or rejects the keystroke. If an invalid key is pressed, then the keystroke is canceled by changing it to ASCII 0. Then, a beep is issued to inform the user that the input was invalid.

In the preceding example, the first Select Case statement checks whether the key pressed is a number between 0 and 9. If it is, then the keystroke is a number, and the subroutine will be exited normally. The next Case statement checks whether a decimal point has been entered. Allowing decimal

points is required for most numeric fields. If a decimal is entered, then the input is allowed and the Case statement and subroutine are exited. The third Case statement checks whether the key pressed was the TAB key, DELETE key, BACKSPACE key, or one of the directional keys. Allowing these keys is needed, to ensure that the text box responds normally to other common keyboard input. The final Case Else statement traps all other input conditions. If the input was something other than the keys that were checked in the preceding Case statements, then a nonnumeric key was pressed. Assigning the KeyAscii variable to 0 cancels the keystroke, and the Beep function issues a warning.

How do I make the text entered into a text box all uppercase?

You can force all uppercase input into a text box by trapping each keystroke with the KeyPress event and then converting each character entered into its uppercase equivalent. The following listing shows how to use a TextBox control's KeyPress event to force all input to be uppercase:

```
Private Sub txtUpper_KeyPress(KeyAscii As Integer)
    KeyAscii = Asc(UCase(Chr(KeyAscii)))
End Sub
```

In this example, the ASCII representation of each keystroke is returned by the KeyPress event of the TextBox control named txtUpper. Within the KeyPress event subroutine, the Chr function is used to convert the ASCII value of the input keystroke to its character equivalent. Then, the UCase function converts the resulting character to uppercase. If the character is a lowercase letter, it is converted to uppercase. Otherwise, the character will not be altered. Finally, the Asc function is used to convert the character value back into its ASCII equivalent, which is then assigned to the KeyAscii variable.

 How can I validate data entered into a text box?

You can use the TextBox control's Validate event subroutine to check the validity of the data entered into a text box. The Validate subroutine is enabled when the CausesValidation property is set to True, and it is fired when the TextBox control loses focus. The following listing shows how to use the Validate event to test data in a text box for the value of "CHECK".

```
Private Sub txtUpper_Validate(Cancel As Boolean)

    If txtUpper.Text <> "CHECK" Then
        MsgBox "You must enter CHECK into this field"
        Cancel = True
    End If

End Sub
```

In this subroutine, the value of the txtUpper.Text property is tested for the value of "CHECK". If the value in the Text property is not equal to the string "CHECK", then a message box is displayed and the Cancel parameter is set to True, which cause the txtUpper TextBox control to retain focus.

 How can I format the data entered into an input field?

The easiest way to perform more advanced formatting is to use the MaskedEdit control. Like the standard TextBox control, the MaskedEdit control enables the user to input data into a window. However, the MaskedEdit control also allows the user's input to be formatted in a variety of ways. The MaskedEdit control is useful when the user needs to input specifically formatted data, such as a social security number, phone number, date, or dollar amount.

The MaskedEdit control's Mask property controls the input mask that's used. The values entered into the Mask property can contain a combination of placeholders and

literals that format the text entered into the MaskedEdit control by users. (*Placeholders* are replaceable characters, while *literals* are actual characters that will appear verbatim in the MaskedEdit control.) Table 8-1 lists the values that can be used in the Mask property of the MaskedEdit control.

One simple use of the Masked Edit box might be to format a multipart number, such as a social security number. Figure 8-5 shows the masks that can be used to facilitate the input of a social security number, a dollar amount, and a phone number.

The social security number (SSN) is formatted as a multipart number, where the first part has three digits, the second part has two digits, and the third part has four digits. In this example, the Mask property uses pound-sign placeholders (#) for the actual numbers that will be entered, while the dash literal is used to separate each part.

The Amount field is treated in a similar fashion. The primary difference is that the dollar-sign literal is used in the beginning of the field to show that the amount is in dollars.

Mask Character	Description
#	Digit placeholder
.	Decimal placeholder
,	Thousands separator
:	Time separator
/	Date separator
\	Treat the next character in the mask string as a literal
&	Character placeholder
>	Convert to uppercase all the characters that follow
<	Convert to lowercase all the characters that follow
A	Alphanumeric character placeholder (entry required)
a	Alphanumeric character placeholder (entry optional)
9	Digit placeholder (entry optional)
C	Character or space placeholder (entry optional)
?	Letter placeholder
Literal	All other symbols are displayed as they are entered in the mask

Table 8-1 MaskedEdit Control Placeholders

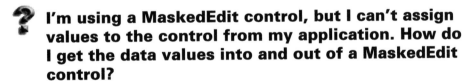

┌─ Masked Edit ──────────────────────────┐
│   │
│   SSN   ###-##-####   │
│   │
│   Amount $ #####.##   │
│   │
│   Phone   (###) ###-####   │
│   │
└──┘

Figure 8-5 Formatted data entry using the MaskedEdit control

Again, a pound-sign placeholder is used for each of the digits that the user enters, and the decimal-point placeholder separates the dollars from cents.

Likewise, the Phone Number field uses parentheses and a space as literals that separate the area code from the remainder of the phone number. The pound-sign placeholders ensure that all of the numbers entered must be valid digits.

 Note: *Although the MaskedEdit control can make it easier for the end user to input complex or multipart data, it does not automatically validate the data that's entered. For instance, you can use a MaskedEdit control to format a Date field for convenient date entry, but the formatting does not check whether the date entered is a valid date.*

I'm using a MaskedEdit control, but I can't assign values to the control from my application. How do I get the data values into and out of a MaskedEdit control?

You can assign data to and retrieve data from the MaskedEdit control by using its Text property, in much the same way as you do with the standard TextBox control. However, there is one important difference: the data that's retrieved from the Text property of the MaskedEdit control contains all the formatting that's applied by the mask. In

other words, if the mask contains an SSN with literal dashes, those dashes are included in the value that can be accessed in the Text property of the MaskedEdit control. Likewise, setting the Text property of a MaskedEdit control requires that the same format be present in the value that's assigned to the Text property. For example, a MaskedEdit control that's used for an SSN will have a dash in the fourth and seventh positions. Any value that's assigned to the Text property of this MaskedEdit control must also have dashes in the fourth and seventh positions.

How do I make a CommandButton control the default control on a form?

The default control automatically receives focus whenever the ENTER key is pressed. Making a control the default control often is useful for data entry forms in which the user input is centered around the keyboard, and using the mouse is inconvenient. You can make a control the default control by assigning the value of True to its Default property. Figure 8-6 illustrates how you can make a CommandButton control the default control.

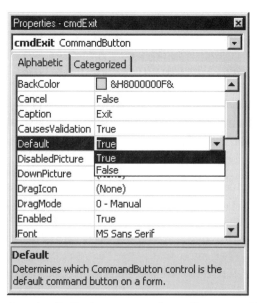

Figure 8-6 Setting the Default property for a CommandButton control

How do I fill a combo box or a list box?

Both the ComboBox control and the ListBox control are filled by using the AddItem method, which adds entries to both types of lists. The AddItem method takes two parameters. The first parameter accepts a string variable that contains the data that will be added to the list box or combo box. The second parameter is optional and specifies the index where the new entry will be added. If the second parameter is not specified, the entry will be added to the bottom of the list, by default. A value of 0 in the second parameter adds the item to the top of the list. The following listing illustrates how to add five entries to a combo box and list box:

```
Dim i As Integer

    For i = 1 To 5
        cboSelect.AddItem "Combo Item " & I
        lstSelect.AddItem "List Item" & I
    Next i
```

This example shows that a For Next loop is used to add five items to the ComboBox control named cboSelect and the ListBox control named lstSelect. Within the For Next loop, the AddItem method is used to add a string value that consists of a constant string that's concatenated with the value of the loop counter contained in the variable named i.

 How do I select items from a combo box?

Clicking an item that's displayed in the drop-down list of a combo box automatically selects that item and copies its value into the ComboBox control's Text property. Once the selected value is in the Text property, it can be accessed just like any other control property. The following listing shows how you can take the value from the selected item of a combo box and assign it to the Text property of another text box:

```
Private Sub cboSelect_Click()

    ' Set the text box from the combo box.
    txtCombo.Text = cboSelect.Text

End Sub
```

This listing shows the Click event subroutine for a ComboBox control. This subroutine is executed when a user left-clicks the drop-down list that's displayed by a combo box. Single-clicking the drop-down list of the combo box automatically places the value of the selected item into the ComboBox control's Text property. From there, the value of the selected item is assigned to the Text property of the TextBox control named txtCombo.

How do I select items from a list box?

Whereas the code required to load a list box is virtually identical to the code required to load a combo box, selecting items from a list box is quite different from selecting items in a combo box. The combo box makes retrieving the value of the selected item easy, by automatically placing that value in the Text property of the ComboBox control. However, the ListBox control doesn't have any equivalent facility. To select items from a list box, you must use the ListBox control's List and ListIndex properties. The List property is a collection of all the items that are contained in the list; the ListIndex property is the value of the currently selected item. The following code illustrates how you can retrieve the value of a specific item in a list box by clicking that item:

```
Private Sub lstSelect_Click()

    ' Select the item based on the list index.
    txtList.Text = lstSelect.List(lstSelect.ListIndex)

End Sub
```

This listing shows the Click event subroutine for a ListBox control named lstSelect. This subroutine is executed when a user left-clicks the list. The ListIndex property of the lstSelect ListBox control is automatically set to the index of the list item that the user clicks. The ListIndex property is used to retrieve the value of one specific item that's contained in the List collection. In other words, if the user clicks the first item in the lstSelect list, the lstSelect.ListIndex property is set to 0. This index is then used with the List collection to retrieve the data contained in the first element of the list, which is then assigned to the variable on the left side of the equal sign. In the previous example, the value of the selected item from the lstSelect list will be assigned to the Text property of the txtList TextBox control.

? I placed the Drive, Dir, and File controls on a form, and, although each seems to work individually, they don't work together. How can I connect these controls so that selections in the Drive control update the Dir control, and changes in the Dir control update the File control?

The Drive, Dir, and File controls all work independently, by default. To get them to work together, you must link the controls together by using their event subroutines. An example window containing the Drive, Dir, and File controls is shown in Figure 8-7.

As Figure 8-7 demonstrates, the Drive, Dir, and File controls provide functions that are very similar to the components that are used in the standard Windows File Open and File Save dialog boxes:

- **Drive control**   Provides a list of all available drives on the system, including both the physical drives that are present on the local system and any mapped network drives.

- **Dir control**   Provides a list of the directories or folders that are in the current path.

- **File control**   Provides a list of files for the current directory.

When these controls are initially placed on a form in the IDE, each provides an immediate list of the respective file system objects. Each control operates independently, and changing any one of the controls has no effect on the other controls. However, you can chain the controls together by using their event subroutines, so that changes on one control cascade through to the other controls. For example, linking the controls through their event subroutines causes a change in the Drive control to automatically change the contents of

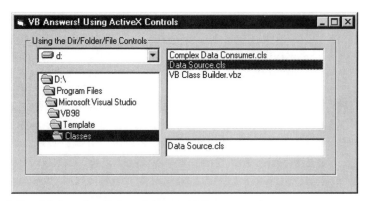

Figure 8-7   Using the Drive, Dir, and File controls

the Dir control to display the contents of the newly selected system drive. Likewise, you can use the event subroutines of the Dir control to automatically update the list of files displayed by the File control when a new directory is selected. The following listing shows how to use the Drive control's Change event subroutine to update the contents of the Dir control:

```
Private Sub drvSystem_Change()
    dirDrive.Path = drvSystem.Drive
End Sub
```

The Drive control's Change event is fired when the user selects a different drive in the list of system drives displayed by the Drive control. The letter of the newly selected drive will be contained in the Drive control's Drive property. Assigning the new value of the Drive property to the Dir control's Path property causes the contents of the Dir control to be updated to reflect the new drive.

Likewise, the Dir control's Change event can be used to update the list of files displayed by the File control. The following listing shows how to use the Dir control's Change event subroutine to update the File control:

```
Private Sub dirDrive_Change()
    filFolder.Path = dirDrive.Path
End Sub
```

The Dir control's Change event is fired when the user changes the selected directory in the list of directories displayed by the Dir control. The path of the newly selected directory is contained in the Dir control's Path property. Assigning the value of the Dir control's Path property to the Path property of the File control updates the list of files displayed by the File control to reflect the contents of the selected directory.

You can also use the File control's Click event to update the contents of a text box with the name of the file selected from the list of files displayed by the File control. The following listing shows how to use the File control's Click event subroutine to update the contents of a text box:

```
Private Sub filFolder_Click()
    txtFile.Text = filFolder.FileName
End Sub
```

The File control's Click event is fired when the user clicks an entry displayed by the File control. The File control's FileName property contains the name of the file that the user clicked. In the previous example, the FileName property is assigned to the Text property of the TextBox control named txtFile when the user selects an entry from the File control.

 On my form, I have a Frame control that I want to contain a group of other controls. However, when I double-click the controls in the Toolbox, they go to the form rather than to the Frame control. How do I make controls appear inside the Frame control?

Double-clicking a control only places the control on the background form. To place new controls within a Frame control, you must drag the controls directly from the Toolbox onto the Frame control. If you want to move a set of controls that is on a form into a Frame control, you need to cut and paste the controls from the form to the Frame control.

For instance, to move a text box that's on a form to a Frame control, you must first click the TextBox control. When the TextBox control's resizing handles are displayed, press

CTRL+X to cut the TextBox control from the form. Next, click the Frame control that is intended to hold the TextBox control. When the resizing handles appear around the Frame control, press CTRL+V to paste the text box onto the Frame control. After the TextBox control has been pasted onto the Frame control, you can move and resize it as usual by clicking the TextBox control and using the resizing handles to move and resize the control as desired.

Can I add graphics to a button?

Yes. The easiest way to display graphics on a button is to use the Image control. The Image control supports the same Click and DoubleClick events that are provided by the standard CommandButton control. However, instead of a Caption property, the Image control provides a Picture property that can be used to specify the name of a graphics file to be displayed in the Image control. Table 8-2 lists the types of graphics files that can be displayed in the Image control.

An Image control's Picture property can be set either at design time, using the Properties window, or at runtime, using the LoadPicture or LoadResPicture function. The LoadPicture function loads the Picture property based on the contents of a graphics file, whereas the LoadResPicture

Graphics File	Description
Bitmap	Ends in the extension .bmp or .dib.
Icon	Ends with the extension .ico. Icons are a type of bitmap file that is either 16 × 16 or 23 × 32 pixels.
Cursor	Ends with the extension .cur. Cursors are a special type of bitmap file that includes a hot-spot pixel that tracks its x and y coordinates.
Metafile	Ends with the extension .wmf for standard metafiles or .emf for enhanced metafiles.
JPEG	Ends with the extension .jpg. A JPEG (Joint Photographic Experts Group) file is a type of compressed bitmap file.
GIF	Ends with the extension .gif. A GIF (Graphic Interchange Format) file is another type of compressed bitmap file.

Table 8-2   Graphic Files Used by the Image Control

function loads the Picture property based on the contents of a resource file that's included with the application.

To load a graphics file into an ImageBox control at design time, click the Image control, and when the resizing handles are displayed, press F4 to display the Properties window. In the Properties window, click the ellipses button that's displayed next to the Picture property. The Load Picture dialog box, shown in Figure 8-8, will be displayed.

The Load Picture dialog box shows only those files whose extension is compatible with the types of graphics files that can be displayed in the Image control. Clicking the desired filename and then clicking the OK button loads the graphic image into the Image control.

You can also load a graphics file into the Image control at runtime. The following listing illustrates how to set the Picture property of an Image control by using the LoadPicture function:

```
imgFile.Picture = LoadPicture _
  (filFolder.Path & "\\" & filFolder.FileName)
```

The LoadPicture function has a single parameter that accepts a string value containing the fully qualified path of the graphics file that will be loaded into the Image control.

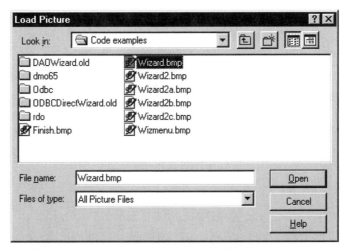

Figure 8-8   Setting the ImageBox control's Picture property

If the format of the file doesn't match the types that are accepted by the Image control, a runtime error is generated.

 Tip: *You can clear the image displayed by an Image control by using the LoadPicture function with no arguments: ImgMyImage.Picture = LoadPicture.*

 ## How can I tell whether an option button has been selected?

You can determine whether an option button has been selected by checking its Value property. The Value property of an OptionButton control contains a Boolean value of True or False. If the Value property is True, then the button has been selected. If the Value property is False, the button has not been selected. The following listing illustrates how to test whether an option button has been selected:

```
If optSelect1.Value Then
    lblOption.Caption = "Option 1 was selected"
ElseIf optSelect2.Value Then
    lblOption.Caption = "Option 2 was selected"
ElseIf optSelect3.Value Then
    lblOption.Caption = "Option 3 was selected"
End If
```

In this example, three option buttons are present on the frame, and an If test is used to check each OptionButton control's Value property. If the Value property is True, then a string is assigned to the Label control named lblOption, indicating which button was selected.

 ## How do I use the ProgressBar control?

The progress bar is typically positioned at the bottom of the window and it is used to visually indicate the status of long running operations. The first step in using the ProgressBar control is to set its Max property to reflect the maximum boundary of the operation that you want the progress bar to track. Next, after you set the upper limit, you increment the ProgressBar control's Value property to indicate the progress of the operation. The bar graph displayed by the ProgressBar

control is automatically repainted as its Value property is updated. The following code illustrates how to use the ProgressBar control:

```
Dim i As Integer

prgCount.Max = txtCount.Text

For i = 1 To txtCount.Text
    prgCount.Value = I
Next i
```

This example shows that the Max property of the ProgressBar control named prgCount has been assigned the value that comes from the TextBox control named txtCount. After the Max property has been set, a For Next loop is used to increment the prgCount.Value property. The graphical progress bar displayed by the prgCount ProgressBar control is expanded each time the Value property is updated. The For Next loop ends when the maximum value assigned to the ProgressBar control is reached.

Visual Basic has several Grid controls. What is the difference between them?

Sometimes you can have too much of a good thing, and the set of different Grid controls that Microsoft provides with Visual Basic 6 is a prime example. Visual Basic 6 provides no less than five different Grid controls, each of which has a slightly different purpose:

- **Microsoft Grid Control (GRID32.OCX)**   The most recent incarnation of the original Grid control that was shipped with Visual Basic 1. This latest Grid control provides the most basic functionality of all the different Grid controls. It displays and operates on tabular data, but it can't display graphics or be bound to a data source.

- **Microsoft Data Bound Grid Control 5.0 (DBGRID32.OCX)**   A version of the Apex TrueGrid, first shipped with Visual Basic 4. It doesn't support graphics, but can be operated in either a data bound or an unbound mode. It is included with Visual Basic 6 in the Tools directory.

- **Microsoft FlexGrid Control 6.0
  (MSFLXGRD.OCX)**   A version of the VideoSoft
  VSFLEX Grid control, first incorporated into Visual
  Basic 5. Like its predecessors, the MSFlexGrid control
  displays and operates on tabular data. It also can put
  text, a picture, or both in any cell, providing the ability
  to sort, merge, and format tables containing strings and
  pictures. The MSFlexGrid control can operate in either
  bound or unbound mode, but it's read-only data when
  bound to a data source.

- **Microsoft Hierarchical FlexGrid Control 6.0
  (MSHFLXGD.OCX)**   New to Visual Basic 6, this
  control is very much like the standard MSFlexGrid
  control. However, A major feature of the new
  MSHFlexGrid control is its ability to display relational
  tables in a hierarchical fashion. Hierarchical recordsets
  are a feature of ADO 2 and have a parent/child
  relationship. For example, the parent might consist of
  an order header record, while the child would be the
  supporting order detail records.

- **Microsoft DataGrid Control 6.0
  (MSDATGRD.OCX)**   Introduced with Visual Basic 6,
  this control is code-compatible with the earlier DBGrid
  control. Like the DBGrid control, the DataGrid control is
  a bound control that displays a series of rows and
  columns representing rows and columns from a
  Recordset object. Unlike the DBGrid control, the
  DataGrid control operates only as a bound control. All
  the bound data displayed by the DataGrid control is
  updateable.

How do I add column headings and set the column in an MSFlexGrid control?

You can set an MSFlexGrid control's column headings
and width by assigning values to the Text and ColWidth
properties. However, the trick to using these properties is to
make sure that your program is accessing the correct cell in
the MSFlexGrid control, before you set these properties. The
MSFlexGrid control uses two basic sets of row and column
coordinates. The first set is used to determine the size of

the grid in terms of number of rows and columns. These coordinates are exposed in the Cols and Rows properties of the MSFlexGrid control object. The second set is used to specify the current cell position in the grid. These coordinates are accessible by using the Col and Row properties.

To effectively set up the column headings for the MSFlexGrid control, you must first size the grid so that it contains the desired number of columns and at least one row. Then, you can begin addressing each cell in the first row of the grid. Setting the column headings for a MSFlexGrid control requires that you first set the Row and Col properties to point to the desired cell. Then, you must set that cell's Text and ColWidth properties. The cell in the upper-left corner of the MSFlexGrid control has a Row property of 0 and a Col property of 0. The immediately adjacent cell in the first row has a Row property of 0 and Col property of 1. The following listing shows how you can set up a MSFlexGrid control with five columns:

```
Dim nCount As Integer

' Set up the grid with one row and five columns.
flxGrid.Redraw = False
flxGrid.Cols = 5
flxGrid.Rows = 1
flxGrid.FixedCols = 0
flxGrid.Row = 0
flxGrid.Col = 0
flxGrid.Clear

' Set up the column headings and width.
For nCount = 1 To flxGrid.Cols
    flxGrid.ColWidth(flxGrid.Col) = _
      TextWidth(String(11, "a"))
    flxGrid.ColAlignment(flxGrid.Col) = 1
    flxGrid.Text = "Column " & nCount
    If flxGrid.Col < flxGrid.Cols - 1 Then
        flxGrid.Col = flxGrid.Col + 1
    End If
Next nCount

' Redraw the grid after adding the headings.
flxGrid.Redraw = True
```

The top of this listing shows that a working variable called nCount is declared to keep track of the columns in the grid. The next section of code sets up the grid. Setting the Redraw property to False prevents the MSFlexGrid control from being redrawn as each cell is updated.

Next, the Rows property is set to 5 and the Cols property is set to 1. As you might expect, this sets up an initial grid size of five columns and one row. The default setting of the FixedCols property is 1, which reserves the first column as a heading area. Setting the FixedCols property to 0 indicates that no fixed columns will be used and data will be displayed in all the grid columns.

Then, the current cell position is set to the upper-left cell in the grid by setting the flxGrid.Row and flxGrid.Col properties to 0. Finally, the grid's Clear method is used to eliminate any residual data that may be present in the flxGrid object.

After the grid has been initialized, the next section of code adds the column heading to the grid and sizes each column. A For Next loop is used to loop through each of the five grid columns. Setting the column width is the first thing that happens inside the loop. The column width of each cell in the grid is set using the ColWidth property, which accepts a value in twips (each twip is 1/20 of an inch). In this example, the TextWidth function is used to retrieve the value, in twips, for a string of 11 lowercase a characters. The resulting twips value is then assigned to the ColWidth property of the MSFlexGrid control column that's specified by the flxGrid. Col index.

Next, the column is configured to use left alignment, by setting the ColAlignment property to 1. After the column width and text alignment properties are assigned, the actual column heading is assigned to the current flxGrid.Text property that's identified by the coordinates contained in the flxGrid.Col and flxGrid.Row properties. At the end of the For Next loop, you can see where the current column pointer is updated by incrementing the flxGrid.Col property. The If test is used to ensure that the setting for the current column doesn't exceed the maximum number of grid columns contained in the flxGrid.Cols property.

The For Next loop ends after headings have been assigned to all five columns. Then, the flxGrid.Redraw property is set to True, which causes the flxGrid object to be repainted on the window.

How do I add data to a grid?

Adding data to a grid is very much like setting the column headings for the grid. You add data to each cell in the grid by setting its Text property. However, before you assign a value to the Text property, you have to make sure to specify the current cell position in the grid by using the grid's Col and Row properties. The following code example illustrates how to add a set of rows to an existing flxGrid object that has been set up to contain five columns:

```
Dim nRowCount As Integer
Dim nColumnCount As Integer

' Set up the grid for writing data.
flxGrid.Redraw = False
flxGrid.Row = 0

' Write out seven rows.
For nRowCount = 1 To 7

    ' Set the number of rows and current position.
    flxGrid.Rows = flxGrid.Rows + 1
    flxGrid.Row = flxGrid.Rows - 1
    flxGrid.Col = 0

    ' Loop for each grid column.
    For nColumnCount = 1 To flxGrid.Cols
        flxGrid.Text = "R:" & nRowCount & _
          " C:" & nColumnCount
        If flxGrid.Col < flxGrid.Cols - 1 Then
            flxGrid.Col = flxGrid.Col + 1
        End If
    Next nColumnCount

Next

' Redraw the grid after all the data has been added.
flxGrid.Redraw = True
```

The top of this code example shows two working variables being declared that will be used to hold row and column counters.

The next section of code prepares the grid for adding data. First, the Redraw property of the MSFlexGrid control named flxGrid is set to False. Although setting the Redraw property to False isn't required to add data to the grid, this setting provides significantly better performance, by avoiding the requirement to redraw the grid after each data item is added. Next, the current grid position is set to the first row in the grid.

In the next section, a For Next loop is used to add seven rows to the grid. The number of rows added to the grid can be consistent, such as in this example, but it can also be based on a dynamic value that's retrieved from a database query or some other operation. Within the For Next loop, the number of total rows in the grid is incremented by adding one to the flxGrid.Rows property. Then, the current row position contained in the flxGrid.Row property is set to one less than the total number of rows in the grid. This prevents the first row of data from overlying any existing column headings.

Next, a second For Next loop is used to loop through the grid columns. The cell's data is assigned by updating the flxGrid.Text property. The actual cell that's updated is specified by the coordinates contained in the flxGrid.Col and flxGrid.Row properties. At the end of this For Next loop, the current column position in the grid is updated by incrementing the flxGrid.Col property. The If test is used to ensure that the value contained in the flxGrid.Col property doesn't exceed the maximum number of grid columns contained in the flxGrid.Cols property. If the value in the flxGrid.Col property is greater than the maximum number of grid columns, then a runtime error is generated.

After adding the data to the grid, the Redraw property of the flxGrid object is set to True, which updates the display of the flxGrid object.

How can I allow user input into a MSFlexGrid control?

The MSFlexGrid control doesn't provide the ability to perform in-cell editing. However, through programming, you can create a relatively simple workaround that gives the

appearance of direct in-cell editing. You can accomplish this by using a standard TextBox control in conjunction with the flxGrid object. When the user double-clicks the grid, the text box is placed over the cell that the user selected. The user can then enter data directly into the text box. When the user either clicks another cell in the grid or presses one of the directional keys, the value that was entered into the text box is copied into the current cell in the MSFlexGrid control.

Before you can begin coding, you must place both a MSFlexGrid control and a TextBox control on the same form. To create a seamless appearance when the TextBox control is displayed over the MSFlexGrid control, the TextBox control's Appearance property must be set to 0 – Flat and its BorderStyle property must be set to 0 – None. In addition, the Visible property of the TextBox control should initially be set to False.

Adding the following code to the MSFlexGrid's DoubleClick subroutine makes the TextBox control appear over the cell that the user double-clicked:

```
Private Sub flxGrid_DblClick()

    ' Select the grid cell.
    txtGridEdit.SelStart = 100

    ' Move the text box over the grid cell.
    txtGridEdit.Left = flxGrid.CellLeft + flxGrid.Left
    txtGridEdit.Top = flxGrid.CellTop + flxGrid.Top
    txtGridEdit.Width = flxGrid.CellWidth
    txtGridEdit.Height = flxGrid.CellHeight

    ' Match the text box font to the grid.
    txtGridEdit.FontName = flxGrid.FontName
    txtGridEdit.FontSize = flxGrid.FontSize

    ' Show the text box and give it focus.
    txtGridEdit.Text = flxGrid.Text
    txtGridEdit.Visible = True
    txtGridEdit.SetFocus

End Sub
```

The flxGrid_DblClick subroutine is executed when the user double-clicks the flxGrid object. At the beginning of this

subroutine, you can see where the SelStart property is set to 100. Setting the SelStart property to a value that's greater than the text length of the cell causes the SelStart property to be set automatically to the cells' existing text length.

Next, the TextBox control named txtGridEdit is positioned over the selected grid cell by setting its Left, Top, Width, and Height properties with the values from the selected cell of the flxGrid object. Then, to make sure that the data displayed in the txtGridEdit TextBox control appears the same as the data displayed by the flxGrid object, the FontName and FontSize properties of the flxGrid object are assigned the txtGridEdit TextBox control.

After the display attributes of the text box have been set up, the value from the current grid cell is assigned to the Text property of the txtGridEdit TextBox control. Finally, the text box is made visible and given focus to direct the user's input to the txtGridEdit TextBox control.

The code in the flxGrid_DblClick subroutine causes the text box to appear seamlessly over a cell in the MSFlexGrid control, and allows the user to enter data into the text box. To get the new data entered in the text box back into the current cell of the MSFlexGrid control, you need to add the following code to the MSFlexGrid control's LeaveCell and GotFocus event subroutines:

```
Private Sub flxGrid_LeaveCell()

    ' Move the value of the text box to the grid cell.
    If txtGridEdit.Visible Then
        flxGrid.Text = txtGridEdit.Text
        txtGridEdit.Visible = False
    End If

End Sub
```

The MSFlexGrid control's LeaveCell subroutine is executed when the user clicks a different cell in the grid. If the txtGridEdit TextBox control is displayed, then the value contained in the Text property is assigned to the current cell of the MSFlexGrid control named flxGrid:

```
Private Sub flxGrid_GotFocus()

    ' Move the value of the text box to the grid cell.
```

```
    If txtGridEdit.Visible Then
        flxGrid.Text = txtGridEdit.Text
        txtGridEdit.Visible = False
    End If

End Sub
```

Likewise, the MSFlexGrid control's GotFocus subroutine is executed when the grid receives focus. This can happen when the user presses one of the directional keys that move the cursor out of the txtGridEdit TextBox control onto the flxGrid object.

Adding the following KeyDown event subroutine to the text box that's displayed over the MSFlexGrid control enables users to use the up and down arrow keys as well as the ESC and ENTER keys with the text box:

Tip: *The KeyDown event can be used to trap directional keys as well as function keys, unlike the KeyPress event, which only captures printable keystroke characters.*

```
Private Sub txtGridEdit_KeyDown _
    (KeyCode As Integer, Shift As Integer)
    Select Case KeyCode
        Case vbKeyEscape
            txtGridEdit.Visible = False
            flxGrid.SetFocus
        Case vbKeyReturn
            flxGrid.SetFocus
        Case vbKeyDown
            flxGrid.SetFocus
            DoEvents
            If flxGrid.Row < flxGrid.Rows - 1 Then
                flxGrid.Row = flxGrid.Row + 1
            End If
        Case vbKeyUp
            flxGrid.SetFocus
            DoEvents
            If flxGrid.Row > flxGrid.FixedRows Then
                flxGrid.Row = flxGrid.Row - 1
            End If
    End Select
End Sub
```

The txtGridEdit_KeyDown subroutine captures the ESC key, the ENTER key, and the up and down arrow keys. If the ESC key is pressed, the text box is made invisible and the MSFlexGrid control is given focus. Because the txtGridEdit TextBox control is invisible, when the flxGrid_GotFocus subroutine fires, the value in the Text property of the TextBox control is not copied to the MSFlexGrid control. Exactly the opposite happens when the ENTER key is pressed. Because the txtGridEdit TextBox control remains visible, the code in the flxGrid_GotFocus subroutine copies the value from the Text property of the txtGridEdit TextBox control into the current cell. If the up or down directional keys are pressed, then the MSFlexGrid control is given focus, which copies the value from the TextBox control to the grid, and then the current row position is set to the new value.

 Tip: *This subroutine doesn't enable the vbLeft and vbRight keys, because their use would prohibit the user from moving the cursor within the text box itself.*

 ## How do I set up multiple tabs using the tabbed dialog control?

The tabbed dialog control is often used to display the option and configuration dialog boxes used by an application. Like the Frame control, the tabbed dialog control is a container control that groups together several other controls, such as TextBox and Label controls. However, unlike the Frame control, the tabbed dialog control essentially provides a separate container for each tab. The user can select the desired group of controls to display by clicking each tab.

To add multiple tabs to the tabbed dialog control, follow these steps:

1. Set the Tabs property to the number of tabs that you want displayed on your control, and then set the TabsPerRow property to the number of tabs that you want to display on each row.

By default, the tabbed dialog control uses the value of 3 Tabs and 3 TabsPerRow to display three tabs on a single row. If you want to display six tabs on two rows, you simply change the Tabs property to 6, leaving the TabsPerRow property at 3.

2. After you set the number of tabs that you want to include, you can assign a heading to each tab by using the tabbed dialog control's custom properties page, shown in Figure 8-9.

The arrow buttons next to the Current Tab field enable you to page forward and backward through the collection of tabs contained in the tabbed dialog control. To change the heading displayed on a given tab, use the arrow buttons to page to the desired tab and then assign a new value to the TabCaption property that's displayed.

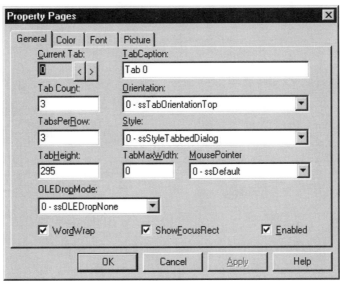

Figure 8-9 Setting the tabbed dialog control's properties

Chapter 9

The Graphical ActiveX Controls

Answer Topics!

The Graphical ActiveX Controls @ a Glance

This chapter presents a set of questions and answers that illustrate the use of the graphical controls that are supplied with Visual Basic 6. For rapid application development with Visual Basic, learning to use these graphical controls may be even more essential than learning the basic ActiveX controls presented in Chapter 8. Many of the graphical controls are very sophisticated and enable you to immediately incorporate tested, robust, and functionally rich routines into your applications. Leveraging the power provided in these controls lets you easily develop powerful applications without the tedious, painstaking effort otherwise required to develop this same level of functionality on your own.

- **Using the Image and PictureBox Controls** answers questions about the two most commonly used graphical controls in VB. This section explains the difference between these two controls and shows how to use them in your VB applications.

- **Using a Resource File** shows how you can load the images used by your application into a resource file that you can easily distribute as a part of your executable program.

- **Using the ImageList Control** shows how to dynamically load images into the ImageList control as well as how the ImageList control is used in conjunction with other graphical controls.

- **Using Additional Common Graphical Controls** answers questions regarding some of the other common graphical controls that are used with VB. Questions in this section cover the Line, Shape, TabStrip, MSChart, and Animation controls.

USING THE IMAGE AND PICTUREBOX CONTROLS

The first part of this chapter explains the use of Visual Basic's Image and PictureBox controls. These controls are the two most commonly used graphical ActiveX controls. The questions and answers in this section detail how to use these controls to display images, as well as how to decide which of these controls is right for a given situation.

How do I display a simple graphic image in my VB application?

Using the Image control is probably the easiest way to display a bitmap file in your application. You can make the Image control display the contents of the bitmap file by setting the Image control's Picture property to the name of that file. The Image control supports the following types of graphics files: bitmap, icon, metafile, enhanced metafile, JPEG, and GIF images.

To set an Image control's Picture property in Design mode, first add an instance of the Image control to your form and then press the F4 key to display the Properties window for the Image control, which will be similar to that shown in Figure 9-1.

Scroll to the Picture property and then click the ellipsis button to display the Load Picture dialog box, presented in Figure 9-2.

The Load Picture dialog box enables you to select the graphics file that will be displayed by the Image control. You can click the arrow to the right of the Look In drop-down list box to navigate to the directory on your hard drive or network that contains the desired graphics files. Although you can certainly use your own custom graphics file, several files are supplied with Visual Basic. By default, these files are found in the \Program Files\Microsoft Visual Studio\Common\Graphics folder. The Load Picture dialog box filters the list of files displayed according to their extensions. Only recognized graphics files with the appropriate file extensions are displayed. Selecting the file from the list and clicking the Open button loads the file into the Image control. After the graphics file has been loaded, its image will be displayed in Visual Basic's Form Designer, as shown in Figure 9-3.

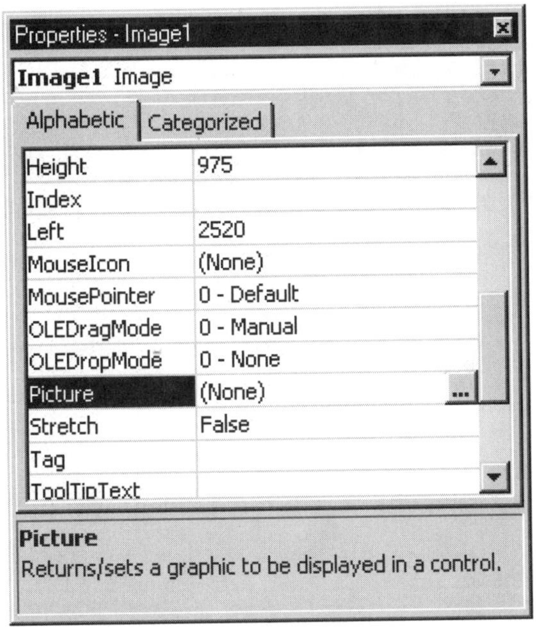

Figure 9-1   The Image control's Picture property

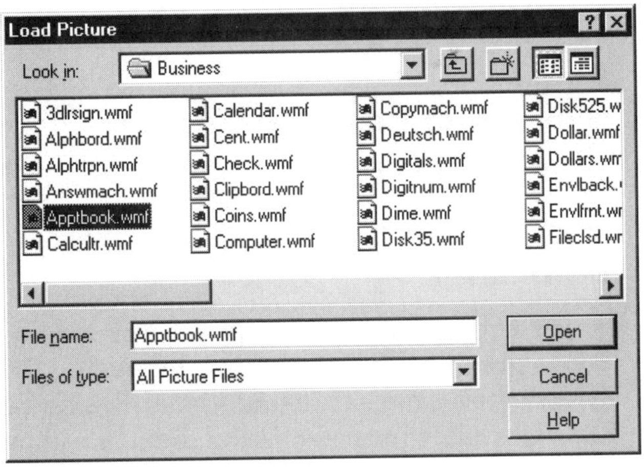

Figure 9-2   The Load Picture dialog box

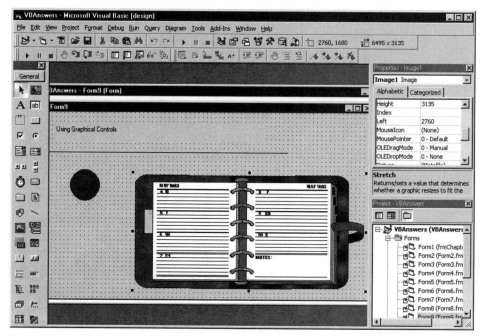

Figure 9-3   Displaying an image in the design environment

When I displayed a graphic image using the Image control, the image was clipped to fit the size of the control. How do I make the Image control display the entire image?

To make files displayed by the Image control fit the size of the control, you need to set the Image control's Stretch property to True.

How do I load an image into the Image control at runtime?

You can make the Image control display the contents of a graphical file at runtime by setting the Image control's Picture property, using Visual Basic's LoadPicture function. The following code listing illustrates how to load an image in this manner:

```
Set Image1.Picture = LoadPicture("graphic.bmp")
```

The LoadPicture function accepts a String parameter that contains the name and path of the bitmap file to be displayed.

The Image and PictureBox controls seem to do the same thing. When should I use an Image control and when should I use a PictureBox control?

The Image control and PictureBox control do seem to be very similar. However, some important differences exist between the two controls. Essentially, the Image control is more specialized as a graphical display control, whereas the PictureBox control is more of a general-purpose control. The following list summarizes the important characteristics of the Image control:

● Uses less resources than the PictureBox control

● Provides better performance than the PictureBox control

● Supports bitmap, icon, metafile, enhanced metafile, JPEG, and GIF images

● Responds to Click events and thus can be used as a button

● Supports stretching images to fit the size of the control

In contrast, the PictureBox control provides capabilities that are more general-purpose in nature. The following list summarizes the important characteristics of the PictureBox control:

● Uses more resources than the Image control

● Supports bitmap, icon, metafile, enhanced metafile, JPEG, and GIF images

● Responds to the Click event and thus can be used as a button

● Can function as a container for other controls

● Can receive the output of graphics methods, such as Circle, Line, and Point

● Displays images only at their original size—the PictureBox control itself changes to accommodate different image sizes

❓ How do I display simple animation?

You can display simple animation in your application by presenting a series of images in either the Image or the PictureBox control. These images can then be displayed in timed sequence by using the Timer control. The changing display of images provides a simple animation effect.

To set up your application to display this type of animation, you must first assign some initial properties to the Timer control and Image control that will be used. Setting up these initial properties is typically performed in the Form_Load subroutine. The following code shows how to set the important properties of the Timer control and the Image control:

```
' Set up the timer.
Timer1.Interval = 100
Timer1.Enabled = False

' Load an initial image.
imgAnimate.Picture = LoadPicture("circle4.bmp")
imgAnimate.Visible = True
```

In this code listing, the Interval property of the Timer control is set to 100, which causes the Timer to fire an event every one-tenth of a second. The Enabled property of the Timer control is initially set to False. Next, an initial image is loaded in the Picture property of the Image control, and the Image control's Visible property is set to True, ensuring that the control is visible to the user.

```
Private Sub Timer1_Timer()

    ' Animate the image.
    Select Case nCircleState

    Case 1
       imgAnimate.Picture = LoadPicture("circle1.bmp")
       nCircleState = 2

    Case 2
       imgAnimate.Picture = LoadPicture("circle2.bmp")
       nCircleState = 3
```

```
   Case 3
      imgAnimate.Picture = LoadPicture("circle3.bmp")
      nCircleState = 4

   Case 4
      imgAnimate.Picture = LoadPicture("circle4.bmp")
      nCircleState = 1

   Case Default
      nCircleState = 1

   End Select

End Sub
```

The real action that controls the animation process takes place inside the Timer event subroutine of the Timer control. The Timer event subroutine is executed each time the timer interval expires. In this example, a simple Select statement is used to display a series of images. The nCircleState variable is used to control which image will be displayed.

Note: *To allow the nCircleState variable to maintain its value between Timer events, it is declared at the module level.*

In each case, the Picture property of the imgAnimate ImageBox control is assigned a new graphic image, using the LoadPicture function. Then, the nCircleState variable is set to the value of the next image in the sequence of images.

To start the animation, the Timer control's Enable property is set to True, as displayed in the following code:

```
Timer1.Enabled = True
```

To end the animation, you simply set the Timer.Enabled property to False, as shown here:

```
Timer1.Enabled = False
```

USING A RESOURCE FILE

Resource files enable you to include the graphic images used by an application as an integral part of the application's executable file. This makes distributing the application much

easier because there is no need to include external bitmap and icon files. The questions and answers in this section show how to create and use resource files.

I'm trying to distribute an application that uses several bitmaps and icons. These graphics files are loaded from separate files located on my hard drive. Do I have to include all of these files with my application? How do I specify the path? There must be a better way.

You're right. A better way does exist. Since release 4, Visual Basic has been able to incorporate resource files into its projects. Resource files are created by using a resource compiler, and they can contain several different types of graphic objects, including bitmaps, icons, and dialog boxes. When your VB project is compiled, all the graphical objects in the resource file are incorporated into your EXE file, and you don't need to distribute a bunch of additional BMP or ICO files with your project. To add a resource file to your VB project, right-click VB's Project window and select the Add option, which will display the pop-up menu shown in Figure 9-4.

The pop-up Add menu enables you to add several different types of files to your VB project. Select the Add File option, which displays the Add File dialog box, shown in Figure 9-5.

The Add File dialog box uses an extension filter that restricts the list to just the file types that Visual Basic expects to use. Resource files end in an extension of .res. Select a RES file from the list and then click OK to add the RES file to your VB project, after which you will see a Related Documents section appear in your VB Project window, similar to the one shown in Figure 9-6.

After you add the file to your project, you can use Visual Basic's LoadResData, LoadResPicture, or LoadResString functions to use the contents of the resource file in your application. An example of the LoadResPicture statement follows:

```
Set Image1.Picture = LoadResPicture(102, vbResBitmap)
```

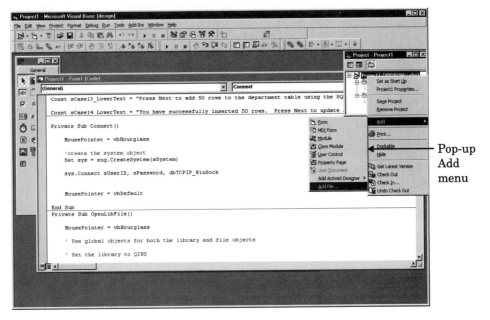

Figure 9-4 Adding a resource file to Visual Basic, step 1

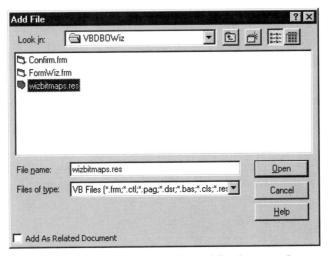

Figure 9-5 Adding a resource file to Visual Basic, step 2

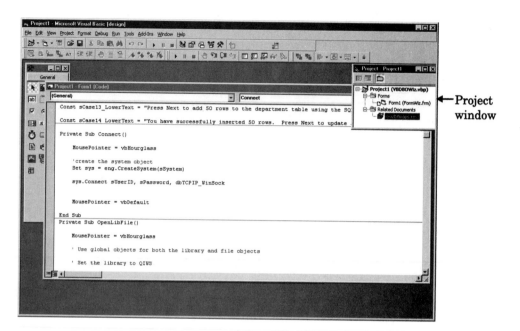

Figure 9-6 Adding a resource file to Visual Basic, step 3

The first parameter of the LoadResPicture function accepts an integer or string that specifies the identifier (ID) of the data in the resource file. The second parameter is a constant that identifies the type of resource. The value of vbResBitmap indicates that the resource is a bitmap.

What's the easiest way to create resource files that I can use in my VB projects?

The easiest method of creating resource files is by using the resource compiler that is included with Visual C++ (VC++). If you have Visual Studio, you should have VC++, as well

as Visual Basic. To create a resource file using VC++, open Microsoft Developer Studio (which is the VC++ IDE) and select File | New, which opens the New dialog box, shown in Figure 9-7.

From the New dialog box, select the Files tab, highlight the Resource Script option in the list, and then click OK to start Visual Studio's Resource Editor. You can use the Resource Editor to create new graphical objects or import existing objects. To import one or more existing bitmaps, right-click the Resource Editor to display the pop-up menu shown in Figure 9-8.

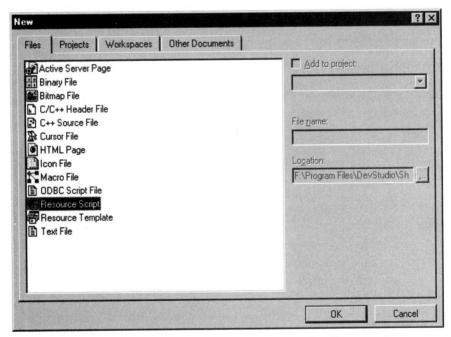

Figure 9-7 Creating resource files using Visual Studio, step 1

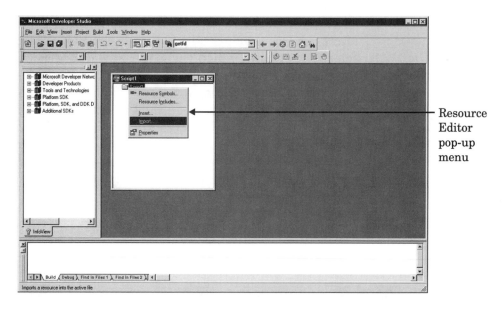

Resource
Editor
pop-up
menu

Figure 9-8   Creating resource files using Visual Studio, step 2

From the pop-up menu, select the Import option, which enables you to incorporate existing bitmaps and icons into your resource file. After you select the Import option, the Import Resource dialog box shown in Figure 9-9 is displayed.

Strangely, the list of file filters used in the Import Resource dialog box doesn't include BMP files. To import BMP files, you need to change the file type from ICO to All Files (*.*), which displays existing BMP files in the Import Resource dialog box. Select the desired bitmap file and then click the Import button to import bitmaps into the resource script file. After you import all the bitmaps that you want, the Resource Editor will look similar to Figure 9-10.

To create a new resource file, select File | Save, which displays the Save As dialog box, shown in Figure 9-11.

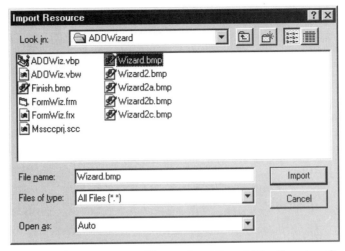

Figure 9-9   Creating resource files using Visual Studio, step 3

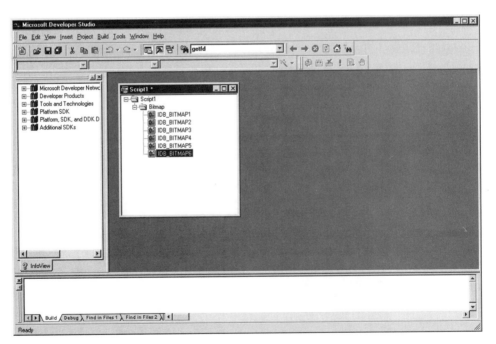

Figure 9-10   Creating resource files using Visual Studio, step 4

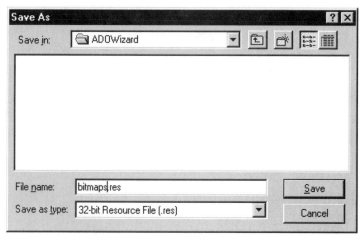

Figure 9-11   Creating resource files using Visual Studio, step 5

In the Save As dialog box, select the file type of 32-bit Resource File from the Save As Type drop-down box at the bottom of the dialog box. Then, enter the name of the RES file that you want to create, and click the Save button. A new RES file is created, which you can incorporate into your VB projects.

 What if I don't have Visual Studio or Visual C++? Can I still make resource files?

Luckily, you can still create resource files even if you don't have Visual Studio or Visual C++. Visual Basic ships with the command-line resource compiler rc.exe, located in the \VB\Wizards directory or the \VB\Tools directory on the CD-ROM. Although rc.exe doesn't provide you with a GUI, you can still use it to produce RES files that you can use in Visual Basic. Creating a resource file is a two-step process:

1. Create a resource script file (RC).
2. Compile the RC file into a resource file.

You can manually create an RC file by using a text editor, such as Notepad. The following listing illustrates a sample RC file named sample.rc that contains the lines needed to compile a set of bitmaps into a resource file:

```
IDB_BITMAP1     BITMAP  DISCARDABLE    "Bitmap.bmp"
IDB_BITMAP2     BITMAP  DISCARDABLE    "Bitmap1.bmp"
IDB_BITMAP3     BITMAP  DISCARDABLE    "Bitmap2.bmp"
IDB_BITMAP4     BITMAP  DISCARDABLE    "Bitmap3.bmp"
IDB_BITMAP5     BITMAP  DISCARDABLE    "Bitmap4.bmp"
IDB_BITMAP6     BITMAP  DISCARDABLE    "Bitmap5.bmp"
```

To run the resource compiler on the RC file, you enter the following command on the command line:

```
rc -v sample.rc
```

The complete instructions for using the resource compiler can be found in the rc.hlp file that accompanies the rc.exe file.

USING THE IMAGELIST CONTROL

The ImageList control enables you to group together collections of images. This is particularly useful because several other graphical ActiveX controls are able to bind to the ImageList control and automatically access the stored images. The questions in this section explain how to add images to the ImageList control as well as how to utilize the ImageList control in conjunction with other graphical controls.

 What is the ImageList control used for?

The ImageList control is used to contain a collection of images that can be referenced by either key or index. Certain other controls are then able to bind to the ImageList control, which enables them to display the images that are contained in the ImageList control. Visual Basic's ListView, ToolBar,

TabStrip, ImageCombo, and TreeView controls are all designed to work with the ImageList control. To use the ImageList control with one of these controls, you must bind the ImageList control to the other control by using the control's appropriate property—usually the ImageList property.

Images can be loaded into the ImageList control at design time by placing an instance of the ImageList control onto your form and then pressing F4 to display the Properties window. From the Properties window, click the Custom property's ellipsis button, shown in Figure 9-12.

From the ImageList control's custom Property Pages dialog box, click the Images tab to add graphics files to the ImageList control. Initially, the Images tab is empty, as shown in Figure 9-13.

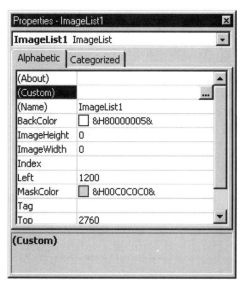

Figure 9-12   The ImageList control's Custom properties

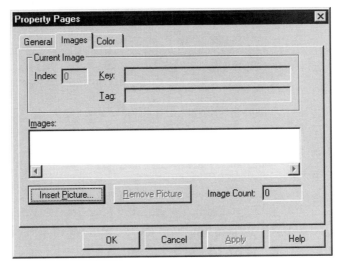

Figure 9-13 The ImageList control's Images tab

Click the Insert Pictures button to begin adding the images contained in graphics files from your hard drive or a network share to the ImageList control. The Select Picture dialog box, shown in Figure 9-14, is displayed. The ImageList control can use the following image file types (extensions in parentheses): bitmap (.bmp), cursor (.cur), icon (.ico), JPEG (.jpg), and GIF (.gif).

From the Select Picture dialog box, navigate to the directory that contains the graphics files that you want to use in the ImageList control. The drop-down box at the top of the control enables you to select different folders that are accessible from your system.

Tip: *Visual Basic supplies several different graphics files in the \Program Files\Microsoft Visual StudioCommon\ Graphics folder. This folder contains various subfolders organized by the type of images. For instance, the \Program Files\Microsoft Visual Studio\Common\Graphics\Bitmaps\ Gauge folder contains a collection of bitmap files that display different gauge images.*

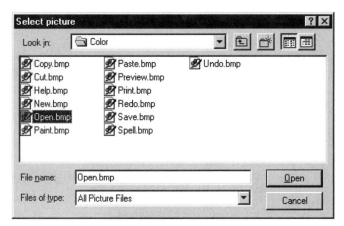

Figure 9-14 Selecting files for the ImageList control

Select the files that you want to add to the ImageList control and then click Open. After you add all the graphics files that you want to the ImageList control, they are displayed in the Images bar, as shown in Figure 9-15.

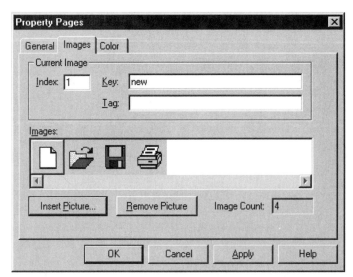

Figure 9-15 Associating keys with the images in an ImageList control

After you add the images to the ImageList control, you can optionally enter a text value to uniquely identify each image. Appropriately, this unique identifier is entered in the Key property. Images contained in the ImageList control can later be displayed by using either the Index value or the Key property. The Index value is assigned according to the order in which the images were added to the ImageList control, whereas the Key property is a unique, meaningful value that you assign to each image. Figure 9-15 shows that the first image has an Index value of 1 and has been assigned the Key property of new. You can assign the Key property for each image in the ImageList control by clicking the image displayed in the Images box and then entering the optional Key and Tag properties.

Can I dynamically add images to an ImageList control?

You can dynamically add images at runtime by using the ImageList control's Add method, which adds an image to the ImageList control's ListImages collection. The following line illustrates how to dynamically add an image to an ImageList control:

```
ilsImages.ListImages.Add ,"cut",LoadPicture("cut.bmp")
```

The ListImages collection's Add method accepts three parameters:

- The first parameter is optional and specifies the index of the item being added to the ListImages collection. If this parameter is blank, as in the preceding example, the image is added as the last member of the ListImages collection, and the Index value is automatically assigned.

- The second parameter also is optional and is used to assign a key to the image. In the previous example, a Key property of "cut" is associated with the image.

● The third parameter is required and specifies the picture that will be added to the collection. If you are loading a file from the hard drive, then you need to use the LoadPicture method to load the graphics file into the ImageList control. The LoadPicture method requires that you supply the filename and path of the graphics file that will be loaded.

How do I use the ImageList control with another control, such as the ImageCombo control?

To use the ImageList control in conjunction with another graphical control, such as the ImageCombo control, you first must add the ImageList control to your form. Then, you need to add a set of graphical images to the ImageList control either by setting the ImageList property at design time or by using the ImageList control's Add method, along with the LoadPicture or LoadResource functions, at runtime. Figure 9-16 shows a set of file system images that are contained in an ImageList control.

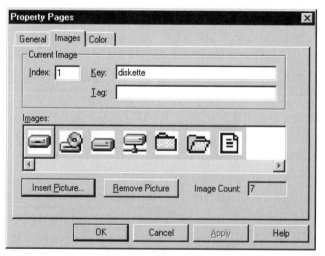

Figure 9-16 File system images in the ImageList control

Next, the ImageList control must be bound to the other graphical control. To bind the ImageList control to an ImageCombo control, for example, create an instance of the ImageCombo control on your form and then press F4 to display its properties. From the properties display, navigate to the Custom properties and click the ellipsis button. The ImageCombo's Property Pages dialog box, shown in Figure 9-17, will be displayed.

Initially, the ImageList property shown on the ImageCombo's Property Pages dialog box is blank. Clicking the drop-down arrow displays a list of any ImageList controls that are on the current form. Clicking the name of the ImageList control in the drop-down list adds the name to the ImageList property. Figure 9-17 shows that the ImageList control named ilsFileSystem has been bound to the ImageCombo control.

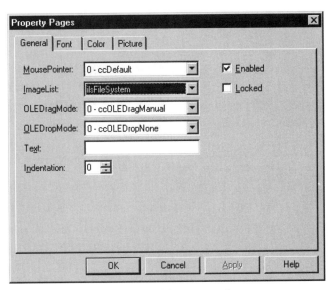

Figure 9-17   Binding to the ImageList control

After you bind the ImageList control to the ImageCombo control, you can display the images in the ImageCombo control. The following listing presents an example of using the ImageList and ImageCombo controls to display a list of system drives and their representative icons that is derived from the FileSystemObject object:

```
Private Sub Form_Load()

    Dim fs As New FileSystemObject

    ' Skip errors for an empty diskette drive.
    On Error Resume Next

    ilsFileSystem.ImageHeight = 17
    ilsFileSystem.ImageWidth = 19

    Dim oDrive As Drive
    Dim oDrives As Drives
    Set oDrives = fs.Drives

    For Each oDrive In oDrives
        ' Put in the correct image for each drive type.
        Select Case oDrive.DriveType
        Case Removable
            icbDrives.ComboItems.Add , _
              oDrive.DriveLetter, _
              oDrive.DriveLetter, "diskette"

        Case Fixed
            icbDrives.ComboItems.Add , _
              oDrive.DriveLetter, _
              oDrive.DriveLetter, "drive"

        Case CDRom
            icbDrives.ComboItems.Add , _
              oDrive.DriveLetter, _
              oDrive.DriveLetter, "cd"

        Case Remote
            icbDrives.ComboItems.Add , _
              oDrive.DriveLetter, _
              oDrive.DriveLetter & _
              oDrive.ShareName, "netdrive"
```

```
        End Select

    Next

End Sub
```

In this example, the ImageCombo control is populated during the Form_Load subroutine. Loading the text and images into an ImageCombo box is often performed before the form is displayed, so that the drop-down box is immediately available for use.

The first action that takes place in the Form_Load subroutine is the creation of an instance of the FileSystemObject. The FileSystemObject is new with Visual Basic 6 and provides a Component Object Model (COM) interface to the different drives, folders, and files that are present on the system. The FileSystemObject is described in greater detail in Chapter 10. For this example, the key point to know about the FileSystemObject is that its Drives collection contains a list of the different drives and their respective types that are available on the system.

After setting the oDrives object with the FileSystemObject's Drives collection, a For Each loop is used to read through the collection of drives. Within the For Each loop, the names and icons of each drive are added to the ImageCombo control. A Select Case statement is used to check the DriveType property of each drive. The first Case statement handles diskette drives, the next adds hard drives, the next adds CD-ROM drives, and the last Case statement adds network shares that have been mapped to local drive letters.

In each case, the Add method of the ImageCombo control named icbDrives is used to add an item to the ImageCombo control:

- The first parameter of the Add method is optional and specifies the index of the item that will be added to the ImageCombo control. Leaving this value blank, as shown in the previous listing, adds the new item at the end of the ComboItems collection.

- The second parameter is the key that is used to identify the given item in the ComboItems list. In this example, the drive letter is used as a key for the items in the list.

● The third parameter is the text that will be displayed in the ImageCombo control's drop-down list. The text and icon that are used vary depending on the type of drive. Standard system drives simply display the drive letter, whereas network shares display the mapped drive letter and the name of the network share that is found in the Drive object's ShareName property.

● The fourth parameter specifies the image that will be displayed. This can be either the numeric index of the image in the ImageList control or the image's key. It's important to note that if the key value is used, it must exactly match the key name that was previously assigned in the ImageList control.

When you click the drop-down arrow of the ImageList control, the drop-down list displays the names and the images that were added to the ImageCombo control. Figure 9-18 shows an example of the ImageCombo control that was filled using the preceding code.

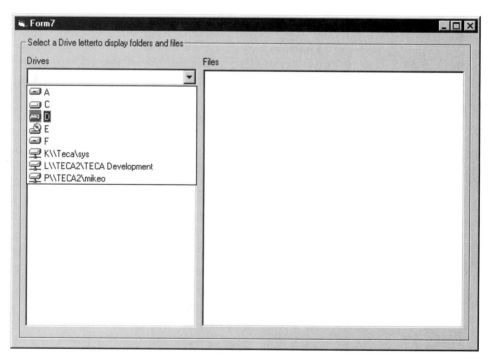

Figure 9-18   An ImageCombo control filled with drive name and icons

 I want to use the TreeView control to create an application with an Explorer-type interface. How do I get the TreeView control to display different images, and how do I create the different levels on the tree?

You can get the TreeView control to display images by using it in combination with the ImageList control. The ImageList control contains a collection of images that can be accessed by other graphical controls, while the TreeView control displays a hierarchical listing of elements, such as the listing used in an index, a tree, or a file system. Linking together the ImageList and the TreeView controls is easy, using the TreeView control's ImageList property. However, the key to effectively combining these two controls is to associate the appropriate images from the ImageList control with the different nodes that are used in the TreeView control.

The following code illustrates how you can populate an Explorer-like form that uses the TreeView control. The TreeView control is used to display a list of folders from a drive that has been selected in an ImageCombo control that lists the different system drives. The TreeView control represents the hierarchy of folders on the selected drive. The open and closed folder images that are displayed in the TreeView control come from the associated ImageList control. The first level of the TreeView control is populated after the user clicks a drive that's listed in the ImageCombo named icbDrives. The following code shows the Click event for the icbDrives ImageCombo box.

```
Private Sub icbDrives_Click()

    Dim nodX As Node
    Dim oFolder As Folder
    Dim oFolders As Folders

    Dim oSubFolder As Folder
    Dim oSubFolders As Folders

    Dim oFile As File
    Dim oFiles As Files

    On Error Resume Next
```

```
' Clear the tree view.
tvwFolders.Nodes.Clear

' Set the root node using the selected drive.
Set nodX = tvwFolders.Nodes.Add(, , _
    Left(icbDrives.Text, 1) & ":", _
    Left(icbDrives.Text, 1) & ":", "closed")
nodX.ExpandedImage = "open"

' Expand the first level of folders for the drive.
ExpandFolders Left(icbDrives.Text, 1) & ":"

' Move the list back to the first folder.
tvwFolders.Nodes.Item(1).EnsureVisible

' Fill the ListView box from the first folder.
Set oFolder = fs.GetFolder(Left _
    (icbDrives.Text, 1) & ":")
Set oFiles = oFolder.Files

' Read through the files collection.
For Each oFile In oFiles
    lvwFiles.ListItems.Add , _
        oFile.Name, oFile.Name, "leaf"
Next

End Sub
```

The code near the top of the icbDrives_Click subroutine declares the working variables that will be used. Regarding the TreeView control, the most important of these variables is the Node object named nodX. A Node object represents each node or item that's displayed on the TreeView control. The Folders, SubFolders, and File objects are all objects that are used to contain the data that's returned from the FileSystemObject.

Note: *In this subroutine, an instance of the FileSystemObject named fs has been declared at the module level. This allows the same FileSystemObject to be shared by different event modules. The common FileSystemObject is declared as Dim fs As New FileSystemObject.*

Next, the VB error handler is enabled. Windows NT systems are capable of implementing file- and folder-level security, and enabling runtime error handling allows the FileSystemObject to bypass nonauthorized files without generating runtime errors.

Next, the TreeView control's Nodes collection's Clear method is used to clear an existing node's data out of the TreeView control named tvwFolders. Then, the Add method of the Nodes collection is used to add the root or base node to the TreeView control. The Nodes collection's Add method accepts six parameters. The first parameter controls the relative position in the Nodes collection where the new item will be added. This parameter can contain either the index or the key value of an existing node. This parameter is left blank to add the root node to an empty Nodes collection. The second parameter defines the type of relationship that the new node has with the node that was specified in the parameter that will be added. Table 9-1 lists the valid node types.

The third parameter of the Nodes collection's Add method specifies the key of the item. The key must be a unique value, and it is used optionally to identify each individual Node object in the Nodes collection. In the previous code listing, the key consists of the drive letter concatenated with a colon. (Concatenating values essentially joins multiple entities together, forming a single new entity.)

Node Type Constant	Value	Description
tvwFirst	0	The node is placed before all nodes specified in the first parameter.
tvwLast	1	The node is placed after all nodes specified in the first parameter.
tvwNext	2	The node is placed after the node specified in the first parameter. (Default)
tvwPrevious	3	The node is placed immediately before the node specified in the first parameter.
tvwChild	4	The node is a child node of the node specified in the first parameter.

Table 9-1   Valid Node Types

The fourth parameter of the Add method specifies the text that will be displayed in the TreeView object. The preceding example code uses the drive letter as the text that will be displayed. The fifth and sixth parameters specify the image from the ImageList control that will be displayed in the TreeView control. This can be either the index or the key that was used in the ImageList control. The previous example sets the image to the ImageList key of "closed." The optional sixth parameter isn't used in the prior example. It sets the image that will be displayed when the TreeView node is selected.

The next statement in the example sets the expanded image of the root node to the open image that's contained in the associated ImageList control.

After you add the root node to the TreeView control, the ExpandFolders subroutine is called to add all the subfolders to the TreeView control. In this case, a subroutine is used because the same code will also be called later to expand each node of the tree when the user drills down through the folder hierarchy displayed by the TreeView control. After the ExpandFolders subroutine completes, the EnsureVisible method is used on the first object in the Nodes collection to reposition the TreeView display to initially show the tree beginning with the root node. Then, a related ListView control is filled with the files that are contained in the root folder.

The ExpandFolders subroutine accepts a single parameter that identifies the parent folder for which all the subfolders will be listed. The ExpandFolders subroutine adds each subfolder as a node in the TreeView control named trvFolders. The ExpandFolders subroutine is shown here:

```
Private Sub ExpandFolders(sFolder As String)
' Pass in the parent node name as a string.

    Dim oFolder As Folder
    Dim oFolders As Folders

    Dim oSubFolder As Folder
    Dim oSubFolders As Folders
```

```
Dim sDrive As String
Dim nodX As Node

sDrive = Left(icbDrives.Text, 1) & ":"
Set oFolder = fs.GetFolder(sFolder)
Set oFolders = oFolder.SubFolders

' If the node already exists, keep going.
On Error Resume Next

' Retrieve the folder names from the Folders
' collection.
For Each oFolder In oFolders

    ' Add folder names to the parent node.
    ' Name the key of each node using the full
    ' path.
    Set nodX = tvwFolders.Nodes.Add(sFolder, _
      tvwChild, oFolder.Path, oFolder.Name, "closed")
    ' Ensure the expanded view of the tree path.
    If sFolder = sDrive Then
        nodX.EnsureVisible
    End If

  ' Add the subfolders as child nodes.
  Set oSubFolder = fs.GetFolder(oFolder.Path)
  Set oSubFolders = oSubFolder.SubFolders

  ' Retrieve the subfolder to expand the tree.
  For Each oSubFolder In oSubFolders
      Set nodX = tvwFolders.Nodes.Add _
        (oFolder.Path, tvwChild, _
        oSubFolder.Path, oSubFolder.Name, "closed")
  Next

  ' Reset the current node to the parent folder.
  Set nodX = tvwFolders.Nodes.Item(sFolder)
  nodX.ExpandedImage = "open"
Next

End Sub
```

Again, at the beginning of the ExpandFolders subroutine, you can see the working objects that are required to deal with the Folders and Files collections contained by the FileSystemObject. In addition, a Node object named nodX is declared, to add new nodes to the TreeView control's Nodes collection.

Next, the GetFolders method of the existing fs FileSystemObject is used to create an instance of the parent folder, and then the SubFolders method is used to retrieve a list of folders from the Folder object.

Then, the VB error handler is enabled. In this case, the main purpose of the error handler is to bypass any duplicate node errors that may be generated when adding new nodes to the TreeView control's Nodes collection.

A For Each loop is used to read all the folder names from the oFolders collection. Within the For Each loop, the Add method of the TreeView control's Nodes collection is used to add each folder name to the TreeView control as a new node. The name of the parent node is used in the first parameter of the Add method. The second parameter uses the tvwChild constant to indicate that the new node will be a child node of the node indicated in parameter one. Child nodes are displayed in the next-lower hierarchical level of the TreeView control. The full path of the folder is used as the unique key, and the folder's name is used as the text that will be displayed in the TreeView control.

Setting the EnsureVisible property of the parent node makes all the new nodes visible in the TreeView control.

Next, the subfolders for the next level of folders are retrieved, so that the TreeView control can display the expand symbol (plus icon) next to each folder that contains subfolders. The expand icon enables the user to drill down through different levels of the tree. If a node in the TreeView control does not have any child nodes, then no expand symbol is displayed by the control and no expansion of that node by the user is possible. Only the next level of folders needs to be retrieved. Any subsequent levels of folders will be retrieved when the user interactively expands each node.

As in the previous example, the Add method of the TreeView's Nodes collection is used to add each subfolder. The parent folder is set as the current folder, the node is added as a child node, the full path of each folder is used as the key, and the folder name is used as the display text. In each case, the image for the unexpanded node is the ImageList image named "closed," and the expanded image has the value of "open."

The previous code displays the root folder and the first level of subfolders in the TreeView control named tvwFolder. This code also allows expand symbols to be displayed next to each folder that contains subfolders. For the TreeView control to work in the way that Windows Explorer works, code also needs to be added that enables each of the folders in the tree to be expanded—showing the subfolders for each level, along with the expand symbol for any of those subfolders that may contain their own subfolders. Adding the following code to the Expand event in the TreeView control allows the user to drill down through the different levels of folders and subfolders:

```
Private Sub tvwFolders_Expand _
    (ByVal Node As MSComCtlLib.Node)

      ' Don't initially expand subfolders.
      If Node.Index <> 1 Then
          ' Add subfolders for the expanded node.
          ExpandFolders Node.Key
      End If

End Sub
```

The Expand event is called when the nodes are initially added to the Nodes collection of the TreeView control, as well as when the user clicks the expand icon that's displayed in front of any node that contains child nodes. You usually want to bypass the Expand event that's called when nodes are first added, but retain the ability to retrieve sublevels of the tree hierarchy when the user clicks the expand symbol. Checking the value of the Node.Index property allows you to do this.

The Node.Index property contains the value of the current node. This value is 0 when the TreeView control is initially expanded, and then contains the index value of the expanded node when the user clicks the expand symbol.

If the Node.Index property points to a node on the TreeView control, then the ExpandFolders subroutine (presented earlier) is used to retrieve the next level of subfolders. The value contained in the Key property of the node is passed to the ExpandFolders subroutine. Its important to note that this Key value was set when the node was initially added to the TreeView control's Nodes collection, and contains the full path of the current Node object. The ExpandFolders subroutine uses this path as the file system path that will be expanded and added to the TreeView control.

Figure 9-19 shows the TreeView control displaying an Explorer-like view of the folders on the current system.

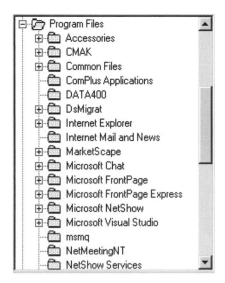

Figure 9-19 Using the TreeView control

How do I use the ListView control together with the ImageList control?

The ImageList control contains a collection of images that can be accessed by other graphical controls, whereas the ListView control displays a list that contains an image and some text. Using the ListView control is similar to using the TreeView control with the ImageList control. In fact, the ListView and the TreeView control are often used together. However, some important differences exist in the way that the ListView control binds to the ImageList control and displays its list elements. First, the ImageList control must be populated with images. This can be done either in design mode or at runtime by using the ImageList Add method in conjunction with the LoadPicture or LoadResource functions. After the ImageList control is populated, it is bound to the ListView control by updating the ListView control's ImageList property with the name of the appropriate ImageList control.

To bind the ListView control to the ImageList control, add an instance of the ListView control to a form and then press F4 to display the ListView control's Properties window. In the control's Properties window, find the Custom property and then click the ellipsis button to display the ListView control's custom Property Pages dialog box. Click the Image Lists tab and then select the ImageList control from the Normal or the Small drop-down lists. Figure 9-20 illustrates binding the ListView control to the ImageList control named ilsFileSystem.

The ListView control can be used to complement the TreeView control in an Explorer-type interface. Whereas the TreeView control can be used to display a hierarchical list of folders, the ListView control can be used to display a list of the files in each folder. To build an Explorer-type interface by using the TreeView and ListView controls, you generally would add file entries to the ListView control when the user clicks a given folder in the TreeView control.

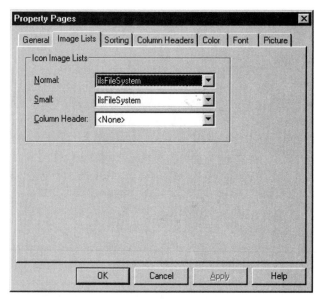

Figure 9-20   Binding the ListView control to an ImageList control

The following subroutine illustrates a sample TreeView Click event subroutine that populates a ListView control that's on the same form. In this example, the TreeView control named tvwFolders contains a listing of system folders, and the ListView control named lvwFiles will display the files that are contained in each folder that the user clicks.

```
Private Sub tvwFolders_Click()

    Dim oFolder As Folder
    Dim oFolders As Folders
    Dim oFile As File
    Dim oFiles As Files

    ' Skip errors like nonauthorization.
    On Error Resume Next

    ' Clear the ListView box.
    lvwFiles.ListItems.Clear

    ' Now fill the ListView box.
    Set oFolder = fs.GetFolder _
        (tvwFolders.SelectedItem.Key)
```

```
    Set oFiles = oFolder.Files

    ' Add the files from the current folder.
    For Each oFile In oFiles
        lvwFiles.ListItems.Add , _
            oFile.Name, oFile.Name, "leaf"
    Next

End Sub
```

At the top of the tvwFolders_Click subroutine, you can see the working objects that are required to deal with the Folders and Files collections contained by the FileSystemObject. Because the FileSystemObject is used by different event subroutines in the same module, the fs FileSystemSystem object has been declared at the module level.

Next, the VB error handler is enabled, which allows the subroutine to bypass runtime errors, such as not having permission to read certain files. Then, the ListItems collection of the lvwFiles ListView control is cleared by using the Clear method. The ListItems collection is used to hold all the entries that will be displayed by the ListView control.

After the ListView control is cleared, the GetFolder method is used to create an instance of the Folder object that was named in the Key property of the TreeView control. Its important to note that for this to work, the Key value of the TreeView control must contain the full path to the folder. Then, the Files collection object named oFiles is set to the collection of files contained within the current Folder object. More-detailed information about the FileSystemObjects and their use is presented in Chapter 10.

A For Each loop is then used to add all the filenames and a representative icon to the lvwFiles ListItems collection. The ListItems collection's Add method accepts five optional parameters:

- The first parameter specifies the index of the item that will be added. If no value is specified, the item is added to the end of the ListItems collection.

- The second parameter is used to give each item in the list a unique key. The name of the file is used.

● The third parameter is the text that will be displayed in the list. In this example, the name of the file is used for this parameter, too.

● The fourth parameter identifies the image from the associated ImageList control that will be displayed in the list when the ListView control is set to Icon view. This parameter can contain either the index of the image from the ImageList control or the image's key. If the key is used, it must match the value of the Key property that was assigned in the ImageList control. The preceding example uses a key of "leaf."

● The fifth, optional parameter is not used in this example, but it is the name of the image that will be used when the ListView control is displayed in SmallIcon mode.

Figure 9-21 illustrates an example of a ListView control that's filled with the filenames from a folder that's displayed in the TreeView control.

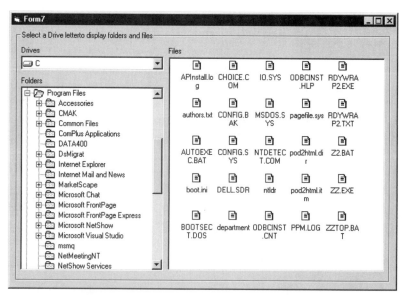

Figure 9-21   Using the ListView control

 Can I bind a single ImageList control to multiple graphical controls?

Yes. A single ImageList control can be bound to multiple other graphical controls that can use the images contained in the ImageList control. For instance, one ImageList control can be simultaneously bound to both a TreeView control and an ImageCombo control. However, the ImageList control contains only a single set of images, so those images must be appropriate for all the different controls that need to bind to the ImageList control.

USING ADDITIONAL COMMON GRAPHICAL CONTROLS

The questions and answers in this section deal with using some of the other commonly used graphical controls that are supplied with Visual Basic. This section begins by covering the simple Line and Shape controls, and then covers the more complicated TabStrip and MSChart controls.

 How do I add lines to a form?

You can add lines to a form by using the Line control, a standard part of the VB Toolbox. But, unlike most other ActiveX controls, the Line control provides support only for the basic Refresh and ZOrder methods and doesn't support any events. The Line control is essentially a tool that's used only for esthetics. To add the Line control to a form, click the Line control in the VB Toolbox; click one of the targeted end points for the line on a form; and then, while holding down the left-mouse button, drag the other endpoint of the line to its desired location. A line is drawn on the form. You can move the line by clicking the Line control and dragging it to its new location on the form.

 ## What is the Shape control used for?

The Shape control is used to display geometric images on the background of a form. Like the Line control, the Shape control does not support any events and supports only minimum methods. The Shape control supports the basic Move, Refresh, and ZOrder methods. Essentially, the Shape control is used only to improve the appearance of a form or to add simple graphic images to your application.

The appearance of the Shape control is governed by its Shape property. Table 9-2 presents the valid setting of the Shape control's Shape property.

In addition to using the Shape control's Shape property to manipulate the shape that is displayed on the form, you can use the BorderStyle, FillColor, and FillStyle properties to alter the appearance of the Shape control. The BorderStyle property controls the type of border, if any, that is used by the control, while the FillColor and FillStyle properties specify how the interior portion of the control will be displayed.

Constant	Value	Description
vbShapeRectangle	0	Displays a rectangle
vbShapeSquare	1	Displays a square
vbShapeOval	2	Displays an oval
vbShapeCircle	3	Displays a circle
vbShapeRoundedRectangle	4	Displays a rectangle with rounded corners
vbShapeRoundedSquare	5	Displays a square with rounded corners

Table 9-2 Shape Property Values

How do I add multiple tabs to a TabStrip control?

Using the TabStrip control is not quite as straightforward as using the simpler TabbedDialog control. The TabbedDialog control displays each tab as a separate container, which makes visually designing the layout of the tab very easy. However, the TabStrip control has several advantages over the TabbedDialog control. The TabStrip control is a single container and uses fewer resources than the TabbedDialog control. In addition, it has the ability to bind with the ImageList control and display graphical images on each tab.

To use the TabStrip control, you first need to configure the number of tabs and the caption that will be displayed on each tab. After you place an instance of the TabStrip control on the form, click the control and then press the F4 key to display its Properties window. In the Properties window, go to the Custom properties and click the ellipsis button to display the TabStrip Property Pages dialog box, shown in Figure 9-22.

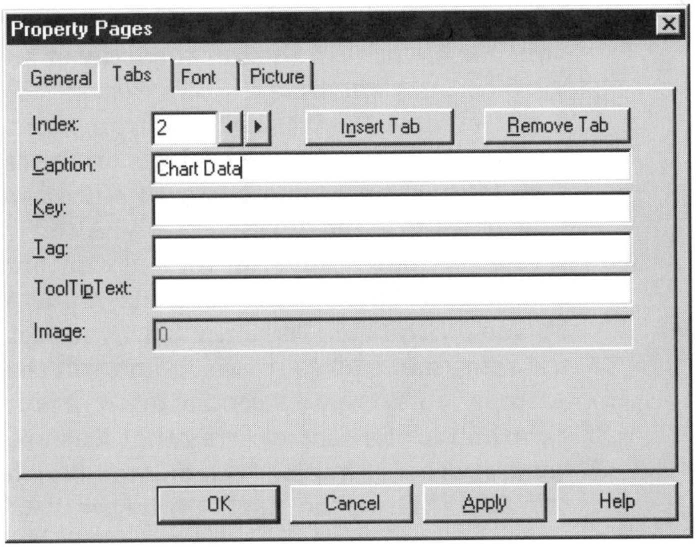

Figure 9-22 Setting the tab properties

To configure the number of tabs that will be displayed by the TabStrip control, click the Tabs column and enter a description to display in the caption of each tab. Each tab is indexed, beginning with tab 1. To add a new tab, click the Insert Tab button. Figure 9-22 shows the second tab being displayed. The Index of the tab is 2, and the description that will be displayed in that tab is Chart Data, as shown in the Caption text box.

Tip: *You can also display images in the caption of each tab by binding the TabStrip control to an ImageList control.*

The next step in using the graphical TabStrip control is to add the GUI elements that will be displayed on each tab. Since the TabStrip control provides only a single container, the best way to keep each set of interface elements separate for each tab is by using a Frame control array to contain each set of interface controls. A control array of Frame controls allows each element on the control array to correspond to a given tab that displays in the TabStrip control. Naturally, only one element in the control array of Frame controls is visible at any one time.

To create a control array of Frame controls, you can simply create two Frame controls on the same form and then give the same name to both controls and set their Index properties to 1 and 2, respectively. Alternatively, you could create the first Frame control and copy and paste it onto the same form. When Visual Basic attempts to paste the second Frame control onto the form, it will see that a control with the same name already exists, and will then automatically prompt you to create a control array. Figure 9-23 shows an example of a control array that was used to group two separate sets of interface elements—one for each of the two tabs that will be displayed by the TabStrip control.

Note: *The Frame controls displayed in Figure 9-23 have been moved for demonstration purposes, so that you can see that two sets of frames are present. In a production environment, these frames would exactly overlay, and the bottom frame would not be visible.*

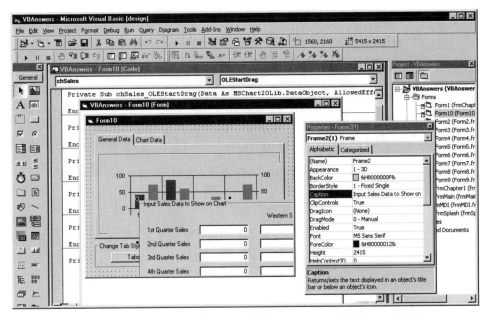

Figure 9-23   Using a control array of Frame controls for each tab

---

Tip: *You can display the contents of different control array elements in the Visual Basic IDE by right-clicking the control array and then selecting either the Bring to Front or the Send to Back option from the pop-up menu.*

After grouping together each set of interface elements into different Frame control arrays, you can cause each element in the control array to be displayed, by adding some code to the TabStrip control's Click event. The following code shows how you can bring a specified element of the control array to the top (thus making it visible) by using the Click event:

```
Private Sub tabGraph_Click()
    frmTabInterface _
        (tabGraph.SelectedItem.Index).ZOrder 0
End Sub
```

In this example, the Index property of the selected TabStrip control named tabGraph is used to indicate which tab has been clicked. Note, importantly, that this index

corresponds with the index that was used in the control array of the Frame controls named frmTabInterface. Then, the ZOrder method is used with the value of 0 to bring to the top the control array element specified by the index. This makes visible to end users the selected element of the Frame control array and any controls that it may contain.

How can I display a bar graph in my application?

You can use the MSChart control that comes with Visual Basic 6 to display a variety of graphs in your application. The MSChart control can display bar charts, line charts, pie charts, and several other graph styles. The MSChart control is not part of the standard VB Toolbox. Before you can use the MSChart control, you need to add it to the Visual Basic IDE by selecting Projects | Components and then checking the Microsoft Chart Control 6.0 option from the list of components. After you add the MSChart control to the Toolbox, you must drop it onto a form in your application and then set its properties by pressing the F4 key.

After placing the MSChart control on your form, you need to set up the graph's Column and Row properties. The MSChart works a bit differently from most of the other graphical controls. Whereas most of the other controls enable you to set the Row and Column properties by using the custom Property Pages dialog box, for the MSChart control, it is easier to set these properties directly from the Properties window. Figure 9-24 illustrates setting the Column property in the Properties window.

First, you must set the ColumnCount property to the number of columns that will be displayed in the graph. In Figure 9-24, the number of columns has been set to 2. Next, you must give each column a heading, by entering in the Column property the index of the column that you want to label, and then entering in the ColumnLabel property the label that you want to display on the graph. Figure 9-24 shows that Column 2 has been given the ColumnLabel Western Sales. Column 1, which is not shown, was assigned the ColumnLabel Eastern Sales.

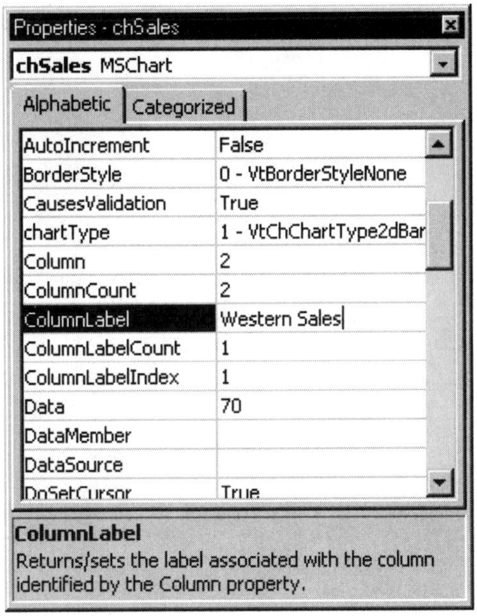

Figure 9-24   Setting the Column property of the MSChart control

The Row properties are set in exactly the same fashion. First, the number of rows that will be included in the graph is set by using the RowCount property. Then, the RowLabel property is assigned for each row. As with columns, you move between the different RowLabel properties by entering the index of the row in the Row property. In this example, four rows were created, and they were assigned the row labels of 1st Quarter Sales, 2nd Quarter Sales, 3rd Quarter Sales, and 4th Quarter Sales.

After you configure the MSChart control's properties, the chart is ready to use. However, the MSChart control requires data to display in the graph. The following listing illustrates how you can set the MSChart control's ChartData property, to supply the graph with data:

```
Public Sub ChartData()
Dim arrSales(1 To 4, 1 To 3)
Dim i As Integer
```

```
For i = 1 To 4
    arrSales(i, 1) = "Qtr " & I
    arrSales(i, 2) = CDbl(txtEastSales(i - 1).Text)
    arrSales(i, 3) = CDbl(txtWestSales(i - 1).Text)
Next
chSales.ChartData = arrSales

End Sub
```

In this example, the array named arrSales is loaded from the input of two sets of four TextBox controls. Each set is part of a control array. One control array exists for the set of four txtEastSales text boxes, and a second control array exists for the four txtWestSales text boxes. Figure 9-25 shows the input screen that captures the sample data that will be shown in the MSChart control.

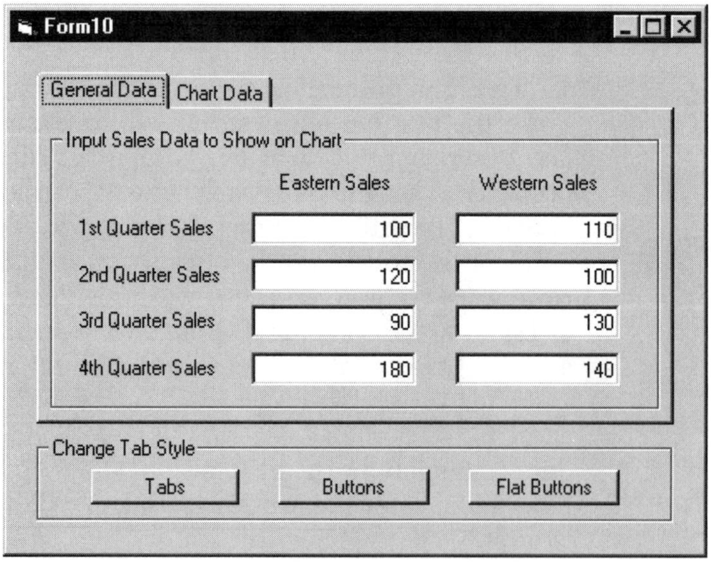

Figure 9-25 Data input for the MSChart control

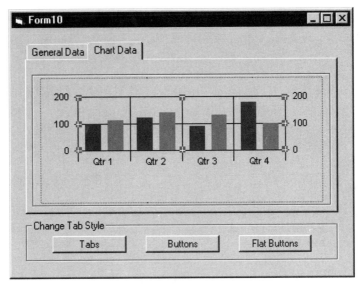

Figure 9-26   Example output of the MSChart control

It's important to note that arrSales is a multidimensional array. Each dimension in the array corresponds to an element of data that is displayed on the MSChart control. The For Next loop gathers the input from each element of the TextBox control array and assigns the value to the appropriate element of the arrSales array. After the arrSales array is loaded with data, it is assigned to the MSChart control's ChartData property, and a graph similar to the one shown in Figure 9-26 is displayed.

How do I display videos and AVI files?

You can display silent videos and animation clips contained in AVI files by using the Microsoft Animation control, which is contained in the mscomct2.ocx file and is installed as part of the Windows Common Controls-2 6.0 component. After you add the Animation control to your project, to use it, you first set its Open property with the name of an AVI file that's located either on your system's hard drive or on a network share.

 Tip: *Visual Basic includes a number of AVI files. By default, these files are installed in the \Program Files\Microsoft Visual Studio\Common\Graphics\Videos folder.*

The following code illustrates how to invoke the Microsoft CommonDialog control to open an AVI file from the Click event of a button named cmdOpenAVI:

```
Private Sub cmdOpenAVI_Click()

    dlgOpenAVI.Filter = "avi files (*.avi)|*.avi"
    dlgOpenAVI.ShowOpen
    anmAVI.Open dlgOpenAVI.FileName

End Sub
```

First, the Filter property of the CommonDialog control named dlgOpenAVI is set to display only files that end in the extension .avi. Next, the ShowOpen method is used to make the CommonDialog control display a File Open dialog box. Finally, the filename that's selected from the CommonDialog control is assigned to the Open property of an Animation control named anmAVI.

After the Open property of the AVI file is assigned the name of a valid AVI file, the animation displayed in the file can be displayed by using the Play method. The following code shows how to call the Play method for the Animation control named anmAVI.

```
Private Sub cmdPlayAVI_Click()
    anmAVI.Play
End Sub
```

When the AVI file is being played in the Animation control, a screen like the one shown in Figure 9-27 will be displayed.

 Tip: *The Animation control must be sized large enough to display the entire image, or else a part of the image will be clipped.*

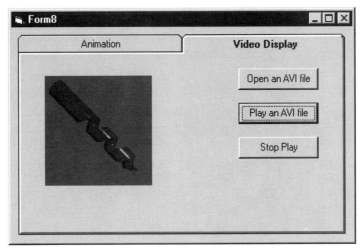

Figure 9-27   Playing an AVI file

The AVI file will play continuously until the Stop method is executed. The following code shows the use of the anmAVI Animation control's Stop method:

```
Private Sub cmdStopAVI_Click()
    anmAVI.Stop
End Sub
```

Chapter 10

The File System

Answer Topics!

The File System @ a Glance

This chapter presents a set of questions and answers that illustrate how to use Visual Basic to access the files that are located on either the local hard drive or a network share. This chapter covers a range of file-related topics, including how to list drives, directories, and files, and how to read and write to files.

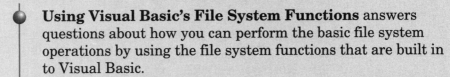

Using Visual Basic's File System Functions answers questions about how you can perform the basic file system operations by using the file system functions that are built in to Visual Basic.

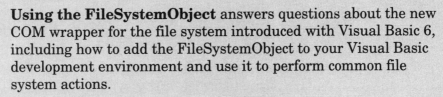

Using the FileSystemObject answers questions about the new COM wrapper for the file system introduced with Visual Basic 6, including how to add the FileSystemObject to your Visual Basic development environment and use it to perform common file system actions.

USING VISUAL BASIC'S FILE SYSTEM FUNCTIONS

The first part of this chapter presents some basic questions and answers that show you how to use the file access functions that are provided with Visual Basic. Most of these functions have been available since Visual Basic 3. They are very stable and provide very good performance. Unlike the newer FileSystemObject, they are not invoked using COM, and you don't need to create any program objects to use them. Instead, you simply add to your application's code the calls to the appropriate functions.

 ## How do I change the current drive that I'm using?

You can change the current drive by using the ChDrive statement, which takes a single String argument that contains the drive letter that will be assigned. The following code shows how you can use the ChDrive function to change the current drive to the drive letter that was selected in the ComboBox control named cboDrives:

```
ChDrive (cboDrives.Text)
```

 ## How do I find the current directory, and how do I change to another directory?

The current directory is the directory or folder that will be used for any unqualified file access. In other words, if your application attempts to open a file but does not provide the entire path to the file—for example, it supplies only the file's name—the application initially attempts to open the file in the current directory.

You can find the current directory by using the CurDir function, and change the current directory by using the ChDir statement:

```
Dim sOriginalDir As String
Dim sCurrentDir As String

' Save the current directory.
sOriginalDir = CurDir
Debug.Print sOriginalDir
```

```
' Change to the c:\temp directory.
ChDir ("c:\temp")
sCurrentDir = CurDir
Debug.Print sCurrentDir

' Now change back to the original directory.
ChDir (sOriginalDir)
```

At the top of this listing, two String variables are declared that will hold the original and the changed directory names. Next, the CurDir function is called to retrieve the name of the current directory and place it into the sOriginalDir variable. The CurDir function returns a String value and does not accept any arguments.

Next, the ChDir statement is executed, which does not return any values and accepts a single String variable as an argument. This variable must contain the path of the new directory. In this example, the current directory is changed to the c:\temp directory. Then, the CurDir function is called again, to report the name of the new current directory. Finally, the ChDir statement is executed again, returning the current directory to its original path.

 ## How can I determine whether a file exists?

You can use Visual Basic's Dir function to check for the existence of a file. The Dir function accepts two parameters. The first parameter is a single String argument that contains the name of either a specific file or a path. Like its command-line namesake, the Dir function can accept wildcard characters, such as the * and the ? characters. The second parameter is optional and contains a constant that controls the type of information that will be returned by the Dir function. The following table lists the valid constants that can be used by the Dir function:

File Type Constant	Value	Description
vbNormal	0	Returns files that do not have special attributes (default)
vbReadOnly	1	Returns read-only files in addition to files with no attributes

File Type Constant	Value	Description
vbHidden	2	Returns hidden files in addition to files with no attributes
vbSystem	4	Returns system files in addition to files with no attributes
vbVolume	8	Returns the volume label of the current disk drive
vbDirectory	16	Returns directories and folders in addition to files with no attributes

The Dir function returns a string containing the first file or folder name of the file that satisfies the argument that was supplied in the first parameter. When multiple matching elements are present, you can repeatedly call the Dir function to return each matching item in succession. The following example illustrates how to use the Dir function to check for the existence of a single file:

```
Dim sFileName As String

sFileName = Dir("Myfile.txt")

If sFileName = vbNullString Then
    MsgBox "File:" & "Myfile.txt" & " does not exist"
Else
    MsgBox "File:" & "Myfile.txt" & " was found"
End If
```

In this example, the Dir function uses the filename Myfile.txt as an input parameter. The filename can contain the qualified path name, which causes the Dir function to search for the file in the specified path. In this case, the filename is not qualified with the path name, so the Dir function looks for the file in the current directory.

If the Dir function finds the file, the name is returned as a String variable. In this example, if the file Myfile.txt is found in the current directory, the sFileName variable will be assigned the value of MyFile.txt. If the file is not found, then the variable sFileName will be set to a null string.

How do I list all the files in a directory?

You can list all the files in a given directory by using the Dir function. In addition to being able to report the existence of a

single file, the Dir function can list all the files within a given folder. To list all the files in a folder, you must provide the Dir function with a string containing the path name of the folder in the first parameter, and the appropriate file attribute constant in the second parameter. The following example shows how you can use the Dir function to list all the files in the c:\temp directory:

```
Dim sFileName As String

    ' Clear any existing list items.
    lstNames.Clear

    ' Call the Dir function with parms to get
    ' the list.
    sFileName = Dir("c:\temp\*.*", vbNormal)

    ' Loop to get all the items.
    Do While sFileName <> ""

        ' Add the files' names to a list box.
        lstNames.AddItem sFileName
        ' Call the Dir function with no parameters
        ' to get the next entry.
        sFileName = Dir

    Loop
```

In the preceding example, a String variable named sFileName is declared, and then the Dir function is called, using the sFileName variable as output. The first argument of the Dir function is a string that specifies the path that the Dir function will search. In this example, the Dir function will list all the files in the c:\temp directory. Note that the Dir function is able to accept wildcard characters. The *.* wildcard characters cause the Dir function to list all the files in the c:\temp directory. If any files are found in the specified directory, the name of the first file found is placed in the sFileName variable.

Next, a loop is used to retrieve the remaining files in the c:\temp directory. Within the loop, each filename returned by the Dir function is added to the ListBox control named lstNames. Calling the Dir function with no parameters causes it to retrieve the next filename from the directory. The

loop ends when the Dir function has read all the entries, at which point it returns an empty string in the sFileName variable.

How do I list the folders that are on the system?

The Dir function can be used to obtain a list of folders from the system in much the same way that it is used to obtain a list of files. The primary difference lies in the arguments that are passed to the function. To get a list of the folders or directories that are on the system, you must use the vbDirectory constant in the second parameter of the Dir function call. The following example illustrates how to use the Dir function to list the folders in the root directory of the C drive:

```
Dim sFolderName As String
Dim sDriveLetter As String
Dim nFolderAttr As Integer

On Error Resume Next

lstNames.Clear

sDriveLetter = "c:\"

sFolderName = Dir(sDriveLetter, vbDirectory)
Do While sFolderName <> ""
    ' Skip the first two . & .. entries.
    If sFolderName <> "." And sFolderName <> ".." Then
      ' Make sure sFolderName is a directory.
      nFolderAttr = GetAttr _
          sDriveLetter & sFolderName)
      If nFolderAttr = vbDirectory Then
          lstNames.AddItem sFolderName
      End If
    End If
    ' Get next folder name.
    sFolderName = Dir
Loop
```

In the beginning of this listing, three working variables are declared. The first String variable contains the folder

names returned by the Dir function. The second String variable contains the drive letter. The third Integer variable is used to contain the attribute bytes of each file or folder name retrieved by the Dir function. The attribute bytes are used to test whether the names retrieved are folder or directory names, as opposed to standard filenames.

Next, the On Error Resume Next statement is used to allow the code to bypass any errors that may be the result of attempting to access unauthorized folders or files. Then, the list box that will contain the folder names is cleared and the sDriveLetter variable is assigned the root path for the C drive.

The Dir function is then called to retrieve the list of directory names. The first parameter contains the base path name from which the subdirectories will be retrieved. The vbDirectory constant in the second parameter specifies that directory names will be retrieved in addition to the standard filenames that are contained in the c:\ path. A Do While loop is used to extract all the names of the files and folders in the c:\ directory.

When using the vbDirectory attribute, the first two entries returned by the Dir function are the . and the .. characters, which you would typically want to skip. Next, because the Dir function returns both file and folder names, you must test the attributes of each object by using the GetAttr function. The GetAttr function requires the fully qualified path to the object and returns an Integer value indicating the object's attributes. In this case, only the objects that have the vbDirectory attribute are added to the list box named lstNames. At the bottom of the loop, the Dir function is called with no parameters, to retrieve the next file or folder name.

Tip: To list the files in a subdirectory, simply pass the name of the subdirectory path to the Dir function. For instance, to list the folders contained in the Windows directory, you use the string c:\Windows\. However, note that the Dir function doesn't accept long filenames, so if you want to list the contents of directories with long names, you must use the shortened DOS-equivalent names.

 Is there a function to list the drives on a system?

No. There is no built-in function that lists the system drives. Probably the easiest way to accomplish this is to use either the DriveListBox control from the Visual Basic Toolbox or the Drives collection exposed by the FileSystemObject.

How do I create a file?

You can create a file by using the Open function with the For Output As keywords. After the file is opened, you can write data to the file by using either Print or Write statements. After you write all the data to the file, you can close it by using the Close statement. The following example shows how to create a file in Visual Basic:

```
Dim i As Integer

' Open the file for output.
Open "file_in.txt" For Output As #1

' Add 50 records.
For i = 1 To 50
    Print #1, "Record: " & Str(i)
Next i

' Close the file.
Close #1
```

The Open statement must always be used before any file operations can be performed. The first parameter of the Open statement is a string that specifies the name of the file that will be opened. The filename used can be either fully qualified with the path or just the name of the file. If the filename is not qualified, it is opened in the current directory. The next part of the Open statement specifies the mode in which the file will be opened. The following table lists the different open modes supported by the Open statement:

Open Mode	Description
Append	The named file is opened for output. If the file exists, all data will be preserved, and any new data will be written to the end of the file.

Open Mode	Description
Binary	The named file is opened in Binary mode. The Binary mode keyword must be combined with one of the other mode keywords, to further identify the type of file access.
Input	The named file is opened for input.
Output	The named file is opened for output. If the file exists, it will be cleared.
Random	A file is opened for random access.

After you specify the open mode, you assign a unique file number, which can have any value from 1–151. However, you must take care to give each file a unique number. In the previous example, the file named file_in.txt has been opened for output and assigned the file number of 1. If the file_in.txt file does not exit, it will be created. If it is present, all existing data will be cleared.

A For Next loop is used to write 50 new records to the file. Inside the loop, the Print statement is used to actually write data to the file. The Print statement uses the file number as the first parameter and uses a string containing the data to be written to the file as the second parameter.

Tip: *The Print statement automatically appends the CR (carriage return) and LF (linefeed) characters to each line it outputs.*

After the loop completes, all 50 records will have been added to the file_in.txt file. Then, the Close statement is executed with the appropriate file number to close the file. After the file is closed, it can be accessed by other applications.

How do I read and write to a text file?

You can read and write to a file by using Visual Basic's Input and Print statements. However, before you can perform any file input or output (I/O) operations, the file must be opened by using Visual Basic's Open statement. The following example illustrates how you can open two files, read the contents of the first file, and then write the contents to the second file.

```
Dim sInputData As String

' Open for sequential access.
Open "file_in.txt" For Input As #1
Open "file_out.txt" For Output As #2

Do While Not EOF(1)
    Line Input #1, sInputData
    Print #2, sInputData
Loop

Close #1
Close #2
```

In the beginning of this example, a String variable named sInputData is declared, which is used to hold each line that's read from the input file. Next, two Open statements are used. The first Open statement opens a file named file_in.txt for input. If this named file doesn't exist, a VB runtime error is generated. The second Open statement opens the file named file_out.txt for output. If the file named output.txt doesn't exist, it is created when the Open statement is executed. It's important to note that each file must be opened using a unique file number. A runtime error will be generated if you attempt to execute the Open statement using a file number that's already in use.

After both the input and the output files are opened, a Do While loop is used to read through the contents of the input file. The Do While loop continues until the EOF function returns a value of True, which indicates that all records in the file have been read. Within the Do While loop, the Line Input statement is used to read each line from the file. The Line Input statement reads a stream of characters until the CR (carriage return) and LF (linefeed) characters are encountered. The stream of input characters (excluding the CR and LF characters) is then assigned to the sInputData variable. Next, the Write statement is used to write the data in the sInputData variable to the output file. Note that the file number used by the Line Input statement matches the file number used by the input file. Likewise, the file number used in the Write statement was used to open the output file.

After all the data from the input file has been read, both files are closed using the Close statement.

How do I read a comma-delimited (CSV) file?

Visual Basic's Input statement makes reading data from a comma-delimited file really easy. (A comma-delimited file is a formatted text file in which each different value is separated by a comma. Further, each record must end with the CR and LF characters, and text strings must be enclosed in quotation marks.) The Input statement uses an open file number as the first parameter, followed by a list of variables. Each variable in the Input statement's parameter list will be filled in with the value from the corresponding field position in the input file. For instance, an example file_in.csv file could contain the following data:

```
"line1field1","line1field2","line1field3","line1field4"
"line2field1","line2field2","line2field3","line2field4"
"line3field1","line3field2","line3field3","line3field4"
```

In this case, the file_in.csv file consists of three lines, each of which has four comma-separated values and ends with the CR and LF characters. The following code illustrates how to open this file for input, read the comma-separated values into program variables, and add the field values to a list box:

```
Dim sField1, sField2, sField3, sField4 As String

lstNames.Clear

' Read through the input file,
' putting each field into a String variable.
Open "file_in.csv" For Input As #1

' Read until EOF.
Do While Not EOF(1)
    Input #1, sField1, sField2, sField3, sField4
    ' Add the fields to a list box.
    lstNames.AddItem sField1 & " " & sField2 & " " _
        & sField3 & " " & sField4
Loop
Close #1
```

In this example, the file_in.csv file is opened for input and is using the file number 1. Next, a Do While loop is used to read through the file. Within the Do While loop, the Input statement reads file number 1 and automatically assigns the contents of each comma-separated value into the four variables: sField1, sField2, sField3, and sField4. The Input statement reads each line in the input file until it encounters the CR and LF characters. The content of each of these variables is then added to the list box named lstNames. When the EOF marker is encountered, the Do While loop is ended and the file is closed.

Is there an easy way to copy a file?

Yes, you can make a complete copy of a file by using the FileCopy function, which is very easy to use. It uses just two arguments. The first is a string that identifies the source file to be copied. The second is a string that identifies the destination file. The following example shows how to use the FileCopy function:

```
FileCopy "file_in.txt", "copyfile_in.txt"
```

This example copies the file named file_in.txt to the new file copyfile_in.txt. If the destination file already exists, it will be overwritten.

How do I delete files in Visual Basic?

Visual Basic's Kill statement is used to delete operating system files. Like the Dir function, the Kill function supports wildcard searches. The following example illustrates using the Kill statement:

```
Dim sFileName As String
sFileName = "copyfile_in.txt"

' Delete one file.
Kill sFileName

' Delete all files that begin with file_.
Kill "file_???.*"
```

```
' Delete all files in the temp directory with
' the extension .tmp.
Kill "c:\temp\*.tmp"
```

The Kill statement uses one parameter that accepts a String variable containing the name and path of the file to be deleted. If no path is specified, the system's search path is used to locate the file. Visual Basic generates a runtime error if the file is not found or is in use by another application.

In the previous example, the first instance of the Kill statement shows how you can delete a single file named copyfile_in.txt. In this case, the name of the file is assigned to a String variable named sFileName.

The second instance of the Kill statement shows how to use the single wildcard character (?) in conjunction with the multiple wildcard character (*) to delete all the files in the current directory that begin with file_. The single wildcard character can substitute one character for the wildcard. For example, since three single wildcard characters are used in the previous example, the target filenames would include file_in.txt, file_out.txt, and file_in.csv.

The third example of the Kill statement shows how you can use the multiple character wildcard (*) to delete all the files in the c:\temp directory that end in the extension .tmp. In this case, files named d00001.tmp and deleteme.tmp would be deleted, but the files named delete.txt and d00001.temp would not be deleted.

How can I determine the size of a file?

You can use the FileLen function to retrieve the number of bytes in a file. The file does not have to be opened to use the FileLen function. The following listing shows how to use the FileLen function:

```
Dim lFileBytes As Long

' Check for input file.
lFileBytes = FileLen("file_in.csv")

lblBytes.Caption = lFileBytes
```

The FileLen function accepts a single argument that identifies the file to be sized. It returns a Long value containing the number of bytes in the file.

Tip: *For fixed-length files, you can determine the number of records in the file by reading the first record, using the Line Input function. Then, you use the Len function to determine the length of the first record, adding 2 bytes to account for the CR and LF characters. Finally, divide the number of bytes by the record length to get the number of records in the file.*

Can I avoid using hard-coded file numbers in VB's Open, Input, Print, and Close file statements?

Yes. Visual basic's FreeFile function can be used to retrieve the first free file number. Using the FreeFile function helps you to avoid the problems that are associated with hard-coding file numbers. Hard-coding file numbers enables you to use a file number that may be in use somewhere else in your program. If you attempt to use a file number that has already been opened, Visual Basic generates a runtime error. The FreeFile function returns the next available file number for your use. The following example illustrates how to use the FreeFile function:

```
Dim nFile As Integer
Dim sTextLine As String

' Get the next free file number.
nFile=FreeFile()
' Open the file, read one line, and close the file.
Open "file_in.txt" for Input as #nFile
Line Input #nFile, sTextLine
Close #nFile
```

USING THE FILESYSTEMOBJECT

The second part of this chapter answers some of the frequently asked questions regarding how to use the new FileSystemObject that is provided with Visual Basic 6. The new FileSystemObject provides most of the same functions that were provided previously in the built-in File functions, and it adds a few new capabilities that are not available in the older file access functions. Like most of the recent Microsoft development tools, the FileSystemObject is COM-based, and it provides a set of easy-to-use object collections and methods.

What is the FileSystemObject?

The FileSystemObject is a COM (Component Object Model)–based object that provides access to the computer's file system. It allows your application to list drives, folders, and fields, as well as read and write to text files and other common file system functions. Although the FileSystemObject was introduced primarily to provide file access to scripting applications, it is equally useful in VB programs.

The FileSystemObject is contained in the Microsoft Scripting Runtime object library, which is part of the scrrun.dll. The scrrun.dll must be present at runtime to use the FileSystemObject. Like all other COM object libraries, the FileSystemObject is organized into an object hierarchy, as shown in Figure 10-1.

As Figure 10-1 indicates, all of the different FileSystemObjects are part of the Scripting object library. The FileSystemObject itself contains the Drives collection,

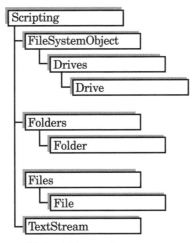

Figure 10-1   The FileSystemObject hierarchy

which contains the listing of the available system drives. The Drive object represents each individual drive. Likewise, the Folders collection is a group of folders or subdirectories, where each Folder object represents a single folder. Also, as you have probably guessed, the Files collection is a group of files contained within a given folder. Each File object represents one operating system file. The TextStream object enables you to create text files and read and write data to them.

How do I use the FileSystemObject in Visual Basic?

You can use the FileSystemObject in Visual Basic by using either *early binding,* in which a reference to the FileSystemObject is added to your VB project, or *late binding,* in which the CreateObject method is used to create an instance of the FileSystemObject at runtime. Although both methods work when you're developing with Visual Basic, using early binding whenever possible is strongly preferable, because it allows the Visual Basic IDE to interact with the object. This provides several interactive development aids, such as the ability to provide IntelliSense prompting during code development and the ability to examine the object's different collections and methods using the Object Browser.

To perform late binding with the FileSystemObject, you must first use the CreateObject method to create an instance of the FileSystemObject. The following code shows how to use late binding to create an instance of the FileSystemObject:

```
Dim fs As Object
Set fs = CreateObject("Scripting.FileSystemObject")
```

After you create the fs FileSystemObject, you can use the various object collections and methods that are provided by the FileSystemObject. However, when you use this method, the Visual Basic IDE can't provide any IntelliSense prompting as you code using the various properties and methods of the FileSystemObject. When you have finished using the object, you should set the object to Nothing, as follows, to make sure that any system resources used by the object are released:

```
Fs = Nothing
```

To add the FileSystemObject to your VB project by using early binding, you must add a reference to the FileSystemObject to your VB project, by selecting Project | Components from the Visual Basic menu, and then selecting Microsoft Scripting Runtime from the list of components in the References dialog box. The following illustration shows the FileSystemObject being added to a VB project:

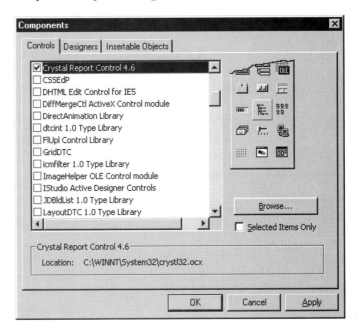

After you add a reference to your project, you can create an instance of the FileSystemObject by declaring it, using the New keyword:

```
Dim fs As New FileSystemObject
```

 How do I use the FileSystemObject to list the drives on a system, and how can I see what type of drives they are?

One of the advantages that the FileSystemObject has over traditional VB file access functions is its ability to easily list

the drives on the system. To list the system drives by using the FileSystemObject, you must create an instance of the FileSystemObject and then interrogate its Drives collection. Each Drive object in the Drives collection has a set of properties that provides information about the Drive. The following example shows how to list the system drive and check the drive type:

```
Dim fs As New FileSystemObject
Dim oDrives As Drives
Dim oDrive As Drive
Dim sDriveName As String

    ' Clear the list box.
    lstFSONames.Clear

    ' Read the Drives collection.
    Set oDrives = fs.Drives
    For Each oDrive In oDrives
        sDriveName = vbNullString
        sDriveName = sDriveName _
            & oDrive.DriveLetter & ": "
        ' Add the share name for network drives.
        If oDrive.DriveType = Remote Then
            sDriveName = sDriveName & oDrive.ShareName
        ' Add the volume name for removable drives.
        ElseIf oDrive.IsReady Then
            sDriveName = sDriveName _
                & oDrive.VolumeName
        End If

        ' Add the name to the list box.
        lstFSONames.AddItem sDriveName
    Next
```

Variables are declared at the top of this listing. The code in this example is able to declare each object by using the specific FileSystemObject type, because a reference to the Microsoft Scripting Runtime object library has been added to the VB project. Adding the reference enables you to use the specific data types of FileSystemObject, Drives, and Drive.

A new instance of the FileSystemObject, named fs, is created using the New keyword. The Drives object will contain the collection of drives contained in the FileSystemObject, and the Drive object will contain the properties associated with each drive.

After clearing the list box that will display the list of drive names, the oDrives object is set to the Drives collection contained by the fs FileSystemObject. Next, a For Each loop is used to process each element in the Drives collection. Within the loop, a string is constructed that consists of the drive letter and the drive share name for network drives, or the drive volume name for removable drives. The oDrive.DriveLetter property contains the drive letter. Then, the DriveType property is checked to determine the Drive type. The following table shows the possible values for the DriveType property.

Drive Type Constant	Value	Description
Unknown	0	Unknown drive type
Removable	1	Diskette or removable disk drive
Fixed	2	Local hard drive
Remote	3	Network share
CDRom	4	Local CD-ROM drive
RamDisk	5	Local RAM disk drive

In this example, if the drive is identified as a network drive, the network share name from the oDrive.ShareName property is appended to the drive letter. Otherwise, the IsReady property is checked. For removable-media drives and CD-ROM drives, the IsReady property is True if there is media inserted into the drive and the drive is ready. If this is the case, then the volume name of the removable drive that's contained in the oDrive.VolumeName property is appended to the drive letter.

After the string containing the drive letter and additional description is assembled, it is added to the list box name lstFSONames.

How do I list the folders for a given drive?

Listing the folders for a drive is conceptually similar to listing the drives. First, you must create an instance of the FileSystemObject. Then, you must populate the Folders collection for a specified directory. Finally, you simply read the Folders collection. The following listing shows how to retrieve a list of folders from a given drive or subdirectory:

```
Dim fs As New FileSystemObject
Dim oFolders As Folders
Dim oFolder As Folder

lstFSONames.Clear

' Create Folder object.
Set oFolder = fs.GetFolder("C:")
Set oFolders = oFolder.SubFolders

' Retrieve the list of folder names from
' the Folders collection.
For Each oFolder In oFolders
    'Add folder names to the list box.
    lstFSONames.AddItem oFolder.Name
Next
```

The top of this listing shows where the FileSystemObject, Folders collection object, and Folder object are declared. These objects are needed to work the folder information returned by the FileSystemObject. After clearing the list box that will be used to display the folder names, the GetFolder method of the FileSystemObject named fs is used to create an instance of a Folder object that represents the c:\ root directory. Next, the SubFolders method of the oFolder object is used to load the oFolders collection with the names of all the subfolders that are in the c:\ directory.

After the oFolders collection is populated with the names of all the subfolders in the c:\ directory, a For Each loop is used to iterate through the collection of folders. Inside the loop, the name of each Folder object is added to the list box named lstFSONames.

How do I list the files that are in a folder?

Listing the files in a folder is almost identical to listing the subfolders in a folder. To list the files in the folder by using the FileSystemObject, you must first create an instance of the FileSystemObject, and then create a Folder object. Then, you populate a Files collection object from the Folder object. The following code shows how to list the files in a directory by using the FileSystemObject:

```
Dim fs As New FileSystemObject
Dim oFolder As Folder
Dim oFile As File

lstFSONames.Clear

' Create Folder object.
Set oFolder = fs.GetFolder("c:\temp")

' Retrieve the list of filenames from
' the Folders collection.
For Each oFile In oFolder.Files
    ' Add filenames to the list box.
    lstFSONames.AddItem oFile.Name
Next
```

This example shows the FileSystemObject, Folder, and File objects that are declared to work with the file information returned by the FileSystemObject. Much like the code that lists the folder names, in the preceding listing, the GetFolder method is first used to create an instance of a Folder object. Here, the Folder object represents the c:\temp directory.

Next, a For Each loop is used to iterate through the Files collection contained in the oFolder object. Inside the For Each loop, the contents of the Name property of each File object is added to the list box named lstFSONames.

How do I write to a text file by using the TextStream object?

You can write to a text file by using the TextStream object, which enables you to manipulate text files. Using the

TextStream object, you can create text files and read and write to them. The following example shows how to create a text file by using the TextStream object, and then write 50 records to that file:

```
Dim oFSO As New FileSystemObject
Dim oTS As TextStream
Dim i As Integer

' Create and open the file for output.
Set oTS = oFSO.OpenTextFile("c:\temp\fileFSO.txt", _
    ForWriting, True)

' Write 50 records in the file.
For i = 1 To 50
    oTS.WriteLine "Record: " & i
Next

' Close the file.
oTS.Close
```

In the beginning of this listing, a new instance of the FileSystemObject named oFSO is created. Next, a TextStream object named oTS is declared, followed by an integer that will be used as a loop counter. Then, the oTS TextStream object is created using the OpenTextFile method of the FileSystemObject. The OpenTextFile method takes four parameters. The first parameter is required and the last three are optional.

The first parameter is a string that identifies the name of the file that will be opened. The second parameter indicates the open mode. The following table lists the valid open modes:

Open Mode Constant	Value	Description
ForReading	1	The file is opened for reading only.
ForWriting	2	The file is opened for output only.
ForAppend	8	The file is opened for output. All data will be appended to the end of the table.

The third parameter accepts a Boolean value that controls the options for opening a file. This parameter controls

whether a new file can be created if the filename specified in the first parameter doesn't exist. A value of True enables the file to be created, while a value of False prohibits the file from being created.

The fourth parameter specifies the system character format that will be used to open the file. The following format options are valid:

Format Constant	Value	Description
TristateUseDefault	−2	Opens the file using the system default character code
TristateTrue	−1	Opens the file as Unicode
TristateFalse	0	Opens the file as ASCII

In the preceding example, the file named fileFSO.txt in the c:\temp directory will be opened for writing, and if it doesn't exist, it will be created. Then, a For Next loop is used to write 50 records to the file. With the For Next loop, the WriteLine method is used to add data to the file. Unlike the Write method, the WriteLine method automatically adds the CR and LF characters to each line that is written.

After all the data is written to the file, the TextStream object's Close method is used to close the file. After the Close method is executed, no more file operations to the File object are allowed until after the file has been reopened.

 ## How do I use the FileSystemObject to read a file?

Reading from a text file by using the FileSystemObject is very much like writing to a file. First, you must create a new instance of the FileSystemObject. Then, you must create an instance of the TextStream object that will be used to read from the file. The following code illustrates how to read all the records contained in a text file, and then display them in a list box:

```
Dim oFSO As New FileSystemObject
Dim oTS As TextStream
Dim i As Integer

' Clear the list box.
```

```
lstFSONames.Clear

' Open the file for input.
Set oTS = oFSO.OpenTextFile("c:\temp\fileFSO.txt", _
    ForReading)

' Read all the records in the file.
Do While Not oTS.AtEndOfStream
    ' Read the line.
    lstFSONames.AddItem oTS.ReadLine
Loop

' Close the file.
oTS.Close
```

At the top of this listing, the FileSystemObject and the TextStream objects are declared. Next, the list box named lstFSONames, which will be used to display the contents of the text file, is cleared.

The FileSystemObject's OpenTextFile method is used to open the file. In this example, the first parameter specifies that the filename fileFSO.txt in the c:\temp directory will be opened. The ForReading open mode constant in the second parameter indicates that this file can be used only for reading.

Next, a Do While loop is used to read all the records in the file. The Do While loop will continue to execute until the AtEndOfStream property becomes True, which indicates that the end of the file has been reached. Inside the loop, the contents of each line is added to the list box named lstFSONames, using the ReadLine method of the oTS TextStream object.

After all the records have been read from the c:\temp\fileFSO.txt file, the file is closed using the TextStream object's Close method.

Can I use the FileSystemObject to write a binary file?

No. The current FileSystemObject works only with text files and can't write binary files. To write a binary file, you must use the older Open and Write file functions.

Is there an easy way to copy a file using the FileSystemObject?

Yes. After you create an instance of the FileSystemObject, you can use its CopyFile method to copy an entire file, using only one line of code. When you use the CopyFile method, you don't need to explicitly open the file or read each record one at a time. The following listing shows how to use the FileSystemObject's CopyFile method:

```
Dim oFSO As New FileSystemObject
oFSO.CopyFile "c:\temp\fileFSO.Txt", _
    "c:\temp\fileFSO2.Txt", True
```

Tip: *You can also use the File object's Copy method to create a copy of a file.*

After creating a new instance of the FileSystemObject, the CopyFile method is used to make a copy of the c:\temp\fileFSO.txt file. The CopyFile method takes three parameters. The first parameter is a string that specifies the source file to be copied. The second parameter is a string that specifies the name and path of the destination file. The optional third parameter controls whether an existing file will be overwritten. A value of True indicates that any existing file with the same name as the destination file will be overwritten, while a value of False indicates that an existing file won't be overwritten. In this example, the file will be copied to a new file named c:\temp\fileFSO2.txt.

Tip: *The CopyFile method supports wildcard characters in the last portion of the the source-file parameter.*

Can I move a file by using the FileSystemObject?

You can easily move a file by using the FileSystemObject's MoveFile method, which is very similar to using the CopyFile method. However, when the MoveFile method completes, the file will be removed from its original location. The following code shows how to use the MoveFile method.

```
Dim oFSO As New FileSystemObject
oFSO.MoveFile "c:\temp\fileFSO2.txt", _
    "c:\fileFSO2.txt"
```

After an instance of the FileSystemObject named oFSO is created using the New keyword, its MoveFile method is used to move the fileFSO.txt file from the c:\temp directory to the c:\ directory. The MoveFile method accepts two parameters. The first parameter is a string that specifies the path and name of the file to be moved. The second parameter is a string that specifies the destination filename and path.

Tip: *You can rename files when using the MoveFile method by giving the file a new name in the destination parameter. In addition, the MoveFile method supports wildcard characters in the source argument.*

 ## How can I tell whether a file exists?

You can tell whether a file exists with the FileSystemObject's FileExists method. The following code shows how to check for the existence of a file:

```
Dim oFSO As New FileSystemObject

If oFSO.FileExists(txtFileName.Text) Then
    MsgBox txtFileName.Text & " exists"
Else
    MsgBox txtFileName.Text & " is not found"
End If
```

Here, an instance of the FileSystemObject named oFSO is created. Then, the oFSO's FileExists method is executed. The FileExists method accepts one parameter, which contains a String value that identifies the path and name of the file to be checked. It returns a Boolean value that reports the results of the test. A value of True indicates that the file was found, while a value of False indicates that the file was not found.

 How do I delete a file with the FileSystemObject?

You can delete a file by using either the File object's Delete method or the FileSystemObject's DeleteFile method. The following listing illustrates both methods of deleting files:

```
Dim oFSO As New FileSystemObject
Dim oFile As File

' Use the File object.
Set oFile = oFSO.GetFile("c:\temp\fileFSO.txt")
' Delete the file.
oFile.Delete

' Alternatively, use the FSO object's Delete method.
oFSO.DeleteFile "c:\fileFSO2.txt"
```

In the beginning of this listing, an instance of the FileSystemObject named oFSO is created, and then a File object named oFile is declared. Next, the File object's Delete method is used to delete the file c:\temp\fileFSO.txt. An instance of the File object named oFile is created using the FileSystemObject's GetFile method. The GetFile method takes one String parameter, which identifies the path and the name of the file. After an instance of the File object has been created, the Delete method is called to delete the file.

The second part of the listing shows how to delete a file by using the FileSystemObject's DeleteFile method. The DeleteFile method is somewhat easier to use than the File object's Delete method, because it doesn't require you to create an instance of the File object. However, the Delete method may be more appropriate in situations where the File object is needed for other operations. The DeleteFile method takes a single String parameter, which specifies the path and the name of the file to be deleted.

 Can I work with only one file at a time?

No. The FileSystemObject contains several methods that allow you to work with entire folders. The folder-level methods that are present in the FileSystemObject include the CopyFolder, CreateFolder, DeleteFolder, FolderExists, and MoveFolder methods. To work with multiple files, you need to take advantage of the wildcard character support provided by each of these methods.

Chapter 11

Printing with Visual Basic

Answer Topics!

Printing with Visual Basic @ a Glance

This chapter presents a series of questions and answers that will show you how to print reports from Visual Basic.

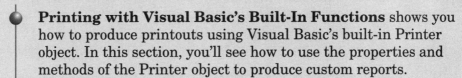 **Printing with Visual Basic's Built-In Functions** shows you how to produce printouts using Visual Basic's built-in Printer object. In this section, you'll see how to use the properties and methods of the Printer object to produce custom reports.

 **Printing with Crystal Reports** introduces you to using the Crystal Reports ActiveX control, supplied with Visual Basic, which provides the ability to design reports interactively and then invoke those reports from within your VB applications.

PRINTING WITH VISUAL BASIC'S BUILT-IN FUNCTIONS

The first part of this chapter deals with using Visual Basic's built-in printing functions. The questions and answers in this section provide an overview of the Windows printing process and address specific issues regarding the use of the VB Printer object and its associated properties and methods.

 How do I print from my Visual Basic application?

Printing is one of the most difficult tasks for a Windows application. Fortunately, Visual Basic's Printer object takes care of most of the difficulties found in the Windows print process. The Printer object relates to a printer in much the same way as a Form object relates to the screen. Essentially, the Printer object is a device-independent logical representation of the physical printer. Your VB application interacts with the Printer object, which in turn sends the Windows-specific print commands to one of the printer device drivers installed on your system. The device driver in turn sends the actual output commands to the printer, which then prints the report. Setting the various properties of the Printer object controls the print quality, orientation, and other output attributes.

From the application standpoint, the Printer object can be thought of as a drawing space. Using the various methods provided by the Printer object, your application draws the text and graphics in the drawing space provided by the Printer object. The Printer object supports many of the same drawing methods to create text and graphics that are used in a form, including Circle, Line, PaintPicture, Print, and PSet. After the Printer object contains the output you want to print, you can use the EndDoc method to send the output directly to the printer. The EndDoc method sends all pending output to the spooler and produces a form feed.

The following example shows how to produce a simple report using Visual Basic's Printer object:

```
Printer.Print "VB Answers! Sample Report Heading"
Printer.Print "This is line one."
Printer.EndDoc
```

Here, the Print method is used to draw two lines on the drawing space provided by the Printer object. The Print method automatically produces a line feed each time it is executed. The drawing space is then sent to the printer by the EndDoc method, which causes the report to be output to the printer.

How can I make my report do page breaks?

When printing longer documents, you can specify when you want a new page to begin, by using the NewPage method. For example, the following code shows how you can use the NewPage method to create a two-page report:

```
Dim nPageCount As Integer

    For nPageCount = 1 To 2
        Printer.Print "VB Answers! Sample Report" _
            & vbTab & vbTab & "Page:" & nPageCount
        Printer.Print "Sample report line."
        Printer.NewPage
    Next nPageCount

    Printer.EndDoc
```

In this example, a For Next loop is used to output two pages to the Printer object. Within the For Next loop, the Print method is used to output one heading line and one report line to each page of the report. The first instance of the Print method prints a sample heading followed by two tab characters and the page number that is contained in the variable nPageCount. The second instance of the Print method outputs the sample report line. A new page is generated when the Printer.NewPage method is executed. After both pages are generated, the EndDoc method is used to send the report to the printer.

Tip: *The NewPage method doesn't send any output to the printer. It only generates a form feed in the drawing space provided by the Printer object. Output is sent to the printer when the EndDoc method is executed.*

 ## How can I use the Print dialog box from my application?

The Print dialog box enables the user to select the printer to use, range of pages to print, print quality, number of copies, printer orientation, and more. This dialog box also enables the user to set a new default printer. You can easily incorporate the Windows Print dialog box into your applications by using the common dialog box object in conjunction with its ShowPrinter method. Before you can use the common dialog box object in your application, however, you must add it to your form by clicking the CommonDialog control in the VB Toolbox and then dragging and dropping it onto your form. After you add the common dialog box object to your form, you can call its ShowPrinter method to display the Print dialog box. The following code displays the Print dialog box when the user clicks the cmdPrinterSetup command button.

```
Private Sub cmdPrinterSetup_Click()
    ' Enable the error handler on cancel.
    dlgSetPrinter.CancelError = True
    On Error GoTo CancelPrintSetup

    ' Display the Print dialog box.
    dlgSetPrinter.ShowPrinter

    ' Get the desired values from the Print
    ' dialog box.
    Printer.Copies = dlgSetPrinter.Copies
    Printer.Orientation = dlgSetPrinter.Orientation

    ' Print the report and exit.
    Printer.Print "VB Answers! Sample Report Heading"
    Printer.Print "This is line one."
    Printer.EndDoc
    Exit Sub

CancelPrintSetup:
    ' Display a message on cancel.
    MsgBox "Printer setup canceled"

End Sub
```

In the beginning of this subroutine, the CancelError property of the dlgSetPrinter common dialog box object is set to True, which causes VB's error-handling routine to be called when the user clicks the Cancel button shown on the common dialog box object. The On Error statement is used to enable error handling for this subroutine. If the user clicks the Cancel button on the Print dialog box, the code will branch to the tag labeled CancelPrintSetup.

The ShowPrinter method of the dlgSetPrinter common dialog box object is then used to display the Print dialog box. An example of the Windows Print dialog box is shown in Figure 11-1.

Like the other common dialog box objects that are used to open and save files, the Print dialog box is modal, and control doesn't return to the application until the user responds to the Print dialog box.

The next section of code assigns two of the values from the Print dialog box to two different Printer properties. All the values that can be configured on the Print dialog box can be returned to your application by using the appropriate

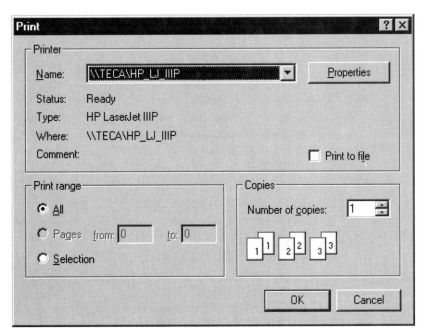

Figure 11-1 Displaying the Print dialog box

properties of the CommonDialog control. In this example, the number of copies set on the dialog box is assigned to the Printer.Copies property, whereas the printer orientation setting is assigned to the Printer.Orientation property.

After the desired values from the Print dialog are returned to your application and assigned to VB's Printer object, you can output the report. In this example, the Print method is used to output two report lines, and then the EndDoc method sends the document to the printer.

At the end of this subroutine is the CancelPrintSetup tag. Program control will branch to this tag if the user clicks Cancel on the Print dialog box. In this example, a message box stating "Printer setup canceled" will be displayed if the user selects the Cancel button.

Can I change printer attributes, such as orientation and output quality, without using the Print dialog box?

Yes. You don't need to use the Print dialog box to assign new values to the different properties of the Printer object. Instead, you can simply assign the appropriate values to the properties that you want to change. The following listing shows how you can change the output orientation, print quality, and number of pages in your application without using the Print dialog box:

```
Dim iSavedOrientation As Integer
Dim iSavedCopies As Integer
Dim iSavedFontSize As Integer

iSavedOrientation = Printer.Orientation
iSavedCopies = Printer.Copies
iSavedFontSize = Printer.FontSize

Printer.Orientation = vbPRORPortrait
Printer.Copies = 2
Printer.FontSize = 16
Printer.Print "VB Answers! Sample Report Heading"
Printer.FontSize = 10
Printer.Print
Printer.Print "This report is using the following _
    settings:"
```

```
Printer.Print "Orientation: " & Printer.Orientation
Printer.Print "Copies: " & Printer.Copies; ""
Printer.Print "Font Size: " & Printer.FontSize
Printer.EndDoc
```

In this example, three variables are declared that will be used to hold the values of some of the various properties of the Printer object. Next, the values from the Printer object's Orientation, Copies, and FontSize properties are assigned to those variables.

The next section of code shows where new values are assigned to the Printer object's Orientation, Copies, and FontSize properties. In this example, the Orientation property is set to portrait mode by using the vbPROPPortriat constant. Then, the number of copies is set to 2 and the FontSize is set to 16-point, which is a good heading size.

Note: *A complete listing of the Printer object constants is provided in Appendix B.*

After you set the Printer object's properties, you output the report by using the Print method. First, the report heading is printed using the 16-point font size. Then, the font size is reduced to 10-point and the body of the report is produced. The Print method with no parameters produces a blank line, and then the next three lines print the current settings of the Printer object's Orientation, Copies, and FontSize settings. Finally, the report is sent to the printer by using the EndDoc method.

How do I change the font and center the heading of a report?

Changing the font that's used in the report heading is a simple matter of setting the correct properties of the Printer object. Centering the title is a bit more complicated, because you need to calculate the correct starting position to begin printing the title text. You can change the font that's used for the heading of a report by adjusting the Printer object's FontSize property. In addition, you can optionally change the FontBold property to print the report heading with a bold

font. Calculating the starting position for the title text requires
you to find the center of the page and then subtract one half
the width of the title text from that median position. The
following PrintHeading subroutine shows how you can print
a bold title in 16-point font that's centered on your report:

```vb
Private Sub PrintHeading()

    Dim bSavedFontBold As Boolean
    Dim iSavedFontSize As Integer
    Dim sHeaderText As String
    Dim iPrtPositionX As Integer
    Dim iPrtPositionY As Integer

    ' Save the current font settings.
    bSavedFontBold = Printer.Font.Bold
    iSavedFontSize = Printer.Font.Size

    ' Set up the header font.
    Printer.Font.Size = 16
    Printer.Font.Bold = True

    ' Set the report title.
    sHeaderText = "VB Answers! Report Title"

    ' Center the title.
    iPrtPositionX = Printer.Width / 2
    Printer.CurrentX = iPrtPositionX - _
        (Printer.TextWidth(sHeaderText) / 2)

    Printer.Print sHeaderText

    ' Reset the font.
    Printer.Font.Size = iSavedFontSize
    Printer.Font.Bold = bSavedFontBold

    ' Left-justify the date.
    sHeaderText = Format(Date, "Long Date")
    Printer.Print sHeaderText
     ' Print a blank line.
    Printer.Print

End Sub
```

At the top of the PrintHeading subroutine, five variables are declared. The bSavedFontBold and iSaveFontSize variables are used to save the Printer object's current font attributes. The sHeaderText string will contain the text that is used for the report heading. The iPrtPostionX and iPrtPositionY variables will be used to hold the current horizontal and vertical coordinates, respectively, of the cursor position within the Printer object's drawing space.

After all the variables are declared, the current font settings from the Printer.Font.Bold and Printer.Font.Size properties are saved in the bSavedFontBold and iSavedFontSize variables. Then, new values are assigned to these properties. The font size is set to 16-point bold.

Next, the report heading is output to the Printer object. First, the report heading text is assigned to the sHeaderText string. Then, the output position for the heading is calculated, as follows:

1. Locate the center of the page, derived by dividing the Printer.Width property in half.

2. Use the TextWidth function to return the width of a text string as it would be printed.

3. Subtract half the width of the heading text from the midpoint of the page.

4. Assign the result of this calculation ito the Printer.CurrentX property, which sets the horizontal print position. Then print the report heading by using the Print method.

After the heading has been centered and output to the Printer object's drawing space, the Print.Font.Size and Printer.Font.Bold properties are restored to their original values, allowing the body of the report to be output in the normal font.

Next, the current date is formatted and assigned to the sHeaderText string, which is subsequently output to the Printer object's drawing space using the Print method. Finally, a blank line is output to the drawing space to allow some separation between the report heading and the report data.

 Note: *Since this subroutine just creates a report header, the EndDoc method is not used to print the contents of the Printer object. This would normally happen after the remainder of the report has been generated.*

How can I print to a specific position of a document?

You can control placement of print output by specifying the drawing coordinates, using the Printer object's CurrentX and CurrentY properties. The Printer object's coordinates are measured from the upper-left corner of the drawing space. The CurrentX property specifies the horizontal output position, while the CurrentY property specifies the vertical output position. The CurrentX property setting is 0 at the Printer object's left edge, and the CurrentY property setting is 0 at the top edge. Coordinates for the Printer object are expressed in twips (each twip is 1/20 of an inch).

By setting the Printer object's CurrentX and CurrentY coordinates before outputting to the drawing space, you can control the specific printing position that your application will use. The following example illustrates how to set the Printer object's CurrentX and CurrentY properties:

```
Dim iPrtPositionX As Integer
Dim iPrtPositionY As Integer
Dim sTextLine As String

' Save the current position.
iPrtPositionX = Printer.CurrentX
iPrtPositionY = Printer.CurrentY

sTextLine = "This will be centered"

' Print in the middle of the page.
Printer.CurrentX = (Printer.Width / 2) - _
    (TextWidth(sTextLine) / 2)
Printer.CurrentY = Printer.Height / 2 - _
    (TextHeight(sTextLine) / 2)

 ' Draw the text.
Printer.Print sTextLine
```

```
' Send to the printer.
Printer.EndDoc

' Restore the current position.
Printer.CurrentX = iPrtPositionX
Printer.CurrentY = iPrtPositionY
```

After the three working variables are declared at the top of this example, the CurrentX and CurrentY coordinates for the Printer object are stored in iPrtPostionX and iPtrPostionY variables. Then, the text that will be printed is assigned to the stextLine String variable.

The next section of code sets the CurrentX and CurrentY coordinates to the center of the page. First, the width of the Printer object is divided in half to find the center of the page. Then, the length of the string that will be printed is divided in half, and that value is subtracted from the center position to get the horizontal starting position of the print string. The midpoint of the height is calculated in exactly the same manner. First, the height of the Printer object is divided in half to find the middle point of the page. Then, the height of the print string is divided in half and subtracted from the middle point to set the beginning vertical coordinates for the print string.

After the CurrentX and CurrentY positions are set, the string is output to the drawing space, and then the EndDoc method is executed to print the page. Finally, the saved CurrentX and CurrentY settings are restored to their initial values.

 ## How can I print graphic images on my reports?

Probably the easiest method to output graphics to a report is to print the contents of an image or picture box by using the Printer object's PaintPicture method, which takes a graphical image and draws it at the output coordinates specified in the method's arguments. For instance, the following code illustrates how you can use the PaintPicture method to print a graphical logo from an image onto the heading of a report:

```
Private Sub PrintGraphicHeading()

    Dim bSavedFontBold As Boolean
    Dim iSavedFontSize As Integer
```

```
Dim sHeaderText As String
Dim iPrtPositionX As Integer
Dim iPrtPositionY As Integer

' Save the current font settings.
bSavedFontBold = Printer.Font.Bold
iSavedFontSize = Printer.Font.Size

' Set up the header font.
Printer.Font.Size = 16
Printer.Font.Bold = True

' Left-justify the picture.
Printer.PaintPicture picLogo.Picture, 0, 0

' Set the report title.
sHeaderText = "VB Answers! Report Title"

' Center the title.
iPrtPositionX = Printer.Width / 2
Printer.CurrentX = iPrtPositionX - _
    (Printer.TextWidth(sHeaderText) / 2)

Printer.Print sHeaderText
' Print a blank line.
Printer.Print

' Set the second-level title.
sHeaderText = "Graphic Heading Report"
Printer.Font.Size = 12

' Center the second.
Printer.CurrentX = iPrtPositionX - _
    (Printer.TextWidth(sHeaderText) / 2)

' Save this line.
iPrtPositionY = Printer.CurrentY
Printer.Print sHeaderText

' Reset the font.
Printer.Font.Size = 10
Printer.Font.Bold = bSavedFontBold
```

```
    ' Reset the line position.
    Printer.CurrentY = iPrtPositionY

    ' Add the date.
    sHeaderText = Format(Date, "Long Date")
    ' Right-justify the date.
    Printer.CurrentX = Printer.Width - _
        (TextWidth(sHeaderText) * 2)

    Printer.Print sHeaderText
      ' Print a blank line.
    Printer.Print

End Sub
```

This example PrinterGraphicHeading subroutine was derived from the PrintHeading subroutine that was presented earlier in this chapter. In the beginning of this subroutine, a set of working variables are declared, and then the Printer object's font size and bold settings are saved to two of those variables. Next, the font size is increase to 16-point and set to bold for the report heading. So far, that's pretty much the same as the standard PrintHeading subroutine. The main difference lies in the use of the PaintPicture method to print the contents of the picture box named picLogo.

 Note: *This example requires a PictureBox control on the current form named picLogo. Its Picture property must be set to the graphic image that you want to display on the form.*

The PaintPicture method draws a graphic into the Printer object's drawing space. The PaintPicture method takes ten parameters. The first three are required, and the remaining seven are optional. The first parameter specifies the picture that will be printed. In this case, the picture is taken from the Picture property of the PictureBox control named picLogo. The second and third parameters specify the X (horizontal) and Y (vertical) coordinates in the drawing space where the picture will be printed. In this example, the

values of 0,0 indicate that the picture will be printed in the upper-left corner of the drawing space. For the PaintPicture method, these coordinates take precedence over any settings that are found in the Printer object's CurrentX and CurrentY properties.

The next two parameters, which are optional, control the width and height of the object that is printed. You can use these parameters to override the size of the printed object. The next two optional parameters control the clipping region of the image that will be printed. The default is 0, which indicates that no parts of the picture will be cut off. The next two optional parameters specify the width and height coordinates from the source object that will be used. Omitting these parameters allows the full width and height of the source image to be used. The final optional parameter accepts an opcode that can alter how bitmap images are painted in the destination drawing space. If this parameter is omitted, a straightforward bit-to-bit copy is used.

 Tip: *You can also use the PaintPicture method to draw graphic images onto a form. This can eliminate the need to place each graphic image into a control.*

The following parts of the PrintGraphicHeading subroutine follow the standard method for printing text. First, the text for the main report heading is assigned to the sHeaderText variable, which is then centered and printed on the document. Next, a second-level heading is centered and output to the drawing space. Before the second-level heading is printed, the vertical coordinate is saved in the iPrtPostionY variable, and the font for the second-level heading is reduced to 12-point. Then, the font is further reduced to 10-point, and the bold is removed before the date is printed in the right side of the drawing space. Immediately before the date is printed, the Printer object's CurrentY coordinate is restored to the same vertical position that was used for the second-level heading.

Following is an example of the report heading that was generated by the PrintGraphicHeading subroutine:

VB Answers! Report Title

Graphic Heading Report   Monday, August 09, 1999

 How do I cancel a print job?

You can terminate the current print job by using the Printer object's KillDoc method. The following example shows how you can use the KillDoc method to cancel a pending report:

```
Printer.Print "VB Answers! Sample Report Heading"
Printer.Print "This is line one."

If vbNo = MsgBox("Print this report?", _
    vbYesNo) Then
  Printer.KillDoc
Else
  Printer.EndDoc
End If
```

In this listing, the first two lines print a simple report heading and data line to the Printer object. Next, the MsgBox function is used to prompt the user to either print the report or cancel the report. The constant vbYesNo used in the second parameter of the MsgBox function causes a Yes button and a No button to be displayed on the message box. The MsgBox function returns a value that indicates which button the user selected. If the user clicks the No button, the value represented by the vbNo constant is returned by the MsgBox function. The If test in the previous example checks for the value of vbNo. If vbNo is returned by the MsgBox function, then the KillDoc method is executed to cancel the report. Otherwise, the EndDoc method is used to send the report to the printer.

 Tip: *The KillDoc method must be executed before the EndDoc method. Otherwise, the EndDoc method will have already sent the output to the printer. If this has happened, then you must cancel the report from Windows Print Manager.*

 ### Does an easy way exist to print a VB form complete with the text and graphics?

Yes. You can use the Form object's PrintForm method to print the current form. The PrintForm method will print an image of all the text, objects, and any graphics that are displayed on the form. The following example shows how you can use the PrintForm method:

```
' Print the form.
Form13.PrintForm
```

The PrintForm method is quite easy to use, and it doesn't accept any parameters. When the PrintForm method is executed, an image of the current form is printed on the default printer.

 Tip: *the KillDoc method works with printouts created with the PrintForm method.*

 ### How do I handle printing errors?

Like other VB runtime errors, printing errors are handled using VB's built-in error handler. However, because printing in Windows is an asynchronous task, any printing errors may not be reported until the subsequent attempt to use the Printer object. This can make printing errors a bit harder to identify than other, more immediate errors. The following table lists some of the most common error codes returned by the Visual Basic error handler.

Error Number	Description
396	Property cannot be set within a page.
482	Printer error.
483	Printer driver does not support the property.
484	Printer driver unavailable.

PRINTING WITH CRYSTAL REPORTS

The second part of this chapter addresses using the Crystal Reports graphical report designer, which entails using the

Crystal Reports ActiveX control. The questions and answers presented here provide a basic understanding about using the Crystal Reports ActiveX control with Visual Basic.

Are any other tools provided with Visual Basic that I can use to print reports?

Yes. VB 6 comes with two additional report designer tools that you can use to create reports. First, VB 6 includes a version of Crystal Reports, a graphical report designer that is licensed to Microsoft by Seagate Software. A version of Crystal Reports has been included with Visual Basic since VB 3. VB 6 includes version 4.6.1, which is the same version that was included with VB 5. Crystal Reports is a very sophisticated and powerful report designer that is primarily oriented toward printing reports that are based on a database. It can use either an Access database or an external ODBC database. With Crystal Reports, you first design the report in design mode and then save the report specifications. Next, you add the Crystal Reports OCX to your form and use it to print the saved report specifications either to the screen or to the printer.

Visual Basic almost always provides you with a choice, and nowhere is that more apparent than in the area of report designers. Starting with VB 6, it also includes the new Microsoft Data Report Designer, which, like Crystal Reports, is designed to print reports based on the data found in an external database. More information about using Data Report Designer is presented in Chapter 15.

I can't find Crystal Reports. How do I install it?

With VB 6, Crystal Reports no longer is installed as a standard part of Visual Basic's setup. However, Crystal Reports is still included on the VB CD-ROM. To install Crystal Reports from the CD-ROM, run the Crystl32.exe Crystal Reports Setup program from the \Common\Tools\ VB\CrysRept directory.

 Note: *Crystal Reports is not included with the Learning Edition of Visual Basic.*

After the Setup program completes, the Report Designer option will be added to VB's Add-Ins menu. Selecting this option starts the Crystal Reports report designer.

Considering the new Microsoft Data Report Designer and the fact that the latest version of Crystal Reports is no longer included with Visual Basic, future versions of Visual Basic may not include the Crystal Reports report designer.

How do I add the Crystal Reports ActiveX control to the VB IDE?

You can add the Crystal Reports ActiveX control to the VB IDE as follows:

1. In Visual Basic, select Project | Components.
2. Scroll to the entry labeled Crystal Report Control 4.6 and click the check box immediately in front of the Crystal Report Control 4.6 entry. The Components dialog box appears, as shown in Figure 11-2.
3. Click OK to add the Crystal Reports ActiveX control to Visual Basic's Toolbox.

Now you can use the ActiveX control in your VB applications by dragging and dropping it onto a form.

What are the basic steps to designing a report?

To design a report by using Crystal Reports, follow these steps:

1. Start the report designer by choosing Add-Ins | Report Designer.
2. Select the New option to design a new report.
3. Choose the desired data source options by using the Create Report Wizard.

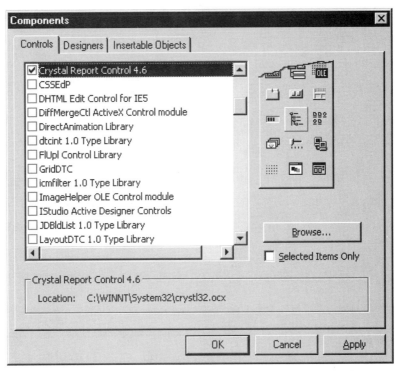

Figure 11-2 Adding the Crystal Reports control to a VB project

4. Interactively design the report by using the report designer. Figure 11-3 shows the Crystal Reports report designer.

5. Save the report specifications.

6. Run the saved report from your VB application.

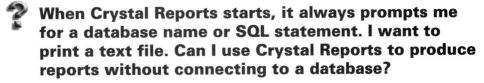 **When Crystal Reports starts, it always prompts me for a database name or SQL statement. I want to print a text file. Can I use Crystal Reports to produce reports without connecting to a database?**

Crystal Reports is expressly designed to connect to an Access or an external ODBC data source, and you can't avoid its prompt for the data source to use. However, Crystal Reports

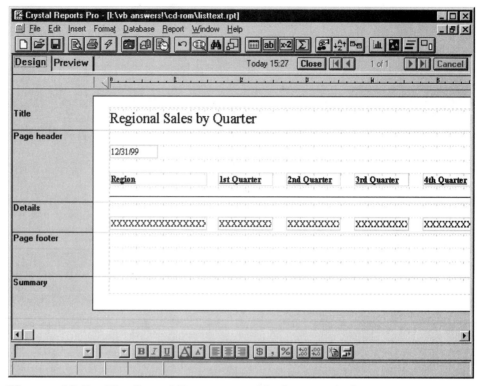

Figure 11-3   The Crystal Reports graphical report designer

can be used to create reports from text files. To use Crystal Reports with data from a text file, you must use the Microsoft ODBC Text Driver. This ODBC driver is supplied with VB, and if it's not present on your system, you can install it by using either the Visual Basic or the Visual Studio Setup program.

To use the Microsoft ODBC Text Driver, follow these steps:

1. Select the New report option from the Crystal Reports menu. The New option automatically runs the Create Report Expert.

2. In Step 1 of the Create Report Expert, choose the SQL/ODBC option.

3. When the Log On Server dialog box is displayed, select the ODBC - Text Files option from the list, as shown in Figure 11-4.

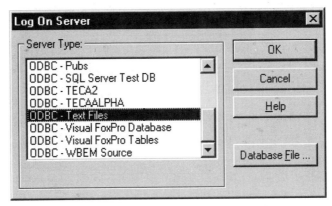

Figure 11-4 Selecting the Microsoft ODBC Text Driver

Select the ODBC Text Driver and click OK to display the Choose SQL Table dialog box, shown in Figure 11-5.

In spite of its name, when used with the Microsoft ODBC Text Driver, the Choose SQL Table dialog box allows you to select the text files to use with Crystal Reports.

4. Select the file or files that you want to use from the list and click the Add button.

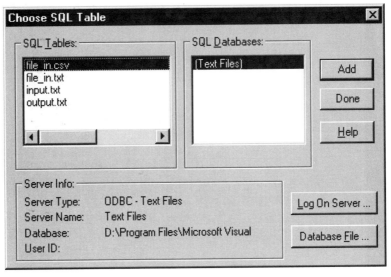

Figure 11-5 Selecting a text file

5. After you select all the files that you want to use, click the Done button.

Now you can continue creating the report by using the Crystal Reports report designer.

 ### How can I use an existing report in my application?

After you create a report using the Crystal Reports report designer and save the report specifications in an RPT file, you can run that report by using the Crystal Reports ActiveX control as follows:

1. First, create an instance of the control on your form by dragging and dropping the control from the Toolbox onto the target form.

2. After you add the control to the form, you must update the control's ReportFileName property with the filename that contains the saved report specifications. Figure 11-6 shows the Crystal Reports ReportFileName property being set with the name of the report specification file.

Tip: *You can also set the ReportFileName property at runtime.*

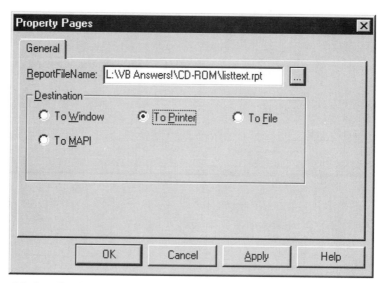

Figure 11-6   Setting the Crystal Reports ReportFileName property

3. After you set the ActiveX control's ReportFileName property to the name of the report specifications that you want to use, you can print the report from your application by executing the PrintReport method, as follows:

```
crwReport.PrintReport
```

Here, the PrintReport method of the Crystal Reports Report Control named crwReport is used to print the report that is specified in the ReportFileName property.

Chapter 12

Dates and Times

Answer Topics!

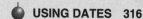

Dates and Times @ a Glance

This chapter presents a series of questions and answers that will show you how to perform some of the most common operations using dates and times.

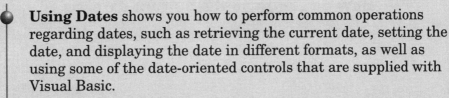

Using Dates shows you how to perform common operations regarding dates, such as retrieving the current date, setting the date, and displaying the date in different formats, as well as using some of the date-oriented controls that are supplied with Visual Basic.

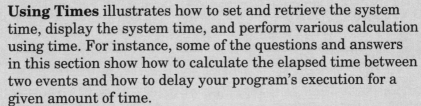

Using Times illustrates how to set and retrieve the system time, display the system time, and perform various calculation using time. For instance, some of the questions and answers in this section show how to calculate the elapsed time between two events and how to delay your program's execution for a given amount of time.

USING DATES

The first part of this chapter presents a series of questions and answers regarding some of the most common date-related development topics.

 ## How do I retrieve the current date?

You can retrieve the current by using Visual Basic's built-in Date function. The Date function does not use any arguments and returns a Variant data type containing the current system date. The following example illustrates how to use the Date function to retrieve the system date:

```
Dim sInfo As String
sInfo = Date
MsgBox sInfo, vbInformation, "Date functions"
```

In this example, a String variable named sInfo is declared to hold the value returned from the Date function. Then, the Date function is executed, and the results are displayed in a message box, as shown here:

 ## How do I format the date to be displayed on the screen?

The Format function can be used to display the date in a variety of different ways. The Format function takes a value to be formatted along with a format keyword that specifies how the formatting should be performed. It returns a Variant data type that is formatted in the manner that was specified. The Format function can be used to reformat many different data types, including numbers and strings, and it provides several handy date-specific keywords. The following code illustrates the date-specific keywords used by the Format function:

```
Dim sInfo As String

sInfo = Format(Date, "Medium Date") & vbCrLf
sInfo = sInfo & Format(Date, "Short Date") & vbCrLf
sInfo = sInfo & Format(Date, "Long Date") & vbCrLf
sInfo = sInfo & Format(Date, "General Date")

MsgBox sInfo, vbInformation, "Date functions"
```

In this example, a String variable named sInfo is declared to hold the different date formats. Then, the Format function is executed four different times. The Format function accepts two parameters. The first parameter contains the expression that will be formatted. In this case, the Date function is used in the first parameter to return the current system date. The second parameter provides the format that will be applied to the value supplied in the first parameter. The format parameter can accept a keyword or a string that contains a set of symbols that control the format that will be applied. In the previous example, each instance of the Format function uses a different date keyword. The following table presents the different date-specific keywords used by the Format function:

Format Keyword	Description
General Date	Displays the date and, optionally, the time. For numbers that include decimal positions, both the date and time are displayed. For integers, only the date is displayed. If there is no integer part, only a decimal value, just the time is displayed.
Long Date	Displays the date using your system's long date format.
Medium Date	Displays the date using your system's medium date format.
Short Date	Displays the date using your system's short date format.

The following illustration displays a message box that shows the results of the different date format keywords.

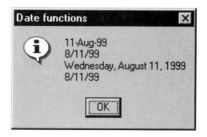

How do I set the date?

You can set the current system date by using the Date statement, as the following example illustrates:

```
Dim tSavedDate As Date
Dim tNewDate As Date

' Save the date and assign a new date.
tSavedDate = Date
tNewDate = #9/1/1999#

' Set the new date.
Date = tNewDate

' Show the changed date.
lblNewDate.Caption = Date

' Restore the original date.
Date = tSavedDate
```

At the top of this listing, two variables are declared using the Date data type. Like most other VB variables, dates can be stored by using either the Date data type or the Variant data type. However, it's best to get into the habit of storing each variable in the correct data type. Next, the current date is assigned to the tSavedDate variable, and the tNewDate variable is set to the date 9/1/1999. Note that date literals are treated differently than strings or numbers. Date literals are enclosed using a pair of matching # symbols.

The next statement sets the system date with the contents of the tNewDate variable. In this example, the new date will be set to 9/1/1999. After the new system date is assigned, the Date function is used to display the new system date in a Label control named lblNewDate. At the end of this listing, the Date statement is used again to restore the current system date to its original value.

How can I check a value for a valid date?

You can use the IsDate function to test the contents of a variable for a valid date. The following code shows how to use the IsDate function:

```
If IsDate(txtDate.Text) Then
    MsgBox "Date OK", vbOKOnly
Else
    MsgBox "Invalid date", vbExclamation
End If
```

This example uses the IsDate function to test the contents of the TextBox control named txtDate. The IsDate function uses a single parameter that contains the date value to be tested. It returns a Boolean value, where True indicates that the value was a valid date, and False indicates that the date was invalid. In this example, if the value contained in the txtDate.Text property is a valid date, a message box will be displayed with the text "Date OK." Otherwise, the message will display "Invalid date."

Note: *For Windows 9x systems, valid dates include January 1, 1980 through December 31, 2099. For Windows NT systems, valid dates range from January 1, 1980 through December 31, 2079.*

How do I calculate the number of days between two dates?

The DateDiff function can be used to determine the number of days between two different dates. It can also perform several other date-related calculations, including determining the number of months between two dates, the number of weeks between today and the end of the year, as well as many other intervals between two dates. An example of using the DateDiff function to determine the number of days between two dates follows.

```
Dim lDays As Long

' Calculate the number of days.
lDays = DateDiff("d", txtDate1.Text, txtDate2.Text)

' Display the results in label.
lblResult.Caption = lDays
```

At the top of this listing, the lDays integer variable is declared, which will be used to hold the results of the DateDiff function. Next, the DateDiff function is used to calculate the number of days between two dates that are supplied in different text boxes. The DateDiff function accepts five parameters. The first three are required and the last two are optional. The first parameter is a string expression that specifies the interval that will be calculated. The following table presents the valid values for the first parameter of the DateDiff function:

Value	Description
yyyy	Year
q	Quarter
m	Month
y	Day of year
d	Day
w	Weekday
ww	Week
h	Hour
n	Minute
s	Second

 Tip: *In spite of its name, the DateDiff routine can also be used to calculate the difference between two times.*

The second and third parameters contain the dates that you want to use in the calculation. The DateDiff function subtracts the date in the third parameter from the date in the second parameter. If the date in the third parameter refers to a later point in time than the date in the second parameter, then the DateDiff function returns a negative number. The optional fourth parameter specifies the first day of the week that will be used in the calculation. If this parameter is not supplied, then Sunday is assumed to be the first weekday. The optional fifth parameter specifies the first week of the year for the calculation. If this is blank, then the week of January 1 is used as the default value.

After the difference between the two dates has been determined, the results are assigned to the lDays variable, which is then displayed in the Label control named lblResult.

Do any controls enable the user to enter dates?

Yes. You can use either the MaskedEdit control or the DateTimePicker control to enter dates. The MaskedEdit control is found in the msmask32.ocx and can be useful for formatting the dates that are entered; however, to present dates or validate dates, it must be used in conjunction with code using Visual Basic's Date function. The DateTimePicker control is found in the mscomct2.ocx and presents a drop-down box that allows the user to choose a desired date for the list.

The MaskedEdit control's Mask property controls the input mask that's used. The values entered into the Mask property may contain a combination of placeholders and literals that format the test that is entered into the MaskedEdit control. (More information about using the MaskedEdit control can be found in Chapter 8.) The following example shows how to set the Mask property of the MaskedEdit control to format a Date input field:

```
Private Sub Form_Load()
    mskDate.Mask = "##-##-##"
    mskDate.Text = Format(Date, "mm-dd-yy")
End Sub
```

This example shows the Mask property of the MaskedEdit control being set during the Form_Load subroutine. The Mask property controls the format that will be available for input. This example presents an input field that allows __-__-__ (two digits separated by a dash). The following table presents some of the common masks that are used for date input:

Mask Property	Description
##-???-##	Medium date: 20-May-92
##-##-##	Short date: 05-20-92

After setting the Mask property, the Format function is used to assign the current date to the Text property of the MaskedEdit control. The Format function is used because the MaskedEdit control requires that data entered into the Text property follow the formatting rules specified in the Mask property.

In addition to formatting the input of the date, you probably will also want to validate the values that are entered in the MaskedEdit control, to make sure that they are valid dates. The following code shows how to validate date input to a MaskedEdit control:

```
Private Sub mskDate_Validate(Cancel As Boolean)

    If Not IsDate(mskDate.Text) Then
        Beep
        MsgBox "You must enter a valid date"
        Cancel = True
    End If

End Sub
```

In this mskDate_Validate subroutine, the IsDate function is used to test the value of the data entered into the mskDate control. If the data is not a valid date, a message box is displayed stating that a valid date must be entered.

Using the DateTimePicker control allows the user to select the desired date either from a month calendar drop-down box or by using a spin button control. The display of the DateTimePicker control is governed by the setting of its UpDown property. If the UpDown property is set to False, then the drop-down month-view box is displayed. If the UpDown property is set to True, then a date spin button control is displayed, as you can see in the following illustration.

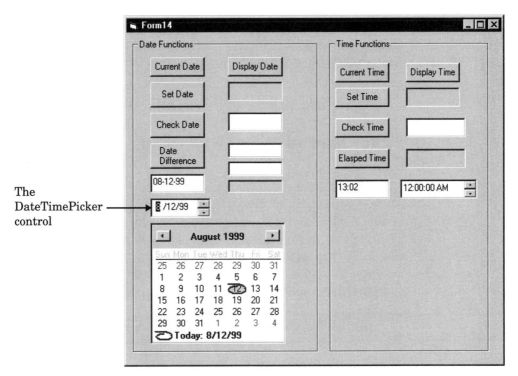

The
DateTimePicker
control

In spin button mode, the up and down buttons increment and decrement the vales displayed in the month, days, and year portion of the control.

The DateTimePicker control's Format property sets the type of values that will be displayed and accepted as input to the DateTimePicker control. The following table lists the allowable values for the Format property:

Format Property	Value	Description
dtpLongDate	0	Long date format
dtpShortDate	1	Short date format (default)
dtpTime	2	Time format
dtpCustom	3	Custom format (controlled by the CustomFormat property)

The MinDate and MaxDate properties can be used to set the allowable range of values that can be entered in the control. The date that's selected by the user can be accessed using the control's Value property. The following code illustrates retrieving the date selected using the DateTimePicker control:

```
lblDate.Caption = dtpDate.Value
```

Does any control allow the user to select a month and year?

Yes. You can use the MonthView control to add a calendar-like display to your VB project. Like the DateTimePicker control, the MonthView control is found in the mscomct2.ocx. Unlike the DateTimePicker control, which displays a calendar window as part of its drop-down box, the MonthView control always displays a calendar on the form. The following illustration shows the MonthView control:

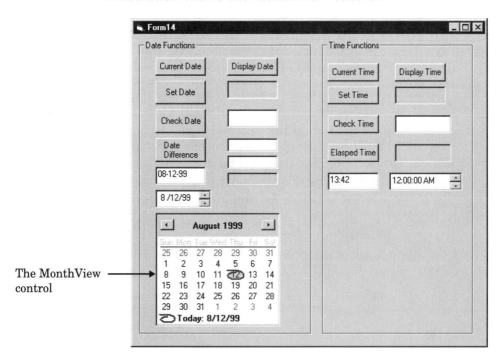

The MonthView control

You can use the left and right arrows at the top of the control to page back and forth between the different months. A red circle indicates the current day selected on the MonthView control. The current day can be accessed by using the control's Value property. The following example shows how to assign the selected day from the MonthView control named mvwDate to the Caption property of a Label control:

```
lblDate.Caption = mvwDate.Value
```

USING TIMES

The second part of this chapter addresses some of the common questions and answers regarding using time data in your VB applications.

 ## How do I retrieve the current time?

You can retrieve the current time by using Visual Basic's Time function. Much like the Date function, the Time function does not use any arguments, and it returns a Variant containing the current system time. The following example shows how to retrieve the system time by using the Time function:

```
Dim sInfo As String
sInfo = Time
MsgBox sInfo, vbInformation, "Time functions"
```

First, a String variable named sInfo is declared to hold the value returned from the Time function. Next, the Time function is executed and the results are displayed in a message box, as shown here:

 ## How do I format the time for display purposes?

The Format function can be used to format the time for output to forms, controls, or reports. The Format function takes a time value to be formatted along with a time-specific format keyword that specifies how the formatting should be performed. It returns a Variant data type that is formatted in the manner that was specified by the format keyword. The following code shows how to format the time using the Format function:

```
Dim sInfo As String

sInfo = Format(Time, "Medium Time") & vbCrLf
sInfo = sInfo & Format(Time, "Short Time") & vbCrLf
sInfo = sInfo & Format(Time, "Long Time") & vbCrLf

MsgBox sInfo, vbInformation, "Time functions"
```

First, a String variable named sInfo is declared to hold the different time formats. Then, the Format function is executed three times using the different time format keywords. The first parameter of the Format function contains the expression that will be formatted. In this example, the Time function is used to return the current system time. The second parameter of the Format function supplies the format keyword that governs how the time will be formatted for output. The format parameter can accept a keyword or a string that contains a set of symbols that control the format that will be applied. The following table presents the different time-specific keywords used by the Format function:

Format Keyword	Description
Long Time	Displays a time using your system's long time format. The long time format includes hours, minutes, and seconds.
Medium Time	Displays a time in 12-hour format using hours, minutes, and the A.M./P.M. indicator.
Short Time	Displays a time using the 24-hour format.

The following illustration displays a message box showing the output of the different time format options:

How do I set the system time?

You can set the current system time by using the Time statement. The following example shows how to use the Time statement:

```
Dim tSavedTime As Date
Dim tNewTime As Date

' Save the time and assign a new time.
tSavedTime = Time
tNewTime = #4:18:11 PM#

' Set the new time.
Time = tNewTime

' Show the changed time.
lblNewTime.Caption = Time

' Restore the original time.
Time = tSavedTime
```

In the first two lines of this listing, two variables are declared using the Date data type. Times can be stored using the Date, Single, or Variant data types. In this case, the two variables will be used to store the saved time and to hold the new time that will be set. Next, the current system time is saved in the tSavedDate variable, and the tNewTime variable is set to 4:18:11 P.M. As with dates, time literals are enclosed using a pair of matching # symbols.

The next statement sets the system date with the contents of the tNewTime variable. Then, the contents of the

tNewTime variable are assigned to the Label control named lblNewTime. Finally, the Time statement is used to restore the current system time to its original value.

 ## How do I check a variable for a valid time?

The IsDate function is used to test a variable for a valid time, exactly as you use it to test for a valid date. The following listing shows how to use the IsDate function to test a time value:

```
If Not IsDate(txtTime.Text) Then
    MsgBox "Invalid time", vbExclamation
End If
```

The IsDate function returns a Boolean value of False if the value in its first parameter is not a valid time. In this example, if the value contained in the txtTime.Text property is an invalid date, then a message will display the text "Invalid time."

 ## How can I calculate the time to execute a given section of code?

To calculate the time to execute a given section of code, use the Timer function to set up a beginning time before the given section of code executes, and then subtract that value from the results of the Timer function that is executed following the given section of code. The Timer function returns a Single variable that contains the number of seconds that have elapsed since 12:00 A.M. The Timer function calculates the fractions of a second six places to the right of the decimal point. The following code illustrates using the Timer function to calculate the execution time for a given section of code:

```
Dim lCount As Long
Dim tStartTime As Single
Dim tDiffTime As Single

' Set the beginning time.
tStartTime = Timer
```

```
' Loop 100,000 times.
For lCount = 1 To 100000
    DoEvents
Next

' Calc the difference from the current time.
tDiffTime = Timer - tStartTime

lblTimeDiff.Caption = tDiffTime
```

In the beginning of this code, three working variables are declared. The Long variable named lCount will be used as a loop counter, while the tStartTime and tDiffTime variables will be used to contain the starting time and the calculated time difference, respectively.

Next, the Timer function is used to set the starting number of seconds in the tStartTime variable, and then a For Next loop is executed 100,000 times. After the loop has completed, the tStartTime variable is subtracted from the current Timer value and the results are placed in the tDiffTime variable, which is then displayed in a Label control.

What controls are available that will help me to enter time values in my application?

You can use either the MaskedEdit control or the DateTimePicker control to enter time values into your applications. The MaskedEdit control simply formats the input area for the time. It must be coupled with the IsDate function if you also need to validate the time values entered by the user. The DateTimePicker control displays either a graphical drop-down box or a spin button control that allows the user to select the time interactively. The following code shows how to use the MaskedEdit control for time input:

```
mskTime.Mask = "##:##"
mskTime.Text = Format(Time, "hh:ss")
```

The Mask property controls the format that governs user input. This example will present an input field (__:__) that allows two digits separated by a colon. The following table presents some of the common masks that are used for date input:

Mask Property	Description
##:## ??	Medium time. Example: 05:36 A.M.
##:##	Short time. Example: 17:23

Next, the Format function is used to assign the current time to the Text property of the MaskedEdit control. The Format function is used because the MaskedEdit control requires that all data entered into the Text property conform to the formatting rules specified in the Mask property.

You can then use the MaskedEdit control's Validate subroutine to verify the time values that are entered in the MaskedEdit control. The following code shows how to use the MaskedEdit control's Validate function for time data:

```
Private Sub mskTime_Validate(Cancel As Boolean)

    If Not IsDate(mskTime.Text) Then
        Beep
        MsgBox "You must enter a valid time"
        Cancel = True
    End If

End Sub
```

The IsDate function is used to test the time value entered into the mskTime control. If the value is not a valid time, then a message box is displayed.

For time input, the DateTimePicker control allows the user to select the desired time from a spin button control. To use the DateTimePicker control with time data, you must first set the Format property to 2 - dtpTime. The user can then increment or decrement the time value by clicking the up and down buttons that are displayed on the DateTimePicker control. For time data, the DateTimePicker control can't display a drop-down calendar, as it can for date values. Following is an example showing the DateTimePicker control used for time input.

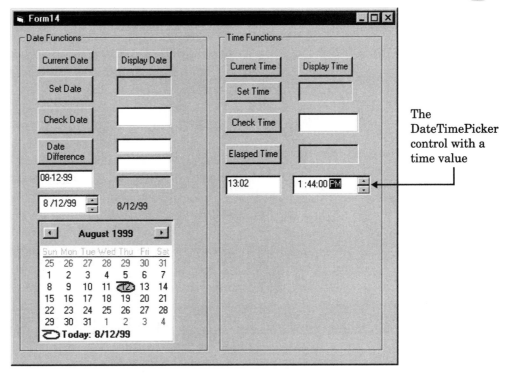

The DateTimePicker control with a time value

The time selected by the user in the DateTimePicker control can be accessed via the control's Value property. The following code illustrates retrieving the selected time from the DateTimePicker control:

```
lblTime.Caption = dtpTime.Value
```

Tip: *To dynamically update the time displayed in the DateTimePicker control, you can add a Timer control to your form and use the Time function to set the DateTimePicker control's Value property when the Timer event fires.*

I tried using a loop and timer to delay my program, but noticed that this drives my CPU usage to 100 percent. Does a better way exist to pause my program?

Yes, you can use the Win32 API Sleep function to implement a pause in your VB applications. The Sleep function suspends

the execution of the current thread for the duration of the interval specified when the Sleep function is called. While the program is suspended, it consumes no CPU. Before you can use the Sleep function in your applications, you must make a declaration for the function, as follows:

```
Public Declare Sub Sleep Lib "kernel32"
    (ByVal dwMilliseconds As Long)
```

In this declaration, the Sleep function is called from the kernel32.dll and accepts a single parameter that specifies the suspend interval, in milliseconds.

After you declare the Sleep function, you can use it in your applications. The following example shows how you can use the Sleep function to pause your program execution for five seconds:

```
Sleep 5000
```

 How can I make my application execute a function at a regular interval?

Visual Basic's Timer control allows your application to execute a section of code at regular intervals. The Timer control is part of the standard VB Toolbox, and before you can use it, you must drag and drop the Timer control onto a Form. To begin using the Timer control, you must first set the Timer control's Interval property and Enabled property. The Interval property accepts values in milliseconds and specifies the duration of time that will elapse between timer events. The Enabled property essentially turns the Timer control on an off. When the Timer control's Enabled property is set to True, the Timer control's Timer event will fire at the interval specified in the Interval property. When the Enabled property is set to False, the Timer event will not fire.

The following code illustrates how you can use the Timer control to display a dynamically updating timer stamp in a Label control:

```
Timer1.Interval = 1000
Timer1.Enabled = True
```

This listing shows how the Timer's Interval property can be set to an interval of one second. Then, the Enabled property is set to True, which starts the Timer.

Once per second, the Timer control will fire a Timer event, and the code that's contained in the Timer control's Timer subroutine will be executed. The following code shows an example Timer subroutine:

```
Private Sub Timer1_Timer()
    lblTimerMsg.Caption = Time
    DoEvents
End Sub
```

In this Timer1_Timer subroutine, the Caption property of a Label control named lblTimer is updated with the current system time each instance that the Timer subroutine is executed. The DoEvent line has been added to ensure that the updated Caption property will be repainted on the screen.

The Timer control's Enabled property can be toggled on or off at any time while your application is running. The following code shows how you can turn the Timer control on and off when the user clicks the button named cmdTimer:

```
Private Sub cmdTimer_Click()

    If Timer1.Enabled = True Then
        Timer1.Enabled = False
        cmdTimer.Caption = "Start Timer"
    Else
        Timer1.Enabled = True
        cmdTimer.Caption = "Stop Timer"
    End If

End Sub
```

Chapter 13

Classes, Objects, and Collections

Answer Topics!

Classes, Objects, and Collections @ a Glance

This chapter presents a series of questions and answers that show you how to create and use classes, objects, and collections in your Visual Basic applications.

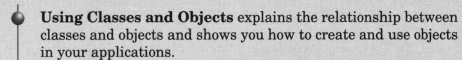

- **Using Classes and Objects** explains the relationship between classes and objects and shows you how to create and use objects in your applications.

- **Using Collections** begins by providing an overview of VB collections and then shows how you can create your own collections and access their elements.

USING CLASSES AND OBJECTS

The questions and answers in this section provide the essential information that you need to know to create and use classes and objects in your VB applications. The first questions and answers in this section explain the relationship between classes and objects, and the later questions and answers show you how to implement objects in your VB applications.

 What's an object?

Objects are quite different from standard VB variables. An object is like a related group of functions and variables all combined into one entity. Objects consist of properties, methods, and events. Properties are similar to variables in that they both contain data. The contents of an object's properties can be assigned and accessed through application code. Object properties are commonly used to customize the way an object functions. An object's methods are similar to functions. Like functions, methods are executed, perform a specific action, and can return data to your application. In other words, methods support the things that you can do with an object. To this combination, objects also add events. Events are hooks into the different actions that an object performs. You can add your own code into the event subroutines that are supported by an object. Events can be thought of as the things that an object does.

If all of this sounds familiar, it should. Although you may not be familiar with creating objects by using Visual Basic, you most certainly are familiar with using them. This same object model of properties, methods, and events is supported by all the VB components that you commonly use to write applications, including both the forms and the various ActiveX controls that an application might use.

What's the difference between a class and an object?

Objects are created from classes. In other words, classes are the source code that is used to define an object's characteristics. Writing the source code to create a class

does not create an object. The source code that comprises the class defines the properties, methods, and events that are possessed by the object. The object itself is a particular instance of the class that is created when your application runs. An instance of the object is created either by adding a reference to your project for the class and then declaring the object in your application by using the Dim As keywords, or by using the generic CreateObject function. After either of these techniques has been executed, an object will have been created, or, to use the object-oriented programming terminology, will have been *instantiated.*

A user-created class normally is prefixed with the letter *c*, indicating that it is a class. When the class is instantiated, the resulting object is typically prefixed with the letter *o*, showing that it is an object. For instance, the class named cNumber might be used to instantiate an object named oMyNumber.

What's the difference between a late bound object and an early bound object?

When an instance of an object is created by adding a reference and then declaring the object by using the Dim statement, the object is known as *early bound.* Early bound refers to the fact that the object is known early—during design time. Otherwise, when an object is created using the CreateObject function, the object is called *late bound,* referring to the fact that the application does not have knowledge about the object until late—during runtime. Although the object created is the same using either method, early binding provides a developmental advantage. Early binding enables the VB IDE to provide IntelliSense prompting and statement completion, as well as syntax checking. These features are not available for late bound objects, because the IDE has no knowledge of the object. The following listings illustrate the difference between creating an object by using early binding and by using late binding. The first example illustrates late binding:

```
Private Sub CreateLateBoundObject()

' This shows how to create a late bound object.
```

```
' Use the generic object data type.
Dim oXL As Object

' Supply the class name.
Set oXL = CreateObject("excel.application")

' Now that the object has been instantiated,
' you can use it.
oXL.Visible = True

End Sub
```

In this example, the oXL object is declared using the generic As Object keyword. This tells Visual Basic that oXL is an object, but it doesn't tell VB what type of object it is. Therefore, the IDE is not aware of the properties, methods, or events that the oXL object may support.

Next, the CreateObject function is used to create an instance of the class named excel.application. For this to work, the Excel.Application class must be registered. This is typically performed as a part of Excel's installation process. After the oXL object has been instantiated, you can access its properties, methods, and events in your application. This example shows its Visible method being set to True, which causes the Excel application to appear.

The next example illustrates how to create an object by using early binding. However, before you begin coding, you must set a reference in your project to the object library that will be created. When you set a reference to an object library, you notify Visual Basic that you may be using the objects in that type library. The VB IDE then loads the type library into memory, enabling it to recognize these objects and their attributes within the IDE. You can set a reference to the Microsoft Excel Object library by using Project | Reference option from Visual Basic's main menu. Then, in the References dialog box, check the entry labeled Microsoft Excel 8.0 Object Library, as shown in Figure 13-1.

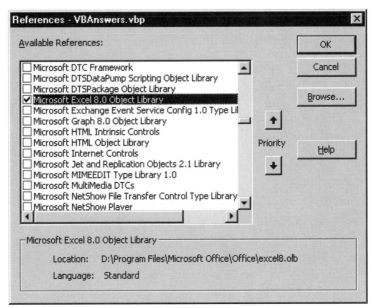

Figure 13-1 Setting a reference for early binding

After you add the reference to the IDE, you can declare the object using its specific data type. The following example shows how to create an object by using early binding:

```
Private Sub CreateEarlyBoundObject()

' This shows how to create an early bound object.
' Use the specific Excel.Application class name.
Dim oXL As New Excel.Application

' Now that the object has been instantiated,
' you can use it.
oXL.Visible = True

End Sub
```

In this example, the oXL object has been declared using the specific Excel.Application object type. Visual Basic knows about this object type because of the reference that was added to the IDE. The New keyword is required to create a new

instance of the oXL object. After you create the oXL object, you can use its properties, methods, and events in your application. Here, again, the object's Visible property is set to True, which causes the Excel application to appear.

When you are done working with the object, you should explicitly release the memory and system resources used by the object, by setting the object to Nothing, as shown in the following code:

```
' Destroy the object.
Set oXL = Nothing
```

How can I find an object's class?

When using late binding and generic object types, it can be difficult to determine the type of a given object. Fortunately, Visual Basic provides two ways that can help you determine the class of a given object:

- **TypeOf keyword** Must be used as part of an If statement and include the name of the class that you are checking for.
- **TypeName function** More powerful than the TypeOf keyword, it accepts the object name as an argument and returns the class name as a String variable.

The following listing demonstrates using the TypeOf keyword and TypeName function:

```
' Use the generic object data type.
Dim oXL As Object

' Supply the class name.
Set oXL = CreateObject("excel.application")

' Check the object type.
If TypeOf oXL Is Excel.Application Then
    MsgBox "oXL is an Excel object"
Else
    MsgBox "oXL is not an Excel object"
End If

' Get the class name.
MsgBox "oXL is: " & TypeName(oXL)
```

After you create an instance of the oXL object by using the CreateObject function, you use the TypeOf keyword to test whether the object is an Excel.Application object. If it is, then a message box will be displayed stating that oXL is an Excel object. Otherwise, the message box will display the string stating that oXL is not an Excel object.

Next, the use of the TypeName function is demonstrated. In this example, the name of the object name oXL is passed as a parameter to the TypeName function. Then, the TypeName function will return a string that contains the class name. That string will then be displayed in a message box.

How do I create a class?

The first step to create a class is to add a class module to your VB project. The class module contains the source code that defines one or more classes. The source files for a class module end with the extension .cls. You can add a class module either by selecting the Project | Add Class Module option from the VB menu or by right-clicking in the Project window and selecting the Add | Class Module option from the pop-up menu. The Add Class Module dialog box, shown in Figure 13-2, will be displayed.

The Add Class Module dialog box allows you to add four different types of class modules. The first option, Class Module, adds a simple class module with no source code. If you select this option, you need to manually add the definition of the class and its properties, methods, and events. The Complex Data Consumer and Data Source options add class modules that contain predefined properties, methods, and events that allow you to integrate your classes with external data sources. Essentially, a Complex Data Consumer works with data retrieved from a data source, whereas the Data Source class itself links the application to an external data source, such as a SQL Server database.

The Class Builder option starts a powerful class design tool that allows you to interactively define the attributes of one or more classes that are contained in your VB project. The Class Builder then automatically generates the source code to implement the various properties, methods, and events that were defined.

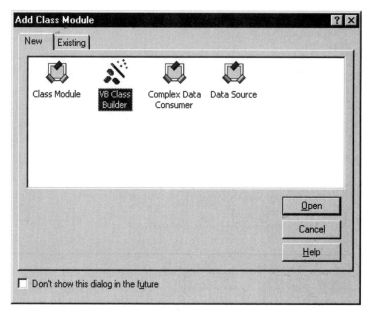

Figure 13-2 Adding a class module using the Add Class Module dialog box

---

 Tip: *The Class Builder can be used both to create new classes and to work with existing classes. When the Class Builder starts, the definitions of any existing classes are automatically displayed in the VB Class Builder window.*

After you select the Class Builder option, you need to use the Class Builder's New | Class menu option, shown in Figure 13-3, to create a new class.

Selecting the New | Class option displays the Class Module Builder, which enables you to name the class and specify the name of another class that this class may be based on. The Class Module Builder is shown in Figure 13-4.

In this example, a simple class to contain a number value has been given the name cNumber. This class isn't based on any other classes. If it were based on another class, the public properties, methods, and events for the named class would be automatically included in the new class. Clicking the OK button adds the base class name to the Class Builder.

The next step in creating a new class by using the Class Builder is to define the properties for the class. In this

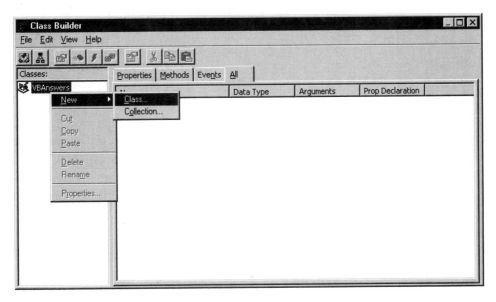

Figure 13-3 Creating a new class by using the Class Builder

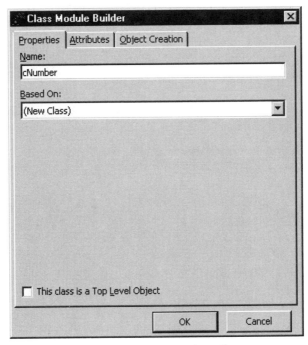

Figure 13-4 Defining the class name and attributes

example, the cNumber class will use a single property named Value that will contain the numeric value of the class. To add a new property to an existing class, click the Properties tab to make it active. Then, right-click the Properties tab and select the New Property option from the pop-up menu. The Property Builder window is displayed, similar to the window shown in Figure 13-5.

Figure 13-5 shows that the new property has been assigned the name Value and has a data type of Variant. It has also been declared Public, which allows it to be accessed by the calling application or other classes. Checking the Default Property box allows the contents of the Value property to be retrieved by default when the cNumber class name is used without a qualifying property, method, or event name. Clicking the OK button adds the Value property to the cNumber class.

The next step to create a new class by using the VB Class Module Builder is to define the methods that will be used by the class. To add methods to a class, first click the Methods tab of the Class Builder window. After the Methods tab is

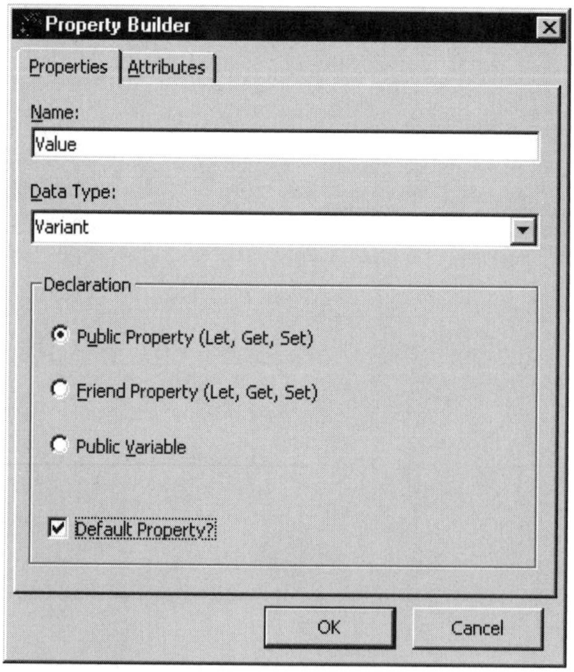

Figure 13-5 Defining the property attributes

active, right-click the tab and select the New Method option from the pop-up menu. A Method Builder window like the one shown in Figure 13-6 will be displayed.

A method named Add is displayed in Figure 13-6. In this example, the Add method will be used to add a number that's supplied as a parameter to the Add method to the number that's stored in the Value property. The Return Data Type field will return the updated value from the Value property to the calling application.

After the name of the method has been defined, the next step is to add any necessary parameters to the method. You can add a parameter by clicking the + button, which displays the Add Argument dialog box, shown in Figure 13-7.

One argument, called ValueToAdd, is being added to the Add method in Figure 13-7. ValueToAdd accepts a Variant data type and is a required parameter. In cases where the parameter is optional, you can check the Optional check box near the bottom of the dialog box. Clicking the OK button

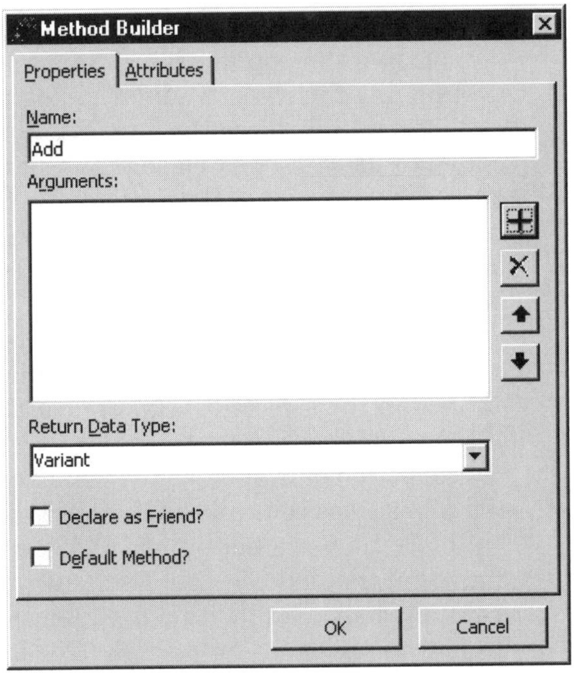

Figure 13-6   Adding methods by using the Class Builder

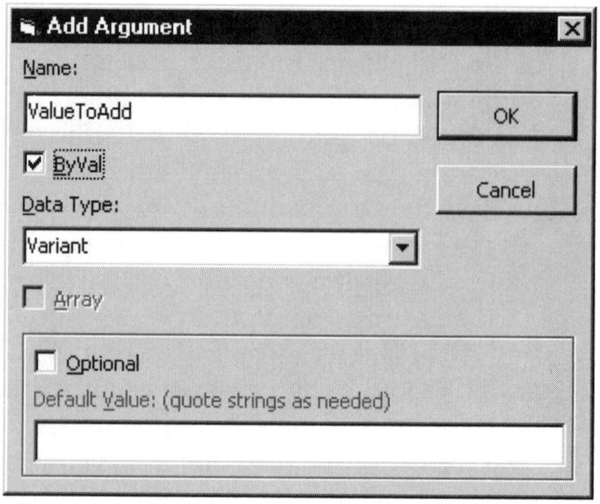

Figure 13-7 Adding arguments to a method

adds the argument to the new Add method. After all the methods and arguments have been added, the last step is to add any events that the class will support. To add a new event, click the Events tab of the Class Builder window, right-click the Events tab, and then select the New Event option from the pop-up menu Figure 13-8 shows adding an event using the Event Builder dialog box.

Figure 13-8 shows that the event named Change has been added to the cNumber class. The Change event is not using any parameters. It will be called any time the value stored in the Value property is changed. The Change event must be called from within the class itself by using the RaiseEvent method.

By clicking the All tab of the Class Builder window, you can see all the properties, events, and methods that are defined in the selected class. Figure 13-9 presents a summary of the example cNumber class.

Here, you can see that the final version of the example cNumber class contains one property, named Value; four Methods, named Add, Subtract, Multiply, and Divide; and one event, named Change. Each different type of member in a class is associated with a unique icon. A small window and hand icon identifies properties. The default property also

Figure 13-8 Adding events by using the VB Class Builder

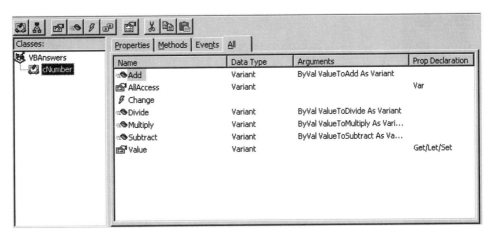

Figure 13-9 Viewing the class members

includes a small blue dot. Methods are displayed next to a green flying-block icon, while events are associated with a lightning-bolt icon.

After you define the class by using the Class Builder, you can choose to update the project, and all the code to implement the class and its properties, methods, and events will be automatically generated. You can update your VB project in any of three ways:

- Close the Class Builder and respond Yes to the prompt to save your changes.
- Select File | Update Project from the Class Builder menu.
- Press CTRL+S.

After the changes are saved, you can add your own custom code inside each of the methods, to make the class perform some actual useful functions. The following listing shows both the code that was generated using the Class Builder and the custom code that was added to support the four methods:

```
Option Explicit

' Local variable(s) to hold property value(s).
Private mvarValue As Variant 'local copy
' To fire this event, use RaiseEvent with the
' following syntax:
' RaiseEvent Change[(arg1, arg2, ... , argn)]
Public Event Change()

Public Function Divide(ByVal ValueToDivide As _
    Variant) As Variant
    ' This is code I added to support the method.
    mvarValue = mvarValue / ValueToDivide
    RaiseEvent Change
    Divide = mvarValue
End Function

Public Function Multiply(ByVal ValueToMultiply As _
    Variant) As Variant
    ' This is code I added to support the method.
    mvarValue = mvarValue * ValueToMultiply
```

```
      RaiseEvent Change
      Multiply = mvarValue
End Function

Public Function Subtract(ByVal ValueToSubtract As _
      Variant) As Variant
      ' This is code I added to support the method.
      mvarValue = mvarValue - ValueToSubtract
      RaiseEvent Change
      Subtract = mvarValue
End Function

Public Function Add(ByVal ValueToAdd As Variant) As _
      Variant
      ' This is code I added to support the method.
      mvarValue = mvarValue + ValueToAdd
      RaiseEvent Change
      Add = mvarValue
End Function

Public Property Let Value(ByVal vData As Variant)
' Used when assigning a value to the property, on
' the left side of an assignment.
' Syntax: X.Value = 5
      mvarValue = vData
End Property

Public Property Set Value(ByVal vData As Variant)
' Used when assigning an object to the property, on
' the left side of a Set statement.
' Syntax: Set x.Value = Form1
      Set mvarValue = vData
End Property

Public Property Get Value() As Variant
' Used when retrieving value of a property, on the
' right side of an assignment.
' Syntax: Debug.Print X.Value
      If IsObject(mvarValue) Then
          Set Value = mvarValue
      Else
          Value = mvarValue
      End If
End Property
```

This listing demonstrates what a powerful productivity tool the Class Builder really is. It created all the code required to implement the cNumber class, and then it automatically wrote it to the cNumber.cls source file. The only code that was not generated was the three lines inside of the Add, Subtract, Multiply, and Divide methods.

The first important point to notice in this listing is the declaration of the mvarValue variable. This Variant variable is created to hold the contents of the Value property. It is declared as a private variable to limit the access of the variable to just the methods of the cNumber class. This prevents the internal value from being altered by any external functions or class. Only the methods in the cNumber class can access this variable.

Next, the Change event is declared using the Public Event statement. The Public Event statement declares a user-defined event that can be fired by using the RaiseEvent statement. The Class Builder doesn't know when you may need to fire this event, so the implementation of the RaiseEvent statement must be performed by the developer.

The next significant section of the code is the declaration of the Add, Subtract, Multiply, and Divide methods. The Class Builder wrote the Function and End Function stubs, which provide the base implementation of the method. However, again, the Class Builder doesn't really know what you want each method to do, so it can't write the implementation code. In this case, all the functions work very much alike. Each accepts one required parameter that is used to alter the value stored in the cNumber class's Private mvarValue variable. After the value is updated, the Change event is fired using the RaiseEvent statement, and then the new value is returned to the caller.

The last significant code routines to implement the cNumber class are in the Let, Set, and Get functions shown near the end of the listing. Like the other methods, these routines were created by the Class Builder. However, in the case of properties, the Class Builder knows what these methods need to do to access the contents of a private variable, and can provide all the code required to implement them.

The Let function is used to assign a value to the property when the property is used with an assignment statement. The Set statement is used to assign an object to the property. In this case, since the cNumber class is mainly intended to work with numbers, the Set method is not really appropriate. The Get method is used to retrieve the value of the property, to assign that value to another class or variable.

How do I use the class that I've created?

After you define the class either manually or by using the Class Builder, you can use it in your application by creating an instance of the class and then using the properties, methods, and events that the class provides. The runtime instance of the class is known as an *object*. Objects that are created from VB classes are typically instantiated using the New keyword, although you can also use late binding and the CreateObject function. If the class supports events, then the WithEvents keyword must be used to enable your application to support the user-defined events provided by the object. The following code illustrates how to declare the oMyNumber object with user-defined events:

```
Option Explicit
Private WithEvents oMyNumber As cNumber
```

The Private WithEvents statement is placed at the module level to declare an object named oMyNumber of the oNumber class. Declaring the object at the module level allows the object to be used in any of the functions that are present in the module. The optional WithEvents keyword is used to enable Visual Basic to respond to the object's events.

Tip: *For objects that do not need to support events, you can use the New keyword at the module level to instantiate the class. However, the New keyword is not compatible with the WithEvents keyword. Therefore, objects with events must be instantiated after they are initially declared.*

After the object has been declared, an instance of the object can be created using the Set statement in conjunction

with the New keyword. The following Form_Load subroutine shows how to instantiate an object that supports events:

```
Private Sub Form_Load()
    Set oMyNumber = New cNumber
End Sub
```

Here, the Set statement is used to create a new instance of the cNumber class. After this statement completes, the object named oMyNumber can be used in your application. The upcoming code examples show how to use the different methods defined in the cNumber class that are exposed by the oMyNumber object.

The first example illustrates using the Add method to update the data contained in the oMyNumber object's Value property. The contents of the TextBox control named txtAddValue is added to the oMyNumber's Value property, and the new result is assigned to the Label control named lblResultAdd.

```
lblResultAdd.Caption = _
    oMyNumber.Add(txtAddValue.Text)
```

The next example shows how to use the oMyNumber object's Subtract method. The value to be subtracted is passed into the Subtract method as an argument, and the resulting value is assigned to the Caption property of the Label control named lblResultSub.

```
lblResultSub.Caption = _
    oMyNumber.Subtract(txtSubValue.Text)
```

The next example shows how the Multiply method is used. Again, the value to multiply by is passed to the Multiply method, and the product of the operation is assigned to a Label control.

```
lblResultMult.Caption = _
    oMyNumber.Multiply(txtMultValue.Text)
```

The Divide method works exactly like the other methods in the oMyNumber object. The value to divide by is passed into the method, and the result of the division operation is assigned to lblResultDiv.Caption.

```
lblResultDiv.Caption = _
    oMyNumber.Divide(txtDivValue.Text)
```

If you look back at the implementation of the oNumber class in one of the earlier listings, you might notice that the Change event is fired by each of the different methods supplied by the cNumber class. In addition, support for user-defined events was added via the Private WithEvents statement that was initially used to declare the oMyNumber object. The following listing shows how to add your own code into oMyNumber object's custom Change event:

```
Private Sub oMyNumber_Change()
    MsgBox "The value of the oMyNumber object _
        has changed."
End Sub
```

Like the event procedures that are supported by ActiveX controls, the event procedures that are supported by custom objects follow a naming convention where the name of the event is concatenated with the object name to form a subroutine name. This subroutine is then called when the object fires the event. In this example, when the oMyNumber Change event is executed, a message box will be displayed.

How do I reuse an existing class in another application?

You can import an existing class simply by adding the class's source file to your VB application. After you add the source file, you can use the class definition to create new objects in your VB applications. Here's how to add an existing class module to a VB application:

1. Select either Project | Add Class Module from the main menu or right-click the Project window and select Add | Class Module from the pop-up menu. The Add Class Module dialog box will be displayed, as shown in Figure 13-10.

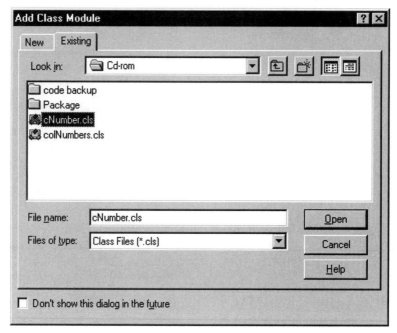

Figure 13-10   Adding an existing class to a VB application

2. In the Add Class Module dialog box, select the Existing tab and then navigate to the CLS module that contains the class that you want to add.

3. Double-click the class module to add it to your project.

 How do I add a property to an object?

Apart from using the Class Builder, the simplest method of manually adding a property to a class is to add a Public variable to the class definition. The following code illustrates adding a property via a Public variable:

```
Option Explicit

' Local variable(s) to hold property value(s).
Private mvarValue As Variant 'local copy
' Public declarations create a property for all access.
Public AllAccess As Variant ' public copy
```

The first Private declaration of the mvarValue property creates a variable that can be accessed only by methods of the same class. You can access the contents of a private property value by using the Let and Get methods and assign the contents by using the Set method. The second Public declaration of the AllAccess variable creates a public property that can be accessed directly by other objects and functions. You don't need to use the Let, Get, and Set methods to access the properties value. As a general rule, it's preferable to store property values in a private variable, because it provides more control over the values that are assigned to the property. For instance, you can add code to the Let method that ensures that only valid data is assigned to a property. Using public variables circumvents the ability to validate the data.

What's the default property?

The default property enables you to make your projects a bit simpler, because you don't need to refer explicitly to the default property to set or access its value. For instance, the Value property of the oMyNumber object that was created in one of the earlier examples was set up as a default property.

Setting up a property as the default property allows you to retrieve and set the value of the property without explicitly naming the property. The following listing shows how to use the Value property as the default property:

```
' Value is the default property of oMyNumber,
' set without explicit reference.
oMyNumber = 1
```

Otherwise, if the Value property were not the default property of the oMyNumber object, you would need to specify the property name before accessing or setting the property, as the following code demonstrates:

```
' Otherwise you'd need to use the name.
oMyNumber.Value = 2
```

You can make a property the default property either by checking the Default check box in the Class Builder or by

using the VB Tools menu. Follow these steps to set a property as the default property from the menu:

1. Select Tools | Procedure Attributes to display the Procedure Attributes dialog box.

2. Click the Advanced button to expand the dialog box, as shown in Figure 13-11.

3. In the Procedure Attributes dialog box, select the name of the property from the Name drop-down box. In Figure 13-11, the Value property is selected.

4. Select (Default) in the Procedure ID box and click the OK button.

 Note: *A class can have only one default member, which can be either a property or a method.*

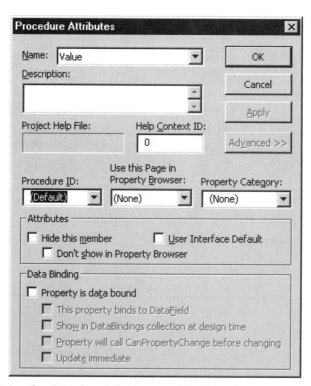

Figure 13-11 Setting the default property by using the Procedure Attributes dialog box

 I'm tired of prefixing the object name before every property. Is there any shortcut?

Yes. You can use the With statement to work with a group of an object's attributes. The With statement specifies the object name that will be worked with, and it begins a block that will contain references to any of that object's properties, methods, or events. Within the With block, the object name does not need to be explicitly referenced. An example of using the With statement is shown in the following code:

```
' Set multiple properties using With.
With oMyNumber
    .AllAccess = "This new value"
    .Value = 25
End With
```

In this example, the With block begins with the With statement, followed by the name of the object that you will be using. In this case, the With statement is using the oMyNumber object, which is an instance of the oNumber class that was created in an earlier example. The oMyNumber object has two properties: AllAccess and Value. Within the With block, the names of the properties that will be used each is prefixed with a period. You don't need to use the object name before a value is assigned to each property. The End With statement marks the end of the With block. If the properties, methods, or events of the oMyNumber object are accessed outside the scope of the With block, then the object name once again is required to access the object's various attributes.

 How can I see all the properties, methods, and events that are supported by an object?

Visual Basic's Object Browser enables you to see an object's properties, events, and methods. The Object Browser can be an invaluable tool to help you understand what an object does and how to use it. You can start the Object Browser by clicking the Object Browser icon in Visual Basic's toolbar, by selecting View | Object Browser from the main menu, or by pressing F2 while the IDE is displayed. Figure 13-12 presents Visual Basic's Object Browser.

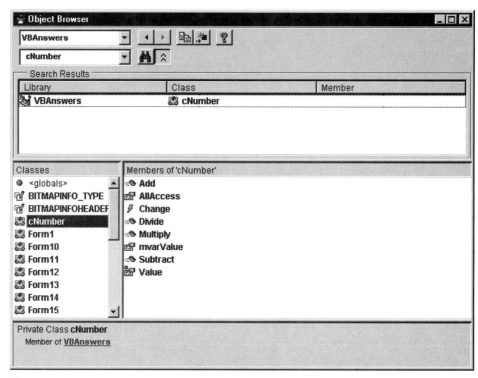

Figure 13-12 Viewing an object with the Object Browser

Figure 13-12 shows the cNumber class displayed in the VB Object Browser. The top drop-down box enables you to select the project or library that you want to display. VB classes that are defined in CLS class modules are always part of the primary project. In this example, the cNumber class is part of the VB project named VBAnswers. For objects that are created by including references in the project, you would select the object's library name from this drop-down box. For instance, if your project includes a reference to the Microsoft Excel 8.0 Object Library, you could view the properties, methods, and events of the Excel object by selecting the Excel object from the top drop-down box.

The second drop-down box enables you to search for an object attribute. You can enter either a whole or partial class, property, method, or event name, and all the matching entries will be displayed in the Search Results window. In the previous example, the search for cNumber displayed the cNumber class from the VBAnswers project in the Search Results window.

The lower portion of the Object Browser window displays the class in each project or library, as well as the properties, methods, and events for each class. Selecting the class name in the left pane of the main Object Browser window displays that class's properties, methods, and events in the right pane. In Figure 13-12, the cNumber class has been selected in the left pane and its attributes are displayed in the right pane. A small window and hand icon identifies properties. The default property also includes a small blue dot. Methods are displayed next to a green flying-block icon, while events are associated with a lightning-bolt icon. Any parameters that are used with the methods or events are displayed at the bottom of the window.

USING COLLECTIONS

The questions and answers in this section show you how to create and use collections in your Visual Basic applications. The topics in this section include an overview of collections as well as information showing how to create a collection and access the items that are contained in the collection.

What's a collection?

A *collection* essentially is an object that serves to group together objects that are alike. Conceptually, collections are a lot like arrays. Resource-wise, a collection is not quite as efficient as an array, but a collection is easier to use because you don't need to manually manage the size of the collection.

You can make collections of user-defined objects or of other objects, such as Form objects. Visual Basic supplies a Collection class that enables you to make your own Collection objects. Since each collection is really an object, it is created exactly like any other object. You create a Collection object by making a new instance of the Collection class. Objects are added to a collection by using the Add method. Collection objects created from the Collection class are *1-based,* meaning that the index of the first item in the collection is one. The For Each loop typically is used to iterate through all the items in a collection. Visual Basic's Collection object stores each item as a Variant, which means that collections must consist of the same data types that can be contained in a

Variant. This includes objects and other standard VB data types, such as Integer, String, and Long, but not user-defined types. Like standard objects, Collection objects are destroyed when they go out of scope or are set to Nothing.

Tip: *Although Collection objects created from Visual Basic's Collection class are 1-based, that's not true for collections of Visual Basic's own objects. VB's own collections of forms and objects are 0-based, meaning that the first object in the collection has an index of zero.*

By default, VB collections come with the following built-in members:

Member	Type	Description
Add	Method	Adds an item to a collection
Count	Property	Contains the number of items in the collection
Item	Method	Returns the value of an item
Remove	Method	Removes an item from a collection

User-created collections usually are prefixed with the letters *col* and end in the letter *s,* indicating plurality. For instance, a collection of oNumber objects would typically be named colNumbers.

 ## How do I create a collection?

Like standard VB classes, collections are defined by using a CLS class module. Collections can be created either by manually writing the code for the collection or by using the Class Builder. The Class Builder is even more useful for collections than it is for classes, because it knows how to implement the primary methods and properties used by the collection. Follow these steps to create a new collection:

1. First add a class module to your VB project by selecting either Project | Add Class Module from the VB menu or right-clicking the Project window and selecting Add | Class Module from the pop-up menu to display the Add Class Module dialog box.

2. Select the VB Class Builder option to open the Class Builder window.

3. Select New | Collection, as shown in Figure 13-13.

The Collection Builder enables you to name the collection and specify the name of an existing class that will be contained in this collection. The Collection Builder is shown in Figure 13-14.

In this figure, a collection named colNumbers has been defined, which will contain a group of cNumber class objects. Clicking the OK button adds the collection and automatically generates all the basic methods and properties required to implement the collection. After generating the members for the collection, the All tab of the Class Builder window is automatically displayed, as shown in Figure 13-15.

Figure 13-15 shows that the Collection Builder created the Add and Remove methods for the colNumbers collection, as well as the Item, Count, and NewEnum properties. These are all the basic members that you need to implement a collection. Updating your project adds a CLS class module source file to your VB project. You can update your VB project in one of the following ways: by closing the Class Builder and responding Yes to the prompt to save your

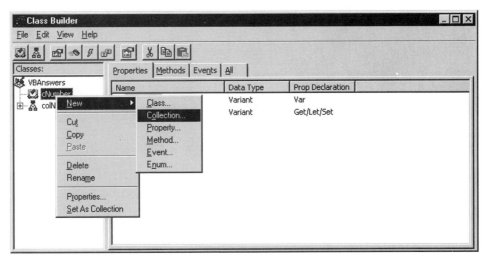

Figure 13-13   Creating a new collection by using the Class Builder

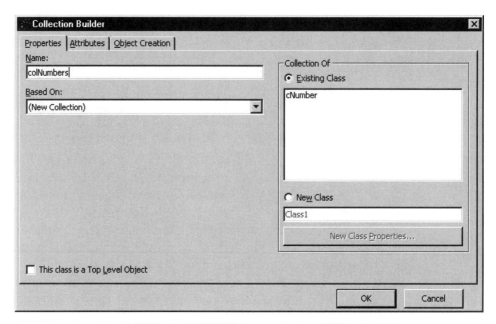

Figure 13-14   Defining the collection name and base class

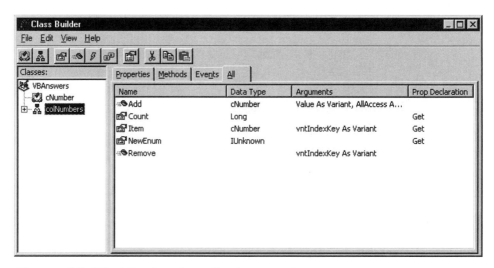

Figure 13-15   Viewing the collection members

changes, by selecting File | Update Project from the menu, or by pressing CTRL+S.

The following listing shows both the code that was generated using the Collection Builder and the custom code that was added to support the four methods:

```
Option Explicit

' Local variable to hold collection.
Private mCol As Collection

Public Function Add(Value As Variant, AllAccess As _
    Variant, Optional sKey As String) As cNumber
    ' Create a new object.
    Dim objNewMember As cNumber
    Set objNewMember = New cNumber

    ' Set the properties passed into the method.
    If IsObject(Value) Then
        Set objNewMember.Value = Value
    Else
        objNewMember.Value = Value
    End If
    If IsObject(AllAccess) Then
        Set objNewMember.AllAccess = AllAccess
    Else
        objNewMember.AllAccess = AllAccess
    End If
    If Len(sKey) = 0 Then
        mCol.Add objNewMember
    Else
        mCol.Add objNewMember, sKey
    End If

    ' Return the object created.
    Set Add = objNewMember
    Set objNewMember = Nothing

End Function
```

```
Public Property Get Item(vntIndexKey As Variant) As _
    cNumber
    ' Used when referencing an element in the
    ' collection vntIndexKey contains either the
    ' Index or Key to the collection. This is why
    ' it is declared as a Variant.
    ' Syntax: Set foo = x.Item(xyz)
    ' or Set foo = x.Item(5)
  Set Item = mCol(vntIndexKey)
End Property

Public Property Get Count() As Long
    ' Used when retrieving the number of elements in
    ' the collection. Syntax: Debug.Print x.Count
    Count = mCol.Count
End Property

Public Sub Remove(vntIndexKey As Variant)
    ' Used when removing an element from the
    ' collection vntIndexKey contains either the
    ' Index or Key. This is why it is declared as
    ' a Variant. Syntax: x.Remove(xyz)

    mCol.Remove vntIndexKey
End Sub

Public Property Get NewEnum() As IUnknown
    ' This property allows you to enumerate
    ' this collection with the For...Each syntax.
    Set NewEnum = mCol.[_NewEnum]
End Property

Private Sub Class_Initialize()
    ' Creates the collection when this class
    ' is created.
    Set mCol = New Collection
End Sub

Private Sub Class_Terminate()
    ' Destroys the collection when this class
    ' is terminated.
    Set mCol = Nothing
End Sub
```

The Collection Builder created all the code required to implement the colNumbers class, and it automatically wrote it to the colNumbers.cls source file. No additional code was required.

The first important point to notice in this listing is the declaration of the mCol Collection object. This Private Collection object is created to hold the different instances of cNumber objects that are added to the collection. Since it is a Private object, only the members of the colNumbers class can access this internal Collection object.

Next, you can see the different methods that the Collection Builder added to the Collection object. As you have probably guessed, the Add method is used to add items to the collection. The Add method essentially makes a new cNumber object and copies the property values from the first two parameters to the new object that's added to the collection. The most important thing to notice about the Add method is the fact that it takes an optional Key parameter. This Key parameter optionally can be used to add a simple key value that can be used later to retrieve the object from the collection. If the Key parameter is not used, then objects must be accessed using their index value, which essentially reflects the order in which the objects were added to the collection.

The Item method is used to retrieve items from the collection. The Item method accepts a single parameter that's used to identify the collection item to be retrieved. This can be either the index of the item or its key value.

Next, the Count property is implemented to retrieve the number of elements in the collection. You might notice that the colNumbers Count method simply is a wrapper for the Count method that's part of the Private mCol Collection object.

The Remove method is used to Remove items from the collection. Like the Item method, the Remove method accepts a single argument that contains either the index of the item to be removed or its key value.

So far, all the properties and methods used by the Collection object are very much like those used by standard objects. Collections are objects, so this fact shouldn't be too

surprising. The NewEnum property shows how collections are a bit different from a standard object. The NewEnum method is implemented to allow the user of the collection to iterate through the collection by using the For Each loop. If the NewEnum property were not present, the For Each loop could not be used with the collection. Within the NewEnum property, the _NewEnum object of the Private mCol collection is used to set a pointer to the next object in the collection.

 Note: *The mCol object's _NewEnum method must be enclosed in brackets, because the name begins with an underscore. Beginning a name with an underscore is a convention that is commonly used to indicate that the method is hidden.*

The remaining Class_Initialize and Class_Terminate methods are used, respectively, to create and then later destroy the internal mCol Collection object.

How do I add objects to a collection?

You can add objects to a collection by using the collection's Add method. However, like any other object, an instance of the Collection object must be created before it can be used. The following line shows how to create a new instance of the colNumbers Collection object that was defined earlier in this chapter:

```
Private oMyNumbers As New colNumbers
```

Exactly like creating an object, a new instance of the colNumbers Collection object is created by using the New keyword. If this Collection object needs to be accessed by different subroutines, it should be declared at the module level.

After the Collection object has been created, items can be added to the collection by using the Add method. The following code shows how to use the Add method of the colNumbers collection to add new instances of the cNumber object to the collection:

```
Dim i As Integer

For i = 1 To 10
    oMyNumbers.Add i, i
Next i
```

In this example, an Integer is declared to act as a loop counter. Next, a For Next loop is used to add ten items to the instance of the Collection object named oMyNumbers. The value of the loop counter is assigned to both property values that are exposed by the oMyNumbers Collection object's Add method.

How can I read all the items in a collection?

You can read through all the objects in an existing collection by using the For Each loop. The following listing shows how the For Each loop can be used to read through all the items in a collection and add the contents of their Value property to a list box:

```
Dim oNumber As cNumber

lstCollection.Clear

For Each oNumber In oMyNumbers
    lstCollection.AddItem oNumber.Value
Next
```

The first line in this listing creates a new instance of the cNumber class named oNumber. Next, the ListBox control named lstCollection is cleared, and then a For Each loop is used to read through all the items in the oMyNumbers Collection object. The For Each loop takes advantage of the Collection object's NewEnum property to set a reference to the next object contained in the oMyNumbers collection. Within the For Each loop, the contents of the oNumber

object's Value property is added to the ListBox control. In this case, the data value contained in the Value property coincides with the item's collection index.

How do I remove objects from a collection?

You can remove items from a collection by using the Collection object's Remove method. For instance, in a previous example, all the items in the oMyNumbers collection were added to the ListBox control named lstCollection. The following code examples show how you can select an item from the list and then remove that item from the oMyNumbers collection by using the Collection object's Remove method.

First, to select an item from the ListBox control, you need to use the ListBox control's ListIndex property, as shown next, to identify the item that the user clicked:

```
Private Sub lstCollection_Click()

    ' Select the item from the list based on the
    ' ListIndex.
    txtItem.Text = _
        lstCollection.List(lstCollection.ListIndex)

End Sub
```

The lstCollection ListBox control's ListIndex property contains the index value of the item in the list that was selected. If this seems familiar, it should. The ListBox control is also an example of a collection. In this case, the ListItem index is used to access one particular item in the collection maintained by the ListBox control. The item selected in the list is then assigned to a TextBox control named txtItem.

The next listing shows how the contents of the txtItem TextBox control can be used to remove the corresponding item from the oMyNumbers collection:

```
Dim iColIndex As Integer

' Convert the string to an integer.
iColIndex = txtItem.Text

' Remove the item shown in the text box.
oMyNumbers.Remove iColIndex
```

First, an Integer named iColIndex is declared to store the value contained by the TextBox control. A numeric data type is required because the collection's index requires a number, but the Text property of the txtItem TextBox control contains a String data type. Assigning the contents of the Text property to the iColIndex Integer variable converts the String data type to an Integer data type that can be used as an index to the oMyNumbers collection. Next, the oMyNumbers Collection object's Remove method is used with the index value contained in the iColIndex variable to remove the item from the collection.

Tip: *Visual Basic's own collections, such as the Forms, Objects, and Controls collections, don't have the Remove method.*

Chapter 14

The Data Control and DAO

Answer Topics!

The Data Control and DAO @ a Glance

This chapter shows you how to access a database using Visual Basic's built-in Data control and DAO (Data Access Objects). The Data control provides a quick and easy method for writing simple data access applications. However, its capabilities are fairly limited. DAO provides a more comprehensive set of functions that enables the development of full-blown database applications. Both the Data control and DAO are intended to be used primarily with single-user or small multiuser applications using an Access database, but they can also be used to connect to multiuser databases such as SQL Server.

 Using the Data Control and Bound Controls shows you how to connect the Data control to an Access database, as well as how to connect data-bound controls to the Data control.

 Using DAO shows you how to add the DAO object library to your VB applications. You'll also see how to use the DAO functions to both query and update the target database.

USING THE DATA CONTROL AND BOUND CONTROLS

The first part of this chapter covers using the Data control and bound controls. The questions and answers in this section explain the relationship of the Data control and the Microsoft Jet database engine (Microsoft Jet). They also illustrate how to bind a control to the Data control, and manipulate the Data control by using program code.

 ## What is the Data control?

The *Data control* is a graphical control that makes it very easy to implement simple database applications. The Data control uses the Microsoft Jet database engine for database access. Microsoft Jet is the same underlying database engine that's used by Microsoft Access.

Although the Data control provides some basic navigational user interface elements, the Data control itself does not display data. Instead, the Data control enables other controls, such as the TextBox, ListBox, PictureBox, and ComboBox controls, to connect to the target database. In other words, the Data control serves as a connector. On one side, the Data control connects to Microsoft Jet, which in turn connects to a database. On the other side, the Data control provides the ability to bind other interface components to specific columns in the target database.

Not all controls can work in conjunction with the Data control. Only data-bound controls support binding to the Data control. Generally, most data-bound controls include a DataSource property. The following table lists the database-oriented properties in a Data control and describes the use of each property.

Property	Description
Connect	Specifies the type of target database connection. The default value is Access.
DatabaseName	Specifies the location of the target database. This typically is an MDB file. This property can include the fully qualified path name.
DefaultType	Specifies the type of data source that will be used. The value of 2 - UseJet specifies that a local Access Jet database will be used. Otherwise, the value of 1 - UseODBC specifies that a remote ODBC data source for a database such as SQL Server will be used.

Property	Description
ReadOnly	Specifies whether the Data control is allowed to update data or the data is read-only.
RecordsetType	Specifies the type of Recordset object that will be opened by the Data control: 0 - Table indicates that an Access table type of recordset will be used. 1 - Dynaset indicates that an indexed Dynaset will be used. 2 - Snapshot indicates the snapshot copy will be used.
RecordSource	Specifies the records that will be included in the Data control's recordset. This property can contain an Access table name, a SQL (pronounced "sequel") statement, or a stored procedure name.

 Note: *The Data control is provided primarily for backward compatibility with existing VB projects. The new ADO Data control introduced with Visual Basic 6 is recommend by Microsoft for new applications. The ADO Data control is discussed in more detail in Chapter 16.*

What's a data-bound control?

A *data-bound control,* sometimes called just a *bound control,* is a control that can be bound or linked to the Data control. Data-bound controls typically are user-interface controls, such as TextBox, ListBox, ComboBox, and ListBox controls. When a data-bound control is bound to the Data control, the contents of the data-bound control are automatically filled with data from the data source specified by the Data control. Data-bound controls typical have special properties that are used both for binding to the Data control and for identifying the specific data element from the data source that will be displayed in the data-bound control. The following table lists the properties of data-bound controls:

Property	Description
DataField	Specifies the name of the field or column that will be used in the target database. A data-bound control typically is associated with only one column in a database table.

Property	Description
DataFormat	Controls the formatting that will be applied to the data value that is displayed. This can be one of several standard numeric formats or it can specify the name of a custom format object.
DataSource	Specifies the name of the Data control to which this data-bound control will be attached.

 ## How do I add the Data control to my project?

You don't have to do anything special to add the Data control to a VB project. The VB Toolbox includes the Data control by default. To use the Data control, you simply drag and drop it onto a VB form and then set its properties to connect to an existing database.

 ## How do I connect my Data control to a target database?

Connecting the Data control to a database is simply a matter of setting the appropriate properties after you place the Data control on the form:

1. Set the Data control's DatabaseName property to the path and filename of the target database. The DatabaseName property of the Data control named datNWCustomers is shown in Figure 14-1.

 Note: *You can either directly enter the filename and path of the database file by typing into the Data control's DatabaseName property, or click the ellipsis button to display the DatabaseName dialog box, shown in Figure 14-2.*

2. In the DatabaseName dialog box, locate the database file that you want to add and click Open. Figure 14-2 shows that the Nwind.mdb database in the /VB98 directory has been selected using the DatabaseName dialog box.

 Note: *Visual Basic comes with two sample database files located in the \VB98 directory. The Nwind.mdb database is a sample customer/order entry type of database, whereas Biblio.mdb is a sample database representing a publishing business.*

3. Select the appropriate data from the database by using the Data control's RecordSource property, shown in Figure 14-3.

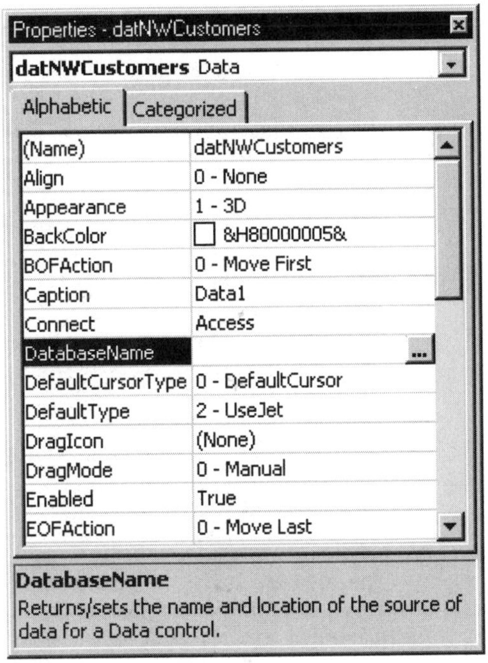

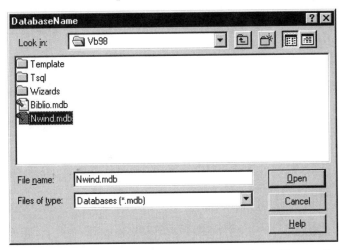

Figure 14-1 Setting the DatabaseName property

The RecordSource property can contain the name of a table, a SQL statement, or the name of a stored procedure. When connected to a Jet/Access database, clicking the drop-down arrow lists the names of the tables in the database, as shown in Figure 14-3.

Figure 14-2 Selecting a database with the DatabaseName dialog box

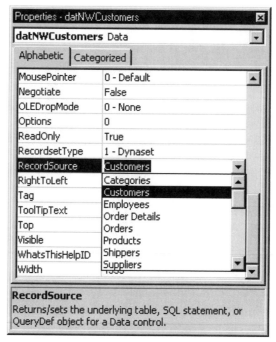

Figure 14-3 Setting the RecordSource property

To connect the Data control to one of the tables in the Access database, simply select the table from the list of tables displayed. In Figure 14-3, the Customers table has been selected from the list of tables displayed in the RecordSource property of the Data control.

 ## How do I bind a control to the Data control?

After you place a Data control on a form and connect it to a data source, you can connect any data-bound controls that are on the form to the Data control. Generally, each data-bound control is linked to one specific field or column of the database table that's identified by the Data control.

1. Specify the name of the Data control in the data-bound control's DataSource property, as shown in the example in Figure 14-4.

   The figure shows a data-bound TextBox control named txtCustID being bound to the Data control named datNWCustomers. Multiple Data controls can be present on one form.

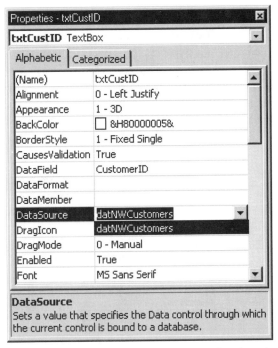

Figure 14-4 Setting the DataSource property of a data-bound control

2. Click the drop-down arrow on the DataSource property to display all the available Data controls in the drop-down list; then select the appropriate Data control by clicking its name in the list.

3. Select the column from the target table by using the DataField property of the data-bound control. Figure 14-5 illustrates using the DataField property of a data-bound control to link to one column from the target table.

Clicking the drop-down arrow displayed next to the DataField property displays all the available columns from the Data control. To select the column to bind to the data-bound control, simply click its name in the drop-down list. In Figure 14-5, the column named CustomerID has been bound to the TextBox control.

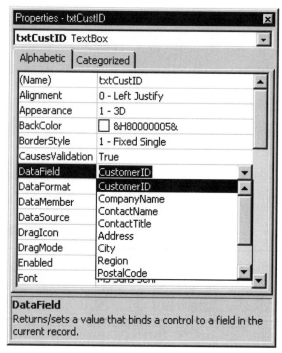

Figure 14-5   Selecting a database column by using the DataField property

Can I bind multiple controls to a single Data control?

Yes. In fact, that's typical of how the Data control is used. A single Data control is usually linked to one target database table. Then, multiple data-bound controls are linked to the Data control. Each data-bound control is used to display a different column from the target table on the form. To link multiple data-bound controls to a single Data control, simply set the DataSource property of each data-bound control to the name of the Data control that's on the form.

Can I have multiple Data controls on a single form?

Yes. You can have as many Data controls per form as you need. Multiple Data controls often are needed, because each different Data control can be linked to only one specific table

or recordset that's specified in the Data control's RecordSource property. However, a typical data entry form displays data from several different database tables. A different Data control is used to accommodate each different table.

How can I create a new database if I don't have Access?

You can create a new database by using Visual Basic's Visual Data Manager, which is supplied with the Visual Basic Professional and Enterprise Editions:

1. You start Visual Data Manager by selecting Add-Ins | Visual Data Manager from Visual Basic's menu.

2. To create a new Access/Jet database, select File | New | Microsoft Access | Version 7.0 MDB, as shown in Figure 14-6.

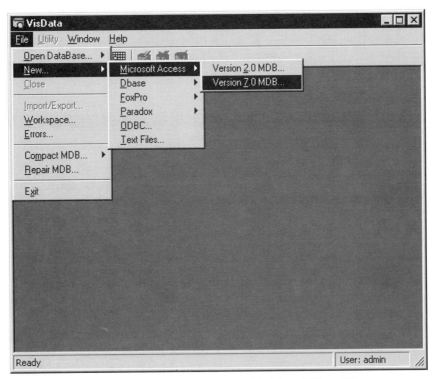

Figure 14-6   Creating a new database with Visual Data Manager

After you select the option to create a new database, Visual Data Manager displays a Save Database dialog box that prompts you to specify the path and name of the database that will be created. Because the Microsoft Access database option was selected as the type of database, the Save Database dialog box automatically prompts you to save the database using the .mdb file extension.

3. Select the database path and name the database.

4. Click the OK button to display the main Visual Data Manager Database Window, shown in Figure 14-7.

After you create the database, you next need to create tables. The database serves as a container to group together all the different database objects. The table is the primary database object that actually contains the data that will be used by your database applications. Tables contain groups of related data elements. For example, an Employee table might contain all the information about employees, such as names, addresses, and phone numbers, and a Department table might contain information about a department, such as its number and name.

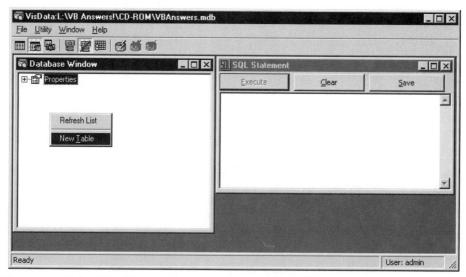

Figure 14-7 The Visual Data Manager Database Window

Follow these steps to create a new table:

1. Right-click the Database Window to display the pop-up menu shown in Figure 14-7.

2. Select the New Table option from the pop-up menu. The Visual Data Manager's Table Structure dialog box is displayed. You can use the Table Structure dialog box to provide a name for the table that you are creating.

3. To add fields to the table click the Add Field button, which displays the Add Field dialog box shown in Figure 14-8.

   The Add Field dialog box enables you to specify the names and data types of all the fields that will be grouped together in the table. The Name and Type boxes are the only required fields in the Add Field dialog box.

4. Enter the name of the field or column in the Name box and specify the field's data type in the Type box.

   In Figure 14-8, a field named Dep_ID is being added to the table. The drop-down arrow next to the Type box displays a list of the valid Access data types. The Dep_ID field is identified as a Long data type, which means that only numbers can be contained in this field.

Add Field

Name:	OrdinalPosition:
Dep_ID	
Type:	ValidationText:
Long	
Size:	ValidationRule:
4	
○ FixedField	DefaultValue:
○ VariableField	
□ AutoIncrField	OK
□ AllowZeroLength	
□ Required	Close

Figure 14-8   Adding new fields to a table by using the Add Field dialog box

5. After you add all the fields that you want to the table, click OK to redisplay the Table Structure dialog box, shown in Figure 14-9.

The Table Structure dialog box lists all the fields that have been added to the table, and displays the attributes for each field. In Figure 14-9, two fields have been defined for the Department table: Dep_ID and Dep_Name. At the bottom of the screen, an index has been created on the Dep_ID field. Microsoft Jet requires a unique index on all tables that will be updated.

6. Select the fields that will be used in the index by clicking the Add Index button, shown in the lower-left corner of Figure 14-9. (Likewise, you can remove fields from the index by clicking the Remove Index button.)

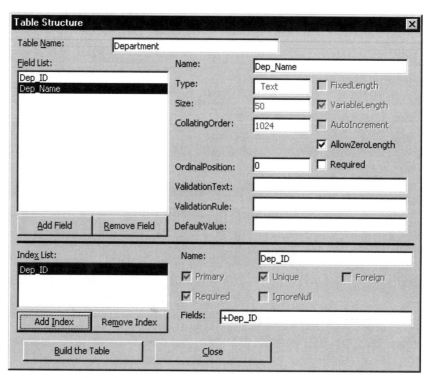

Figure 14-9 The Table Structure dialog box, listing all the fields

7. After you define all the fields and indexes for the table, click the Build the Table button at the bottom of the Table Structure dialog box.

The table and all of its fields will be added to the database. Figure 14-10 shows the Department table and its Dep_ID and Dep_Name fields displayed in the Visual Data Manager Database Window.

 Tip: *Visual Data Manager is provided as a sample application in the Professional and Enterprise Editions of Visual Basic. All of its source code can be found in the Samples\VisData directory located under the \Program Files\Microsoft Visual Studio\MSDN directory. The VisData.exe executable program is provided in the \Program Files\Microsoft Visual Studio\VB98 directory.*

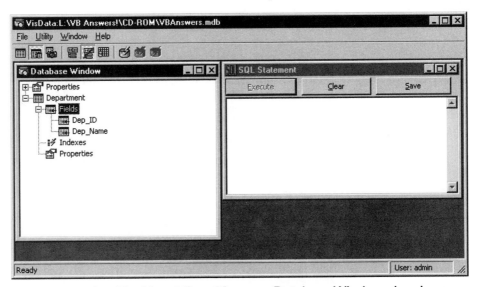

Figure 14-10 The Visual Data Manager Database Window showing a table and fields

 How do I bind multicolumn controls, such as the DBGrid control, to the Data control?

Complex, multicolumn controls, such as the DBGrid control, can be bound to a Data control in much the same way as simple, single-column controls, such as the TextBox and Label controls, are bound to a Data control.

1. Set the Data control's DataSource property to the name of the database file that you want to use.

2. Set the Data control's RecordSource property either to the name of the table that you want to query or to a SQL statement that will select the database records that you want to display. For instance, to connect the Data control to a table named Department in the VBAnswers.mdb database, you would set the DataSource property to VBAnswers.mdb.

3. Click the RecordSource property's drop-down box and select the Department table from the list of tables found in the VBAnswer's database.

4. After you set the properties in the Data control, you must bind the DBGrid control to the Data control by setting its DataSource property to the name of the Data control. For instance, if the Data control that is bound to the Department table is named datDepartment, you need to set the DataSource property of the DBGrid control to datDepartment.

So far, all of these steps are identical to the steps that are required to bind a simple data-bound control to a Data control. However, whereas a simple data-bound control uses the DataField property to select a single column or field from the target database, a complex, multicolumn control such as the DBGrid control typically allows you to select multiple columns by using the Property Pages dialog box. Figure 14-11 illustrates the custom Property Pages dialog box used by the DBGrid control.

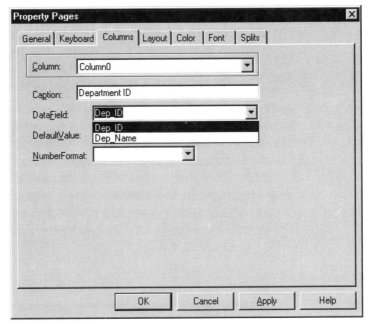

Figure 14-11 Selecting database columns by using the DBGrid control

5. In the Columns tab, select the columns that will be bound and displayed using the DBGrid control, and fill out the following boxes:

● The Column drop-down list box at the top of the dialog box allows you to work with each column from the target table. Column0 specifies the first column in the DBGrid control.

● The Caption list box enables you to add a more user-friendly and meaningful heading for the current column.

● The DataField drop-down box enables you to select the field or column from the target table that will be bound to this column in the DBGrid control.

● The NumberFormat drop-down box allows you to choose the format that will be used to display the data in the cell. For instance, the Number format allows you to select to display the data value as currency, with a fixed number of decimal positions, or as a date/time field.

In Figure 14-11, the Dep_ID field from the target database is being bound to Column0 (the first column) in the DBGrid control. You can continue to select and bind different grid columns to database columns by selecting new DBGrid control columns in the Column drop-down box and binding them to different database fields selected using the DataField drop-down box. Figure 14-12 shows the DBGrid control bound to the Department table.

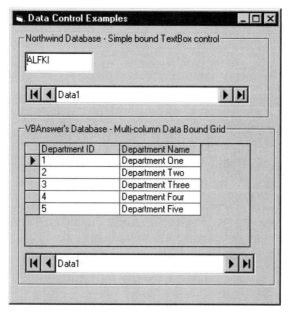

Figure 14-12   Binding the DBGrid control to the example Department table

 Can I programmatically control the operation of the Data control?

Yes. Although the Data control is primarily intended to be used for building simple database access applications, it also supports more sophisticated data access, by using the methods and properties that are exposed by the Data control. The Data control exposes many of the same functions that are provided by the DAO (Data Access Objects) database programming object framework. For instance, the following listing illustrates how you can add 50 records to the example Department table by using the Data control:

```
Dim nCount As Integer

For nCount = 1 To 50
    With datDepartment.Recordset
        .AddNew
        .Fields("Dep_ID").Value = nCount
        .Fields("Dep_Name").Value = "Department " & _
            CStr(nCount)
        .Update
    End With
Next

dbgDepartment.ReBind
```

This listing illustrates how you can programmatically use the Data control in your applications. The Data control provides a Recordset object that enables you to manipulate the data in a target data source. The Recordset object that's exposed by the Data control provides the same properties, methods, and events that are supported by the DAO object library's Recordset object. In the preceding example, a For Next loop is used to add 50 records to the Department table in the database that's connected to the datDepartment Data control. Inside the For Next loop, a With block is used to simplify access to the datDepartment.Recordset object.

First, the Recordset object's AddNew method is used to allocate a buffer that will contain the new record values. Next, the Value property of each Field object is assigned new values that will be added to the table. In this case, the Dep_ID Field object will be assigned the value of the loop counter contained in the nCount variable. The Dep_Name Field object will be assigned the value of Department concatenated with the string representation of the nCount variable. After the new values have been assigned to the Field objects, the Recordset object's Update method is executed to write the new values to the database. Finally, the ReBind method of the dbgDepartment DBGrid control object that's bound to the underlying Department table is executed to display the new data values in the DBGrid control.

Likewise, to programmatically delete all the records on the Department table, you could execute the following code:

```
datDepartment.Recordset.MoveFirst

Do While datDepartment.Recordset.EOF = False

    With datDepartment.Recordset
        .Edit
        .Delete
        .MoveNext
    End With

Loop

dbgDepartment.ReBind
```

In this example, the Recordset object's MoveFirst method is used to position the cursor to the first record contained in the Recordset object. Next, a Do While loop is used to delete all the records contained in the Recordset object. The Do While loop continues until the Recordset object's EOF property is no longer False—which indicates that all records in the Recordset object have been read. Inside the Do While loop, a With block is used to simplify access to the datDepartment .Recordset object. Within the With block, the Recordset object's Edit method is used to put the current record into the update mode. Next, the Delete method is used to delete the current record. Then, the Recordset object's MoveNext method is used to move the cursor to the next record in the Recordset object.

After all records in the datDepartment.Recordset object have been deleted, the ReBind method of the dbgDepartment DBGrid object is executed to update the data values displayed in the DBGrid control.

More detailed information about using the DAO object framework and the Recordset object is presented in the second part of this chapter.

USING DAO

The second part of this chapter covers using the DAO (Data Access Objects) object library to write database applications. This section explains why you might want to use DAO rather than the Data control. In addition, the questions and answers in the latter part of the chapter provide detailed explanations showing how to implement some of the most common database operations by using Visual Basic and DAO.

What is DAO and why would I want to use it instead of the Data control?

DAO (Data Access Objects) is Visual Basic's default data access technology. DAO has been a part of Visual Basic since DAO 1 was released with Visual Basic 3. Like the Data control, DAO was primarily intended to provide VB applications data access to local Access databases, but now it can also be used to provide access to several other databases, including dBase, Paradox, and even multiuser client/server databases such as Oracle and SQL Server. However, whereas the Data control is intended to provide quick and easy data access, DAO is intended to be the basis for writing full-blown

database applications. The Data control is simple to use, but it also is limited and not very flexible. More sophisticated database applications require the power and flexibility that are offered by DAO's object-based approach to database access.

What is the Microsoft Jet database engine and how does it relate to DAO?

The Microsoft Jet database engine (Microsoft Jet) is used by Microsoft Access. This same database engine is also delivered with Visual Basic, which enables VB to build database applications. DAO is a COM-based object framework that's built over Microsoft Jet. DAO's COM foundation makes it easy to access DAO functions from Visual Basic. Unlike ODBC or other DLL-based APIs, for which you must manually declare all the functions and their parameters in a BAS or CLS module, to use DAO, you only need to add the DAO reference to your project. Adding a reference to the DAO object library loads the DAO ActiveX DLL into your application. After that, you can immediately begin creating the desired objects using VB code.

How do I add a reference to the DAO object library?

Before you can begin to use DAO from Visual Basic, you must set a reference to the DAO object library. The files that provide the basic support for DAO are installed on the system when you first installed either the Professional Edition or the Enterprise Edition of Visual Basic. However, even though the files are installed, before you can use them, you need to set a reference to the DAO object library in Visual Basic's integrated development environment (IDE). Follow these steps to add a reference to the DAO 3.6 object library in Visual Basic 6:

1. Select Project | References, which displays the References dialog box shown in Figure 14-13.

2. Scroll through Visual Basic's references dialog box until you see Microsoft DAO 3.6 Object Library and click in its check box.

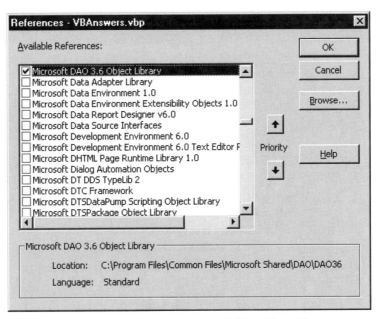

Figure 14-13   Adding a reference to the DAO object library

3. Click OK to add the DAO object library to Visual Basic's IDE.

Unlike adding ActiveX controls, adding a reference to Visual Basic's IDE doesn't create any visual objects in the VB Toolbox.

What are the primary objects found in the DAO object framework?

DAO is implemented using a hierarchical object framework. Figure 14-14 presents an overview of DAO's object model.

The DBEngine is at the top level of the DAO object hierarchy. The DBEngine object represents Microsoft Jet. Only one DBEngine object can be created per application. All other DAO objects are contained within the DBEngine object.

The Workspaces, Errors, and Groups object collections are at the second level of the DAO framework. The Workspaces collection contains a set of Workspace objects. Each Workspace

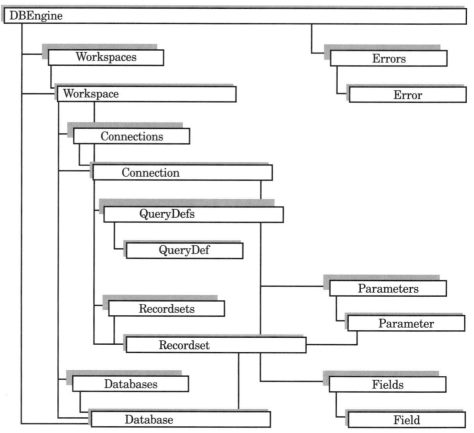

Figure 14-14 The DAO object model

object represents a database session. The Workspace object is used to control database login security and transaction scope. Each Workspace object contains a collection of Database objects.

The Database object is the central object in the DAO object hierarchy. As its name suggests, each Database object represents a local or remote database. A Database object is added to the Databases collection when Microsoft Jet opens a local or remote database. The Database object contains the other primary DAO object collections that are used for database access: TableDef objects, Recordset objects, and QueryDef objects. In addition, the Database object contains

Relations and Containers collections that are used for local Jet databases.

Each TableDef object contains a description of one table in the database, along with its columns and indexes. The TableDef object contains a collection of Field objects and Index objects, where each Field object corresponds to a column in a database table and each Index object corresponds to an index for the table. The Index object itself contains a collection of Field objects that comprise the columns that are used by the particular index. The TableDef object is populated with the appropriate database schema information when the TableDef object is first referenced or attached.

The collection of Recordset objects within the Database object represents a set of data that satisfies one or more database queries. The Recordset object also defines the type of cursor that will be supported. Microsoft Jet supports Table, Dynaset, and Snapshot types of Recordset objects. The differences and implementations of these different cursor types are covered later in this chapter. Each Recordset object contains a collection of Field objects. Like the Field objects that are contained by the TableDef object, each Field object within a Recordset object represents a data column in the Recordset object.

The collection of QueryDef objects represents a set of stored query definitions. Each QueryDef object contains a collection of Parameter objects as well as a collection of Field objects. Each Parameter object describes a parameter that is passed to a QueryDef object. Like the Fields collection that is contained by the TableDef and Recordset objects, the Fields collection of the QueryDef objects represents the data columns contained by the QueryDef object.

The Database object also contains a collection of Relations and a collection of Containers. The Relations collection describes the relationships between database tables, while the Containers collection provides a generic object store capability.

The Errors collection of the DBEngine object contains the DAO Error objects. Each Error object corresponds to an error that is generated by one of the Microsoft Jet operations.

When a new DAO error occurs, any existing Error objects are cleared from the DAO Errors collection and replaced by the most recent Error objects. DAO errors can be trapped by using Visual Basic's On Error handler. Within the On Error handler, you can retrieve the specific error information from the DAO Errors collection.

In addition to these primary objects, the DBEngine object also contains collections of Groups and Users. The local Microsoft Jet uses the Groups and Users collections to implement security.

 ## How do I retrieve data from a database by using DAO?

After you add a reference to Visual Basic's IDE, you're ready to use the DAO objects in your VB applications. The first step in using DAO is to create an instance of the DBEngine and Workspace objects. However, you don't need to create these objects explicitly by using code. Both the DBEngine and Workspace objects are automatically created the first time one of the DAO objects is referenced. The first piece of DAO code that's typically required is the creation of a Database object.

After a Database object has been instantiated, you can use the Database object to create a TableDef object, a QueryDef object, or a Recordset object. The Recordset object is the primary mechanism for querying a database using DAO. A Recordset object represents the contents of a table or it can represent the results of a query. A Recordset object is created using the Database object's OpenRecordset method. You can choose the type of Recordset object you want to create by using the type argument of the OpenRecordset method. If you don't specify the type of Recordset, DAO will automatically use a Recordset object with the most functionality. DAO starts with the Table Recordset object. If it isn't available, DAO then attempts to use a Dynaset Recordset object, followed by a Snapshot, and finally a Forward-Only Recordset object.

● **Table Recordsets** A Table Recordset object is a representation of a local Microsoft Jet table. Table Recordset objects support forward and backward scrolling and are updateable. Table Recordset objects can be used to open more than one base table and can also be used for ISAM data sources. (ISAM, or Indexed Sequential Access Method, is an older database technology that was used to access nonrelational databases.)

- **Dynaset Recordsets**   DAO's Dynaset Recordset object supports forward and backward movement through the Recordset object, as well as updating of the Recordset object. When a Dynaset Recordset object is opened, Microsoft Jet builds a local set of keys, whereby each key is associated with a row in the Recordset object. When your application accesses rows in the Recordset object, the local index value for the row is used to retrieve the corresponding row's data from the data source.

- **Snapshot Recordsets**   A Snapshot Recordset object provides a frozen copy, or "snapshot," of the data source at the time the Recordset object was opened. Snapshot Recordset objects are not updateable. Because of their static nature, they generally are less resource-intensive than Dynaset Recordset objects. However, since Snapshot Recordset objects make a copy of the data, you need to be careful about using this type of Recordset object with large amounts of data.

- **Forward-Only Recordsets**   The Forward-Only Recordset object provides the best performance and the least overhead of any of the other DAO Recordset objects, but it's also less capable than either the Dynaset or Snapshot Recordset object. Forward-only Recordset objects only support one-way forward movement through the Recordset object. Forward-only result sets are updateable, but they can only update the current row.

- **Dynamic Recordsets**   Like a Dynaset, a Dynamic Recordset object uses a local set of indexes that correspond to each row in the data source. Also like Dynasets, Dynamic Recordset objects are fully updateable. However, they offer additional functionality beyond the Dynaset Recordset objects. Dynamic Recordset objects can automatically reflect all the changes that are made to the original data source and are available only when using the ODBCDirect object framework—they are not supported when using a local Jet database.

The following code illustrates how to read through a database table by creating a Table Recordset object:

```
Dim ws As DAO.Workspace
Dim db As DAO.Database
Dim rs As DAO.Recordset


Set ws = Workspaces(0)
Set db = ws.OpenDatabase("VBAnswers.mdb")
Set rs = db.OpenRecordset("Department", dbOpenTable)

DisplayRSGrid rs, flxDepartment

rs.Close
```

Note: *It's not always necessary to prefix a DAO object name with the DAO class name, as this example illustrates. However, sometimes this is needed if multiple objects with the same name exist in one project. For instance, if you use both DAO and ADO in the same project, then you must prefix the objects that have common names by using the object's class name.*

In the previous code example, the Workspace object called ws is created. Then, the OpenDatabase method of the ws Workspace object is used to create a new Database object. The first parameter of the OpenDatabase method is a String data type that identifies the name of the database that will be opened. This example shows the VBAnswers.mdb database being opened.

Next, the OpenRecordset method of the db Database object is used to create a new Recordset object. The OpenRecordset method takes four parameters. The first parameter is required, and the last three parameters are optional. In this case, the first parameter contains a String data type that identifies the table in the database that will be opened. This example shows that the Department table will be opened by the OpenRecordset method. The second parameter of the OpenRecordset method specifies the type of Recordset object that will be opened. The following table lists each of the DAO constants that specifies a type of Recordset object:

DAO Constant	Recordset Object Type
dbOpenTable	Table type
dbOpenDynamic	Dynamic type
dbOpenDynaset	Dynaset type
dbOpenForwardOnly	Forward-Only type
dbOpenSnapshot	Snapshot type

Using the constant dbOpenTable specifies that a Table Recordset object will be opened, which allows both forward and backward movement, as well as updating. The third and fourth parameters of the OpenDatabase method are not used in this example. However, you still need to understand their use. The third parameter controls the behavior of the Recordset object. The following table lists the constants that are allowed for the third parameter:

OpenRecordset Option Constants	Description
dbAppendOnly	Rows can be appended to the Recordset object, but no rows can be updated or deleted.
dbSQLPassthrough	The SQL statement will not be processed by Microsoft Jet. Instead, it will be sent to the server. This can only be used with Snapshot Recordset objects.
dbSeeChanges	Generates a DAO error if Microsoft Jet detects that a row contained in a Dynamic or Dynaset Recordset object has been updated by another application.
dbDenyWrite	Prevents other users from updating any rows that are contained in the Recordset object. This is only for local Jet databases.
dbDenyRead	Prevents other users from reading a Table Recordset object. This is only for local Jet databases.

OpenRecordset Option Constants	Description
dbForwardOnly	Creates a forward-only Recordset object. Note that this option exists only for backward-compatibility. You should use the dbOpenForwardOnly constant in the second parameter of the OpenRecordset method to create a forward-only Recordset object.
dbReadOnly	Prevents other users from changing a Recordset object.
dbReadAsync	Submits SQL to create the Recordset object asynchronously.
dbExecDirect	Executes a dynamic SQL statement on the database server. This is only for ODBCDirect connections.
dbInconsistent	Allows an update of a multitable join to write inconsistent one-to-many updates.
dbConsistent	All one-to-many table updates of a multitable join must be written consistently.

The fourth parameter of the OpenDatabase function sets the type of locking that Microsoft Jet uses to control the concurrency of the data in the Recordset object. The following table lists the values that are valid for the fourth parameter of the OpenRecordset function:

DAO Locking Constant	Description
dbReadOnly	Sets the Recordset object to read-only. No updates are allowed.
dbPessimistic	Sets the Recordset object to use pessimistic locking (whereby the page or record containing the edited row is locked until the Update method is executed).
dbOptimistic	Sets the Recordset object to use optimistic locking (whereby the page or record containing the edited row is not locked until the Update method is executed) based on a unique index.

DAO Locking Constant	Description
dbOptimisticValue	Sets the Recordset object to use optimistic locking based on the row values. This is only for ODBCDirect workspaces.
dbOptimisticBatch	Sets the Recordset object to use ODBC batch updating (whereby sets of local updates are sent to the server in blocks or batches). This is only for ODBCDirect workspaces.

After the Recordset object is created, the DisplayRSGrid function is executed, which displays the contents of a Recordset object by using an MSFlexGrid control. Unlike the Data control, DAO does not support the use of data-bound controls. Therefore, the contents of the Recordset object must be assigned to user interface objects, such as an MSFlexGrid control, by using code. The following listing shows the source code for the DisplayRSGrid function:

```
Private Function DisplayRSGrid(rs As DAO.Recordset, _
    grid As MSFlexGrid)

    Dim fld As DAO.Field

    On Error Resume Next

    grid.Redraw = False

    ' Set up the grid.
    grid.Cols = rs.Fields.Count
    grid.Rows = 1
    grid.Row = 0
    grid.Col = 0

    rs.MoveFirst

    ' Set up the grid headings.
    For Each fld In rs.Fields
        grid.Col = fld.OrdinalPosition
        grid.ColWidth(grid.Col) = _
```

```
              TextWidth(String(fld.Size + 9, "a"))
        grid.ColAlignment(grid.Col) = 1
        grid.Text = fld.Name
    Next fld

    ' Move through each row in the recordset.
    Do Until rs.EOF

        grid.Rows = grid.Rows + 1
        grid.Row = grid.Rows - 1

        ' Loop through all fields.
        For Each fld In rs.Fields
            grid.Col = fld.OrdinalPosition
            grid.Text = fld.Value
        Next fld

        rs.MoveNext

    Loop

    grid.Redraw = True

End Function
```

The DisplayRSGrid function accepts two required
parameters. The first parameter is the name of a DAO
Recordset object, and the second parameter must contain
the name of an MSFlexGrid object. The first thing that
happens inside the DisplayRSGrid function is that an
instance of the DAO Field object is declared to access the
properties of each column contained in the Recordset object.
Next, the VB error-handling function is enabled to allow the
DisplayRSGrid function to continue running if it tries to
process an empty Recordset object. Then, the grid's Redraw
property is set to False, to prevent the grid from being
repainted on the screen each time an item is added to
the grid.

The next section of code sets up the grid. The number of
columns in the grid is set to the number of columns that were
contained in the Count property of the Fields collection of the

rs Recordset object. Then, the number of rows is set to 1, and the current row and column are set in the upper-left grid cell (grid coordinates 0,0).

After the grid has been set up, the Recordset object is positioned at the first record using the MoveFirst method. Then, the column headings of the Recordset object are retrieved, using a For Each loop to iterate through the Fields collection of the rs Recordset object. For each Field object contained in the Fields collection, the OrdinalPosition property is used to put it into a unique column of the grid, and then the column name is retrieved from the fld.Name property. Next, using the MSFlexGrid's ColWidth method, the column width of each MSFlexGrid column is set at nine positions larger than the size of the Recordset object's column. Then, the cell alignment is set to 1, which causes the entries in each cell to be left-justified. Finally, the column name from the fld.Name property is assigned to the current cell.

After setting up the grid's column headings with the column names from the Recordset object, a Do Until loop is used to read through all the rows in the Recordset object. When the end of the Recordset object is reached, the rs.EOF property becomes True and the code drops out of the Read loop.

As each record is retrieved from the rs Recordset object, the number of rows in the grid is reset to allow the grid to display the new record. To list all of the Recordset object's column values in the grid, a For Each loop is used to iterate through the Fields collection. Again, the OrdinalPosition of each column is used to assign the Recordset column value to the appropriate column in the grid. The fld Field object's Value property is then used to retrieve the actual column data, whereupon it is assigned to the grid's Text property. After all the data values from the row have been moved to the appropriate location in the grid, the rs.MoveNext function is used to position the cursor to the next row in the Recordset object.

When all the information from the Recordset object has been assigned to the MSFlexGrid object, the Redraw property is set to True, which causes the grid to display the new data.

How do I add data to a database using DAO?

In addition to retrieving data, Recordset objects can be used to update data. However, not all Recordset objects are updateable. The ability to update a Recordset object depends on the type of Recordset object that is opened and the options that were used in the call to the OpenRecordset method. A summary of the Recordset object types and their ability to support data-update methods is listed in the following table:

Result Set	Updateable
dbOpenForwardOnly	Yes (current row only)
dbOpenSnapshot	No
dbOpenDynaset	Yes
dbOpenDynamic	Yes
dbOpenTable	Yes

If a Recordset object had been created using one of the updateable Recordset types, then you can use the AddNew method in combination with the Update method to add rows to the DAO Recordset object. The following code illustrates how you can add rows to an updateable DAO Recordset object:

```
Dim ws As DAO.Workspace
Dim db As DAO.Database
Dim rs As DAO.Recordset

Dim i As Integer

Set ws = Workspaces(0)
Set db = ws.OpenDatabase("VBAnswers.mdb")
Set rs = db.OpenRecordset("Department", dbOpenTable)

Screen.MousePointer = vbHourglass

For i = 0 To 50
    rs.AddNew
    rs!Dep_ID = i
    rs!Dep_Name = "Department " & CStr(i)
    rs.Update
```

```
Next

DisplayRSGrid rs, flxDepartment

rs.Close

Screen.MousePointer = vbDefault
```

After the Workspace and Database objects have been instantiated, the OpenRecordset method is used to create a new Recordset object named rs. The first parameter of the OpenRecordset method accepts a string that contains either a SQL statement that defines the Recordset object or the name of a table. In this case, the string is set to the name of the Department table in the VBAnswers database. The second parameter of the OpenRecordset method uses the constant dbOpenTable to specify that the Recordset object will be an updateable Table Recordset object.

After the Recordset object has been created, a For Next loop is used to add a series of rows to the result set. Within the For Next loop, the AddNew method is called to create a new row buffer for the row that will be added to the Recordset object. After the AddNew method has been executed, the value of each of the columns is assigned. The value of the Dep_ID column is set using the unique integer supplied by the loop counter variable (i), while the Dep_Name column is assigned the value of a string that is formed by concatenating the literal "Department" and the string representation of the loop counter. After the new row values have been set, the Update method is called to add the row to the Recordset object, which also results in the update of the base Department table.

After all 50 rows have been added to the Department table, the DisplayRSGrid function is called to display the new contents of the Department table in an MSFlexGrid control named flxDepartment. Finally, the Recordset object is closed using the Close method.

 ### How do I update data using DAO?

The Edit and Update methods of the Recordset object can be used to update rows in an updateable recordset. The following code illustrates how you can update the rows in a Table Recordset object:

```
Dim ws As DAO.Workspace
Dim db As DAO.Database
Dim rs As DAO.Recordset


Set ws = Workspaces(0)
Set db = ws.OpenDatabase("VBAnswers.mdb")
Set rs = db.OpenRecordset("Department", dbOpenTable)

Dim sTemp As String

Screen.MousePointer = vbHourglass

Do Until rs.EOF
    rs.Edit
    ' Jet returns blank filled strings -- truncate
    ' at the first blank.
    sTemp = RTrim(rs!Dep_Name)
    rs!Dep_Name = "Updated " & sTemp
    rs.Update
    rs.MoveNext
Loop

DisplayRSGrid rs, flxDepartment

rs.Close

Screen.MousePointer = vbDefault
```

In this example, the Workspace and Database objects are declared and instantiated. Then, the OpenRecordset method is used to create a new Recordset object named rs. Again, the first parameter of the OpenRecordset method contains a string that defines that the Department table will be used as the source for the Recordset object. The dbOpenTable constant in the second parameter indicates that the Recordset object will be scrollable and updateable.

After the Recordset object has been created, a Do Until loop is used to read all the rows contained in the recordset.

The loop is ended when the EOF property of the Recordset object becomes True. Within the Do loop, the Edit method is used to put each row into edit mode. Next, because Microsoft Jet returns string values and all trailing blanks, the nonblank data value of the Dep_Name column is moved into a temporary string variable. This prevents the updated column value from exceeding the length of the column. Next, the value of the Dep_Name column is set to the new string value that begins with the literal "Updated". You might note that the Dep_ID field is not updated, because it is the table's primary key.

After the new values have been assigned to the Dep_Name column, the Update method is called to update the row in both the Recordset object and the data source. Then, the MoveNext method of the rs Recordset object is used to move to the next row in the Recordset object. After all the rows have been updated, the DisplayRSGrid function is called to display the new contents of the rs Recordset object, and then the Recordset object's Close method is used to close the recordset.

How do I delete data using DAO?

The Delete method of the Recordset object is used to remove rows in an updateable DAO recordset. The following code illustrates how you can delete rows in a Table Recordset object:

```
Dim ws As DAO.Workspace
Dim db As DAO.Database
Dim rs As DAO.Recordset


Set ws = Workspaces(0)
Set db = ws.OpenDatabase("VBAnswers.mdb")
Set rs = db.OpenRecordset("Department", dbOpenTable)

Screen.MousePointer = vbHourglass

Do Until rs.EOF
    rs.Delete
    rs.MoveNext
Loop
```

```
DisplayRSGrid rs, flxDepartment

rs.Close

Screen.MousePointer = vbDefault
```

Like the previous examples, the OpenRecordset method is used to create a new Recordset object based on the Department table in the VBAnswers database. The value of dbOpenTable in the second parameter of the OpenResultset ensures that the rs Recordset object is updateable. After the Recordset object has been created, a Do Until loop is used to read through all the rows of the recordset. Each row is deleted by using the Delete method, and then the MoveNext method is used to position the cursor to the next row in the result set. Finally, the empty Recordset object is displayed using the DisplayRSGrid function, and the Close method is used to close the Recordset object.

Are any good examples of using DAO available that can help me to get started?

One of the best examples of using DAO can be found in the source code for Visual Data Manager. In fact, many of the forms used in Visual Data Manager were designed to be used in other applications with very little modification. The forms in the Visual Data Manager do contain some global variables, which can make them a little difficult to move; but they are listed in the "global variables" section of the VisData.bas file, so they are relatively easy to find. You can add the following forms to your application:

- **frmAttachments**   Displays a list of attached tables, allowing the user to add new attachments and reattach existing attachments

- **frmDataControl**   A form that dynamically loads a recordset and then displays its contents

- **frmDataGrid**   Displays a recordset in a bound grid

- **frmDynaSnap**   Loads a Dynaset or Snapshot Recordset object and provides the ability to zoom in on a memo field or large text fields and use a scroll bar to move around the recordset

- **frmGroupsUsers**   A dialog box that allows you to administer the permissions of the groups and users of the database

- **frmQuery**   A fairly full-featured query builder

- **frmSQL**   Allows a user to enter and execute SQL statements

- **frmTableObj**   Displays a Table Recordset object with the ability to search and set the current index

Chapter 15

The ADO Data Control and Object Library

Answer Topics!

The ADO Data Control and Object Library @ a Glance

This chapter shows you how to access a database using Visual Basic's new ADO Data control, and explains the basics of developing database applications using the ADO (ActiveX Data Objects) object library. The ADO Data control provides a quick and easy method for creating simple data access forms. However, like the standard Data control, its capabilities are fairly limited. The ADO object framework provides a more comprehensive set of functions that enables you to develop both local single-user and multiuser client/server database applications.

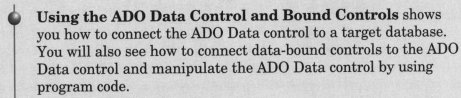 **Using the ADO Data Control and Bound Controls** shows you how to connect the ADO Data control to a target database. You will also see how to connect data-bound controls to the ADO Data control and manipulate the ADO Data control by using program code.

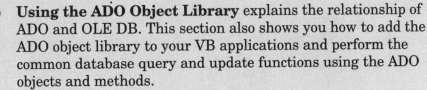 **Using the ADO Object Library** explains the relationship of ADO and OLE DB. This section also shows you how to add the ADO object library to your VB applications and perform the common database query and update functions using the ADO objects and methods.

USING THE ADO DATA CONTROL AND BOUND CONTROLS

The first part of this chapter covers using the ADO Data control with the standard VB data-bound controls. The questions and answers in this section show you how to connect the ADO Data control to a target database. They also illustrate how to bind a data-bound control to the ADO Data control and manipulate the ADO Data control by using program code.

What's the difference between the ADO Data control and the standard Data control?

Functionally, the ADO Data control is very much like its predecessor, the standard Data control. Both controls enable you to quickly connect your VB application to a target data source, and both controls enable you to connect data-bound controls to individual fields in the target data source. However, whereas the standard Data control is built on top of DAO (Data Access Objects) and the Microsoft Jet database engine, the ADO Data control is built on the foundation of ADO (ActiveX Data Objects) and OLE DB.

DAO and Microsoft Jet were primarily designed to enable database access to a local Access database. Although DAO and Microsoft Jet evolved to support other data sources, such as networked databases (SQL Server, for example), they were neither optimized for that type of functionality nor really intended to be used with nonrelational data sources. OLE DB and its ADO object library provide data access to a number of different data sources, including both relational data sources, such as Access and SQL Server, and nonrelational data sources, such as Active Directory (AD), text files, and Excel spreadsheets. Basically, any data that can be represented in tabular form (rows and columns) can be accessed using OLE DB and ADO. This broader base of functionality allows the ADO Data control and the ADO object library to be used for a much greater variety of tasks than what DAO and the standard Data control can be used for.

How do I add the ADO Data control to my VB project?

Before you can use the ADO Data control in your VB application, you must add the Microsoft ADO Data Control 6.0 ActiveX control to your project. To do so, follow these steps:

1. Select Project | Components, which displays the Components dialog box, shown in Figure 15-1.

2. Scroll through Visual Basic's Components dialog box until you see Microsoft ADO Data Control 6.0 (OLEDB) entry.

3. Click the check box and then click the OK button to add the ADO Data control to the VB Toolbox. You can then drag and drop the control onto the forms in your application.

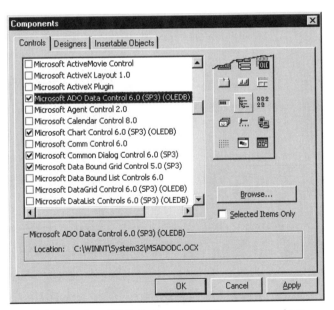

Figure 15-1   Adding the ADO Data control to your project

How do I connect the ADO Data control to a target database?

To connect the ADO Data control to a target data source, you first set the ConnectionString property to identify the desired OLE DB provider and target data source. Next, you need to set the RecordSource property to select the data that will be retrieved by the ADO Data control. These properties can be set at either design time or runtime by using program code.

To set the ConnectionString property in VB's integrated design environment (IDE), follow these steps:

1. Drag and drop an instance of the ADO Data control onto a form.

2. Then, display the ADO Data control's properties by pressing the F4 key.

3. Scroll to the ConnectionString property and click the ellipsis button to display the ADO Data control's custom Property Pages dialog box, shown in Figure 15-2.

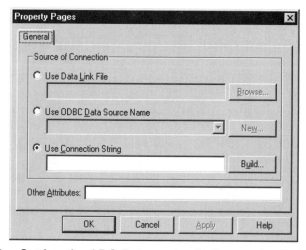

Figure 15-2 Setting the ADO Data control's ConnectionString property

The ADO Data control's Property Pages dialog box enables you to select the type of connection that will be used by the ADO Data control. You have three options:

- You can choose a data link file, a file that ends in the extension .udl and contains a saved OLE DB connection string.

- You can choose an ODBC data source name, which defines the connection to a relational database and is typically built using the ODBC Administrator.

- You can interactively build an OLE DB connection string.

To build an OLE DB connection string, follow these steps:

1. Click the Build button, which displays the Data Link Properties page shown in Figure 15-3.

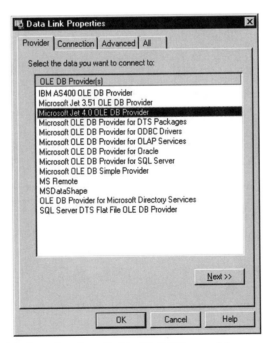

Figure 15-3 Setting the data link's OLE DB provider

2. Specify the OLE DB provider. In Figure 15-3, Microsoft Jet 4.0 OLE DB Provider has been selected.

3. Click the Next button to display the Connection tab of the Data Link Properties dialog box, shown in Figure 15-4.

   The specific values that are displayed on the Connection tab vary according to the OLE DB provider that you have selected. For the Microsoft Jet 4.0 OLE DB Provider, you must specify the name of the Access MDB database file that will be used.

4. Click the ellipsis button next to the Select or Enter a Database Name field to display an Open dialog box that can be used to interactively locate the desired database file.

5. After you enter the database name, you can optionally test the connection by clicking the Test Connection button. Those are the only parameters that are required.

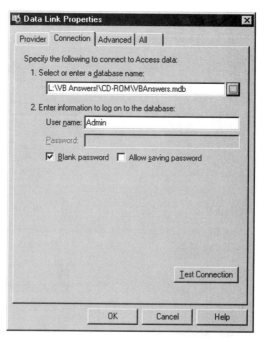

Figure 15-4   Setting the data link's connection properties

6. Click OK to save all the selections in a new ConnectionString property that will be used by the ADO Data control.

 Note: *This example uses the sample VBAnswers database. Instructions for creating this database using the Visual Data Manager are presented in Chapter 14.*

Now, the RecordSource property of the ADO Data control must be set as follows:

1. Scroll through the ADO Data control's properties until the RecordSource property is visible, and click the ellipsis button to display the RecordSource Property Pages dialog box, shown in Figure 15-5.

2. Set the RecordSource property for the ADO Data control to the name of a table, the name of a stored procedure, or a SQL statement. In Figure 15-5, the CommandType has been set to 2 - adCmdTable, which indicates that the RecordSource will be a table in the target database.

3. Set the Table or Stored Procedure Name field to the name of the target. Clicking the drop-down arrow next to this field displays a list of all the tables in the data source.

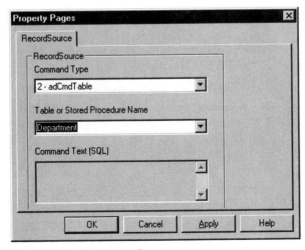

Figure 15-5 Setting the RecordSource property

In Figure 15-5, the table named Department has been selected from the VBAnswers.mdb database.

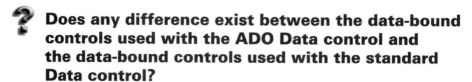 **Does any difference exist between the data-bound controls used with the ADO Data control and the data-bound controls used with the standard Data control?**

No. The data-bound controls used with the ADO Data control are the same as the data-bound controls used with the standard Data control. The exact same controls that can be bound to the standard Data control can also be bound to the ADO Data control. The only change that you need to make is to set the DataSource property of the data-bound control to point to an available ADO Data control.

How do I connect data-bound controls to the different database fields using the ADO control?

Data-bound controls can be connected to the ADO Data control by setting their DataSource and DataField properties. After you place an ADO Data control on a form and connect it to a data source, the data-bound controls that are on the form can be connected to the ADO Data control. As a general rule, each data-bound control is associated with only one specific field or column of the data source that is being used by the ADO Data control.

1. First, specify the name of the ADO Data control in the data-bound control's DataSource property.

   Figure 15-6 shows the DataSource property of the TextBox control named txtDepID being set. The data-bound txtDepID TextBox control is being bound to the adoDepartment ADO Data control.

2. Click the drop-down arrow in the DataSource property to display all the ADO Data controls that are available on the current form.

3. To assign the name of an ADO Data control to the data-bound control's DataSouce property, simply click the

Figure 15-6   Setting the DataSource property of a data-bound text box

ADO Data control name that's displayed in the drop-down list.

Next, you need to select the field that will be bound to the data-bound control, by using the data-bound control's DataField property. Figure 15-7 shows the DataField property of the txtDepID TextBox control being set with the Dep_ID field from the data source.

4. Click the DataField property's drop-down arrow to display all the fields or columns that have been made available by the ADO Data control.

5. To bind a specific field to the data-bound control, simply click the desired field name in the drop-down list. Figure 15-7 shows the Dep_ID field from the Department table being bound to the txtDepID TextBox control.

Just as with the standard Data control, multiple data-bound controls can be bound to a single ADO Data control. To bind additional data-bound controls to the ADO

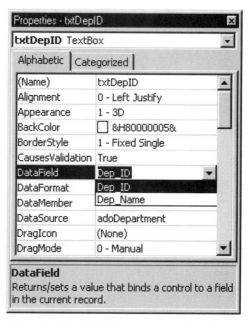

Figure 15-7 Setting the DataField property of a data-bound control

Data control, simply set the DataSource property to the name of the ADO Data control and then set the DataField property to the individual field in the data source that will be bound to each data-bound control.

 I'm trying to use the ADO Data control with the MSFlexGrid control, but it doesn't seem to work. How do I use the ADO Data control with the MSFlexGrid control?

The ADO Data control is not compatible with the MSFlexGrid control. The MSFlexGrid control can only be bound to the standard Data control or the RemoteData control, which is designed for use with networked ODBC data sources, such as SQL Server or Oracle. If you want a bound Grid control that works with the ADO Data control, then you need to use the new Microsoft Hierarchical FlexGrid (MSHFlexGrid) control introduced with VB 6.

Like the standard FlexGrid control, the MSHFlexGrid control displays a spreadsheet window presenting rows and columns of data. It allows sorting and formatting of data, and it can be used with both character data and binary images, such as bitmaps and WAV files. When bound to a Data control, the MSHFlexGrid control is read-only. A major new feature of this control is its ability to display hierarchical recordsets—relational tables displayed in a hierarchical fashion. In other words, the MSHFlexGrid control can display related recordsets in a parent-and-child fashion. This feature is useful for actions such as displaying an order header record followed by all the related order detail records.

The MSHFlexGrid control is bound to the ADO Data control in the same way as other data-bound controls are bound to the ADO Data control. First, the ConnectionString and RecordSource properties of the ADO Data control must be set to the desired data source. Then, the DataSource property of the MSHFlexGrid control is set to the name of the ADO Data control.

When bound to the ADO Data control, the MSHFlexGrid control, unlike the DBGrid control, doesn't allow me to choose the fields from the table that I want to display in the grid. How do I choose the data fields that will be displayed in the MSHFlexGrid control?

The MSHFlexGrid control performs automatic recordset-to-column bindings, and has no facilities that allow you to bind a given column in the ADO Data control's recordset to a specific grid column. Although you can't specify the column binding by using custom Property Pages, as you can in the DataBound Grid control, you can still selectively display columns in the MSHFlexGrid control by taking advantage of the ADO Data control's ability to define its recordset by using a SQL statement. The SQL Select keyword not only provides the ability to select certain columns from the data source, but also provides other features, such as the ability to select data from multiple tables and then group and sort the data that's retrieved. You can specify a SQL Select statement in the

ADO Data control's RecordSource property, as Figure 15-8 illustrates.

In Figure 15-8, the Command Type drop-down list box has been set to adCmdText, which indicates that a SQL statement will be used to specify the data that will be retrieved by the ADO Data control. The actual SQL statement is then entered into the Command Text property. This SQL Select statement retrieves just the CustomerID, CompanyName, and Phone columns from the Customers table in the Northwind database.

 Tip: *It's important to note that when using SQL statements in the RecordSource property, the column names used in the Select statement must exactly match the column names in the data source. This means that you must be familiar with the structure (or schema) of the target table. If the column names don't match, the ADO Data control will generate a runtime error.*

You can see the resulting output in the MSHFlexGrid control that's displayed in Figure 15-9.

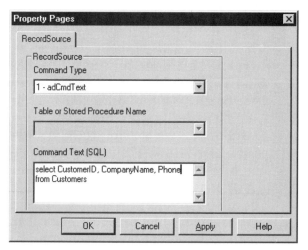

Figure 15-8 Using a SQL statement for the RecordSource property

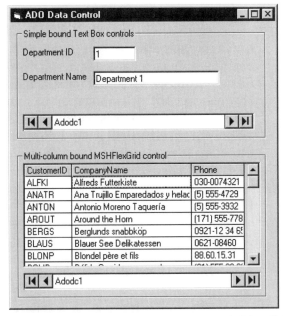

Figure 15-9   Displaying the SQL results in the MSHFlexGrid control

USING THE ADO OBJECT LIBRARY

The second part of this chapter covers using the ADO (ActiveX Data Objects) object framework to write database applications. This section begins by explaining the relationship between OLE DB and ADO, as well as the purpose of the different objects that comprise the ADO object library. The questions and answers in the latter part of the chapter provide detailed examples showing how to implement database queries and how to perform some of the common database update operations using ADO.

 ## How is ADO related to OLE DB?

OLE DB and ADO are the most recent data access programming interfaces developed by Microsoft. Microsoft has positioned OLE DB as the successor to ODBC. Considering

the widespread success of ODBC, this leaves OLE DB with some big shoes to fill. The ODBC API has enjoyed near universal acceptance. It is supported by most shrink-wrapped desktop applications, such as Microsoft Office, and ODBC drivers exist for virtually all the major database systems. However, ODBC was designed primarily to handle relational data. The ODBC API is based upon SQL and, although it works very well for relational database access, was never intended to work with other nonrelational data sources. Like ODBC, OLE DB provides access to relational data, but OLE DB extends the functionality provided by ODBC. OLE DB has been designed as a standard interface for all types of data. In addition to relational database access, OLE DB provides access to a wide variety of data sources, including tabular data (such as Excel spreadsheets), ISAM files (such as dBase), Windows 2000 Active Directory, and even IBM host DB2 data.

Applications that use OLE DB are classified as either of the following:

● **OLE DB consumers** Applications that are written to use the OLE DB interface.

● **OLE DB providers** Applications that are responsible for accessing data sources and supplying data to OLE consumers via the OLE DB interface.

However, the OLE DB programming interface is a low-level interface that requires support for pointers, data structures, and direct memory allocation. This makes the direct use of OLE DB providers unsuitable for development environments that do not provide this type of low-level functionality, which includes Visual Basic, VBA, VBScript, Java, JScript, JavaScript, and many others. This is where ADO (ActiveX Data Objects) comes in to use. ADO is a COM layer for OLE DB that allows OLE DB providers to be accessed by interactive and scripting languages that do not support low-level memory access and manipulation. ADO essentially is an OLE DB consumer that provides application-level access to OLE DB data sources. ADO is implemented as a COM object library that can be accessed by most OLE-compliant development and scripting environments.

What do I need to do to use the ADO object library in my applications?

Before you can use ADO from Visual Basic, you must set a reference to the ADO object library. To add a reference to the ADO 2.5 object library in Visual Basic 6, follow these steps:

1. Select Project | References, which displays the References dialog box, shown in Figure 15-10.

2. Scroll through Visual Basic's References dialog box and click the Microsoft ActiveX Data Objects 2.5 Library check box.

3. Click OK to add the ADO object library to the VB IDE.

Unlike ActiveX controls, such as the ADO Data control, adding a reference to a VB project doesn't create any visual objects in the VB Toolbox. To see the ADO objects, properties, and methods, you need to use Visual Basic's Object Browser. Figure 15-11 displays the ADO object library using Visual Basic's Object Browser.

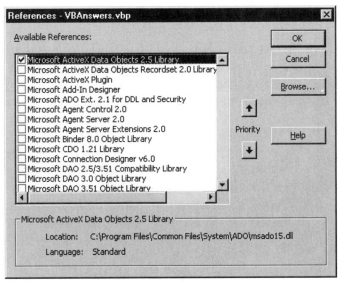

Figure 15-10 Setting a reference to the Microsoft ADO 2.5 Library

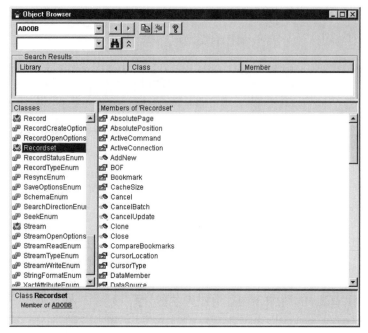

Figure 15-11 Displaying the ADO 2.5 object library in the Object Browser

What are the primary objects found in the ADO object framework?

ADO is not implemented using a hierarchical object framework like DAO. However, the ADO object model is simpler and flatter than either the DAO or RDO object frameworks that were introduced in the earlier versions of Visual Basic. Figure 15-12 shows an overview of ADO's object hierarchy.

The Connection, Recordset, and Command objects are the three primary objects in the ADO object model. The Connection object represents a connection to the remote data source. In addition to establishing the connection to a data source, Connection objects can be used to control the transaction scope. A Connection object can be associated with either a Recordset object or a Command object.

The Recordset object represents a result set that is returned from the data source. An ADO Recordset object can either use an open Connection object or establish its own connection to the target data source. Recordset objects enable

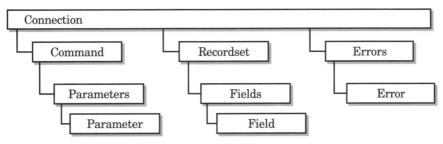

Figure 15-12   ADO object hierarchy

you to both query and modify data. Each Recordset object
contains a collection of Field objects, in which each Field
object represents a column of data in the Recordset.

The Command object is used to issue commands and
parameterized SQL statements. Command objects can be
used for both action SQL statements and SQL queries that
return recordsets. Like the ADO Recordset object, the
Command object can either use an active Connection object or
establish its own connection to the target data source. The
Command object contains a Parameters collection, in which
each Parameter object in the collection represents a
parameter that is used by the Command object. In the case
where a Command object is used to execute a parameterized
SQL statement, each Parameter object represents one of the
parameters in the SQL statement.

Directly beneath the Connection object in the ADO
hierarchy is the Errors collection. Each Error object
contained in the Errors collection contains information about
an error that was encountered by one of the objects in the
ADO object framework.

In addition to the main objects shown in Figure 15-12, the
Connection, Command, Recordset, and Field objects all have
a Properties collection, which consists of a set of Property
objects. Each Property object can be used to get or set the
various properties associated with the object.

At first glance, the ADO framework may seem just as
hierarchically structured as DAO, but that really isn't the
case. Unlike the other data access object frameworks, all the
ADO objects, such as the Connection, Command, and
Recordset objects, can be created directly without needing to

be accessed through a higher-level object. This makes the ADO object framework simpler to use than the other data access object models.

 ## How do I retrieve data from a database using ADO?

ADO enables you to retrieve data using either the Recordset or the Command object, both of which can either be used with an active Connection object or open their own connections. However, the Recordset object is the primary object to use to retrieve data, because it enables access to the individual columns contained in the recordset, and allows your application to traverse the contents of the recordset. The ADO Recordset object represents a result set that's returned from a database query.

The specific functionality offered by the ADO Recordset object depends on the type of recordset that is used. The ADO Recordset object's CursorType property governs the type of recordset that will be used by the ADO Recordset object. ADO provides support for Forward-Only, Static, Keyset, and Dynamic Recordset objects. The type of cursor used in an ADO Recordset object must be set before the Recordset is opened. If you don't specify the type of Recordset object that you want to use, ADO will automatically use a Forward-Only cursor.

- **Forward-Only cursors** The default cursor used by ADO. Forward-Only cursors provide the best performance and the least overhead of any of the ADO cursor types, but they also are less capable than other ADO cursors, because they only support forward scrolling through the rows in the recordset. ADO Recordset objects that use Forward-Only cursors are updateable, but only the current row can be modified.

- **Static cursors** Provide a snapshot of the data at the time the cursor was opened. ADO Recordset objects that use Static cursors are not updateable and do not reflect any changes that are made in the base tables unless the cursor is closed and reopened. Because of their static nature, Recordset objects created by Static cursors generally are less resource-intensive than Recordset objects that use Keyset or Dynamic cursors. However,

since the Static cursor makes a local copy of the data, you need to be careful about using this type of cursor with large result sets.

● **Keyset cursors**   Build a local set of keys, wherein each key is an index to a row in the result set. When your application accesses a Recordset object that uses a Keyset cursor, the key value from the local keyset is used to retrieve the corresponding row from the base table. Recordset objects that use Keyset cursors are updateable and support both forward and backward movement through the recordset.

● **Dynamic cursors**   The most powerful and capable type of ADO cursors, but also the most resource-intensive. Dynamic cursors are very similar to Keyset cursors. Both use a local set of keys that correspond to each row in the result set and both are fully updateable. However, unlike Recordset objects that use a Keyset cursor, Recordset objects that use Dynamic cursors are able to automatically reflect any changes that other applications make to the base tables. Dynamic cursors typically are used only with networked data sources, such as SQL Server.

The following listing illustrates how to use a Recordset object to read and display the contents of a database table:

```
Dim cn As New ADODB.Connection
Dim rs As New ADODB.Recordset

Screen.MousePointer = vbHourglass

' Set up the Jet 4.0 OLE DB connection string.
cn.ConnectionString = _
    "Provider=Microsoft.Jet.OLEDB.4.0;" & _
    "Data Source=C:\Program Files\Microsoft Visual _
    Studio\VB98\NWIND.MDB;" & _
    "Persist Security Info=False"
' Open the Connection.
cn.Open

' Open the Recordset object by using the Connection
' object.
```

```
rs.Open "customers", cn, , , adCmdTable

' Display the Customers table in the grid.
DisplayRSGrid rs, flxDisplayData

' Close the Recordset and Connection objects.
rs.Close
cn.Close

Screen.MousePointer = vbDefault
```

The Dim statements at the beginning of this listing create a new ADO Connection object named cn and a Recordset object named rs. After the ADO objects are declared, the ConnectionString property of the cn Connection object is set up to use the OLE DB provider for Jet 4 and connect to the Nwind.mdb. Then, the Connection object's Open method is used to connect to the data source.

Next, a Forward-Only cursor is opened using the Recordset object's Open method, which takes five optional parameters. The first parameter is a Variant data type that defines the data source. It can accept the name of an existing Command object, a SQL statement, a table name, or the name of a stored procedure. In this example, the first parameter contains the name of a table in Nwind.mdb database.

The Open method's optional second parameter can be used to associate the Recordset object with an ADO Connection object. This parameter can accept either a String that contains an OLE DB connection string or a Variant that contains the name of an active ADO Connection object. If you specify an OLE DB connection string rather than the name of a Connection object, ADO implicitly creates a Connection object and uses it to establish a link to the target data source. In this example, the ADO Connection object, cn, is used in the second parameter.

The third optional parameter of the Open method is used to specify the cursor type that the Recordset object will use. If this parameter is not designated, then the cursor type will be set to Forward-Only by default, which is the simplest and the best-performing option. Table 15-1 presents the ADO

ADO Constant	Cursor Type
adOpenForwardOnly	Forward-Only cursor (default)
adOpenStatic	Static cursor
adOpenKeyset	Keyset cursor
adOpenDynamic	Dynamic cursor

Table 15-1   ADO Recordset Cursor Types

constants that are used to specify the type of cursor that will be used by an ADO Recordset object.

The fourth optional parameter is used to specify the type of locking that will be used by the OLE DB provider. If this parameter is not designated, the lock type will be set to read-only by default. Table 15-2 presents the ADO constants that are used to specify the lock type that will be used by an ADO Recordset object.

The fifth optional parameter is used to specify the options of the Open method. The options parameter is used to tell ADO explicitly how to handle the first parameter if the first parameter does not contain the name of an ADO Command object. In this example, the constant of adCmdTable indicates that the first parameter contains the name of a table in the target data source.

After the Open method completes, the data in the Recordset is available for processing. In the previous example, the DisplayRSGrid subroutine is called to display the contents of the rs Recordset object in a grid, and then both the Recordset object and the Connection object are closed.

Lock Type	Description
adLockReadOnly	Read-only (default)
adLockPessimistic	Pessimistic locking
adLockOptimistic	Optimistic locking
adLockBatchOptimistic	Optimistic locking using batch mode updates

Table 15-2   ADO Recordset Lock Types

 Note: *In the examples presented in this chapter, the Connection object is closed at the end of each code section. This would not be the case for a typical production application, in which the Connection object normally would be opened at the beginning of the application and then closed when the application ends.*

The following listing shows the DisplayRSGrid subroutine being used. In this listing, you can see how to move through the rows in the Recordset object and how to access the individual database column information that's contained in the Fields collection.

```
Public Function DisplayRSGrid(rs As ADODB.Recordset, _
  Grid As MSFlexGrid)

    Dim fld As ADODB.Field
    Dim nFldCount As Integer

    On Error Resume Next

    Grid.Redraw = False

    ' Set up the grid.
    Grid.Cols = rs.Fields.Count
    Grid.Rows = 1
    Grid.Row = 0
    Grid.Col = 0

    rs.MoveFirst

    nFldCount = 0
    ' Set up the grid headings.
    For Each fld In rs.Fields
        Grid.Col = nFldCount
        Grid.ColWidth(Grid.Col) = _
            TextWidth(String(fld.ActualSize + 4, "a"))
        Grid.ColAlignment(Grid.Col) = 1
        Grid.Text = fld.Name
        nFldCount = nFldCount + 1
    Next fld

    ' Move through each row in the recordset.
```

```
    Do Until rs.EOF

        Grid.Rows = Grid.Rows + 1
        Grid.Row = Grid.Rows - 1

        nFldCount = 0
        ' Loop through all fields.
        For Each fld In rs.Fields
            Grid.Col = nFldCount
            Grid.Text = fld.Value
            nFldCount = nFldCount + 1
        Next fld

        rs.MoveNext

    Loop

    Grid.Redraw = True

End Function
```

At the very beginning of this subroutine, an instance of the ADO Recordset object named rs is passed as the first parameter, and an instance of the MSFlexGrid object is passed as the second parameter of the DisplayRSGrid subroutine. This allows the same subroutine to be reused with many different Recordset and Grid objects. The Dim statement that follows creates an instance of an ADO Field object named fld.

Note: *Unlike the previous ADO examples, the preceding listing didn't need to use the New keyword to declare either the ADO Recordset object or the ADO Field object, because both of these variables refer to an instance of a Recordset object that has already been created.*

After the ADO objects have been declared, the next portion of the DisplayRSGrid subroutine sets up the grid to display the Recordset object. First, the grid's Redraw property is set to False to prevent the grid from being repainted as each item is added to the grid. Then, the number of grid columns is set using the Count property of the Recordset object's Fields

collection. Next, the grid's Rows property is set up to have at least one row, which will contain the column heading information. Then, the grid's Row and Col properties are used to set the current grid cell at row 0, column 0 (the upper-left corner of the grid).

Once the grid's initial number of rows and columns have been set, the heading values and sizes for each of the grid's columns are set up. Every column in the result set will have a corresponding Field object in the Recordset object's Fields collection. A For Each loop is used to iterate through all the Field objects contained in the Fields collection. The first action within the For Each loop sets the column width of the grid by using the grid's ColWidth property. To set the width of the correct column, the ColWidth property requires the index of the current grid column that is supplied by the grid's Col property. The ColWidth property must be assigned a value in twips, so Visual Basic's TextWidth function is used to return the number of twips required for each Field object. The correct number of twips is determined by creating a placeholder string using the Field object's ActualSize property plus four extra characters that help to prevent the grid columns from appearing too crowded. Next, the grid's ColAlignment property for each column is set to left-justify the cell text. Then, the Field object's Name property is used as heading text for the grid columns. Finally, the current column is incremented using the nFldCount variable.

Next, a Do Until loop is used to read through all the columns in the Recordset object. The Do Until loop continues until the Recordset's EOF (End of File) property becomes True—which indicates that all the rows in the Recordset have been read. Inside the Do Until loop, the grid's Rows property is incremented to expand the size of the grid, and the Row property is incremented to move the current position to the new grid row. Then, the current grid column is set to the first column, and a For Each loop is used to move the data values contained in the Fields collection to the grid columns. Again, the nFldCount variable is used to keep track of the current grid column. After all the Field values have been processed, the

Recordset object's MoveNext method is used to move the cursor to the next row in the Recordset object.

How do I add data to a database using ADO?

Probably the easiest way to add data to a data source is to use the ADO Recordset object. The Recordset object's AddNew method, in combination with the Update method, can be used to add rows to an updateable ADO result set. The following code illustrates how you can add rows to a Recordset object that was created using a Keyset cursor:

```
Dim cn As New ADODB.Connection
Dim rs As New ADODB.Recordset
Dim i As Integer

Screen.MousePointer = vbHourglass

' Set up the Jet 4.0 OLE DB connection string.
cn.ConnectionString = _
    "Provider=Microsoft.Jet.OLEDB.4.0;" & _
    "Data Source=VBANSWERS.MDB;" & _
    "Persist Security Info=False"
' Open the Connection object.
cn.Open

' Pass in the SQL, Connection, Cursor type, lock type
' and source type.
rs.Open "Select Dep_ID, Dep_Name FROM department", _
        cn, adOpenKeyset, adLockOptimistic, adCmdText

' Add 50 rows to the department table.
For i = 1 To 50
    rs.AddNew
    rs!Dep_ID = i
    rs!Dep_Name = "Department " & CStr(i)
    rs.Update
Next

' Display the new rows in a grid.
DisplayRSGrid rs, flxDisplayData

' Close the connections.
```

```
rs.Close
cn.Close

Screen.MousePointer = vbDefault
```

In the first part of this listing, the new ADO Connection and Recordset objects are declared. Then, the connection string is established, and a connection to the target data source is started using the Connection object's Open method.

Next, the Recordset object is opened using the Open method. The first parameter of the Recordset object's Open method accepts a string that contains a SQL statement that defines the result set. In this case, the result set consists of the Dep_ID and the Dep_Name columns from the Department table that is contained in the Northwind (Nwnd.mdb) database. The second parameter of the Open method contains the name of an active Connection object named cn. The third parameter uses the constant adOpenKeyset to specify that the Recordset object will use a Keyset cursor. The fourth parameter contains the value adLockOptimistic. The third and fourth parameters indicate that this Recordset object set is updateable and that it will use optimistic record locking.

After the result set has been opened, a For Next loop is used to add 50 rows to the Recordset object. Within the For Next loop, the AddNew method is called to create a row buffer that will contain the new row values. Within the For Next loop, note how the individual columns are addressed using the column name and Bang (!) notation.

 Tip: *This notation is case-sensitive. When using the Bang notation, you must specify the column names exactly as they appear in the database. Otherwise, a runtime error will be generated.*

The value of the Dep_ID column is set using a unique integer value that is obtained by using the loop counter. The Dep_Name column is set using the string that is formed by concatenating the literal "Department" and the string representation of the loop counter. After the row values have

been set, the Update method is called to add the row to the Recordset object and the data source. Next, the DisplayRSGrid subroutine is called, which will display the new row values in a grid. Finally, the Close method is used to close both the Recordset and the Connection objects.

How do I update data using ADO?

The Recordset object's Update method can be used to update rows in an updateable ADO result set. The following code illustrates how you can update the rows in an ADO Recordset object that was created using a Keyset cursor:

```
Dim cn As New ADODB.Connection
Dim rs As New ADODB.Recordset
Dim i As Integer
Dim sTemp As String

Screen.MousePointer = vbHourglass

' Set up the Jet 4.0 OLE DB connection string.
cn.ConnectionString = _
"Provider=Microsoft.Jet.OLEDB.4.0;" & _
    "Data Source=VBANSWERS.MDB;" & _
    "Persist Security Info=False"
' Open the connection.
cn.Open

' Pass in SQL, Connection, cursor type, lock type,
' and source type.
rs.Open "Select Dep_ID, Dep_Name FROM department", _
        cn, adOpenKeyset, adLockOptimistic, adCmdText

Do Until rs.EOF
    ' Trim off the blanks, because ADO doesn't
    ' truncate the data.
    sTemp = Trim(rs!Dep_Name)
    rs!Dep_Name = "Updated " & sTemp
    ' Update the row.
    rs.Update
    rs.MoveNext
Loop

' Display the updated rows in a grid.
```

```
DisplayRSGrid rs, flxDisplayData

rs.Close
cn.Close

Screen.MousePointer = vbDefault
```

Like the other examples, in the first part of this listing, the new ADO Connection and Recordset objects are declared, and a connection to the target data source is started by using the Connection object's Open method.

Then, the Recordset object's Open method is used to create a new ADO Recordset object named rs. The first parameter of the Open method accepts a string that specifies the result set. In this case, the Recordset object consists of the Dep_ID and the Dep_Name columns from the Department table. The active Connection object named cn is used in the second parameter. The adOpenKeyset and asLockOptimistic constants used in the third and fourth parameters indicate that the Recordset object will use an updateable Keyset cursor and optimistic record locking.

After the Recordset object set has been created, a Do Until loop is used to read through all the rows in the Recordset object. The loop ends when the Recordset object's EOF property turns True. Within the Do loop, the value of the Dep_Name column is set to a new string value that begins with the literal "Updated", which is concatenated with the current column value. Then, the Update method is called to update the Recordset object, and the MoveNext method positions the cursor to the next row. After all the rows in the Recordset have been updated, the DisplayRSGrid function is used to display the contents of the updated Department table. Finally, the Close method is used to close the Recordset object and the Connection object.

 ## How do I delete data using ADO?

The ADO Recordset object's Delete method can be used to remove rows in a target data source. The following code illustrates how you can use an updateable Recordset to delete rows in the sample Department table:

```
Dim cn As New ADODB.Connection
Dim rs As New ADODB.Recordset
Dim i As Integer

On Error Resume Next

Screen.MousePointer = vbHourglass

' Set up the Jet 4.0 OLE DB connection string.
cn.ConnectionString = _
    "Provider=Microsoft.Jet.OLEDB.4.0;" & _
    "Data Source=VBANSWERS.MDB;" & _
    "Persist Security Info=False"
' Open the connection.
cn.Open

' Open the Department table for update.
rs.Open "department", cn, adOpenKeyset, _
    adLockOptimistic, adCmdTable

' Delete all of the rows.
Do Until rs.EOF
    rs.Delete
    rs.MoveNext
Loop

' Display the empty Recordset object in a grid.
DisplayRSGrid rs, flxDisplayData

' Close the connections.
rs.Close
cn.Close

Screen.MousePointer = vbDefault
```

As in the previous examples, in the first part of this listing, the new ADO Connection and Recordset objects are declared, and a connection to the target VBAnswers database is started by using the Connection object's Open method.

Next, the Recordset object's Open method is used to create a new ADO Recordset object based on the Department table in the VBAnswers database. The second parameter contains the name of an active Connection object named rs. The third

and fourth parameters contain the constants **adOpenKeyset** and **adLockOptimistic**, which specify, respectively, that the result set will use a Keyset cursor that supports updates using optimistic record locking.

After the Recordset object has been created, a Do Until loop is used to read through all the rows contained in the Recordset object. The rs Recordset object's Delete method is used to delete each row, and the MoveNext method positions the cursor to the next row in the result set. After all the rows have been deleted, the DisplayRSGrid subroutine is used to display the empty Department table. Finally, the Close method is used to close the Recordset object.

How do I handle ADO Errors?

Runtime errors that are generated using the ADO object framework are placed in the ADO Errors collection. When an ADO runtime error occurs, Visual Basic's error handler is fired, which enables you to trap and respond to runtime errors. This tight integration with Visual Basic makes it easy to handle ADO errors. The following cmdShowError_Click subroutine illustrates how ADO's error handling can be integrated with Visual Basic's On Error function:

```
Private Sub cmdShowError_Click()

    Dim cn As New ADODB.Connection
    Dim rs As New ADODB.Recordset

    On Error GoTo ErrorHandler

    Screen.MousePointer = vbHourglass

    ' Set up the Jet 4.0 OLE DB connection string.
    cn.ConnectionString = _
        "Provider=Microsoft.Jet.OLEDB.4.0;" & _
        "Data Source=VBANSWERS.MDB;" & _
        "Persist Security Info=False"
    ' Open the connection.
    cn.Open

    ' Use a Select statement that will generate
    ' an error.
    rs.Open "Select * FROM bad_table_name", cn
```

```
    rs.Close
    cn.Close

    Screen.MousePointer = vbDefault
    Exit Sub

ErrorHandler:
    DisplayADOError cn
    cn.Close

    Screen.MousePointer = vbDefault

End Sub
```

The previous cmdShowError function first opens a connection to the data source, and then it attempts to open a Recordset object against a nonexistent table. Near the beginning of this function, Visual Basic's error handler is enabled using the On Error statement. In this case, the On Error statement causes the program to branch to the ErrorHandler label when a trappable error is encountered.

Executing the Open method with a nonexistent table causes the ADO object framework to generate a runtime error. This causes the program execution to resume with the first statement following the label. In this example, the DisplayADOError subroutine will be executed following the invalid Open attempt.

The following listing shows how the DisplayADOError subroutine uses ADO's Error object and Errors collection to display information about an ADO error condition in a simple message box:

```
Private Sub DisplayADOError(cn As ADODB.Connection)

    Dim er As ADODB.Error

    For Each er In cn.Errors
        MsgBox "Number: " & er.Number & vbCrLf & _
        "Source: " & er.Source & vbCrLf & _
        "Text: " & er.Description
    Next

End Sub
```

In this subroutine, an ADO Connection object is passed in as a parameter. The Connection object is required, because the ADO Errors collection is contained in the Connection object. Next, a new ADO Error object named er is declared and a For Each loop is used to iterate through the ADO Errors collection. The loop is required, because the ADODB.Errors collection can contain multiple Error objects, where each Error object represents a different error condition. With the loop, the values of the Number, Source, and Description properties are displayed in a message box. The Number property of the ADO Error object contains the ADO error message number, while the Source property identifies the source object that fired the error. As you might expect, the Description property contains the error condition's text description. The message box that's displayed by the DisplayADOError subroutine is shown here:

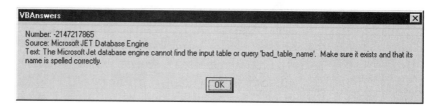

Chapter 16

Visual Database Tools

Answer Topics!

Visual Database Tools @ a Glance

In this chapter, you'll see how to take advantage of Visual Basic's new Visual Database Tools to help you quickly and easily create database applications that access both local single-user database applications such as Access, and multiuser database systems, such as SQL Server.

Using the Data Environment shows you how to create new DataEnvironment and Connection objects that link your VB application to a target database. You'll also see how to create Command objects that run queries against those databases.

Using Data Views shows you how to use the Data View window to list the available DataEnvironment and Connection objects. This section also shows you how to use the Data View window to view the contents of database tables.

Using the Query Designer covers using the new graphical Query Designer to build both data retrieval queries and action queries that can update data in the target database.

Using the Data Report Designer shows you how to create database reports using the new Data Report Designer. In this section, you see how to use the data report's graphical report designer, as well as how you can link a data report to an existing data environment Command object.

USING THE DATA ENVIRONMENT

The Data Environment Designer is a graphical, interactive, design-time tool for setting up the database access objects that can be used by your application. These database access objects can be used to connect either to a local Access database or to a networked database, such as SQL Server or Oracle.

Using Visual Basic's integrated development environment (IDE), you can create a new DataEnvironment object and then set the property values for its Connection and Command objects. The Connection objects are used to specify the target database, and the Command objects define the types of data access that will be used by your application. The questions and answers in this section show you how to use the DataEnvironment object in your applications, as well as how you can add your own Connection and Command objects to a data environment.

 I don't have the Data Environment in my project. How do I add it?

The data environment is normally available as one of the default references for the Visual Basic Professional and Enterprise Editions 6 (it isn't available in the Learning Edition). However, if the data environment has been removed, you won't be able to use the Data Environment Designer in the VB IDE. To add a reference to the Data Environment 1.0 object library in Visual Basic, first select Project | References, which displays the References dialog box, shown in Figure 16-1.

Scroll through the References dialog box until you see the Data Environment 1.0 object library. Click the check box and then click the OK button to add the Data Environment 1.0 object library to Visual Basic's IDE, which enables you to use it in your applications.

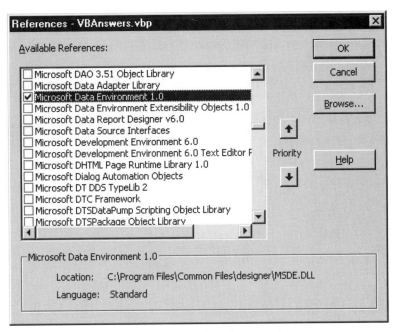

Figure 16-1 Adding a reference to the data environment

How do I create a new data environment and connect it to a target data source?

You can add a new data environment to your VB project by selecting Project | Add Data Environment. Immediately after you select this option, the Data Link Properties dialog box, shown in Figure 16-2, is displayed. (For an existing data environment, you can display the Data Link Properties dialog box by right-clicking the Connection object in your data environment and then choosing Properties from the pop-up menu.)

First, select an OLE DB provider on the Provider tab of the dialog box. In Figure 16-2, the Microsoft Jet 4.0 OLE DB

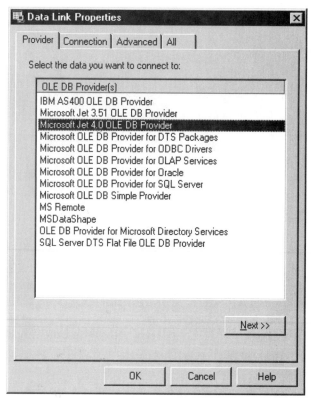

Figure 16-2 Selecting the data environment's OLE DB provider

Provider has been selected. Then, click Next to enter the connection information on the Connection tab of the dialog box. The layout of the Connection tab varies depending on the OLE DB provider selected on the Provider tab. Figure 16-3 shows the Connection tab layout that is required to connect to the sample Access Northwind database by using Microsoft Jet 4.0 OLE DB Provider, which was selected on the Provider tab.

On the Connection tab, the path to the database file is entered as the value for the database name prompt, and the default value of Admin is used for the logon prompt. These

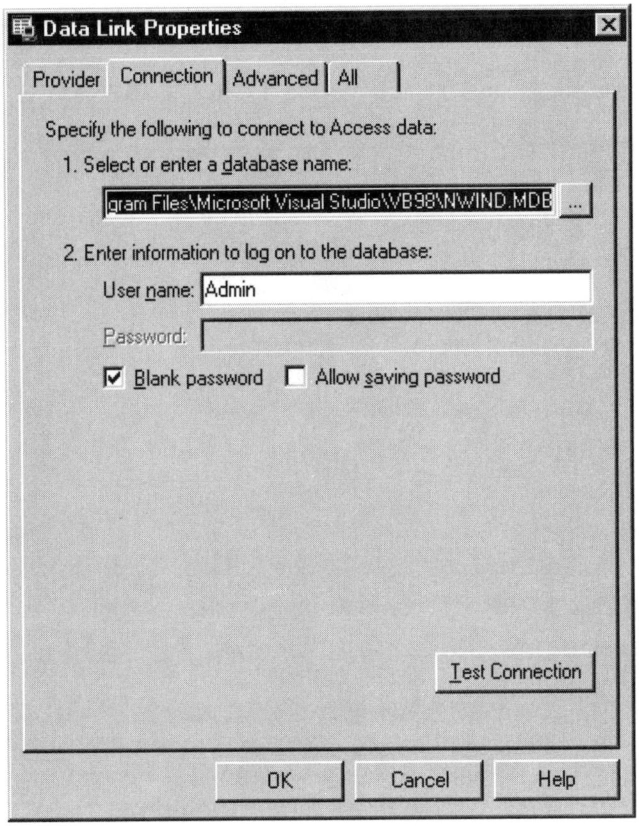

Figure 16-3 Setting the OLE DB provider's connection properties

are the only required fields. After you complete them, you can optionally test the connection by clicking the Test Connection button. Click the OK button to create the new DataEnvironment object along with a new Connection object. Figure 16-4 shows the Data Environment Designer.

In Figure 16-4, by default, the new data environment is named DataEnvironment1 and its Connection object is named Connection1. You can rename both the DataEnvironment and the Connection objects by using the VB Properties window: press the F4 key or select View | Properties Window. In Figure 16-5, the data environment has been renamed deVBAnswers.

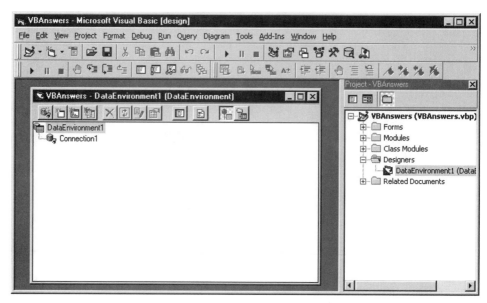

Figure 16-4 The default data environment

After the data environment has been renamed, you can save it using the new name. Saving the data environment adds a DSR file to your VB project. In the case of the data environment shown in Figure 16-5, the file named deVBAnswers.dsr will be added to your project.

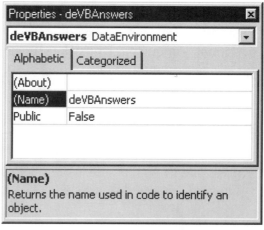

Figure 16-5 Renaming the data environment

 ## Can a data environment use more than one Connection object?

Yes. A single data environment can contain multiple Connection objects and multiple Command objects, and each Connection object can use both a different OLE DB Provider and a different target data source. To add a new Connection object to an existing DataEnvironment object, either click the Add Connection icon in the Data Environment Designer's toolbar or right-click the data environment entry to display the pop-up menu. From the pop-up menu, select the Add Connection option, as shown in Figure 16-6.

After you select the Add Connection option, the Data Link Properties dialog box is displayed, allowing you to select the OLE DB provider to use with the new Connection object. After you select the OLE DB provider, you must set the provider's Connection properties.

Tip: *Because the data environment can contain multiple Connection objects, and each Connection object can potentially use a different database, it's generally a good idea to name your data environment after the application. Each Connection object should then be named to represent the target data source.*

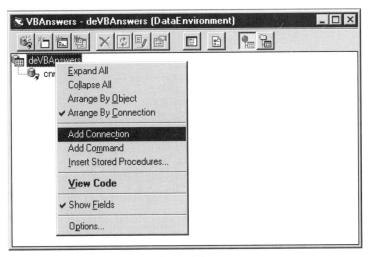

Figure 16-6   Adding a Connection object

? How do I create a new data environment Command object?

Data environment Command objects are used to run queries and execute commands on the target database. You can create a new data environment Command object either by clicking the Add Command button on the Data Environment Designer's toolbar or by right-clicking the Connection object in the data environment window and choosing Add Command from the pop-up menu. The Command Properties dialog box, shown in Figure 16-7, will be displayed, in which you can then specify the Command object's name, the connection it uses, and the source of its data.

In Figure 16-7, the Command object name has been set to cmdCustomers. You can select the Connection object that will be used by clicking the drop-down arrow in the Connection box. Here, the Command object's Connection property has been set to the name of the previously created Connection object named cnnNorthwind.

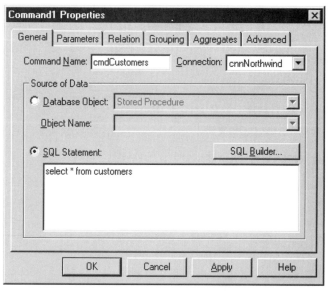

Figure 16-7   Setting the Command object's properties

Next, you must define the data source for the Command object. The data source can be either the name of a database object, such as a stored procedure name or a table name, or a SQL (pronounced "sequel") statement. The example in Figure 16-7 is using a SQL statement that selects all the records from the Customers table as a data source. To specify a more complex SQL statement, you can optionally click the SQL Builder button. More information about using the Query Designer is presented later in this chapter, in the section "Using the Query Designer."

Can I bind a data-bound control to the data environment?

Yes. The data environment can function as a data source in exactly the same way as the ADO Data control functions as a data source. The DataEnvironment object will appear in the drop-down list of the DataSource property of a data-bound control just as if it were an ADO Data control. You can also specify the columns from the DataEnvironment object by using the data-bound control's DataField property. The only difference is that when using the DataEnvironment object as a data source for a bound control, you must also specify the name of a Command object that is contained in the data environment. Unlike the ADO Data control, which identifies the records that will be bound using its RecordSource property, the DataEnvironment object doesn't possess a RecordSource property. Moreover, the data environment can contain multiple Connection and Command objects. If multiple Connection and Command objects are present, then you need a mechanism that enables you to select the desired object or member of the DataEnvironment object. The DataMember property serves as this mechanism. Figure 16-8 illustrates setting the DataSource, DataMember, and DataField properties of the data-bound TextBox control to bind to the CustomerID column from the cmdCustomer Command object in the deVBAnswers data environment.

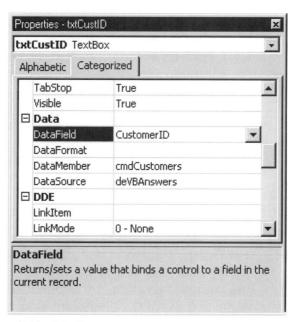

Figure 16-8 Binding a data-bound control to a data environment command

How do I execute a Command object in my application?

After you create a Command object in the data environment, you can execute it in very much the same way that you execute a standard ADO Command object created by using the ADO object library. However, some differences do exist. When a data environment Command object is created, Visual Basic automatically adds a special property to the DataEnvironment object to contain the Recordset object that is created by the Command object. This recordset property is named by taking the name of the data environment Command object and prefixing it with *rs*. For example, if a data environment Command object named cmdCustomers is created, then the special rscmdCustomers property will be added automatically to the data environment. The rscmdCustomers property contains a Recordset object and can be used just like a normal ADO Recordset object. The following code example shows how to use the

rscmdCustomers property to execute the cmdCustomers object and then display the query results in a Microsoft Hierarchical FlexGrid (MSHFlexGrid) control:

```
' Execute the cmdCustomers object.
   deVBAnswers.rscmdCustomers.Open

    ' Display the recordset in the MSHFlexGrid.
    DisplayHFlexGrid deVBAnswers.rscmdCustomers, _
        hflxDisplayData

    ' Close the recordset.
    deVBAnswers.rscmdCustomers.Close
```

In this listing, the Open method of the rscmdCustomer object is used to execute the cmdCustomer Command object. In this case, the cmdCustomer Command object contains a SQL Select statement that will return all the rows and columns from the Customers table found in the sample Northwind database. After the Open method is executed, the rscmdCustomer Recordset object will be populated with the rows and columns from the Customers table in the Northwind database. The rscmdCustomers Recordset object can then be processed using the same methods that can be used with any other ADO Recordset object.

In the previous listing, after the rscmdCustomer recordset has been opened, it is passed as the first parameter to the DisplayHFlexGrid subroutine, and the name of an existing MSHFlexGrid object is passed as the second parameter. The DisplayHFlexGrid subroutine is essentially the same as the DisplayRSGrid subroutine presented in Chapter 15, except that the DisplayHFlexGrid subroutine accepts the name of a Hierarchical FlexGrid object in the second parameter rather than the name of a standard MSFlexGrid object. The DisplayHFlexGrid subroutine reads through the contents of the rscmdCustomer Recordset object and displays the data in the MSHFlexGrid control named hflxDisplayData.

After the contents of the rscmdCustomers Recordset object have been displayed in the grid, the Close method of the deVBAnswers.rscmdCustomer Recordset object is executed to release the system resources used by the Recordset object.

Alternatively, you could take advantage of the new MSHFlexGrid control's ability to be bound to an ADO Recordset object and to dynamically bind the MSHFlexGrid control to the DataEnvironment object. The following listing illustrates how to set the DataMember and DataSource properties of the MSHFlexGrid control to use an existing DataEnvironment and Command object at runtime:

```
' Point to the correct DE member.
   hflxDisplayData.DataMember = "cmdCustomers"

   ' Set the DataSource property to the DE.
   Set hflxDisplayData.DataSource = deVBAnswers
```

This code example shows how the data environment can be used as the data source for the data-bound MSHFlexGrid control. First, because the deVBAnswers data environment can contain multiple Command objects, the hflxDisplayData MSHFlexGrid object's DataMember property is assigned a string that identifies the name of the desired Command object. In this example, the DataMember property is set to use the cmdCustomers Command object that is a part of the VBAnswers data environment. The cmdOrders Command object contains the simple Select * From Customers SQL statement that retrieves all the rows and columns from the Customers table.

 Tip: *Setting the DataMember property first allows the MSHFlexGrid object to bind to the desired Command object as soon as the DataSource property is assigned.*

Next, the DataSource property of the MSHFlexGrid control named hflxDisplayData is set to the name of the deVBAnswers data environment. Setting the DataSource property at runtime has exactly the same effect as setting the DataSource property at design time—the MSHFlexGrid control will be bound to the target data source. Because the data is automatically placed in the MSHFlexGrid control via binding, you don't need to manually move the data into the grid. However, because the MSHFlexGrid control's data binding is automatic, you have no control over how the data will be displayed in the grid.

 ## What is a child Command object and how would I use one?

A child Command object is essentially an ADO data environment Command object that's nested within another ADO data environment Command object. The child Command object is contained within the parent Command object as if it were just another column of the parent recordset. However, instead of simply retrieving the data from the column, when the data environment encounters a child Command object, it is executed, and the results are returned as a Recordset object. Child Command objects take advantage of ADO's ability to support *hierarchical recordsets*—recordsets contained within other recordsets. Child Command objects are useful for retrieving related data elements from two or more tables. For instance, you could use a child Command object to retrieve all the Order Detail rows for a given Order header record, or to show all the line items for a particular order.

To create parent and child Command objects that can be used to show all the orders for each customer in the example Northwind database, you first need to create a DataEnvironment object in your application. Then, you can add a standard Connection object that uses the Microsoft Jet OLE DB Provider to connect to the target data source. An example of creating a data environment and this kind of Connection object was presented earlier in this chapter in the question, "Can a data environment use more than one Connection object."

Creating the parent Command object is also essentially the same as creating a standard Command object. To add a new Command object to an existing Connection object, simply right-click the Connection object and select the Add Command option from the pop-up menu. This will add a new Command object. Then, right-click the new Command object and select Properties from the pop-up menu to access the Properties dialog box, shown in Figure 16-9, in which you can set the properties for the parent Command object.

In Figure 16-9, the parent Command object is named cmdCustOrders and consists of a SQL statement that selects the CustomerName and CustomerID fields from the Customers table of the sample Northwind database.

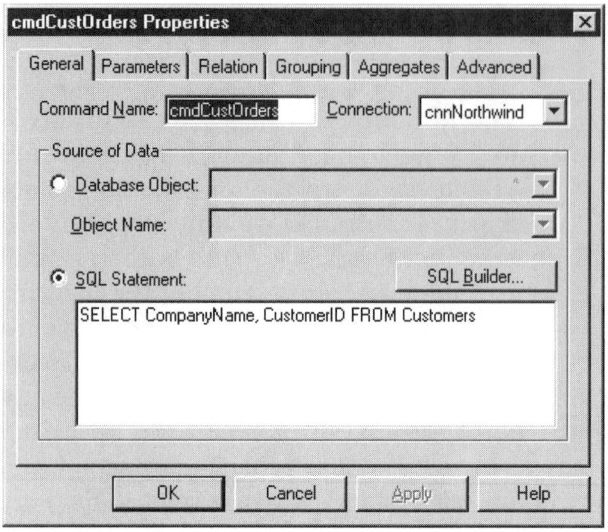

Figure 16-9 Setting the parent Command object properties

After you create the parent Command object, you can create the child Command object by right-clicking the cmdCustOrders parent Command object in the Data Environment design window and then selecting Add Child Command from the pop-up menu. A Properties dialog box similar to the one shown in Figure 16-10 will be displayed.

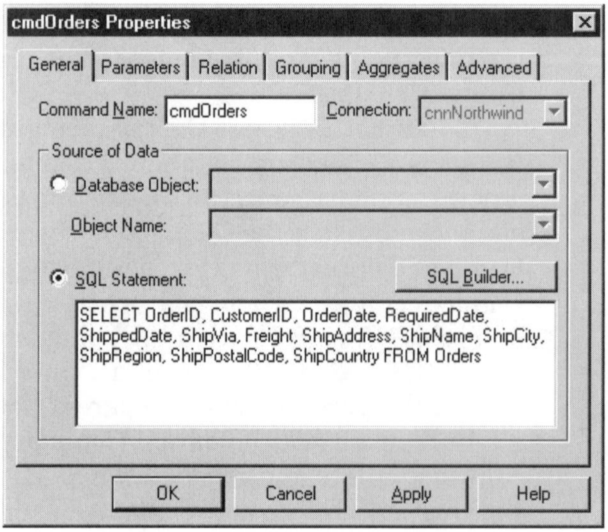

Figure 16-10 Setting the child Command object's properties

Figure 16-10 shows that the child Command is named cmdOrders and is also using a SQL statement to retrieve a selected group of columns from the Orders table. So far, this is very much like creating a standard Command object. However, for a child Command object, you must also set the Relation Definition attributes. Click the Relation tab, which displays the Relation Definition properties shown in Figure 16-11.

To establish the relationship of the child Command object to the parent Command object, you need to check the Relate to a parent Command Object check box and then specify the name of the parent object by using the parent Command drop-down box. In Figure 16-11, the parent Command object has been set to cmdCustOrders.

Next, the column that's used to relate the parent and child tables must be defined. In Figure 16-11, the CustomerID column found in both the Customers table and the Orders table is used as the relation. In relational databases, a standard practice is to use the same name to link fields in different tables. In this case, the linking fields from the parent Customers table and the child Orders table are both named CustomerID. The Data Environment Designer automatically matches like-named columns in the

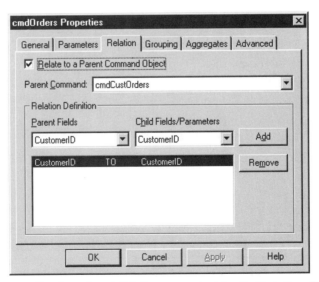

Figure 16-11 Setting the child Command object's Relation Definition properties

dialog box. Clicking the Add button adds the relation to the Command object. The Data Environment Designer reflects the relationship by displaying the two commands as a hierarchy, as shown in Figure 16-12.

You can execute the parent and child Command objects through the parent Command object. The following listing shows the parent cmdCustOrders Command object being dynamically bound to an MSHFlexGrid control:

```
' Point to the child_grouping DE member.
hflxDisplayData.DataMember = "cmdCustOrders"

' Set the DataSource property to the DE.
Set hflxDisplayData.DataSource = deVBAnswers
```

First, the name of the parent Command object is assigned to the DataMember property of the MSHFlexGrid object named hflxDisplayData. Then, the hflxDisplayData DataSource property is set to the name of the VBAnswers DataEnvironment object that contains both the parent and child Command objects. Figure 16-13 illustrates the resulting hierarchical recordset displayed using the MSHFlexGrid control.

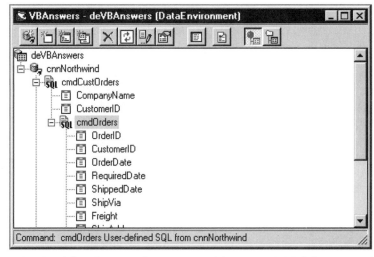

Figure 16-12 The data environment with parent/child Command objects

	CompanyNa	CustomerID	OrderID	CustomerID	OrderDate	▲
⊟			10643	ALFKI	9/25/95	
			10692	ALFKI	11/3/95	
	Alfreds Futte	ALFKI	10702	ALFKI	11/13/95	
			10835	ALFKI	2/15/96	
			10952	ALFKI	4/15/96	
			11011	ALFKI	5/9/96	
⊟			10308	ANATR	10/19/94	
	Ana Trujillo E	ANATR	10625	ANATR	9/8/95	
			10759	ANATR	12/29/95	
			10926	ANATR	4/3/96	
⊟	Antonio Mor	ANTON	10365	ANTON	12/28/94	▼

Run Command   Bind to Grid   Child Command   Clear Grid

Figure 16-13   Displaying parent/child Command objects in the MSHFlexGrid control

What's the quickest way to create a data entry form?

By far, the quickest way to create a data entry form is to drag and drop an existing Command object from the Data Environment Designer onto a blank form. Visual Basic then will automatically create a set of data-bound Label and TextBox controls for all the fields that are contained in the Command object. Figure 16-14 illustrates a simple data entry form that was created by dragging and dropping the cmdOrders Command object from the VBAnswers data environment onto a blank form.

How can I create a master/detail data entry form?

You can quickly and easily create a basic master/detail data entry form by dragging and dropping an existing parent Command object that contains a child Command object from the data environment onto a blank form. After the parent/child Command object is dropped onto the blank form, Visual Basic will automatically create a set of data-bound Label and TextBox controls for all the fields that are contained in the parent Command object. A data-bound

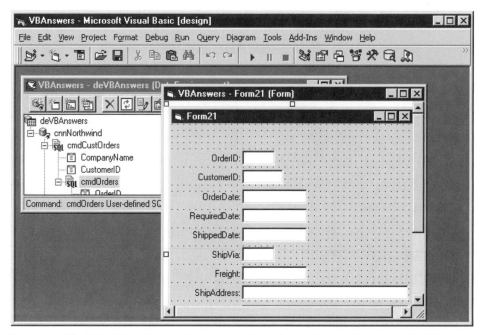

Figure 16-14   Creating a data entry form based on a Command object

MSHFlexGrid control will be created for the fields in the child Command object. Figure 16-15 illustrates a simple data entry form that was created by dragging and dropping the cmdCustOrder Command object from the VBAnswers data environment onto a blank form.

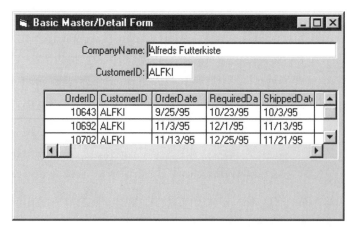

Figure 16-15   A master/detail form created from a parent/child Command object

USING DATA VIEWS

The Data View window presents a view of one or more database connections, providing access to the entire structure of the database on a particular connection. The Data View window provides the means to use the Microsoft Visual Database Tools (Query Designer and Database Designer) to visually manipulate the structure of a database.

 How do I open the Data View window?

To open the Data View window, select View | Data View, or click the Data View button on Visual Basic's standard toolbar, which displays a Data View window like the one shown in Figure 16-16.

The Data View window lists the available data link and data environment objects that are present in the current project. In Figure 16-16, the Data View window includes one data environment Connection object named cnnNorthwind, which defines a connection to the sample Northwind database. Clicking the plus symbol enables you to view the structure of the target data source. In Figure 16-17, the cnnNorthwind Connection object is expanded to show all the tables contained in the Northwind database.

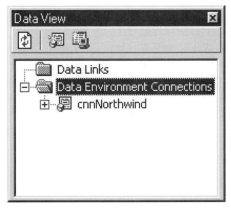

Figure 16-16 Using the Data View window

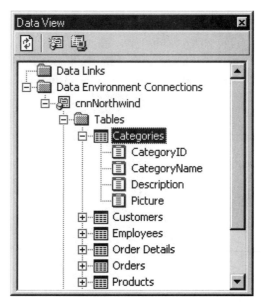

Figure 16-17 Expanding the Data View Connection object

The Data View window enables you to drag and drop the displayed database objects to the Database Designer and Query Designer tools, which can be launched from the Data View window.

 ## How do I use the Database Designer?

The Database Designer is a visual tool that enables you to create, edit, or delete database objects in a database that's connected using the data environment. You interact with the server database by using *database diagrams,* which graphically represent the tables in your database. These tables display the columns they contain, the relationships between the tables, and indexes and constraints attached to

your tables. When you establish a connection to a database, you can use database diagrams to view database tables and see their relationships, or to create new tables or change the structure of existing tables. However, the Database Designer is only available when connected to a SQL Server database. It can't be used with local Access/Jet databases.

Can I see the contents of a table by using the Data View window?

Yes. To view the contents of a table by using the Data View window, you must first open the Data View window and then expand the Connection object to reveal the database tables that are present in the connected database. To display the contents of a table, simply right-click the table and select the Open option from the pop-up menu. The Run Table window is displayed, similar to the one shown in Figure 16-18.

Figure 16-18 illustrates using the Data View window's Open table command to view the contents of the Categories table.

Run Table: Categories

CategoryID	CategoryName	Description	Picture
1	Beverages	Soft drinks, coffee:	<Binary>
2	Condiments	Sweet and savory :	<Binary>
3	Confections	Desserts, candies,	<Binary>
4	Dairy Products	Cheeses	<Binary>
5	Grains/Cereals	Breads, crackers, p	<Binary>
6	Meat/Poultry	Prepared meats	<Binary>
7	Produce	Dried fruit and bea	<Binary>
8	Seafood	Seaweed and fish	<Binary>

Figure 16-18 Displaying the contents of a table

USING THE QUERY DESIGNER

The Query Designer is a powerful tool for creating SQL commands using a graphical user interface (GUI). Using the Query Designer, you can create complex, multitable queries simply by dragging tables from the Data View window into the Query Designer. After you select the tables, you can further define the columns and other query options that will be used, from the Query Designer's GUI.

The Query Designer includes both a graphical pane that enables you to build your query visually and a SQL pane that displays the SQL text generated by the Query Designer. You can work in either the graphical or SQL panes, and the Query Designer will keep both panes in sync. For multiple tables, the Query Designer can automatically suggest how to join any related tables. You can use the Query Designer for both SQL Select statements that query the database and action queries, such as Update, Insert, and Delete, that update the database. The results of queries are displayed in a grid that allows you to view and edit records in the database.

 How do I start the Query Designer?

You can start the Query Designer when you create a new data environment Command object. After you create a new Command object, right-click the object and select Design from the pop-up menu. The Query Designer, shown in Figure 16-19, will be started. The Data View window will also be opened (if it isn't already active).

Initially, the Query Designer window is blank. You can use the Query Designer to build a new query either by directly entering the desired SQL statements into the SQL pane or by dragging and dropping tables from the Data View window onto the Query Designer.

 How do I create a query using the Query Designer?

You can create a query using the Query Designer in two ways:

● Directly enter into the SQL pane in the middle of the Query Designer window the SQL statement that you want to execute.

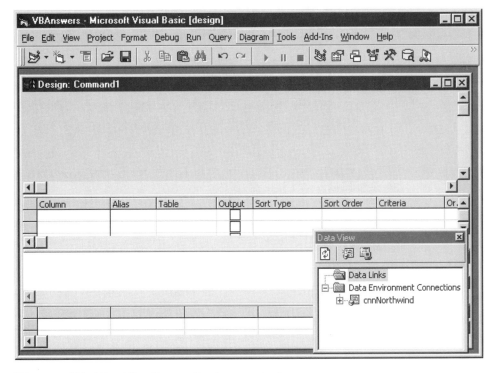

Figure 16-19   The Query Designer window

● Drag and drop tables from the Data View window into the upper Diagram pane of the Query Designer and then visually choose the columns and join actions that you want to perform.

You can freely move between the graphical representation of the query and the query's SQL statement. The Query Designer automatically takes any changes made to the SQL statement and applies them to the graphical representation of the query. Likewise, all changes made to the graphical portion of the query automatically re-create a new SQL statement.

To create a new query that uses the Northwind database to show all the products that have been ordered for each customer, you first open the Data View and expand a Connection object that's using the sample Northwind database. (See "Can a data environment use more than one Connection object?," earlier in this chapter for instructions on

how to create a Connection object that uses the Jet OLE DB
Provider to connect to the Northwind database.) From the
Data View window, you then left-click the Customers table
and drag and drop the Customers table onto the upper, gray
portion of the Query Designer, called the Diagram pane. A
box listing all the columns for the Customers table will be
displayed in the Query Designer. Next, repeat this process
for the Orders table, the Order Details table, and the
Products table. When you have finished, four table boxes
will be listed at the top of the Query Design window, as
shown in Figure 16-20.

Near the top of Figure 16-20, in the Diagram pane of the
Query Designer window, the Query Designer automatically
joined all the tables by using the matching column names for
each table. Next, you select the columns from each table that
you want to include, by checking the box that's displayed
immediately before each column name. As each column is
checked, it is added to the grid near the center of the Query
Designer window. This grid displays the column name, the
parent table, and whether the column will be output in the
recordset created by the query or just used for internal
calculations. Adding tables, selecting column names, and

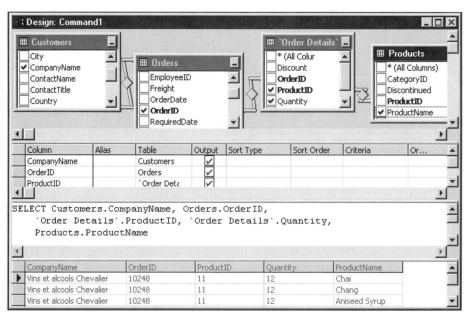

Figure 16-20   Building a Customer-Products query with the Query
Designer

specifying other query criteria causes the Query Designer to automatically build the SQL statement shown in the center of the window.

After you add the tables and select the desired columns, you can test run the query by selecting Query | Run from the VB menu. The results of the query will be output to the grid shown at the bottom of the Query Designer window. When you've finished building the query, click the Exit window button, and the Query Designer will prompt you to save the query into a data environment Command object.

 ## How do I create an action query that updates data in a table?

Unlike queries that use the SQL Select statement to retrieve data, action queries can add, update, and delete data in a target database. As you might expect, the underlying SQL that supports each of these types of queries is quite different. The SQL Select statement is used to query and retrieve data from a target data source, whereas the SQL Insert, Update, and Delete statements are used to update the data in the target data source. The Query Designer supports both data retrieval queries and action queries that update the data in a target data source.

To create an action query by using the Query Designer, you must first create a Connection object that will link your data environment to the target data source. For this example, a Connection object is used that opens the example Department table in the VBAnswers.mdb database. After the Connection object is created, you can create a new Command object and open its Properties page. To start the Query Designer, click the SQL Builder button on the General tab. After the Query Builder is running, open the Data View window and expand the tables that are found in the Connection object. Drag and drop the table that will be updated from the list of tables in the Data View window to the Diagram pane of the Query Designer. In Figure 16-21, the Department table from the VBAnswers database is displayed in the Diagram pane of the Query Designer.

After you add the table to the Diagram pane, convert the default query type to an Update query either by right-clicking the Query Designer and selecting Update from the pop-up menu or by choosing Query | Change Type | Update from

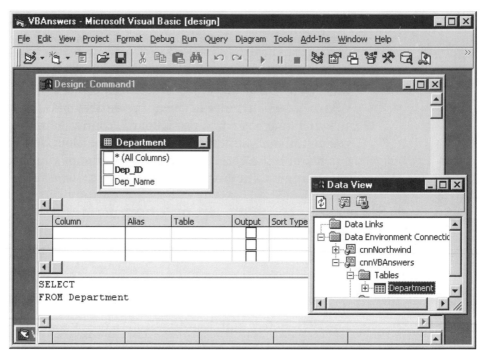

Figure 16-21 Adding the Department table to the Query Designer

the standard VB menu. After selecting this option, the SQL pane will be updated to show the SQL Update statement.

Tip: *Action queries can only update a single table.*

Next, select the data columns to update by checking the box immediately before the name of each column that's displayed in the Diagram pane. Only those columns that are selected will be updated. In the case of the Department table, select the Dep_Name column to be updated. Again, as you select columns, notice that the column names are added to the Grid pane, and the Update statement in the SQL pane is modified to show the columns selected.

After you select the columns, enter the new value that will be assigned to the column by typing a value in the New Value column in the Grid pane. The New Value column can contain a literal value, a column name, or an expression. In this example, enter the literal **New Department Name** in the New Value column.

After you set the data that will be used in the update operation in the New Value column, the next step required to create an update action query is to set up the criterion that identifies the rows that will be updated. If you do not specify an update criterion, then all the rows in the table will be updated, which generally isn't the desired result. To define the update criterion, enter a search condition in the Criteria column. For instance, to update just the Dep_Name column for department records that have a value of 1 in the Dep_ID column, you would enter the value =1 in the Criteria column from the Dep_ID field. This tells the Query Designer that you want to update the Dep_Name column only in those rows where the Dep_ID is equal to 1. Figure 16-22 shows the completed Query Designer window for the update query.

You run an action query exactly like a standard Select query. To run the Update query, either select Query | Run or right-click the Query Designer and select the Run option from the pop-up menu. When you execute an action query, no results are displayed in the Results pane at the bottom of the Query Designer window. Instead, a message box is displayed that reports the number of rows that were affected. Closing the Query Designer prompts you to save the query specifications in the Command object.

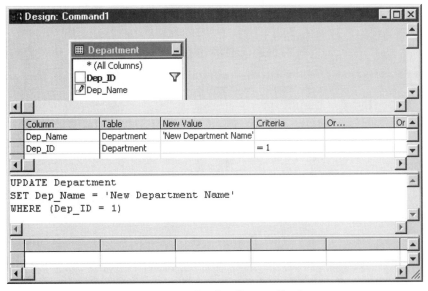

Figure 16-22 An update query in the Query Designer

USING THE DATA REPORT DESIGNER

By using the Data Report Designer, you can easily create database reports from within the Visual Basic IDE. You can use the Data Report Designer to lay out a report visually. You can position literal text and data fields on the report and then bind the report to a data source.

 No option for the Data Report Designer is shown in my project. How can I add the Data Report Designer to my VB IDE?

The Data Report Designer typically is installed as a default option for the Visual Basic Professional and Enterprise Editions 6 (it isn't available in the Learning Edition). However, if it wasn't installed or has been removed, you can add it by first selecting Project | Components and then selecting the Designers tab to display the Components dialog box, shown in Figure 16-23.

Click the check box in front of the Data Report option and then click OK to add the Data Report Designer to your VB IDE.

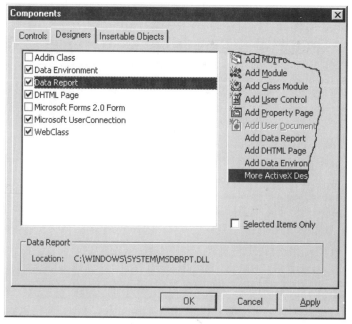

Figure 16-23 Adding the Data Report Designer

 ## How do I create a data report?

To add a data report to your project, either select the Project |
Add Data Report or right-click in the Project window and
select the Add | Data Report option. The Data Report
Designer shown in Figure 16-24 will be displayed.

The Data Report Designer provides five preformatted
sections that you can use when designing your database
reports, as described in the following table:

Report Section	Description
Report Header	Presents information that appears one time at the very beginning of a report; often used for overall values, such as the department, author, or database name.
Page Header	Presents information that is printed at the top of every page; typically used for the report's title.
Detail	Presents the core database information in the body of the report; typically used for database fields.
Page Footer	Presents information that goes at the bottom of every page; typically used for the page number.
Report Footer	Presents information that appears at the very end of the report; often used for summary information.

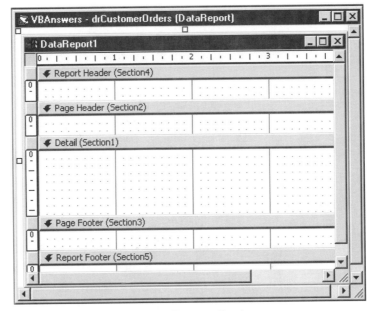

Figure 16-24 Starting the Data Report Designer

After adding a new data report to your project, the next step is to connect the DataReport object to the database. To do so, first display the DataReport object's properties by clicking the Data Report Designer and then pressing the F4 key. Next, set the DataSource and DataMember properties to the target database. Figure 16-25 illustrates setting the DataReport object's properties.

In Figure 16-25, the DataReport object's DataSource property is set to the name of an existing deVBAnswers data environment. The DataMember property is set to the name of the cmdCustOrders Command object that's contained in the data environment.

After setting up the database connection attributes, the next step in creating a data report is to set the structure of the report to match the hierarchical structure of the data returned by the Command object. To assign a new structure to the data report, right-click the Data Report Designer and then select the Retrieve Structure option from the pop-up

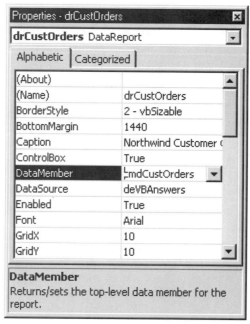

Figure 16-25   Setting the Data Report's DataSource properties

menu. Once the structure of the report has been retrieved, you can begin designing the report layout by dragging and dropping the Data Report Designer controls that are displayed in the VB Toolbox onto the Data Report design window.

What are the Data Report Designer controls and how do I used them on a data report?

Adding a new Data Report Designer to a VB project automatically adds the collection of Data Report Designer controls to the VB Toolbox. The Data Report Designer controls, shown in Figure 16-26, are a set of ActiveX controls specifically designed for use in the Data Report Designer.

The following Data Report Designer controls are included in Visual Basic 6:

- **Pointer**   Used to resize or move a control that has already been drawn on a report.

- **RptLabel**   Used to display text that cannot change, such as the report's title; can't be used to display database fields.

- **RptTextBox**   Used to display database fields; bound to a database field by setting the DataField and DataMember properties.

Figure 16-26   The Data Report Designer controls

- **RptImage** Used to display a graphical image on the report; can display bitmaps, icons, or metafile images, and often is used for company logos.

- **RptLine** Used to draw an assortment of line styles on the report. Lines are used to separate sections of your report and make it easier to read.

- **RptShape** Used to draw shapes on your report; can be used to display a rectangle, rounded rectangle, square, rounded square, oval, or circle.

- **RptFunction** Used to perform calculations based on the values of selected data fields; can compute Sum, Average, Minimum, Maximum, Row Count, Value Count, Standard Error, and Standard Deviation.

You use the Data Report Designer controls on the DataReport object in very much the same way as you use standard ActiveX controls on a VB form—you drag and drop the desired controls from the Data Report Toolbox to the Data Report Designer. Then, you set the properties of each control to alter its appearance or to bind the control to an appropriate database field. Figure 16-27 shows how the DataMember and DataField properties of the RptTextBox control can be set to bind it to one of the columns exposed by a data environment Command object.

In Figure 16-27, the DataMember property has been set to the cmdOrders Command object, while the DataField property has been set to the OrderID field that's returned by the cmdOrders object.

 Note: *You don't need to set a DataSource property for the Data Report Designer controls. The DataSource property is assigned at the DataReport object level—not at the individual control level. You can see an example of setting the DataReport object's DataSource property in Figure 16-28.*

After adding the Data Report Designer controls to the data report and setting their properties, the data report is

Properties - Text1 [×]

Text1 RptTextBox [▾]

Alphabetic | Categorized

BackColor	☐ &H00FFFFFF&
BackStyle	0 - rptBkTransparent
BorderColor	■ &H00000000&
BorderStyle	0 - rptBSTransparent
CanGrow	False
DataField	OrderID [▾]
DataFormat	General
DataMember	cmdOrders
Font	Arial
ForeColor	■ &H00000000&
Height	240
Left	288

DataField
Returns/sets the name of a field the object is
bound to.

Figure 16-27   Binding the RptTextBox control to a database field

ready to be used in your application. You can see an example
of a completed data report in Figure 16-28.

In this example, the Report Header and Report Footer
sections were not used, so they were deleted from the report
by right-clicking the Data Report Designer and toggling off
the Show Report Header/Footer option. Also notice the
addition of a Group Header section, which is automatically
added to the data report when a parent/child Command
object is used as the DataReport object's DataMember
property and then the Retrieve Structure option is executed.
Here, the Group Header is used to print the relevant
Customer data, while the Detail section is used to print the
Order information for each customer. In the Group Footer
section, the RptFunction Data Report Designer control was
used to count the total number of orders for each customer.
To enable the RptFunction control to count the number of

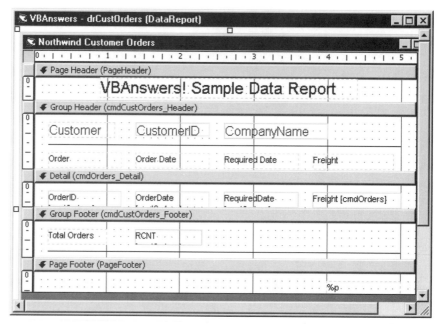

Figure 16-28   Sample data report

orders, the DataField property of the RptFunction control first was set to the OrderID field in the cmdOrders Command object. Then, the FunctionType property was set to 4 - rptFuncRCnt, which counts the number of rows. Finally, in the Page Footer section, a page counter was added by right-clicking the Data Report design window and then selecting the Insert Control | Current Page Number option from the pop-up menu.

After you complete the data report layout, closing the Data Report Designer prompts you to save the data report. In this example, the data report was named drCustOrders before the window was closed. This caused the data report to be saved in a file named drCustOrders.dsr.

 How do I make a data report print from my application?

You can print a data report by using the PrintReport method. The following code illustrates using the PrintReport method for the DataReport object named drCustOrders:

```
drCustOrders.PrintReport False
```

The PrintReport method accepts four optional parameters. The first parameter is a Boolean value that controls whether the Print Setup dialog box is displayed. A value of False indicates that the dialog box will not be shown and the report will be printed immediately to the default printer. The second parameter is an Integer value that controls whether the entire report is printed or only a range of the report that was identified in the data report's Setting property is printed. The following table presents the valid values for the second parameter:

Constant	Value	Description
RptRangeAllPages	0	All pages will be printed (default).
RptRangeFromTo	1	Only the range of pages specified in the Settings property will be printed.

The last two optional parameters are Integer values that are used to set the lower and upper boundaries of the pages that will be printed.

 Can I preview a report before printing it?

You can preview a data report before printing by using the Show method. The following example illustrates using the drCustOrders DataReport object's Show method. When the Show method is executed, a window containing a formatted

data report is displayed, similar to the one shown earlier in Figure 16-28.

```
drCustOrders.Show
```

The Show method accepts two optional parameters. The first parameter controls the style of the window that will be displayed. Leaving this parameter at 0, the default, causes the window to be modeless. A value of 1 causes the print preview window to be modal, which requires that the user close the window before any other program actions can be performed. The second optional parameter specifies the window that will be the owner of the print preview window. The default is the form from which the print preview window was launched. The current form can be identified by using the value of Me.

An example of the data report print preview window is shown in Figure 16-29.

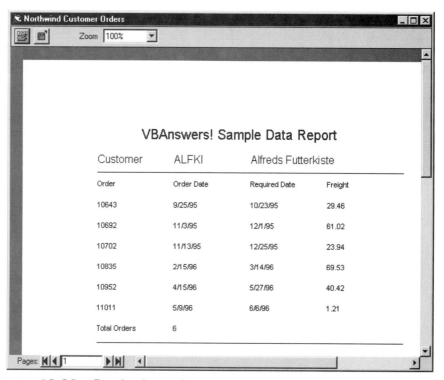

Figure 16-29 Previewing a data report

The horizontal and vertical scroll bars allow you to navigate through the report. In addition, the Printer button in the upper-left corner of the print preview window can be used to send the report to the printer.

I don't want to spend a lot of time creating a pretty report. What's the quickest way to print the values in a database?

The quickest way to generate a simple report is to drag a Command object from the data environment onto the Data Report Designer. This works in much the same way as designing simple data-bound forms. Dropping the Command object onto the Data Report Designer's Detail section causes the Data Report Designer to automatically create a set of RptLabel and RptTextBox controls to display data from the Command object's recordset. The RptTextBox object's DataMember and DataField properties will be automatically bound to the fields in the recordset. No fancy report headings, page numbering, or formatting will be performed, but a simple list of the data values from the data source can be immediately printed or previewed.

How do I create a page break?

Custom page breaks can be used to improve the formatting of your printed reports, which can make your data reports easier to read. You can add custom page breaks before or after any group header or footer, or after the report header or before the report footer.

To force a page break before the group header that contains the CompanyID field, you first click the Group Header section to select it. Next, press F4 to display the properties for the Group Header section. On the Properties window, click the drop-down arrow next to the ForcePageBreak property and then select the 1 - rptPageBreakBefore value from the list of page break options displayed. When the data report is executed, a page break will be performed before each group header.

Chapter 17

ActiveX Controls and Web Projects

Answer Topics!

ActiveX Controls and Web Projects @ a Glance

This chapter shows you how to use two of the more advanced types of development projects that are supported by Visual Basic 6.

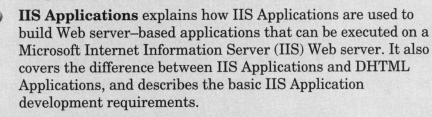

- **ActiveX Controls** shows you how to create ActiveX controls using Visual Basic. You'll also see how to test the controls by using a VB project group.

- **DHTML Applications** covers using the newest Web-oriented features that are provided as part of Visual Basic 6. It also explains how to create DHTML (Dynamic Hypertext Markup Language) projects that are executed by a Web browser.

- **IIS Applications** explains how IIS Applications are used to build Web server–based applications that can be executed on a Microsoft Internet Information Server (IIS) Web server. It also covers the difference between IIS Applications and DHTML Applications, and describes the basic IIS Application development requirements.

ACTIVEX CONTROLS

Taking advantage of ActiveX controls is one of the core components of the highly productive VB integrated development environment (IDE). In fact, Visual Basic not only can use ActiveX controls, it can also create them. The questions and answers in the first section of this chapter discuss how ActiveX controls created using Visual Basic compare to third-party commercial controls. You will also see how to create and test ActiveX controls using Visual Basic.

What's the difference between ActiveX controls created using VB and those that come with VB or can be bought from another software vendor?

From a Component Object Model (COM) perspective, there's no difference between ActiveX controls created with VB and those created in other environments, such as Visual C++. COM is the underlying technology used by ActiveX controls, and ActiveX controls created using VB use COM in exactly the same way as ActiveX controls created using other languages. However, definite differences do exist from the implementation and deployment perspectives.

In exactly the same way that Visual Basic hides the complexities of Windows application development, it hides the complexities of developing COM-based components, such as ActiveX controls. This makes the development of COM components much easier, but it also restricts the developer from the entire range of COM capabilities. Only those capabilities that have been exposed through a VB interface can be used. From a deployment perspective, ActiveX controls that are created using Visual Basic have the same runtime requirements as standard VB applications. In other words, the VB msvbvm60.dll runtime dynamic link library (DLL) must be present on the target system to execute the ActiveX controls. ActiveX controls created using Visual C++ or Delphi don't share this requirement.

How do I create an ActiveX control?

Follow these steps to create an ActiveX control:

1. Start Visual Basic and then select File | New Project. The New Project dialog box, shown in Figure 17-1, will be displayed.

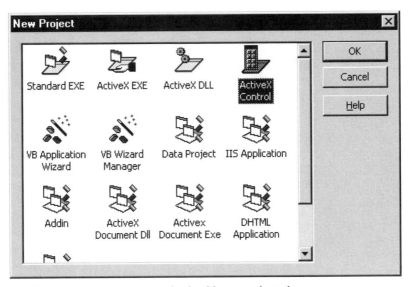

Figure 17-1 Creating a new ActiveX control project

 Note: *You can also add ActiveX controls to an existing project by selecting Project | Add User Control.*

2. In the New Project dialog box, select the ActiveX Control option and then click the OK button to create a new ActiveX control project.

A UserControl object is presented in a window that looks quite similar to the standard VB form design window. In fact, you can do many of the same things with the UserControl design window that you can do with the standard form design window. For example, as with the form design window, the UserControl design window enables you to drag and drop one or more ActiveX controls from the Toolbox to the UserControl design window.

ActiveX controls can be as simple as a single TextBox-like control, or as complex as complete dialog boxes that display multiple ActiveX controls. However, although there are exceptions, most ActiveX controls are limited to a single user interface object, such as a TextBox or ComboBox control.

 Note: *Although an ActiveX control can contain other ActiveX controls, the other controls can't be accessed independently of the parent control. The container or form can only access the properties and events that are exposed by the parent ActiveX control. For example, if you create an ActiveX control named MyControl that contains four Label controls and four TextBox controls, these eight internal controls are only addressed by the parent MyControl ActiveX control. Any actions that involve the internal Label and TextBox controls must be performed by the MyControl ActiveX parent control.*

3. After the UserControl design window is presented, you can assign values to the properties and add the user interface objects to the control.

For example, to create an ActiveX control that works like the TextBox control but only allows numeric input, you first press F4 to assign a new name to the ActiveX control. If you don't assign a name to the control, it will assume the default name of UserControl1, which is not very user-friendly. Figure 17-2 shows the UserControl

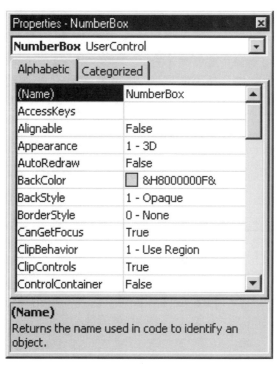

Figure 17-2 Assigning a name to the UserControl object

Properties dialog box, in which the Name property has been assigned the value of NumberBox.

4. To allow the ActiveX control to accept user input, drag and drop a TextBox control from the VB Toolbox onto the upper-left corner of the UserControl design window. Then, press F4 to assign the name txtNumber to the TextBox control.

5. To enable the NumberBox control to appear like the normal TextBox control, reduce the UserControl design area to the same size as the TextBox control by using the UserControl's resizing handles. Figure 17-3 presents the completed NumberBox user interface design in the UserControl window.

At this point, the NumberBox control looks and acts like the standard TextBox control.

6. To enable the NumberBox control to accept only numeric input, add some code to the NumberBox ActiveX control to capture and test all the keystrokes entered into the TextBox control portion of the NumberBox control.

The following listing shows how the event subroutine txtNumber_KeyPress of the txtNumber TextBox control

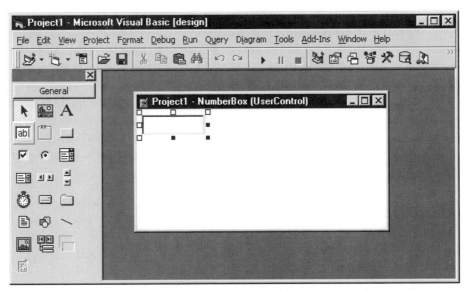

Figure 17-3 The completed NumberBox ActiveX control interface

that's contained in the NumberBox control can be used to test each keystroke for a numeric value:

```
Private Sub txtNumber_KeyPress(KeyAscii As Integer)
    Select Case KeyAscii

        ' Allow numbers.
        Case vbKey0 To vbKey9

        ' Allow the decimal.
        Case vbDecimal

        ' Allow TAB and directional keys.
        Case vbKeyBack, vbKeyClear, vbKeyDelete, _
            vbKeyLeft, vbKeyRight, vbKeyTab, _
            vbKeyUp, vbKeyDown

        ' Cancel all other keystrokes.
        Case Else
            KeyAscii = 0
            Beep

    End Select

End Sub
```

The KeyPress event is fired each time the user enters a keystroke into the txtNumber TextBox control. A Select Case block is used to test each keystroke. If the keystroke entered is a number, a decimal point, or one of the directional arrows, then it is accepted. Otherwise, the keystroke is canceled by setting its value to ASCII 0, and a beep is issued to inform the user of an input error.

The implementation of the numeric validation code in the NumberBox control is no different from the code that's required to perform this type of input validation for a standard TextBox control. However, implementing this as an ActiveX control has two distinct advantages:

- *The ActiveX control greatly facilitates code reuse.* Instead of manually adding the numeric validation code to each instance of the TextBox control that should accept numeric input, you can simply use the NumberBox

control. This greatly simplifies downstream development, because all the coding has already been performed and you can readily incorporate it into other projects.

● *The overhead and management of the code are reduced.* There is only one instance of the validation routine rather than one instance for each TextBox control. This can be significant in large projects with hundreds of numeric input fields.

How do I add properties to an ActiveX control?

You can add custom properties to an ActiveX control by using the Tools | Add Procedure option from the standard VB Toolbar. To use the Add Procedure option, you must first display the code view of the ActiveX control by right-clicking the control in the Project window and then selecting the View Code option from the pop-up menu. Figure 17-4 illustrates adding a Number property to the ActiveX control named NumberBox.

In the Add Procedure dialog box shown in Figure 17-4, Number has been given as the name of the new procedure, and the Property radio button has been selected, indicating the new procedure will be a property of an ActiveX control. In addition, the scope of the property has been set to Public, which allows the property value to be set and accessed by the parent container. Clicking the OK button causes the Add procedure to generate the Get and Let methods for the new property.

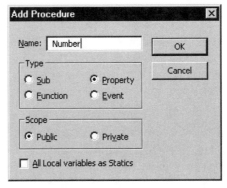

Figure 17-4 Adding properties to an ActiveX control

The Get and Let methods that are generated are only the stubs. Since the VB IDE doesn't know how you want the property to be used, no additional code is provided within each of these stub methods. You have to add the code for whatever action you want taken on the property. In the case of the NumberBox example, the Number property is analogous to the Text property of a TextBox control. The Number property will be used to store and display the numeric value that is entered by the end user. Since the NumberBox control contains a TextBox control, the simplest action is to take the value entered into the Number property and assign it to the Text property of the internal txtNumber TextBox control. An alternative implementation method would be to assign the value to a private variable contained by the NumberBox control. However, since the Text property of the internal TextBox control is available and unused, it is simpler just to use it. The following code shows the completed Get and Let methods used to implement the Number property of the NumberBox control:

```
Public Property Get Number() As Variant
    Number = txtNumber.Text
End Property
```

The Get method is used to retrieve the value contained in an ActiveX control property. As the previous code indicates, the Get method is quite simple. It merely takes the value that is currently stored in the txtNumber.Text property and returns it to the caller of the Get method.

The following code illustrates how to implement the Let method:

```
Public Property Let Number(ByVal vNewValue As Variant)
    txtNumber.Text = vNewValue
    PropertyChanged "Number"
End Property
```

The Let method is slightly more involved. It is used to assign a new value to the ActiveX control property. In this case, the value passed into the Let method in the vNewValue Variant variable is assigned to the txtNumber.Text property. This changes the internal value contained in the ActiveX

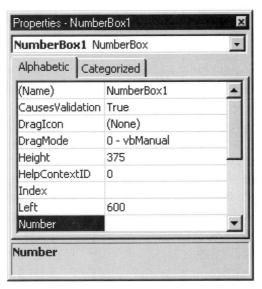

Figure 17-5 Adding the Number property to the NumberBox control

control. Next, the PropertyChanged method is executed to notify the container that a property's value has been changed. The PropertyChanged method accepts a single string parameter that identifies the name of the property that has been modified.

After implementing the Get and Let methods, the new Number property will be available for use both in the IDE and at runtime. Figure 17-5 illustrates the Properties dialog box of the NumberBox control, showing the new Number property.

 How can I test my ActiveX control?

The easiest way to test your ActiveX control is by creating a VB project group. Essentially, a project group enables you to combine multiple related projects. This is especially important for testing ActiveX controls and VB object classes, because these types of COM objects can be executed only from a parent process. In other words, they require a container and they can't be executed as stand-alone applications.

To create a project group to test an ActiveX control, follow these steps:

1. Select File | Add Project while your ActiveX project is currently displayed in the VB IDE. The Add Project dialog box appears, as shown in Figure 17-6.

2. From the Add Project dialog box, select the Standard EXE option from the list of project types and then click OK. A project group will be automatically created, and the new Standard EXE project will be added to the project group along with the existing UserControl project.

3. After the new Standard EXE project has been added, add a form to that project and test the ActiveX control on that form.

   The ActiveX control that was developed in the User Control project is automatically displayed in the Standard EXE project's Toolbox. Figure 17-7 shows the VB project group containing both a User Control ActiveX control project and a Standard EXE project used to test the ActiveX control.

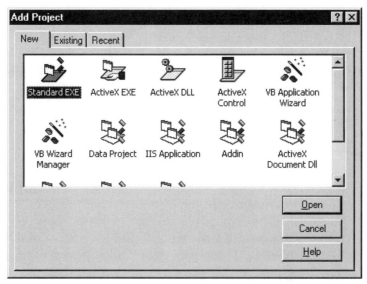

Figure 17-6   Adding a Standard EXE project to an ActiveX project group

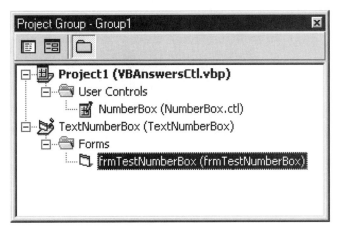

Figure 17-7 A project group containing ActiveX and Standard EXE projects

 I have an ActiveX control that works, but I can't seem to resize it on the test form. How can I make my control resize properly?

In many respects, ActiveX controls are a lot like standard executable programs. Because they contain properties, events, and methods, they are even more closely related to the COM-based class objects presented in Chapter 14. However, there is one significant difference between the implementation of ActiveX controls and these other VB project types: many events in ActiveX controls are executed at design time while the control is displayed in the VB IDE, which is a significant departure from Standard EXE projects and class-based objects, whose code is executed only at runtime.

The Resize event is an example of one of the events that is executed in the design environment. When an ActiveX control is placed on a form and then resized by dragging its resizing handles, its Resize event is fired. For the ActiveX control to react to the Resize event, code must be added to the Resize event subroutine. If no code is placed in the control's Resize event subroutine, nothing will happen when the Resize event is fired. The following listing illustrates the Resize event subroutine that's used by the NumberBox control to allow it to be dynamically resized in the Visual Basic IDE:

```
Private Sub UserControl_Resize()
    ' Size the txtNumber control to fill the
    ' visible UserControl area.
    txtNumber.Move 0, 0, ScaleWidth, ScaleHeight
End Sub
```

This example shows the UserControl_Resize event that's used for the NumberBox control. It's important to note that the code for the Resize event is implemented in the UserControl object rather than in the TextBox control contained in the UserControl object. The UserControl object receives the Resize messages from the container and must then react to these messages by resizing any of the ActiveX controls that are contained by the UserControl object.

In the case of the NumberBox control, the task is simple, because there is only one TextBox control, and it assumes the entire visible area provided by the UserControl object. When the UserControl's Resize event is fired, the txtNumber TextBox object's Move method is executed to resize the TextBox control. The first two parameters of the Move method position the txtNumber TextBox control in the upper-left corner of the UserControl object. The second two parameters set the width and height of the txtNumber Text TextBox control to the same values that are found in the UserControl object. This allows the NumberBox to react to design-time Resize events.

 How do I make the class name of my control appear in the Text property and automatically increment the number of each instance, similar to how the TextBox control works?

To make the control's class appear as the default value in one of the control's properties, you need to add code to the

ActiveX control's InitProperties event. The InitProperties event is executed at design time before the control is displayed. By hooking into this event, you can take the name that the container has assigned to the control and display it in the control at design time. This enables your control to behave exactly like the standard VB controls. For instance, this allows the first instance of the NumberBox control to be given the default name of NumberBox1, the second instance of the NumberBox control to be named NumberBox2, and so on. Assigning a class name to the control makes it easier to identify each control in the design environment. The following InitProperties event subroutine illustrates how to assign the class name and the instance count to each instance of the ActiveX control that's placed on a form:

```
Private Sub UserControl_InitProperties()
    txtNumber.Text = Extender.Name
End Sub
```

This listing shows how the value from the Extender object's Name property is assigned to the Text property of the txtNumber TextBox control contained in the example NumberBox control. This causes each instance of the NumberBox control to display a different value in the text display that appears in the design window. The Extender object's properties are really provided by the container your control is placed on. These properties include the unique name assigned to the control that's stored in the Extender object's Name property, as well as position attributes that are stored in the Top and Left properties of the Extender object. The Extender object provides access to these properties that are stored in the container object.

Figure 17-8 shows two instances of the NumberBox control placed on the test form. In each case, the unique default text that was assigned to each control came from the Extender object's Name property.

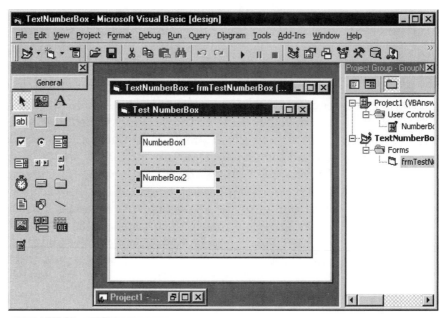

Figure 17-8 Two instances of the NumberBox control displaying the default name

 ## What events from an ActiveX control are executed at design time?

ActiveX controls contain several events that can be executed in the design environment. The following table lists the different events that can be fired when an ActiveX control is loaded into the design environment.

Event	Order	Description
Initialize	1	Occurs when the control is being created, for instance, when it is added to the design environment.
InitProperties	2	Occurs after the control is created. Initial values such as the name are assigned to the control's properties.
Resize	3	Occurs after the control is positioned or moved in the design environment. It allows any internal objects to be resized.
ReadProperties	4	Occurs before an instance of the control is displayed. This allows any saved values to be read out of the FRM file. It doesn't occur for the first instance of the control placed on the design environment.
Show	5	Occurs before the control is displayed, for instance, after it is resized.

Event	Order	Description
Paint	6	Occurs after the Show method, to refresh the screen area covered by the control.
Terminate	7	Occurs when the control is being destroyed, for example, when the design environment is ended.

 ## How do I add events to an ActiveX control?

ActiveX controls must be concerned with two types of events: *received* events, which are generated by the various controls that are contained by your UserControl project, and events that your ActiveX control can send to its container. Events your control receives enable your application to perform some action, whereas events that your control raises (sends) enable the developer who uses your control to perform some action based on the state of your control.

To add an event to an ActiveX control, first open the code-editing window for the UserControl object and then select the Add Procedure option from the VB tools menu. An Add Procedure dialog box, similar to the one shown in Figure 17-9, will be displayed.

To add an event by using the Add Procedure dialog box, first click the Event radio button in the Type area and then enter the name of the event that your control will raise. For instance, in Figure 17-9, an event named Change is being added. Clicking the OK button adds the following public declaration to the General Declarations section of your UserControl project:

```
Public Event Change()
```

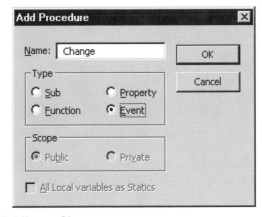

Figure 17-9 Adding a Change event

After the Public Event declaration has been added, you can fire the event from your UserControl project by executing the RaiseEvent function. The following example shows how the RaiseEvent function can be used from within the NumberBox object's internal TextBox control:

```
Private Sub txtNumber_Change()
    RaiseEvent Change
End Sub
```

The txtNumber TextBox control's Change event is received by the NumberBox UserControl object when the value in the txtNumber.Text property is changed. To surface this Change event to the application that contains the NumberBox control, you can use the RaiseEvent function within the TextBox control's Change event subroutine. The RaiseEvent function accepts two parameters. The first, required parameter identifies the event name that will be fired. The second, optional parameter contains an argument list that can be passed to the event subroutine. In the previous example, the RaiseEvent function is used to fire the UserControl object's Change event.

DHTML APPLICATIONS

The expanding use of the Web as an application development platform has brought new Web development capabilities to almost all development platforms, and Visual Basic is no exception to this trend. Visual Basic 6 includes both the new DHTML Application and the new IIS Application project types for developing Web-based applications with Visual Basic. The questions and answers in this section show you how to create a DHTML project and how to access data on DHTML pages.

What's a DHTML project?

A DHTML project is a Web-based application that is run from a Web browser, such as Internet Explorer. DHTML projects use a combination of DHTML and compiled Visual Basic to create a browser-based application. In other words, the DHTML project code is actually executed by the client browser. This type of client-side execution gives DHTML

Applications the type of responsiveness that users would expect from a local application.

A DHTML Application typically is sent from the Web server to the client system, where the Web browser on the client's system executes it. Once the code is present on the client system, the Web browser presents the application to the end user through the browser and interprets and responds to the events generated by the end user. DHTML applications are created using the VB IDE, and they consist of a combination of HTML files and ActiveX DLLs.

How do I create a DHTML Application?

Follow these steps to create a new DHTML project:

1. Start Visual Basic and then select File | New Project. The New Project dialog box is displayed, as shown in Figure 17-10.

2. In the New Project dialog box, select the DHTML Application option and then click the OK button to create a new DHTML Application. The DHTML Page Designer and HTML Toolbox are displayed, similar to those shown in Figure 17-11.

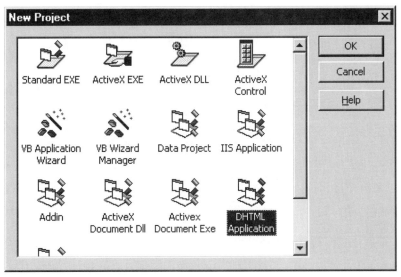

Figure 17-10 Creating a new DHTML project

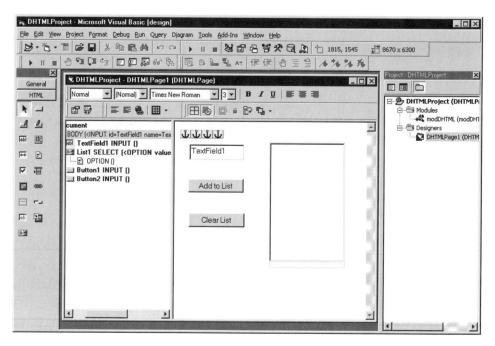

Figure 17-11 Designing a DHTML page with the DHTML Page Designer

Using the DHTML Page Designer is very much like using the standard VB form design window. You add HTML items to the form by dragging and dropping them from the HTML Toolbox. After you add the HTML objects to the page, you can resize and move each object by clicking it. When the object's resizing handles are displayed, you can move the object to the new location by clicking and dragging the object to the target location.

In Figure 17-11, an HTML TextField object, a List object, and two Button objects have been created on the DHTML page.

3. After creating the user interface, add DHTML code to work with the interface objects. Then, you can save the DHTML page as either a designer file or as an external HTML file.

 What's the difference between saving my DHTML project as designer files and saving it as external files?

Saving a DHTML Application as designer files enables you to easily move the DHTML project to different developers and systems and results in designer filenames that end in the extension .dsr. For instance, saving the project named DHTMLProject as designer files results in the files DHTMLProject.vbp, which contains the project definition; modDHTML.bas, which contains the DHTML source code; and DHTMLPage1.dsr, which contains the visual design specifications. When a DHTML Application is saved as designer files, you don't need to worry about the relative path names that may be required to access any of the pages that are contained in the project. However, to change the application, you must use the VB IDE.

Saving the project as external files saves the design elements as HTML files to the specified location on your computer. The external HTML files are referenced in the designer's SourceFile property by an absolute path that you specify when you select to save the project using external files. When you save to external files, you can use the Launch Editor feature to edit the page in an external HTML editor or text editor. This enables you to edit the HTML by using a variety of other Web development tools.

To set the project's SourceFile property, click the DHTML Page Designer Properties button displayed on the DHTML Page Designer window. This displays the DHTML Page Properties dialog box, shown in Figure 17-12.

By default, the project's HTML is saved as part of the VB designer file. To change that option, select the Save HTML in an External File option and then enter the path name of the file that will contain the HTML specifications.

 What are the basic DHTML Application objects?

DHTML Applications are created using the COM-based DHTML object model, which enables you to access the various objects that are presented on an HTML page. Each

DHTMLPage1 Properties   ? ×

General

┌─ Save Mode ────────────────────────────────
│ ⊙ Save HTML as part of the VB project
│
│ ○ Save HTML in an external file:
│
│ ┌──────────────────────────────────────┐
│ └──────────────────────────────────────┘
│
│ ┌───────────┐
│ │ New...   │   Create a new HTML file
│ └───────────┘
│ ┌───────────┐
│ │ Open... │   Use existing HTML file
│ └───────────┘
└───

         [OK]   [Cancel]   [Apply]

Figure 17-12   Setting the save options for a DHTML file

basic HTML element is exposed as an object that can be used
in your DHTML Applications. Just like other COM objects,
DHTML objects are used by setting their properties and by
calling methods. The object model also exposes events, such
as keystrokes and mouse clicks. The basic DHTML object
framework is shown here:

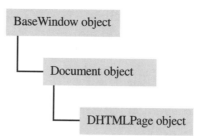

The BaseWindow object represents the browser and
contains the Document object. The Document object represents
an HTML page that is displayed in the Web browser. It
enables you to access user events and contains the
DHTMLPage object. The DHTMLPage object represents
a dynamic HTML application page.

How do I work with the data displayed on a DHTML page?

You work with the data that's input on a DHTML page similar to the way in which you work with a standard VB form. For example, you can access the value that was entered into an HTML TextField object through the Value property, and you can also assign a new value to the Value property. The following code illustrates setting the contents of one TextField object when the user clicks a button that's displayed on the DHTML page:

```
Private Function Button1_onclick() As Boolean
    TextField2.Value = TextField1.Value
End Function
```

The Button1_onclick function will be executed when the user clicks the Button1 object that's displayed on the DHTML page. In this example function, the contents of the Value property of the TextField1 object will be assigned to the TextField2.Value property.

Can any Web browser be used for DHTML applications?

No. DHTML applications require the use of Microsoft Internet Explorer 4.01 Service Pack 1 or Internet Explorer 5 or higher. Earlier versions of Microsoft Internet Explorer will not work. Other Web browsers may work, but Microsoft does not support them for DHTML applications.

Is the VB runtime DLL required on the system that executes a DHTML Application, or is the Web browser enough?

Unfortunately, the VB runtime DLL, msvbvm60.dll, is required on all client systems that run DHTML Applications. The Web browser itself is not adequate. If msvbvm60.dll is not present on the client system, it must be downloaded as part of the deployment process.

IIS APPLICATIONS

The questions and answers in this section cover how an IIS Application is different from a DHTML Application. You'll also learn about the development and runtime requirements of IIS Applications.

What's an IIS project and how is it different from a DHTML project?

Unlike DHTML Applications, which are processed entirely by the Web browser, an IIS (Internet Information Server) Application is a server-based application that runs on an IIS Web server. IIS applications are designed to perform most of their processing on the Web server, whereas DHTML Applications perform their processing on the browser machine. You do not create any Web server components when you create a DHTML Application.

An IIS Application presents its user interface by using standard HTML that is sent to the browser. It responds to Web client requests by using compiled VB code that is executed on the IIS server. To the browser-based client, an IIS Application appears no different from any other HTML Web page. In other words, like Active Server Pages (ASP) applications, IIS Applications send only HTML to the browser-based clients. This means that IIS Applications have no special Web browser requirements and run on almost all versions of Internet Explorer and Netscape Navigator.

An IIS Application is developed using the new WebClass object that was introduced with Visual Basic 6. Each WebClass object is essentially an ASP Web page that takes advantage of the WebClass runtime components. WebClass applications present content to the Web browser by using either of the following:

- **HTML templates** Standard HTML code that is developed using an external HTML editor.

- **Custom WebItems** Program resources that consist of one or more event handlers. They do not contain any HTML source code.

Figure 17-13 provides an overview of the structure of an IIS Application.

An IIS Application begins when a Web browser requests an ASP Web page from an IIS Application. The IIS Web server processes the ASP page by using the mswcrun.dll runtime DLL that is present on the Web server. The WebClass runtime processes the ActiveX DLL code that was generated by the IIS Application. The WebClass runtime DLL then returns the results to the ASP page, which the IIS Web server processes. The results are then sent back to the Web client as a standard HTML stream.

How is an IIS Application different from an ASP application?

ASP and IIS Applications are very closely related. Both types of applications perform their processing on the server rather

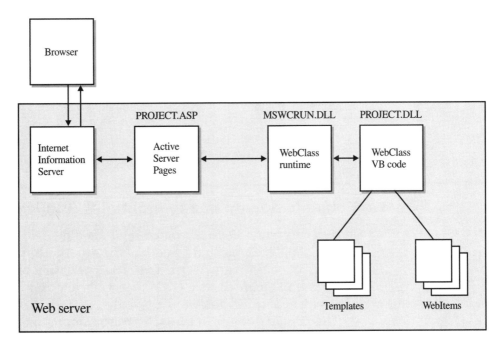

Figure 17-13 An overview of an IIS Application

than on the client, and both present standard HTML to the Web browser. However, ASP applications are primarily for script developers who are interested in authoring Web pages, and they are built using either VBScript or JScript. ASP applications freely mix this script with HTML.

IIS Applications are for VB developers who are building Web-based applications. IIS Applications use Visual Basic as the development language and don't allow the developer to mix the VB code and HTML. Instead, IIS Applications join HTML templates to VB code in the IDE. They are then used to generate ASP files and VB ActiveX DLL's that are deployed on the Web server.

What are the requirements for developing an IIS Application?

To develop an IIS Application, you must be running Visual Basic on one of the following platforms:

Operating System	Web Server
Windows NT Server 4 or later	Internet Information Server 3 or later, with Active Server Pages
Windows NT Workstation 4 or later	Peer Web Services 3 or later, with Active Server Pages
Windows 95 or later	Personal Web Server 3 or later, with Active Server Pages

IIS applications can be run using almost all standard Web browsers.

What objects do you use to create IIS Applications?

Considering their close relationship, it should be no surprise that IIS Applications share many of the objects that are used by the ASP object framework. The IIS Application object model is implemented as a COM object library and has the hierarchical object framework presented in Figure 17-14.

The primary object in the ASP programming model is the WebClass object, which contains the six primary IIS Application objects. The first five of these objects, Request, Response, Session, Application, and Server, are shared by

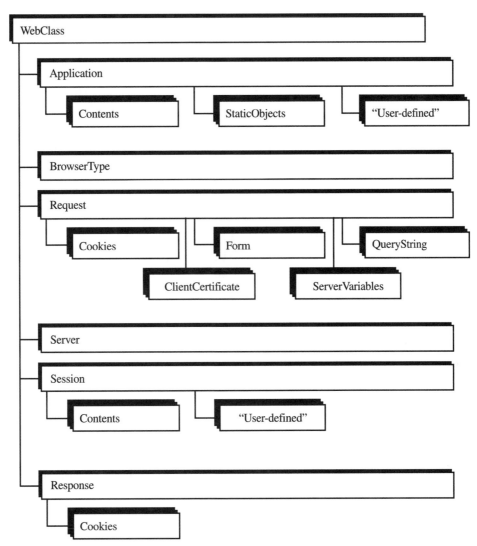

Figure 17-14 The IIS Application object model

ASP applications. The last object, BrowserType, is unique to IIS Applications. The following list describes these six objects:

- **Request** Receives requests from the Web clients. It can receive all the data on the form plus information about the current user. It contains several other

collections, each of which represents different sets of information that can be returned for the Web client. Each ClientCertificate object in the ClientCertificate collection represents a certificate field that's returned from the Web client that identifies the client. The Cookies collection contains a set of Web cookies, where each cookie contains a small amount of information about the Web user. The Forms collection contains a set of Form objects, where each object represents an HTML form. The QueryString collection contains a set of added URL arguments. The ServerVariables collection contains a set of server environment variables.

● **Response** Writes information into the HTML stream and sends that information to the client browser. It also supports a Cookies collection, where each Cookie object contains information that can be written to the client system. The Request object can later read these cookies.

● **Session** Maintains information that relates to the current Web session. The collection of Contents objects contained in the Session object contains all the items that have been added to the Web session using script commands. The ObjectContext object provides access to the current object's context. It typically is used to instantiate MTS (Microsoft Transaction Server) objects or to control database transactions.

● **Server** Used to create other COM objects that your Web application will use. For instance, the Server object's CreateObject method can be used to create the ADO objects that can be used to access database information.

● **Application** Shared by all active Web sessions and used to manage the state for all the instances of the Web application. It can also be used to store information about multiple users who are connected to the Web. It is very much like the Session object, except the Application object pertains to all Web users, whereas the Session object refers only to the current Web session. The Application object contains the Contents collection and the StaticObjects collection. Each Contents object in the Contents collection contains all the items that have been

added to the Web application using ActiveX script commands. The StaticObjects collection contains all the objects added to the Web application using the HTML <Object> tag. In addition, the Application object can contain user-defined objects that are created by the Web application, and can be shared by multiple users.

- **BrowserType** Determines the capabilities of the Web client's Web browser.

How do I create an IIS project?

To create a new IIS Application, follow these steps:

1. Select File | New Project, which displays the New Project dialog box, shown in Figure 17-15.

2. Select the IIS Application icon and then click the OK button. If the VB IDE can detect the local Web server, the WebClass Designer will be started.

3. After the WebClass Designer has started, add an HTML template to the IIS Application project. The HTML template must be developed outside of the IIS Applications. You can create the template by using

Figure 17-15   Creating a new IIS Application project

Notepad or a specialized HTML editor. The following listing presents a simple HTML file that can be used as a template:

```
<!-- start.htm -->
<html>
<head><title>Sample IIS Application Template</title>
</head>
<body>
<h1>Select an option</h1><br><hr>
<p>Select from the following options to view the next
page:</p>
<form method="POST" id="WebPage1"><input type="submit"
value="Show page1" name="btnPage1"></form>
<form method="POST" id="WebPage2"><input type="submit"
value="Show page2" name="btnPage2"></form>
</body>
</html>
```

4. To add the HTML template to the IIS Application, right-click the WebClass name in the left pane of the WebClass Designer and then select the Add HTML Template option from the pop-up menu.

An Open dialog box is displayed that allows you to select the HTML file to use as a template. After you add the HTML template to your project, the WebClass Designer appears, similar to Figure 17-16.

In the figure, each of the objects identified by the HTML tags appears in the right pane of the WebClass Designer. After the HTML templates have been added, you should save the project, which causes Visual Basic to make copies of all the HTML files, for use by the IIS Application. Using copies of the HTML files prevents the IIS Application from being affected by any changes that might be made to the original HTML files.

5. Set the startup options for the application by using the WebClass object's Start event. The code for the sample Start event is shown here:

```
Private Sub WebClass_Start()

    Set NextItem = Start

End Sub
```

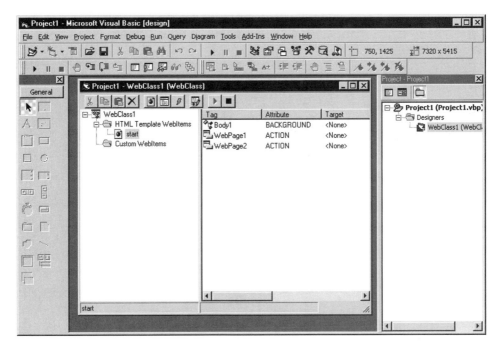

Figure 17-16 Adding an HTML template to an IIS Application

After the WebClass object is created, the Start event is executed. The Start event is used to pass the processing to the WebItem's Respond event, by setting the NextItem property to the name of the template that will be shown. The Respond event is responsible for displaying the Web page. A sample Respond event is shown in the following listing:

```
Private Sub start_Respond()
    Start.WriteTemplate
End Sub
```

The Start object's WriteTemplate event will cause the HTML form to be displayed in the Web browser.

To make the buttons on the start page work, you must create custom WebItems and then pass the processing to the appropriate WebItem when the button is clicked. This is quite similar to the way standard VB event subroutines are used.

Follow these steps to create a custom WebItem and connect it to the HTML Form element:

1. Right-click the Custom WebItems entry in the right pane of the WebClass Designer and then select the Add Custom WebItem option from the pop-up menu. You can create a separate event for each menu option.

2. To connect the HTML Form element to the custom WebItem, right-click the HTML elements in the right pane of the WebClass Designer to display the pop-up menu shown in Figure 17-17.

3. Select the Connect to WebItem option from the pop-up menu. Then select the name of the custom WebItem from the list that is displayed in the next dialog box. This will connect the HTML buttons to the event actions described in the custom WebItem.

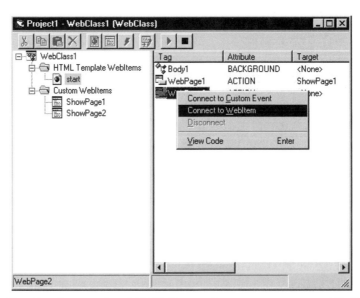

Figure 17-17 Connecting HTML Form elements to custom WebItems

4. Add code in the custom WebItem's Respond event subroutine to respond to the user's button click. The following code illustrates how the custom WebItem's Respond event can then be used to output an HTML page that displays the user's selection:

```
Private Sub ShowPage1_Respond()
    Response.Write "<HTML><BODY><H1>You
        selected Web Page 1</H1><HR>"
    Response.Write "</table></BODY></HTML>"
End Sub
```

After you finish designing your IIS Application project, select File | Make to compile the ActiveX DLL and create the resulting ASP page. These can then be deployed to the target Web server. Refer to Chapter 18 for more information about deploying projects.

Chapter 18

Deploying Applications

Answer Topics!

Deploying Applications @ a Glance

In this chapter, you'll see how to take advantage of Visual Basic's Package and Deployment Wizard to create installation programs that you can use to distribute both the desktop applications and the Web projects that you create using Visual Basic.

- **Using the Package and Deployment Wizard** shows you how to use the new Package and Deployment Wizard. You'll see how to add the wizard to your VB integrated development environment (IDE), as well as how to create setup programs that can be used for both your standard VB applications and your Web applications.

- **Using Third-Party Products** shows you how to add third-party custom controls to your deployment packages. It also discusses alternatives to the VB Packaging and Deployment Wizard.

USING THE PACKAGE AND DEPLOYMENT WIZARD

The first several questions and answers in this section illustrate how to run the Packing and Deployment Wizard from the desktop and add it your VB IDE. Then you'll see how to create setup programs using the wizard.

 ## How do I start the Package and Deployment Wizard?

You can start the Package and Deployment Wizard in one of two ways:

- **By opening it in Visual Studio**   Choose Start | Programs | Visual Studio | Visual Studio 6.0 Tools | Package and Deployment Wizard.

- **By starting it as an add-in to the VB IDE**   Using the Package and Deployment Wizard from the VB Add-Ins menu has the advantage of automatically filling in the name of the current VB project on the wizard's initial screens. However, before it can be used from the Add-Ins menu, you need to load it by using the VB Add-In Manager:

  1. Select the Add-In Manager option from the Add-Ins menu. The Add-In Manager, shown in Figure 18-1, will be displayed.

  2. Click the Package and Deployment Wizard option in the list of available Add-Ins.

  3. Check the Loaded on Startup check box. The words Startup/Unloaded will appear under the Load Behavior caption.

  4. Click the OK button to confirm the change.

The next time VB starts, an option for the Package and Deployment Wizard will appear under the Add-Ins menu.

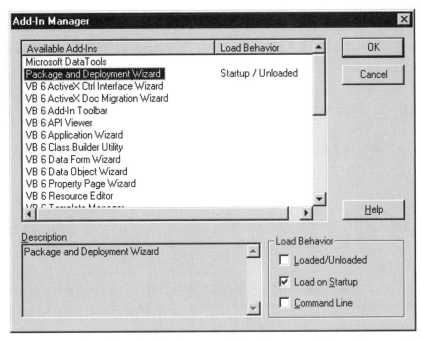

Figure 18-1 Loading the Package and Deployment Wizard as an add-in

What's the difference between the Package and Deploy options presented by the Package and Deployment Wizard?

The Package and Deploy options in Visual Basic's Package and Deployment Wizard each perform different tasks. The Package option is used to group all the components together that are used in a VB project. The Package option scans the VB project for dependent DLL and OCX files and then prompts you to group these files together into one or more CAB files. The contents of the CAB files are compressed to make it easier to distribute them on diskette, CD-ROM, or across the Internet.

The Deploy option enables you to copy the files that were produced by the Package option to a target destination. The Deploy option is used to copy the CAB and Setup.exe files

that were produced by the Package option to either a networked folder or a target Web server.

 Note: *To deploy files to a target Web server, the Visual Studio server extensions must be applied to the destination Web server.*

What are the basic steps to create an installation program for my VB project?

To create a setup program, follow these steps:

1. Ensure that the most recent changes to your VB project have been saved and that a current copy of the executable file has been created.

2. Open the Package and Deployment Wizard, shown in Figure 18-2, by selecting its option from the VB Add-Ins menu.

3. Make sure the Active Project text box is set.

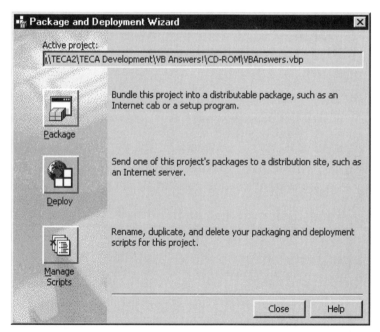

Figure 18-2 The Package and Deployment Wizard dialog box

When you run the Package and Deployment Wizard from the Add-Ins menu, the Active Project text box automatically contains the name of the current project. If you want to run the wizard for a different project, you must manually enter the new project name and path into the Active Project text field. In Figure 18-2, the Active Project text box has been set to the VBAnswers.vbp project.

4. Choose either the Package or the Deploy option.

   If this is the first time you have created an installation package for your project, you must choose the Package button before proceeding on to the Deploy button.

5. Click the Package button to display the Package Type dialog box, shown in Figure 18-3, which enables you to select the type of package that will be created.

   ● The Standard Setup Package option is used to create standard setup programs. This option creates one or more compressed CAB files along with a Setup.exe program.

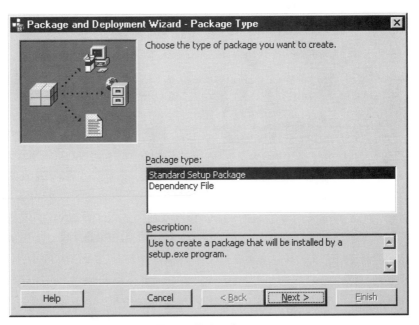

Figure 18-3 The Package Type dialog box

⬤ The Dependency File option creates a DEP file that
contains a listing of all the project files needed by
the application.

6. Select the Standard Setup Package option and click
Next to display the Package Folder dialog box, shown in
Figure 18-4.

This dialog box enables you to choose the folder that will
contain the CAB files and Setup.exe program that are
created by the Package option. By default, the wizard
places the setup files in a subdirectory of the current
folder named Package. You can optionally change this
location by using the drive and directory list boxes at
the bottom of the dialog box.

7. Select the location of the setup files and click Next to
display the Included Files dialog box, shown in Figure 18-5,
which lists all the files that the Package and
Deployment Wizard has located in the VB projects.

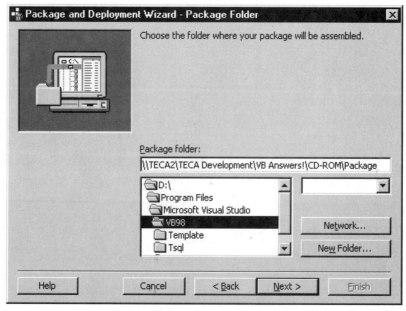

Figure 18-4 The Package Folder dialog box

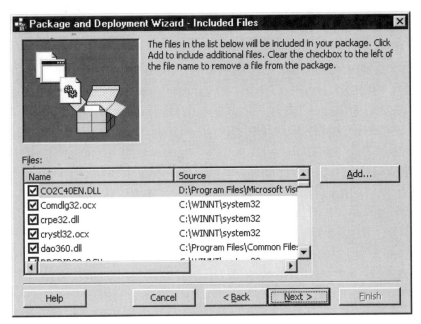

Figure 18-5 The Included Files dialog box

Note: *The Package and Deployment Wizard scans the VPB and FRM files to identify the DLLs and ActiveX controls that are used by the current project.*

Checking the box in front of the component's name causes the component to be included in the packaging process. By default, all the files identified by the Package and Deployment Wizard are selected.

- To omit a file, uncheck the box immediately before the filename.

- To include other files, such as the project's source files or any third-party ActiveX controls that were not automatically detected by the wizard, click the Add button to display a File Open dialog box that enables you to locate and add any missing files.

8. Include all the desired files and click Next to display the Package and Deployment Wizard's CAB Options dialog box, shown in Figure 18-6.

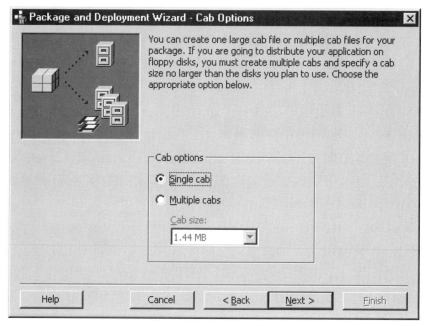

Figure 18-6   The CAB Options dialog box

This dialog box allows you to specify the type of
CAB files that will be created by the Package and
Deployment Wizard.

- **Single cab**   By default, the wizard creates a
  single CAB file. This is typically the best option for
  distributing applications on CD-ROM or across
  the Internet.

- **Multiple cabs**   You can also specify a CAB file size,
  to cause the wizard to produce multiple CAB files.
  Multiple CAB files typically are used when you must
  distribute the application on diskettes.

9. Select the type of CAB file that will be generated and
   click Next to cause the wizard to display the Installation
   Title dialog box, shown in Figure 18-7.

   This dialog box allows you to input the name that will
   be displayed when the Setup.exe program is run. In
   Figure 18-7, the Installation Title box has been set to
   VBAnswers.

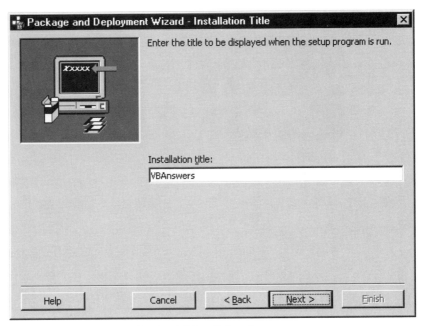

Figure 18-7 The Installation Title dialog box

10. Enter a name in the Installation Title box and click Next to display the Package and Deployment Wizard's Start Menu Items dialog box, shown in Figure 18-8, which governs the menu items that are added to the Window's Start menu.

   By default, the menu options are added under the Programs menu, under the name that was used in the Installation Title dialog box. You can change the default menu options by using the New Group, New Item, Properties, and Remove buttons.

11. Click Next to display the Package and Deployment Wizard's Install Locations dialog box, shown in Figure 18-9, which enables you to select the target location for the files that will be installed.

   This dialog box lists each component that will be included in the package, as well as the source location on the development system and a macro that identifies the target directory. Using macros to identify the target directory makes it possible to use the same script to

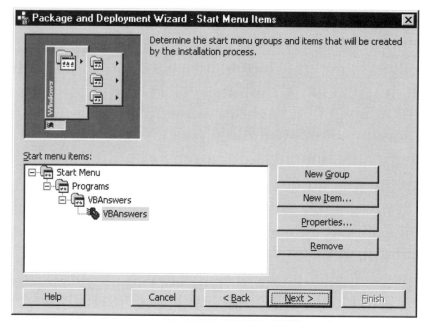

Figure 18-8 The Start Menu Items dialog box

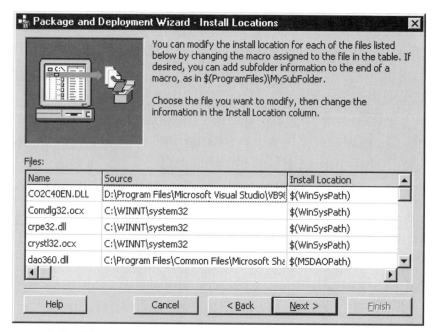

Figure 18-9 The Install Locations dialog box

perform the installation, even when the target system might use different drive letters. The following table presents the different folder macros that are available to the Package and Deployment Wizard.

Macro	Directory
$(WinSysPath)	\Windows\System (Windows 95 and 98)
	\Winnt\System32 (Windows NT and 2000)
$(WinSysPathSysFile)	\Windows\System (Windows 95 and 98 System file)
	\Winnt\System32 (Windows NT and 2000 System file)
$(WinPath)	\Windows (Windows 95 and 98 System file)
	\Winnt (Windows NT and 2000 System file)
$(AppPath)	The application directory specified
$(CommonFiles)	\Program files\Common files
$(CommonFilesSys)	\Program files\Common files\System
$(ProgramFiles)	\Program files

12. Select the target directories for the installation files and click Next to display the Shared Files dialog box, shown in Figure 18-10, which lists the files that have been tagged as shared files.

    Shared files are typically objects, such as ActiveX controls, that can be used by multiple executable programs. Identifying a file as shared can prevent it from being removed when the project's uninstall routine is run. A shared file is removed only if all the programs that reference that file have also been removed.

    ● Checking the box immediately in front of the filename marks that file as shared.

    ● Leaving the check box empty indicates that the file should not be installed as a shared file.

13. Click Next to display the Finished! dialog box, shown in Figure 18-11, which signifies that you have completed all the steps necessary to create an installation package.

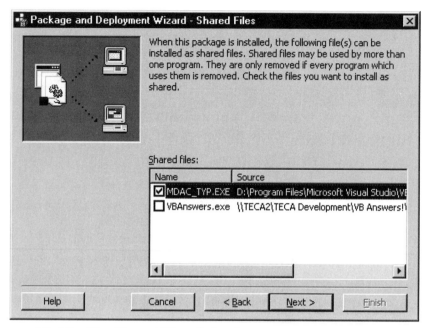

Figure 18-10 The Shared Files dialog box

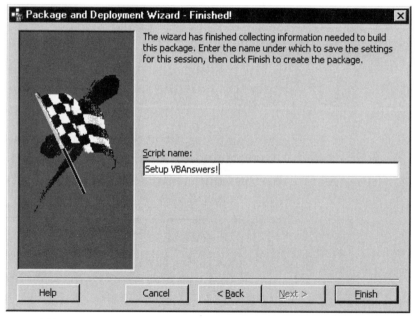

Figure 18-11 The Finished! dialog box

14. Click Finish to create the CAB files and the Setup.exe program. When the Package and Deployment Wizard has finished creating the installation package, the Packaging Report dialog box, shown in Figure 18-12, is displayed.

This report displays the results of running the Package and Deployment Wizard.

15. Click the Save Report button if you want to write the contents of the dialog box to a text file.

After you complete the packaging step, you can either copy the resulting CAB and Setup.exe files to distribution media or run the Package and Deployment Wizard's Deploy option to copy the package files to a networked folder or a Web server.

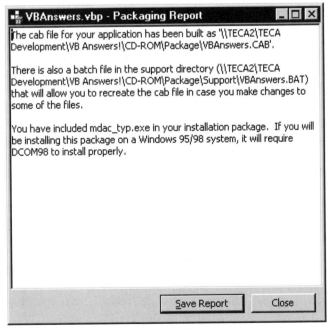

Figure 18-12 The Packaging Report dialog box

 What are all the runtime files that I need to include in my installation?

The specific files needed for each individual project varies according to the different components that are used in the project. However, all VB projects need the following list of files:

- Msvbvm60.dll
- Stdole2.tlb
- Oleaut32.dll
- Olepro32.dll
- Comcat.dll
- Asyncfilt.dll
- Ctl3d32.dll

Tip: *As a general rule, if you add either a component or a reference to your project, at least one OCX or DLL file will need to be distributed at runtime. Both the Components and the References dialog boxes list the actual filename of each component.*

Can I view all the files that will be installed by the Setup.exe program?

Yes. When the Package and Deployment Wizard creates the CAB and Setup.exe files, it also creates a Setup.lst file that lists all the files that will be installed. The Setup.lst file is a plain text file that contains a complete list of installation instructions and files.

How do I uninstall the applications that were installed using the Package and Deployment Wizard?

Applications that are installed using the Package and Deployment Wizard can be removed as follows:

1. Open the Control Panel and select the Add/Remove Programs option.

2. Scroll through the list of installed applications until you find the name of the application you want to remove.

3. Click the Add/Remove button to remove the application.

 Tip: *The St6unst.exe program is used by the Application and Deployment Wizard to remove unwanted applications.*

USING THIRD-PARTY PRODUCTS

This chapter ends by showing how to use the Package and Deployment Wizard to install third-party ActiveX controls. It also discusses some of the third-party installation programs that can be used as an alternative to the VB Package and Deployment Wizard.

 The Package and Deployment Wizard didn't include the third-party ActiveX controls that are in my project. How can I add them to my installation package?

The Package and Deployment Wizard automatically recognizes most third-party ActiveX controls. However, if the control is not automatically recognized, you can add it during the packaging process manually by using the Package and Deployment Wizard's Included Files dialog box, shown in Figure 18-13.

1. Click the Add button to display the Add File dialog box, shown in Figure 18-14.

2. Select from the list the component you want to add to the installation package

3. Click OK to add it to the installation package.

After you finish adding the third-party component, the Package and Deployment Wizard resumes with the Included Files dialog box.

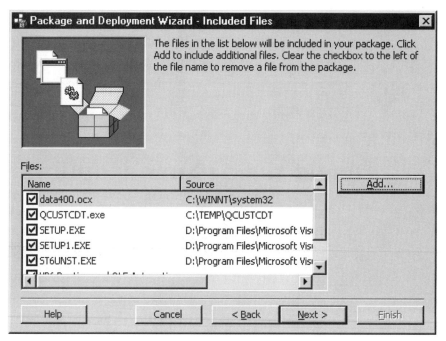

Figure 18-13   The Included Files dialog box

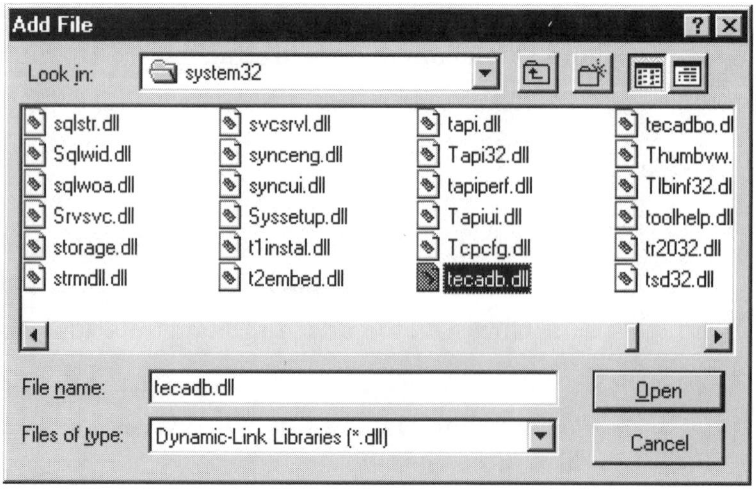

Figure 18-14   The Add File dialog box

 The Application and Deployment Wizard won't create a self-extracting executable program. Do any third-party installation tools work with VB projects?

Although the VB Package and Deployment Wizard is a big improvement over the installation tools that were provided with the earlier versions of Visual Basic, it still doesn't offer all the options that are available with the leading third-party installation tools. For instance, the Package and Deployment Wizard can't create self-extracting executable files, which often are used to distribute applications across the Internet. Two of the leading third-party installation tools that can be used for VB projects are InstallShield Professional, by InstallShield, and Wise InstallBuilder, by Wise Solutions. You can find more information on these products at www.installshield.com and www.glbs.com.

Appendix A

Naming Conventions

Using a standard naming convention means that the name assigned to each program object and variable helps to identify its data type. Following a standard naming convention is optional in Visual Basic. It has no built-in requirement for you to use any predetermined names for your program's objects and variables. However, adopting a standard naming convention has definite benefits, both while you're developing your application and when you later need to maintain that application. Standard naming conventions make it easier to develop your projects, by helping to eliminate any ambiguity that may exist regarding an object's type. Different objects provide different methods and can be used with different functions and operators.

When no naming conventions are in place, it's easy to attempt to use an object or variable with an incompatible function or operator. When you encounter this kind of error, you must take the time to find the declaration of the object or variable in question and then correct your code. For a large application with tens or even hundreds of different variable and object declarations, this can result in a significant waste of time. Even worse, sometimes a function or operator can be applied to two different objects, and it can have different effects depending on the type of object that it is used with. This can result in subtle and very difficult-to-find bugs.

However worthwhile the benefits of a standard naming convention are during the development process, they are even more beneficial for program maintenance. When the workings of a program are fresh in your memory, as they are during the development process, you may be able to recognize the different variables that are used in an application and remember their data types. However, when you haven't made changes to that program for six months or a year and then you or some other developer returns to it to make a set of modifications, the data type of each program variable or object will certainly not be clear. Then, you or some other developer will be forced to spend the time to research the type of most of the different variables that your changes may affect. Adopting a standard naming convention eliminates this kind of problem, because the type of the variable or object is identified as a part of the object's name.

The naming convention that you adopt is not nearly as important as the fact that you do use a standard naming convention. The following tables present a recommended set of naming conventions. You can adopt these naming conventions for your own development or use them as a basis for implementing your own set of naming conventions.

FILE-LEVEL OBJECTS

Object	Prefix	Example
Form	frm	frmMyForm
MDI form	mdi	mdiMyMDIForm
Module	mod	modMyModule
Class module	cls	clsMyClassModule
User control	uctl	uctlMyUserControl
Property page	pp	ppMyPropertyPage
User document	udoc	udocMyUserDocument
Web class	wcls	wclsMyWebClass
DHTML page	dpag	dpagMyDHTMLPage
Data environment	de	deMyDataEnvironment
Data report	Dr	drMyDataReport

VARIABLES
Standard Three-Character Naming Convention

Object	Prefix	Example
Boolean	bln	blnMyBoolean
Byte	byt	bytMyByte
Collection	col	colMyCollection
Currency	cur	curMyCurrency
Date/time	dtm	dtmMyDateTime
Double	dbl	dblMyDouble
Integer	int	intMyInteger
Long	lng	lngMyLong
Object	obj	objMyObject
Single	sng	sngMySingle
String	str	strMyString
User-defined	udt	udtMyUserType
Variant	vnt	vntMyVariant

Alternative Single-Character Naming Convention

Object	Prefix	Example
Boolean	b	bMyBoolean
Byte	y	yMyByte
Collection	o (beginning) s (ending)	oMyObjects
Currency	m	mMyCurrency
Date/time	t	tMyDateTime
Double	d	dMyTime
Integer	i	iMyInteger
Long	l	lMyLong
Object	o	oMyObject
Single	n	nMySingle
String	s	sMyString
User-defined	u	uMyUDT
Variant	v	vMyVariant

CONTROLS

Object	Prefix	Example
3-D panel	pnl	pnlMyPanel
ActiveX data	ado	adoMyAdodc
Animated button	ani	aniMyAnimation
Check box	chk	chkCheckBox
Combo box	cbo	cboMyComboBox
Command button	cmd	cmdMyCommandButton
Common dialog	dlg	dlgMyCommonDialog
Communications	com	comMyMSComm
Data	dat	datMyData
Directory list box	dir	dirMyDirListBox
Drive list box	drv	drvMyDriveListBox
File list box	fil	filMyFileListBox
Frame	fra	fraMyFrame
Gauge	gau	gauMyGauge
Graph	gra	graMyGraph

Object	Prefix	Example
Grid	grd	grdMyGrid
Horizontal scroll bar	hsb	hsbMyHScrollBar
Image	img	imgMyImage
Image list	ils	ilsMyImageList
Label	lbl	lblMyLabel
Line	lin	linMyLine
List box	lst	lstMyListBox
List view	lvw	lvwMyListView
MAPI message	mpm	mpmMyMAPIMessages
MAPI session	mps	mpsMyMAPISession
MS chart	ch	chMyMSChart
MS flex grid	flx	flxMyMSFlexGrid
OLE container	ole	oleMyOLE
Option button	opt	optMyOptionButton
Picture box	pic	picMyPictureBox
Picture clip	clp	clpMyPictureClip
Progress bar	prg	prgMyProgressBar
Remote data	rd	rdMyMSRDC
Rich text box	rtf	rtfMyRichTextBox
Shape	shp	shpMyShape
Slider	sld	sldMySlider
Spin	spn	spnMySpinButton
Status bar	sta	staMyStatusBar
System info	sys	sysMySysInfo
Tab strip	tab	tabMyTabStrip
Text box	txt	txtMyTextBox
Timer	tmr	tmrMyTimer
Toolbar	tlb	tlbMyToolbar
Tree view	tre	treMyTreeView
Up-down	upd	UpdMyUpDown
Vertical scroll bar	vsb	vsbMyVScrollBar

DATA ACCESS OBJECT FRAMEWORKS
Data Access Objects (DAO)

Object	Prefix	Example
Container	con	conMyContainer
Database	db	dbMyDatabase
Database engine	dbe	dbeMyDBEngine
Document	doc	docMyDocument
Field	fld	fldMyField
Group	grp	grpMyGroup
Index	ix	ixMyIndex
Parameter	prm	prmMyParameter
Query definition	qry	qryMyQueryDef
Record set	rs	rsMyRecordSet
Relation	rel	relMyRelation
Table definition	tbd	tbdMyTableDef
User	usr	usrMyUser
Workspace	wsp	wspMyWorkspace

Remote Data Access Objects (RDO)

Object	Prefix	Example
rdoEngine	rdo	rdoMyRDOEngine
rdoError	err	errMyError
rdoEnvironment	en	enMyEnvironment
rdoConnection	cn	cnMyConneciton
rdoTable	tbl	tblMyTable
rdoResultset	rs	rsMyResultset
rdoColumn	cl	clMyColumn
rdoParameter	prm	prmMyParameter
rdoQuery	qry	qryMyQuery

ActiveX Data Objects (ADO)

Object	Prefix	Example
Connection	cn	cnMyConnection
Command	cmd	cmdMyCommand
Parameter	prm	prmMyParameter
Record set	rs	rsMyRecordset
Field	fld	fldMyField
Error	err	errMyError
Property	prp	prpMyProperty

SCOPING

Scope	Prefix	Example
Global	g	gstrText1
Module	m	mstrText1
Local	(none)	strText1

Chapter B

Visual Basic Constants

Visual Basic comes with numerous constants that can be used both to set properties and to set parameter values for different function calls. Using these constants makes your application code much easier to read and maintain. Literally hundreds of constants are available for use both from the VB runtime objects and from other COM object libraries that can be referenced in your projects. This appendix presents the most commonly used VB constants.

BORDER STYLE CONSTANTS

Constant	Value	Description
vbBSDash	2	Dashed-line border style
vbBSDashDot	4	Alternating dash and dot border style
vbBSDashDotDot	5	Dash with two dots border style
vbBSDot	3	Dotted-line border style
vbBSInsideSolid	6	Solid inside-line border style
vbBSSolid	1	Solid-line border style
vbTransparent	0	Transparent border style

BUTTON CONSTANTS

Constant	Value	Description
vbButtonGraphical	1	Graphical command button style
vbButtonStandard	0	Normal command button style

CHECK BOX CONSTANTS

Constant	Value	Description
vbChecked	1	The check box is checked.
vbGrayed	2	The check box is grayed out.
vbUnchecked	0	The check box is unchecked.

COLOR CONSTANTS

Constant	Value	Description
vbBlack	0	Black
vbBlue	16711680 (&HFF0000)	Blue
vbCyan	16776960 (&HFFFF00)	Cyan
vbGreen	65280 (&HFF00)	Green
vbMagenta	16711935 (&HFF00FF)	Magenta
vbRed	255 (&HFF)	Red
vbWhite	16777215 (&HFFFFFF)	White
vbYellow	65535 (&HFFFF)	Yellow

COMBO BOX CONSTANTS

Constant	Value	Description
vbComboDropdown	0	Drop-down only combo box style
vbComboDropdownList	2	Drop-down list combo box style
vbComboSimple	1	Simple combo box style

DRAG CONSTANTS

Constant	Value	Description
vbBeginDrag	1	The mouse drag event was started.
vbCancel	0	The mouse drag event was canceled.
vbEndDrag	2	The mouse drag event was ended.

FILE ATTRIBUTES CONSTANTS

Constant	Value	Description
vbAlias	64 (&H40)	The File object name is an alias.
vbArchive	32 (&H20)	The File object has the Archive attribute set.
vbDirectory	16 (&H10)	The File object is a directory.
vbHidden	2	The File object has the Hidden attribute set.
vbNormal	0	The File object has no attributes set.
vbReadOnly	1	The File object has the Read-Only attribute set.
vbSystem	4	The File object has the System attribute set.
vbVolume	8	The File object is a disk volume.

FORM BORDER TYPE CONSTANTS

Constant	Value	Description
vbBSNone	0	Don't display a border.
vbFixedDialog	3	Display as a fixed dialog.
vbFixedSingle	1	Display with a fixed single border.
vbFixedToolWindow	4	Display as a fixed tool window.
vbSizable	2	Allow the form to be resized.
vbSizableToolWindow	5	Display as a resizable tool window.

FORM DISPLAY CONSTANTS

Constant	Value	Description
vbModal	1	The form is modal.
vbModeless	0	The form is modeless.

FORM STARTUP POSITION CONSTANTS

Constant	Value	Description
vbStartUpManual	0	The startup position is manually set.
vbStartUpOwner	1	The startup position is centered over the form's owner.
vbStartUpScreen	2	The startup position is centered over the screen.
vbStartUpWindowsDefault	3	The startup position of the form is in the upper-left corner of the screen.

FORM TYPE CONSTANTS

Constant	Value	Description
vbMaximized	2	Maximize the form.
vbMinimized	1	Minimize the form.
vbNormal	0	Display the form as a normal window.

FORM WINDOWING CONSTANTS

Constant	Value	Description
vbArrangeIcons	3	Automatically arrange icons.
vbCascade	0	Display cascaded windows.
vbTileHorizontal	1	Tile windows horizontally.
vbTileVertical	2	Tile windows vertically.

KEYBOARD CONSTANTS

Constant	Value	Description
vbKey0	48 (&H30)	0
vbKey1	49 (&H31)	1
vbKey2	50 (&H32)	2
vbKey3	51 (&H33)	3
vbKey4	52 (&H34)	4
vbKey5	53 (&H35)	5
vbKey6	54 (&H36)	6
vbKey7	55 (&H37)	7
vbKey8	56 (&H38)	8
vbKey9	57 (&H39)	9
vbKeyA	65 (&H41)	A
vbKeyAdd	107 (&H6B)	+ (plus on numeric keypad)
vbKeyB	66 (&H42)	B
vbKeyBack	8	BACKSPACE
vbKeyC	67 (&H43)	C
vbKeyCancel	3	Cancel
vbKeyCapital	20 (&H14)	CAPS LOCK
vbKeyClear	12	Clear
vbKeyControl	17 (&H11)	CTRL
vbKeyD	68 (&H44)	D
vbKeyDecimal	110 (&H6E)	. (decimal point on numeric keypad)
vbKeyDelete	46 (&H2E)	DELETE
vbKeyDivide	111 (&H6F)	/ (divide sign on numeric keypad)
vbKeyDown	40 (&H28)	DOWN ARROW
vbKeyE	69 (&H45)	E

Constant	Value	Description
vbKeyEnd	35 (&H23)	END
vbKeyEscape	27 (&H1B)	ESC
vbKeyExecute	43 (&H2B)	Execute
vbKeyF	70 (&H46)	F
vbKeyF1	112 (&H70)	F1
vbKeyF10	121 (&H79)	F10
vbKeyF11	122 (&H80)	F11
vbKeyF12	123 (&H81)	F12
vbKeyF13	124 (&H82)	F13
vbKeyF14	125 (&H83)	F14
vbKeyF15	126 (&H84)	F15
vbKeyF16	127 (&H85)	F16
vbKeyF2	113 (&H71)	F2
vbKeyF3	114 (&H72)	F3
vbKeyF4	115 (&H73)	F4
vbKeyF5	116 (&H74)	F5
vbKeyF6	117 (&H75)	F6
vbKeyF7	118 (&H76)	F7
vbKeyF8	119 (&H77)	F8
vbKeyF9	120 (&H78)	F9
vbKeyG	71 (&H47)	G
vbKeyH	72 (&H48)	H
vbKeyHelp	47 (&H2F)	F1 (Help)
vbKeyHome	36 (&H24)	HOME
vbKeyI	73 (&H49)	I
vbKeyInsert	45 (&H2D)	INSERT
vbKeyJ	74 (&H4A)	J
vbKeyK	75 (&H4B)	L
vbKeyL	76 (&H4C)	L
vbKeyLButton	1	Left mouse button
vbKeyLeft	37 (&H25)	LEFT ARROW
vbKeyM	77 (&H4D)	M
vbKeyMButton	4	Middle mouse button
vbKeyMenu	18 (&H12)	MENU

Constant	Value	Description
vbKeyMultiply	106 (&H6A)	* (multiply on numeric keypad)
vbKeyN	78 (&H4E)	N
vbKeyNumlock	144 (&H90)	NUM LOCK
vbKeyNumpad0	96 (&H60)	0 (on numeric keypad)
vbKeyNumpad1	97 (&H61)	1 (on numeric keypad)
vbKeyNumpad2	98 (&H62)	2 (on numeric keypad)
vbKeyNumpad3	99 (&H63)	3 (on numeric keypad)
vbKeyNumpad4	100 (&H64)	4 (on numeric keypad)
vbKeyNumpad5	101 (&H65)	5 (on numeric keypad)
vbKeyNumpad6	102 (&H66)	6 (on numeric keypad)
vbKeyNumpad7	103 (&H67)	7 (on numeric keypad)
vbKeyNumpad8	104 (&H68)	8 (on numeric keypad)
vbKeyNumpad9	105 (&H69)	9 (on numeric keypad)
vbKeyO	79 (&H4F)	O
vbKeyP	80 (&H50)	P
vbKeyPageDown	34 (&H22)	PAGE DOWN
vbKeyPageUp	33 (&H21)	PAGE UP
vbKeyPause	19 (&H13)	PAUSE
vbKeyPrint	42 (&H2A)	PRINT SCREEN
vbKeyQ	81 (&H51)	Q
vbKeyR	82 (&H52)	R
vbKeyRButton	2	Right mouse button
vbKeyReturn	13	ENTER
vbKeyRight	39 (&H27)	RIGHT ARROW
vbKeyS	83 (&H53)	S
vbKeyScrollLock	145 (&H91)	SCROLL LOCK
vbKeySelect	41 (&H29)	Select
vbKeySeparator	108 (&H6C)	ENTER (on numeric keypad)
vbKeyShift	16 (&H10)	SHIFT
vbKeySnapshot	44 (&H2C)	Snapshot
vbKeySpace	32 (&H20)	SPACEBAR
vbKeySubtract	109 (&H6D)	– (subtract on numeric keypad)
vbKeyT	84 (&H54)	T
vbKeyTab	9	TAB

Constant	Value	Description
vbKeyU	85 (&H55)	U
vbKeyUp	38 (&H26)	UP ARROW
vbKeyV	86 (&H56)	V
vbKeyW	87 (&H57)	W
vbKeyX	88 (&H58)	X
vbKeyY	89 (&H59)	Y
vbKeyZ	90 (&H60)	Z

LIST BOX CONSTANTS

Constant	Value	Description
vbListBoxCheckbox	1	Display list box with check box style.
vbListBoxStandard	0	Display standard list box style.

MESSAGE BOX BUTTON CONSTANTS

Constant	Value	Description
vbAbortRetryIgnore	2	Display Abort, Retry, and Ignore buttons.
vbDefaultButton1	0	Make the first button the default selection.
vbDefaultButton2	256 (&H100)	Make the second button the default selection.
vbDefaultButton3	512 (&H200)	Make the third button the default selection.
vbDefaultButton4	768 (&H300)	Make the fourth button the default selection.
vbOKCancel	1	Display OK and Cancel buttons.
vbOKOnly	0	Display an OK button only.
vbQuestion	32 (&H20)	Display a question mark.
vbRetryCancel	5	Display Retry and Cancel buttons.
vbYesNo	4	Display Yes and No buttons.
vbYesNoCancel	3	Display Yes, No, and Cancel buttons.
vbMsgBoxHelpButton	16384 (&H4000)	Display a Help button.

MESSAGE BOX DISPLAY CONSTANTS

Constant	Value	Description
vbApplicationModal	0	Display an application modal message box.
vbCritical	16 (&H10)	Display a red stop icon.
vbExclamation	48 (&H30)	Display an exclamation point.
vbInformation	64 (&H40)	Display a yellow information icon.
vbMsgBoxRight	524288 (&H80000)	Align text on the right.
vbMsgBoxRtlReading	1048576 (&H100000)	Display text in right-to-left format.
vbMsgBoxSetForeground	65536 (&H10000)	Display the message box as the foreground window.
vbSystemModal	4096 (&H1000)	Display a system modal message box.

MESSAGE BOX REPLY CONSTANTS

Constant	Value	Description
vbAbort	3	The Abort button was selected.
vbCancel	2	The Cancel button was selected.
vbIgnore	5	The Ignore button was selected.
vbNo	7	The No button was selected.
vbOK	1	The OK button was selected.
vbRetry	4	The Retry button was selected.
vbYes	6	The Yes button was selected.

MISCELLANEOUS CONSTANTS

Constant	Value	Description
vbCRLF	Chr(13) & Chr(10)	Carriage return linefeed
vbCR	Chr(13)	Carriage return
vbLF	Chr(10)	Linefeed
vbNewLine	Chr(13) & Chr(10)	Carriage return linefeed

Constant	Value	Description
vbNullChar	Chr(0)	Null
vbNullString	""	String variable containing no data
vbObjectError	–2147221504	Starting value for user-defined errors
vbTab	Chr(9)	TAB
vbBack	Chr(8)	BACKSPACE

MOUSE BUTTON CONSTANTS

Constant	Value	Description
vbLeftButton	1	The left button was clicked.
vbMiddleButton	4	The middle button was clicked.
vbRightButton	2	The right button was clicked.

MOUSE POINTER CONSTANTS

Constant	Value	Description
vbArrow	1	Display the mouse pointer as an arrow.
vbArrowHourglass	13	Display the mouse pointer as an arrow with an hourglass.
vbArrowQuestion	14	Display the mouse pointer as an arrow with a question mark.
vbCrosshair	2	Display the mouse pointer as crosshairs.
vbCustom	99 (&H63)	Display the mouse pointer using the cursor bitmap indicated in the MouseIcon property.
vbDefault	0	Display the mouse pointer as a standard pointer arrow.
vbHourglass	11	Display the mouse pointer as an hourglass.
vbIbeam	3	Display the mouse pointer as an I-beam.
vbIconPointer	4	Display the mouse pointer as a double-arrow resizing pointer.
vbNoDrop	12	Display the mouse pointer as a red circle.

Constant	Value	Description
vbSizeAll	15	Display the mouse pointer as a double arrow.
vbSizeNESW	6	Display the mouse pointer as a double arrow for the upper-right and lower-right corners of a window.
vbSizeNS	7	Display the mouse pointer as a double arrow for the top and bottom edges of a window.
vbSizeNWSE	8	Display the mouse pointer as a double arrow for the upper-left and lower-left corners of a window.
vbSizePointer	5	Display the mouse pointer as a double arrow.
vbSizeWE	9	Display the mouse pointer as a double arrow for the left and right edges of a window.
vbUpArrow	10	Display the mouse pointer as an up arrow.

PRINTER COLOR MODE CONSTANTS

Constant	Value	Description
vbPRCMMonochrome	1	Monochrome output
vbPRCMColor	2	Color output

PRINTER DUPLEX PRINTING CONSTANTS

Constant	Value	Description
vbPRDPSimplex	1	Single-sided printing
vbPRDPHorizontal	2	Double-sided horizontal printing
vbPRDPVertical	3	Double-sided vertical printing

PRINTER ORIENTATION CONSTANTS

Constant	Value	Description
vbPRORPortrait	1	Print with the top at the narrow side of the paper.
vbPRORLandscape	2	Print with the top at the wide side of the paper.

PRINTER PAPER BIN CONSTANTS

Constant	Value	Description
VbPRBNUpper	1	Use paper from the upper bin.
VbPRBNLower	2	Use paper from the lower bin.
VbPRBNMiddle	3	Use paper from the middle bin.
VbPRBNManual	4	Wait for manual insertion of each sheet of paper.
VbPRBNEnvelope	5	Use envelopes from the envelope feeder.
VbPRBNEnvManual	6	Use envelopes from the envelope feeder, but wait for manual insertion.
VbPRBNAuto	7	(Default) Use paper from the current default bin.
VbPRBNTractor	8	Use paper fed from the tractor feeder.
VbPRBNSmallFmt	9	Use paper from the small paper feeder.
VbPRBNLargeFmt	10	Use paper from the large paper bin.
vbPRBNLargeCapacity	11	Use paper from the large capacity feeder.
VbPRBNCassette	14	Use paper from the attached cassette cartridge.

PRINTER PAPER SIZE CONSTANTS

Constant	Value	Description
VbPRPSLetter	1	Letter, 8 1/2 × 11 in.
VbPRPSLetterSmall	2	+A611Letter Small, 8 1/2 × 11 in.
vbPRPSTabloid	3	Tabloid, 11 × 17 in.
vbPRPSLedger	4	Ledger, 17 × 11 in.
vbPRPSLegal	5	Legal, 8 1/2 × 14 in.
vbPRPSStatement	6	Statement, 5 1/2 × 8 1/2 in.
vbPRPSExecutive	7	Executive, 7 1/2 × 10 1/2 in.
vbPRPSA3	8	A3, 297 × 420 mm
vbPRPSA4	9	A4, 210 × 297 mm
vbPRPSA4Small	10	A4 Small, 210 × 297 mm
vbPRPSA5	11	A5, 148 × 210 mm

Constant	Value	Description
vbPRPSB4	12	B4, 250 × 354 mm
vbPRPSB5	13	B5, 182 × 257 mm
vbPRPSFolio	14	Folio, 8 1/2 × 13 in.
vbPRPSQuarto	15	Quarto, 215 × 275 mm
vbPRPS1&H14	16	10 × 14 in.
vbPRPS11x17	17	11 × 17 in.
vbPRPSNote	18	Note, 8 1/2 × 11 in.
vbPRPSEnv9	19	Envelope #9, 3 7/8 × 8 7/8 in.
vbPRPSEnv10	20	Envelope #10, 4 1/8 × 9 1/2 in.
vbPRPSEnv11	21	Envelope #11, 4 1/2 × 10 3/8 in.
vbPRPSEnv12	22	Envelope #12, 4 1/2 × 11 in.
vbPRPSEnv14	23	Envelope #14, 5 × 11 1/2 in.
vbPRPSCSheet	24	C size sheet
vbPRPSDSheet	25	D size sheet
vbPRPSESheet	26	E size sheet
vbPRPSEnvDL	27	Envelope DL, 110 × 220 mm
vbPRPSEnvC3	29	Envelope C3, 324 × 458 mm
vbPRPSEnvC4	30	Envelope C4, 229 × 324 mm
vbPRPSEnvC5	28	Envelope C5, 162 × 229 mm
vbPRPSEnvC6	31	Envelope C6, 114 × 162 mm
vbPRPSEnvC65	32	Envelope C65, 114 × 229 mm
vbPRPSEnvB4	33	Envelope B4, 250 × 353 mm
vbPRPSEnvB5	34	Envelope B5, 176 × 250 mm
vbPRPSEnvB6	35	Envelope B6, 176 × 125 mm
vbPRPSEnvItaly	36	Envelope, 110 × 230 mm
vbPRPSEnvMonarch	37	Envelope Monarch, 3 7/8 × 7 1/2 in.
vbPRPSEnvPersonal	38	Envelope, 3 5/8 × 6 1/2 in.
vbPRPSFanfoldUS	39	U.S. Standard Fanfold, 14 7/8 × 11 in.
vbPRPSFanfoldStdGerman	40	German Standard Fanfold, 8 1/2 × 12 in.
vbPRPSFanfoldLglGerman	41	German Legal Fanfold, 8 1/2 × 13 in.
vbPRPSUser	256	User-defined

PRINTER QUALITY CONSTANTS

Constant	Value	Description
vbPRPQDraft	−1	Draft print quality
vbPRPQLow	−2	Low print quality
vbPRPQMedium	−3	Medium print quality
vbPRPQHigh	−4	High print quality

RESOURCE FILE CONSTANTS

Constant	Value	Description
vbResBitmap	0	Display the resource as a bitmap.
vbResCursor	2	Display the resource as a cursor.
vbResIcon	1	Display the resource as an icon.

SCROLL BAR CONSTANTS

Constant	Value	Description
vbBoth	3	Display both a horizontal and a vertical scroll bar.
vbHorizontal	1	Display a horizontal scroll bar.
vbSBNone	0	Don't display a scroll bar.
vbVertical	2	Display a vertical scroll bar.

SHAPE CONSTANTS

Constant	Value	Description
vbShapeCircle	3	Display a circle.
vbShapeOval	2	Display an oval.
vbShapeRectangle	0	Display a rectangle.
vbShapeRoundedRectangle	4	Display a rectangle with rounded corners.
vbShapeRoundedSquare	5	Display a square with rounded corners.
vbShapeSquare	1	Display a square.

TIME CONSTANTS

Constant	Value	Description
vbGeneralDate	0	Display date using the general date/time format.
vbLongDate	1	Display date using the long date format.
vbLongTime	3	Display time using the long time format.
vbShortDate	2	Display date using the short date format.
VbShortTime	4	Display time using the short time format.

VARIANT DATA TYPE CONSTANTS

Constant	Value	Description
vbVCurrency	6	Currency
vbVDate	7	Date
VbVDouble	5	Double
vbVEmpty	0	Empty string
vbVInteger	2	Integer
vbVLong	3	Long
vbVNull	1	Null
vbVSingle	4	Single
vbVString	8	String

ndex

NOTE: Page numbers in *italics* refer to illustrations or charts.